Centro de Estudios Puertorriqueños

CENTRO JOURNAL

VOLUME XXXI • NUMBER II • SUMMER 2019

El Huracan (2014). Photograph taken at the Bombazo Fandango after party at La Bodega, Santa Ana, California. Pictured in the photograph is Chicago bombera Ivelisse "Bombera de Corazón" Díaz (drumming) and Mayda del Valle (dancing). Photograph by Piero L. Guinti.

ISSN: 1538-6279 (Print); ISSN: 2163-2960 (Online)
ISBN: 978-1-945662-34-8 (Print); 978-1-945662-35-5 (Ebook)

Hunter College / City University of New York
695 Park Avenue, E-1429, New York, NY 10065
212.772.5690 • Fax 212.650.3673 • http://centropr.hunter.cuny.edu

CENTRO Journal is indexed or abstracted in: Academic Search Complete (EBSCO host); Alternative Press Index; America: History and Life; Cabell's Whitelist; Caribbean Abstracts; CONUCO–Consorcio Universitario de Indización; Gale; HAPI—Hispanic American Periodical Index; Historical Abstracts; Left Index; MLA International Index; OCLC PAIS; Pro Quest; Scopus; Social Services Abstracts; Social Scisearch; Sociological Abstracts; Ulrich's Periodicals Service; H.W. Wilson Humanities Abstracts; Worldwide Political Science Abstracts.

CENTRO

Journal of the Center for Puerto Rican Studies

VOLUME XXXI • NUMBER II • SUMMER 2019

SPECIAL ISSUE / NÚMERO ESPECIAL

Puerto Rican Bomba: Syncopating Bodies, Histories, and Geographies / Bomba puertorriqueña: sincopando cuerpos, historias y geografías

GUEST EDITORS / EDITORES INVITADOS

JADE POWER-SOTOMAYOR AND PABLO LUIS RIVERA

VOLUME XXXI • NUMBER II • SUMMER 2019

INTRODUCTION / INTRODUCCIÓN

Puerto Rican Bomba: Syncopating Bodies, Histories, and Geographies

JADE POWER-SOTOMAYOR AND PABLO LUIS RIVERA

Over the last two decades, Puerto Rican *bomba* has become increasingly popular across disparate cultural landscapes and far-flung sites. There are now *bomberxs* and active bomba practices in almost all the major US cities, and in the island, there are bomba events nearly every day of the week.[1] Ten years ago, this was uncommon, twenty years ago, *ni hablar*.

This special issue of *CENTRO Journal* provides an in-depth acknowledgement and examination of the many stories, dynamics, and bodies that currently comprise bomba's cipher-like *batey*.[2] We look to the locations to which this movable portal has been brought, the routes it has taken, and ultimately, how bomba has affected Puerto Rican practices of living. As such, the essays in this volume comprise a syncopated arrangement that evokes the spaces of possibility that bomba, as practice and product, has to offer. Syncopation, a key musical feature of this genre as well as many other Afrodiasporic musics, is accomplished through a set of unpredictable rhythmic

Jade Power-Sotomayor (powersoto@gmail.com) is Assistant Professor in the Department of Theatre and Dance at the University of California, San Diego. She is a Cali-Rican performance scholar and a bomba cultural worker and dancer. Research interests include: Latinx theatre and performance, dance studies, epistemologies of the body, feminist of color critique, bilingualism, and intercultural performance in the Caribbean diaspora. Her current book project, *!Habla!: Speaking Bodies in Latinx Dance and Performance*, theorizes Latinidad and Latinx communities of belonging as constituted through doing versus being.

Pablo Luis Rivera (xiorro@gmail.com) holds a Ph.D. in history from the Centro de Estudios Avanzados de Puerto Rico y el Caribe. He is a teaching researcher in the educational system of Puerto Rico, director of the Restauración Cultural organization, and co-director of the AFROlegado Educational Program and the Proyecto Unión. He is a well known bomba performer, composer, presenter and social activist, and has offered university creadit-bearing courses on bomba at the University of Washington and the University of Puerto Rico.

El Huracán (2014). Photograph taken at the Bombazo Fandango after party at La Bodega, Santa Ana, California. Pictured in the photograph is Chicago bombera Ivelisse "Bombera de Corazón" Díaz (drumming) and Mayda del Valle (dancing). Photograph by Piero L. Guinti. © Piero F. Giunti. Reprinted by permission.

irregularities executed in patterns that cycle through a steady downbeat. It thrillingly breaks with the expected, and yet returns us to the satisfaction of alignment with that which we have heard before. As with *balancé*—another concept central to bomba that involves falling towards the state of imbalance only to be pulled back to a center—syncopation's power to move us emanates not only from its beats, but equally, from the interstitial spaces, the moments of in-betweenness, what Fred Moten refers to as the fugitive possibilities of "the break" (Moten 2003). Thus, as these essays punctuate the various and sometimes contradictory interests, investments, aesthetics and locations that different players increasingly attach to bomba, we draw attention to the repetitions and irregularities across the genre's history, its rhizomatic linkages between people and places, and the dynamic exchange between bodies that actualizes the batey. This special issue is not meant to be comprehensive, nor is it meant to be entirely celebratory. It attends to previous silences and new modalities while inevitably signaling other spaces and silences yet to be addressed. It engages with bomba as a living tradition that is simultaneously music and dance, culture and cultural product, political tool and fetishized commodity, community engagement and professional performance, historical archive and embodied repertoire.

New bodies are always finding their way to the batey and new ways of being in it. Seasoned drummers hold it down for the amateurs. Songs about *"se acabaron las promesas*" and double entendres about "María" are interspersed with others whose lyrics are sung in Kreyol, French, or other African-derived dialects of a different time. Line-ups of women drumming, although still not the norm, have certainly become a more common occurrence. Skirts fly with the muscled action force of variously gendered bodies, and movement styles shift between space-taking, aggressive and fierce delicacy. Women dancers extend arms unencumbered by skirts, using the syncopated and intricate footwork previously in the domain of male dancers. A small girl seated in her wheelchair gracefully flourishes her skirt and rhythmically moves her wheels in opposition. The non-verbal grown-to-man son with Down syndrome won't go home until he gets his moment in the batey, *pa' hablar*. Stories of new loves and new losses, new dreams and new memories are woven into songs. Artisans make a life—and in doing so make a living—through their carefully cultivated study of the secrets in the *higüeras* and seeds, wood and skins that make bomba sound.[3] Elders sit on the sidelines, discerningly waiting for the song that will get them up to dance, give them the canvas on which to *pedir piquete, pintar figura,* to awe everyone there with the particular *sabor y estilo* lost to new generations. Children run in and around, tracing the bounds of the batey's reach, occasionally rooting themselves in its center. Ancestors take it all in.

And, of course, there are all the people who have been custodians of the practice through long centuries of racialized silencing.

Boricuas *de pura cepa* without a word of Spanish in their vocabulary save the occasional *wepa!*, witness bomba for the first time, feel the deep bass vibrations of the *barril*, see the multidirectional flow of conversation between voice, body and sound, and say: "I want to learn to do *that*." And they do. Latent gestural, rhythmic and affective languages rise to the surface. Some grow up on the island and don't come to know bomba until the experience of diaspora sends them looking for a way to connect home. Often, they are other AfroCaribeñxs, other AfroLatinxs, to whom bomba signals a place of reuniting with family, of remembering, of re-remembering.[4] For many, learning bomba is part of a larger process of cultural and political awakening, often happening in relation to educational spaces such as the University of Puerto Rico. Black Puerto Ricans find their way to bomba and recognize its unique capacity for tethering them to the corporeality and aesthetics of a black Puerto Rican knowledge system while also requiring creative expression that exceeds "representation." On the other hand, some grow up with essentialized ideas about "Loíza" and "lo negro"—as *mulatxs, blanquitxs* and even *negrxs*—and the rigorous practice and study of bomba helps them disaggregate the stereotype from the deep well of knowledge contained in sites of cultural history. Still, more often than not, bomba becomes a conduit for accessing both an imagined blackness and a real black history, highlighting and celebrating it as fundamental to *puertorriqueñidad* while continuing the widespread Puerto Rican practice of sidestepping the specificities of anti-blackness, and even more so, willfully circumventing acknowledgements of white(r) privilege.[5] And, of course, there are all the people who have been custodians of the practice through long centuries of racialized silencing. Those who are responsible for its survival when it was not popular or trendy, when to practice bomba meant to risk one's safety, one's potential access to a better social standing, exposing oneself to stigmas of primitivity and backwardness. Those for whom the magic and beauty of bomba's medicine is nothing new but in fact a long-held truth.

Outside the batey, politicians and artists varyingly cite and appropriate bomba for its symbolic power as a sign of resistance and as an oftentimes fetishized artifact of black life. For example, in 2019, Spike Lee's Netflix remake of *She's Gotta Have It* featured characters attending a *bombazo* on the beach in Loíza. In 2018, Carmen Yulín Cruz, San Juan's self-proclaimed *soberanista* mayor got onstage to sing with Chicago's Bomba con Buya: "Candeeeeela, candela le damos, si quieres candela, candela le damos." This occurred directly after her public criticisms of Donald Trump for his callous mishandling of the post-María hurricane recovery, for which she received various racist and sexist replies from the President's Twitter account. In 2012, Jennifer López and Marc Anthony's *Q'Viva: The Chosen* culminated a Latin America-wide talent search in a Las Vegas spectacle *The Greatest Latin Show Ever* featuring a bomba dancing and drumming act that, in having survived multiple rounds of competitive elimination, further affirmed the Diasporican hosts' claims to authentic Puerto Ricanness and of the inherent value of said identity. Finally, in the 2017 internet-breaking hit video "Despacito," we see a less "folkloric" citation that nonetheless demonstrates the particular racialized labor that bomba performs when the camera gradually reveals bomba drummers in the background as the "heat" on the dance floor intensifies, effectively locating Puerto Rico in the Caribbean and marking the corporeal pleasures attached to both.

Why bomba, why now?

As bomba practitioners ourselves—who, from our respective locations and positionalities, have spent years in bomba and the community spaces that sustain it—we believe that bomba is worthy of study in its own right as an art form, a cultural practice and a historical object. However, as scholars we also believe that bomba helps us understand something about Puerto Rican life in this current moment, about Puerto Rican racial attitudes and practices, about Puerto Rican sociality. Bomba also reveals to us how music and dance ensconce silenced stories of survival through the brutal realities of racial-colonial capitalism. Yet it has also helped us imagine a future beyond insurmountable economic and political impasses in which a group of individuals make themselves attentively receptive towards each other as they mutually instantiate a moment of collective energy and liberation, as dancers, drummers and singers do in a batey. Bomba is a genre that has largely resisted/been

On percussion (front to back): Amarilys Ríos, Marién Torres López, Víctor Vélez, Jesús Cepeda, Jorge Emmanuelli. Standing behind the drums: Rafael Maya (on the microphone) and George Rosario. Photographer Kimberly Williams (2008). © Kimberly Williams. Reprinted by permission.

excluded from mass distribution through the recording industry due in part to the difficulty in capturing the deep tones and texture of the barril. Combined with its necessary spontaneity, it resists ways of being experienced other than in the flesh, *en vivo*, as something to be lived and not merely consumed. The call-and-response singing, the dancer-drummer communication, the proximity necessary to see and hear, pull bodies into shared communication. As such, it necessitates the sharing of real time and space and the structuring of a relational affect that the participants seek to reproduce and experience again and again. Thus, even as we celebrate the unprecedented burgeoning of bomba compositions and recordings that create a substantial archive of wide-ranging projects featuring virtuosic and innovative bomba artists, we also wish to underscore the central importance of the batey in cultivating new generations of bomberxs.[6] We continue to decry bomba's relegation to the "folkloric" and away from that deemed broadly "popular" while also asking that we learn from that which takes place in the batey and in its name, that which happens in this still marginal, and as such semi-protected, space.

As evidenced in this issue's collection of essays, bomba means different things to different people. These nuances reflect distinct positionalities in relation to race, class, gender, sexuality, nation, and geography. Given long-time investments in bomba's use-value as emblematic symbol of the *tercera raíz* formulation of puertorriqueñidad, we asked contributors to consider what it might mean to think about bomba beyond the bounds of the heteropatriarchal nationalist discourses that have historically framed conversations about bomba. In other words, what happens when we think of bomba beyond "representing puertorriqueñidad," indeed beyond "representation" and instead locate it within a family of AfroCaribbean expressive practices with which it shares not just rhythmic, linguistic and aesthetic similarities but also social function (R. Z. Rivera 2010)? What does that do to our sense of identity, shifting from thinking of ourselves as islanders to thinking of ourselves as people in an archipelago filled with movement and connection but also truncated filiations and affective interruptions? What happens, as Bárbara Abadía-Rexach here asks, when we reflect on how Puerto Rican identity and the need to "celebrate" and "know" it is instrumentalized to exalt the genre of bomba as valuable? Does thinking about it beyond its capacity to "represent puertorriqueñidad" make bomba any less valuable? Or more? Does this challenge how we think of the boundedness of puertorriqueñidad? Of the real consequences of constructed blackness? How can we address the ritualistic and spiritual dimensions of bomba history and experience while contending with erasures and absences colonially imposed on AfroCaribbean religious practice? What are the dynamics that ensue when Diasporicans, awakened to a deep sense of knowing, approach bomba with unmitigated fervor yet lack the resources—money, flexible time, cultural literacy—to study deeply and broadly, to travel to the island to experience immersion in not just the techniques but the worlds that sustain bomba practice? What about the bomba worlds they create in their own localities? How have leadership roles taken on by women and queer folks changed not just how women practice bomba but how gendered identities are imagined in bomba spaces, how music and dance are gendered in relation? What can we learn when we look at practices other than drumming, dancing and singing to think about cultural custodianship—such as Melanie Maldonado's examination of women's historical use of *enaguas*? And finally, as scholars writing about bomba, we are obligated to reflect on what is at stake when bomba becomes the subject of scholarly interest, enters institutional spaces and, as Shannon Dudley discusses, "goes to college."

AfroBoricua Music: Entre Bomba y Plena

While we recognize the interlocking roots and cross pollinations that exist between legions of musicians who play salsa, plena, rumba, música jíbara, reggaetón and even trap, we are grateful for the opportunity to linger here in the specificity of bomba as a genre. We follow in the footsteps of cultural workers and scholars who have worked to distinguish bomba from plena, two AfroBoricua popular music genres that together comprise what Hal Barton refers to as the "folkloric dyad" *bombiplena* in which historically the instrumentation and stylistic norms of plena have been privileged (Barton 1995).[7] Yet, given their shared histories of marginalization in relationship to the mass production of salsa, hip hop and reggaetón, and subsequent ability to symbolize a countercurrent of "tradition," they are still often collapsed. Many Puerto Ricans regularly use the metonym to signal generalized festive, folkloric black percussive sound. Though the two share vocabularies and certainly many musicians make a living by expertly playing both—indeed many *bomberos* were first *pleneros*—they are distinct in instrumentation and history. Plena, a 20th century working-class genre known as "the people's newspaper" is played on portable hand-held drums. As such, it is often present from parrandas to political protests. Coming into popularity alongside and in direct relation to labor movements of the early 20th century, its lyrics richly capture proletarian life, including labor unrests, oppressive working conditions, and survival through emigration. Bomba is played on large, heavy drums and is the centuries-old antecedent to plena. Traditional songs also sing of the material conditions of labor and exploitation but additionally open windows into earlier worlds, epistemologies and spiritual beliefs, giving lasting life to those whose dancing, deeds, and dramas were deemed of importance.[8] As such, bomba songs, especially when it comes to the presence of refrains sung not in Spanish but in French-based Kreyol, index an earlier epoch of forced labor and migrations and polyglot communities.[9] Furthermore, the evolution of the unique "corporeal sounding" relationship between the dancer and the lead drummer where the dancer moves, not just in response to the music, but locked into deep conversation with the *primo* drummer to *make* the music itself, has made dance integral to bomba as opposed to its adjacent relationship in plena (Power-Sotomayor 2020).[10]

They followed trans-Caribbean links that led to a deeper understanding of bomba's Bantu-Kongo origins and looked to women as bomba protagonists.

Research on music and affective culture in Puerto Rican life has been foundational in formulating Puerto Rican Studies as a field of inquiry since its early stages and though bomba is often cited, it has rarely been dealt with specifically (Glasser 1995; Aparicio 1998; Flores 2000; R. Z. Rivera 2003; Rivera-Rideau 2015; Fiol-Matta 2017). However, some of the most important scholarship on 20th and early 21st century bomba practice was first published in *CENTRO Journal* in 2004 marking a new frame of engagement (Cartagena 2004; Barton 2004). Thus, the scholarship in this volume has been made possible by the work of an earlier generation of researchers who noted and harnessed the increasing interest and activity around bomba practice in the late 1990s, following the 2001 historic release of the Banco Popular special *Raíces* and the transition from a previous model of folkloric groups to bombazo-centered activities. These early pioneers in research and documentation—in the diaspora Raquel Z. Rivera, Hal Barton, Juan Cartagena, Ramón López, Alex LaSalle, Melanie Maldonado and, of course, the legacy of Juan Gutíerrez of Los Pleneros de la 21 among others—created archives, scholarships, newsletters, conferences, dedicated spaces to study and perform bomba, which consequently inspired the generation that comprises today's batey.[11] They delved into the stakes of untethering bomba from folkloric blackness, to the racialized political economy encountered by bomba musicians, the embodied specificities that uniquely mark the genre, thinking beyond representing the "past" and instead searching for long-surviving alternate knowledges actualized in the batey. They followed trans-Caribbean links that led to a deeper understanding of bomba's

Bantu-Kongo origins and looked to women as bomba protagonists.

In Puerto Rico, knowledge about bomba has long-resided in the oral cultures of the protected family spaces of the Cepedas (Cangrejos/Santurce) and the Ayalas (Loíza)—who are largely responsible for the institutional recognition of bomba on a national and international scale—as well as in other less commonly touted but nonetheless important families throughout the island, for example: Negrón and Pizarro (Cataño), Mangual and Nadal (Mayagüez), Villodas, Flores, Lind, and Texidor (Guayama and Arroyo), Archeval (Ponce) and many others. Following the 1990s, the documentation and study of bomba went from the generalized to the more specific and began to focus on the value of practice as research and oral historiography. Drawing on a limited number of earlier 20th century published texts on bomba (Álvarez Nazario 1960; Muñoz 1966; López Cruz 1967, Vega Druet 1979), the eventual digitalization of anthropologist John Alden Mason's 1915 recordings (Viera Vargas 2008b), and the writings of María Cadilla de Martínez (1933), researchers turned to their own communities and local knowledges to learn more about the different eras of bomba's varied and long history, exploring diverse regional practices, bringing to life important figures previously swept into oblivion—La Ponchinela, Domingo Negrón, Eustacio Flores, Andrés Laguer, Pablo Lind, Mamá Tontón among others.[12] In doing so, they folded these new understandings into their practice, their storytelling songs, their *toques* and *repiques*.[13]

This issue pays homage to this early work, adding new discoveries, observations, and methodological formations. It is thus intended as a *retomada* of some of this foundational research to both extend its scope and to reflect on how the conditions of Puerto Rican life have created shifts in conversations and practices that provide new ways of engaging with historical and contemporary bomba. Our ability to critically address the multiple vectors through which the practice is gendered, to discuss bomba accounting for sexuality and heteropatriarchy, to name anti-black racism *within* bomba, and to conceive bomba through non-essentializing identities has significantly evolved in the last two decades. Activist intellectual projects in the island and in the diaspora have made this shift possible in the batey and we wish to create and foster scholarship that mirrors this.[14] Thus, what we offer here is intended as a snapshot of the current moment when it comes to discourse and practice, a documentation of some of the key figures in today's bomba worlds, a questioning of some previously—and currently—held assumptions. Because we realize that readers for this special issue have arrived here from a variety of formations and critical angles, we take some time to provide the reader with an introduction to bomba by outlining its histories, geographies and its moving bodies, concluding with a description of each of the essays presented in the volume. Through the syncopation of voices that follows we hope to clarify some ambiguities while also signaling other spaces of possibility.

Syncopating Histories

As Puerto Rico's oldest extant music and dance genre, the history of bomba is deep and richly complex. To begin to unravel it requires that we grapple with bomba's fragmented and asynchronous yet simultaneously emergent and repeated historical trajectories. Having had been corporeally transferred and enacted, then partially remembered before the next generational transfer, bomba as a historical signifier does not refer to a singular set of cohesive practices. Rather, it signifies a collection of musical embodiments organized around drumming and created in the name of a collective communion that was varyingly social and sacred, used to escape harsh social realities and to enact shared belief systems (Quintero Rivera 2009). Archival mentions of bomba embodiments date back to the early 18th or possibly late 17th century and are contradictory and revelatory, ranging from letters, travel narratives, slave codes, and literary mentions.[15] Nomenclature, location and description vary but the theme of black bodies exuberantly dancing, drumming and singing repeatedly appears in these sources. Thus, the punctuating exchange between the "archive and the repertoire"—as performance scholar Diana Taylor has termed it—together confirm bomba's long historical trajectory in Puerto Rico, albeit one impossible to frame through teleological claims (Taylor 2003). It instead requires broad gestures that mark migratory movements, social and political dynamics, and that follow the thread of the drum.

Derived from West and Central African cultural practice, bomba is a "big drum" tradition linked to many others in the Caribbean and the Americas, eventually folding in distinctive elements that would set it apart from other genres across this diaspora. It became a layered conversation drawing from the traditions that traveled with people from the diverse ethnic groups that were kidnapped directly from Africa, brought as enslaved people from other islands, or as black *ladinos* from Spain. Furthermore, as a music-dance-song brought to life both within plantation and *hacienda* spaces as well as in sites of fugitivity and beneath radars of surveillance, bomba likely acquired remnants of Taíno performative practices preserved in the bodies and communities that resisted complete genocide. Political movements in the region such as the Haitian revolution brought other migratory waves of enslaved and free people to Puerto Rico, including those from New Orleans and other places disrupted by the creation of a black republic. In so doing, they brought with them their own cultures and languages as well as political ideologies of revolt. La Real Cédula de Gracias in 1815 marked a steep rise in all populations in the archipelago bringing many non-Spanish settlers and both enslaved and free blacks (Kinsbruner 1996, 41–2).

Archival references to bomba throughout the 18th and 19th century voice a combination of the delight, disgust, dismissal, and fear with which Afrodiasporic music and dancing had historically been framed. Following the abolition of slavery in 1873, as before, *bailes de bomba* were surveilled by authorities, deemed irreputable and a threat to an ordered society, a scrutiny that became further reified in the 20th century as criollo elites vied to represent Puerto Ricans as "modern," "civilized" and white or at least near-white subjects.[16] Moreover, as these elites attempted to centralize hierarchies of power over *gente de color*, they asserted their superiority by exerting sexual control over women and by activating discourses of lasciviousness and depravity ascribed to poor and AfroPuerto Rican women. Not only did this result in an exclusion of these women from 'the community of respectability" still seen today, but it also posed them as a threat to such respectability, activating a mechanism of "blackening" women who moved in ways deemed sexual and thereby furthering practices of control and surveillance (Findlay 1999, 24). Despite such dynamics, mostly poor but not exclusively black and mulatx Puerto Ricans continued to attend the bomba events that were held in private residences, local establishments and other public places for specific celebrations as well as for general socializing. And yet, this stigma of "irreputability" was ultimately strong enough for many —though certainly never all—bomba enthusiasts and practitioners to actively distance themselves and their families from these spaces, leading to the commonly-touted idea that by the mid-20th century bomba had become "nearly extinct."[17]

The foundation of the Institute of Puerto Rican Culture in 1955 created a structure and an imperative for cataloguing and incorporating all aspects of Puerto Rican culture, and bomba—together with plena—became the emblematic signifier for AfroPuerto Rican culture. At this point, famed AfroBoricua musicians Rafael Cortijo and Ismael Rivera had been composing popular music, drawing on traditional bombas and plenas, playing music in elite establishments and ultimately giving their music great exposure through their widely circulated recordings popular amongst various sectors of Puerto Rican society. Furthermore, the arrival of television also amplified bomba's visibility on a national scale as many of these musicians were regularly invited to perform. Now appearing on stage in a variety of contexts, such as in Francisco Arriví's play *Vejigantes* (1958) and in shows sponsored by tourist companies at hotels featuring performances by folkloric companies, bomba was curated as an artistic product that was both sensational and "historic."

Known today as "the patriarch of bomba" and "el roble mayor," in 1957, Rafael Cepeda Atiles, a seasoned bomba and plena musician and composer from Cangrejos/ Santurce, together with his wife Caridad Brenes Caballero, his son Modesto Cepeda and his many other children, created Grupo Folklorico Trapiche, marking a new era for bomba's visibility and national import. Members of the Cepeda family would go on to form Ballet Folklórico de la Familia Cepeda (1973) that would in turn seed the vast majority of the bomba projects that we have subsequently witnessed. The Cepeda legacy, coupled with that of the Ballet Fólklórico de los Hermanos Ayala created in 1959 by Castor Ayala with his family and community members in Loíza after being approached by a television producer seeking demonstrations of bomba dances, gave bomba a massive injection of cultural and institutional capital (Los Ayala-Bomba Puertorriqueña-Datos 2001). These projects distinguished themselves from other groups of the era aiming to theatrically represent the variety of the island's folklore, of which bomba and plena comprised but only one part, such as Areyto (1968), Tony D'Astro y el Ballet Folklórico Nacional de Puerto Rico (1962), and Gíbaro de Puerto Rico (1973). Bomba appeared in these productions as choreographies created internally by the Cepeda family or by inviting them as special guests. Finally, the creation of the Escuela de Bomba y Plena Rafael Cepeda Atiles in the 1970s was a pivotal moment in this history, as it made bomba not just a performed product of consumption and enjoyment but also a site of official study and practice for those outside designated families or performance groups, thereby consolidating and codifying disparate knowledges into standards and norms that today make up the *fundamentos* of the practice. The 1973 founding of the Festival de Bomba y Plena by Pedro "Capitol" Clemente would harness these currents, modeling structures (festivals) and practices (visual art) for engagements with AfroBoricua identity that had been taking shape in a range of cultural spheres.

Mayagüez is a particularly critical site in bomba history given its strategic location as a port city receiving merchants, landowners and enslaved people fleeing the Haitian revolution.

Given the varying impulses propagating interest in bomba throughout this era, bomba histories have tended to elide practices outside of the Santurce/San Juan area, though they have been varied and continuous, especially in the Western region and in the South. Mayagüez is a particularly critical site in bomba history given its strategic location as a port city receiving merchants, landowners and enslaved people fleeing the Haitian revolution. Though played consistently in different barrios throughout the city, new attention was brought to bomba throughout the 1960s and 70s by people such as Enrique "El Chino" Vázquez Báez and projects like Ballet Sepia de Mayagüez which were exclusively dedicated to cultivating a rebirth of bomba, drawing on the knowledges of important figures that would go on to create their own projects. These include Félix Alduén y sus Tambores (1970) and Don Ramón "Papo" Alers' Yagüembé de Mayagüez and La Escuela de Bomba de Mayagüez. In the South, in 1979, Isabel Albizu, known as "*la matriarca de la bomba*" formed the group Bambalué drawing on her family's history of the practice in Ponce and their exchanges with others from Guayama, Salinas, and Arroyo.[18] Following in the tradition of *la bomba del sur*, Nellie J. Lebrón Robles and Emmanuel Dufrasne González, created Paracumbé in 1979 as both a performance group and a project that recuperated histories of this region. Gladys Rivera's Los Mayombe de Loíza and later Raíces de Loíza would also become key in crystallizing a particular style of *bomba loiceña*.

As critical interest in and knowledge about bomba continued to spread, other bomba groups, schools, platforms manifested themselves.[19] The many projects that have since taken shape across the island have relied on arduous work, a spirit of *autogestión*, an unwavering commitment to bomba and its communities, and have thrived in spite of what Raquel Z. Rivera coyly describes as "a fair share of impostors and troublemakers" (R. Z. Rivera 2013, 24).[20]

The most defining moment of this resurgence was the beginning of the "bombazo movement" in 1993. "Bombazo" was a new word for an old concept that had been largely overshadowed by the prolifertion of bomba experiences through the framework of group performances in proscenium settings. Through the combined vision and efforts of the Emmanuelli Náter brothers (José, Jorge and Víctor) of the group Raíces Eternas, Jesús Cepeda, and members of Paracumbé, the first bomba *bailes de marque-*

sina were held in Carolina. They would later be supported and promoted by the Centro de Investigación Cultural Raíces Eternas (CICRE) project with Halbert Barton at the University of Puerto Rico (UPR), and by the end of the 1990s bombazos had begun to stick as a concept, marking a return to the batey, to the *soberao*, and to the social settings that reflected daily Boricua living (Barton 2004, 75).[21] Though already cross-nurtured by the steady and multidirectional cultural flow between island and diaspora (e.g., Ángel Luis Reyes, who came to Puerto Rico from New York, recruited the Emmanuellis into the genre), bombazos at this point also began to take on new momentum in the diaspora, and bomba practices between different regions becoming even more complexly rhizomatic and producing their own *sabores*, aesthetics, politics and trajectories of exchange.

Syncopating Geographies

Though the majority of the contributions in this issue focus on bomba practices on the island, we wish to highlight the increasing importance of exchanges that have taken place across island and diaspora, generating a plethora of projects and new modalities. We know from archives, oral histories and song lyrics that, in the early and mid 20th century, people would travel across the island to share in bomba events, especially as transportation became more accessible. As interest in bomba coalesced, the hunger for new knowledges and interlocutors drove bomberxs in search of each other, though certainly many also suspiciously guarded their worlds from outsiders. For instance, many believe that much of what is today known as the Cepeda Cangregos/Santurce bomba tradition was in part inspired by exchanges with bomba *mayagüezana*—also the birthplace of Rafael Cepeda's great-grandfather—though we also know that there was already a tradition in Cataño and within the islet of San Juan.[22] Indeed, as a tradition that evidences the coerced movement of bodies across islands and continents, bomba was collectively created through the dynamic interweaving of the local and the *lejano* and the need to bring the two into communication. Yet, like today, even as bomba would bring people together, the conditions of colonial life separated them, most often painfully. The lyrics of an early 20th century song about Domingo Negrón, an esteemed dancer and convener of bomba events from Cataño recount such a separation, "*Domingo Negrón se embarcó pa' Nueva York y dejó a sus hijos, a sus hijos de corazón.*" Bomba's routes of travel and exchanges between the island and the diaspora in many ways reflect this earlier history. The advent of social media and the increased accessibility of air travel over the last decades have been transformational in creating a web of connections that today sustain communities separated by land and water. Not only has social media helped generate regular and lasting contact and intimacy between different parties, but the videos and images shared —from early YouTube videos of Alma Moyó bombazos in New York, to the uploading of historical footage, to the now-ubiquitous livestreaming of bombazos—have served as resources, especially in the diaspora, to learn about bomba practice, the batey thereby extending its presence into the digital realm.[23]

While technology shrinks distance, it does not replace embodied presence, therefore bomberxs regularly and frequently travel to each other's events near and far, by car, by bus, by train and by plane to share in food and drink, sleep in each other's living rooms, bringing their voices, hands, and bodies to the batey. The *fiebre de bomba* that we have witnessed over the last two decades is in large part due to this willingness of people to travel—despite challenges—to continue to build and learn. The exchanges have been varied in scope and practice. For instance, the biennial *BomPlenazo* in New York was started in 2000 at the Hostos Center for Arts & Culture by its director Wally Edgecomb, Héctor "Tito" Matos (Viento de Agua), Juan Gutiérrez (Pleneros de la 21), Roberta Singer (City Lore), and José "Chema" Soto (Rincón Criollo) as a weekend of performances, workshops, *conversatorios* and *convivios* organized around a central theme and featuring different groups and regions from both the island and the diaspora. The creation of projects like Proyecto Unión started by Pablo Luis Rivera and Rafael Maya in 2009 linked groups across the diaspora not only to bomba teachings from the island, but just as importantly, to each other. These areas include: Florida, Chicago, New York, the Bay Area, Los Angeles, San Diego, Virginia, Seattle, Cleveland, Denver, the Antillean islands of Guadalupe and Martinique, and cities as international as Valencia, Brehmin and Dubai. La Bomba es Nuestra started in 2007 in the Bay Area and the following year, it went on to create *Cimarronaje,* a historic collection of original performances that used bomba to explore the lives of revolutionary Puerto Rican women from Sylvia Del Villard to Carmen Valentín, Lola Rodríguez de Tió, Luisa Capetillo to Lolita Lebrón with a broad-ranging group of bombera elders and apprentices (Awilda Sterling Duprey, Oxil Febles, Norka Hernández Nadal, Marién Torres López, Amarilys Ríos, Denise Solis, Cynthia Renta, Sarazeta Ragazzi, Melanie Maldonado, Priscilla Renta and Jade Power-Sotomayor) many of whom were or have become leaders in a variety of music and performance projects, and especially those nurturing the presence of women in bomba. In 2009, the late professor and folklorist Norma Salazar created the annual *Encuentro de Tambores* in Puerto Rico, a gathering of hundreds of barrilerxs representing "delegations" from different municipalities and regions including the diaspora. Today, the *Encuentro* is organized and directed by Marién Torres López. Mutually benefitting those seeking to study and deepen knowledge as well as those whose expertise and talents deserve remuneration and reverence, these exchanges have in turn created others that continue to grow in scope and frequency.[24]

Although islanders continue to be shocked at the presence, dedication, and, ultimately, the skill exhibited by many non-Puerto Rican bomberxs, Diasporicans have become accustomed to navigating shared vectors of difference and subalterneity in complex and nuanced ways.

Though musical groups and bands had performed bomba in New York and Chicago as part of their repertoires for decades, and the racial and cultural politics of the post-Civil Rights era had brought renewed attention to AfroBoricua music and identity, diasporic engagements with bomba through a practice defined by the inter-relation of different elements of the genre—drum, dance, song—were limited until the late 20th century. This kind of practice first made its way into diasporic communities through the work of organizations that supported bomba-specific projects like Los Pleneros de la 21 and the La Casita Rincón Criollo in New York, and Segundo Ruíz Belviz Cultural Center in Chicago, but also through La Peña in Berkeley and The Puerto Rican Cultural Center in Austin, Texas. New York street-corner rumbas were also an early impetus for the bombazo-like setting of live music and dance exchange, and it comes as no surprise that bomba in both the diaspora and the island was for many years played on congas instead of barriles due to the lack of accessibility to the genre-specific drums which until recently were difficult to purchase, their acquisition depending on personal knowledge in barril-making.[25] Key visits and prolonged residences from different members of the Cepeda family—together with their disciples and other knowledge holders that traveled and performed with them—in the late 1980s and 1990s enriched and guided bomba practice here,[26] catalyzing and synergizing with local talents.[27] Bomba was developing as a new site for exploring, articulating and performing Puerto Rican identity: a distinctly, if often still folkloric, AfroBoricua identity. As such, bomba projects in the diaspora have tended to be aligned—though many exceptions exist—with nationalist-leanings or social justice-oriented currents, creating distinct points of entry for those in the communities amongst which Diasporicans variously live: Dominican, Chicanx, African American. In this way, they enact what Raquel Z. Rivera calls "liberation mythologies" that are "less concerned with identity and honor than with social justice and liberation" in terms of "class and race rather than nation" (R. Z. Rivera 2012, 9). Although islanders continue to be shocked at the presence, dedication, and, ultimately, the skill exhibited by many non-Puerto Rican bomberxs, Diasporicans have become accustomed to navigating shared vectors of difference and subalterneity in complex and nuanced ways.

Despite the fact that diasporic bomberxs have continued to seek teachings from "master" knowledge holders on the island, the exchanges have flowed in both directions. In doing so, they enact Juan Flores' insistence on the cultural remittances offered by Diasporicans and the need to disrupt assumptions about the island as the primary source for puertorriqueñidades that then flow in the direction of the diaspora (Flores 2009). In the process of imagining and creating bomba projects in the diaspora, bomberxs have variously followed and pushed back against the "official" bomba teachings from the island. Sometimes doing both at the same time, creating productive ruptures in bomba practice norms that have ultimately served as "cultural remittances" to island Ricans. Certainly, most diasporic bomberxs recognize the importance of the protocols of humility, reverence and respect for eldership built into all aspects of bomba's practice —song, drum, dance—and at the same time express anxiety about the responsibility of properly "representing" bomba and by extension Puerto Rico. However, this has also sometimes resulted in looking to embody hegemonic teachings of bomba that prioritize "original" practices that define bomba in relation to folkloric attire, heterosexual pairing in dancing, strict adherence to movement vocabularies ascribed to men and women, and even doubts about women playing drums.[28] These norms, embedded in heteropatriarchal nationalist discourses of puertorriqueñidad—and by extension black puertorriqueñidad—as something needing protection from both extinction and contamination, have gradually been unraveled and reworked from both sides of the proverbial *charco*.

Even as we hope to extend our understanding of diasporic bomba practice as taking place beyond New York, this region has been the hub from which many of these *movidas* were first made, rippling out to other communities who grew from the examples set by these innovators. For instance, Alma Moyó, a project founded by Alex LaSalle in New York in 2002, in many ways served as the gravitational center of a nascent diasporic bomba praxis that insistently framed bomba not as expressly Puerto Rican but as Afrodiasporic, creating song compositions inspired by knowledges and imaginings of maroon history and life, and seeking to deemphasize staged codification of the genre. While similar expressions were happening on the island, especially with the historic work of Son del Batey taking bomba to San Juan nightlife settings, local resistances to this framing oftentimes effectively silenced these deviations (Barton 2004). Without a doubt, the unapologetic claims staked by Alma Moyó and their surrounding community served as inspiration for bomberxs in Puerto Rico. Another way these "remittances" functioned was simply how folks in the New York area set an example by centering bomba (and plena) as something valuable and worthy of study as evidenced by Juan Cartagena's bilingual *Güiro y Maraca* newsletter from Segunda Quimbamba Folkloric Center in Jersey City, the first-ever publication dedicated exclusively to discussing and documenting the happenings and histories of bomba and plena practice.[29] An appearance by the Pleneros de la 21 with Roberto Cepeda on the children's show *Sesame Street* in 1993 is another example of how bomba was specifically visibilized and featured in New York settings.

As bombazo-like performances became more common occurrences, other sartorial, corporeal and musical practices were instituted, not necessarily in direct contestation of practices at the time, but rather emerging from contextual social realities. On the island, the bombazo movement had relied greatly on the talents of dancers that came of age dancing hip hop and electro-boogie brought over from New York. The eventual appearance of the *pañuelo*, scarf, or *pashmina* as a replacement for the skirt was a gradual process born out of logistical imperatives. Women, coming in to a bombazo off the street in a wintry New York, often not having the requisite skirt, always had a scarf.[30] Pashminas specifically were in fashion in this era, sold at subway stations in all variety of colors to match an outfit. Untethered from a skirt, movement styles became more quotidian and infused with embodiments drawn from other repertoires—hip hop's swag and rumba's graceful swing, the pulsing movements of *orisha* dances and the forceful groundedness of *palos*—underscoring links between practices. Once deemed "*inventos de allá afuera,*" today it is the norm to see dancers at any bombazo on the island or in the diaspora dancing without a skirt and often in its place a pañuelo, except on the island, instead of being the thick wool of a winter scarf, they are the thin cotton of a beach wrap or a head scarf. Rather than reifying ideas about "backwards insularism" and "politically evolved" Diasporicans, just as we also denounce ideas about islanders as the source of untainted culture and Diasporicans as Puerto Rican knock-offs, we wish to show these transformative exchanges as dynamic, multi-sited, parallel and often imperceptible while they are happening.

Syncopating Bodies

Bomba's batey today is produced by a dynamic exchange between bodies that syncopate sound and flesh. As such, it is sustained by an ethos of listening that includes both finding the rhythmic gaps into which dancers insert their flesh and carve space, and an equal attention to expressive movement as a sound-producing agent and not just a visual object. Because of this, determining who gets to do what with their bodies in the batey continues to be a subject of concern for all generations of bomberxs. This concern, of course, exists in tension with the reality of the need to follow certain protocols—the slippage between "tradition" and "protocol" often being ambiguous—in order for the genre to function and the exchange between dancer and drummer be executed: respect, listening, control and clarity of movement, precision of timing, attention to others. As such, there exists a legitimate imperative to continually stress the *fundamentos* of the genre as people sloppily adhere to technique, inventing what they do not know, or have not taken the time to learn. Oft misperceived by novices as simplistic, successfully articulating bomba languages requires study and practice, even if they happen outside of formalized spaces. And yet, as we have been positing throughout, these concerns also intersect—at times imperceptibly—with the logics of patriarchy and homophobia that, together with a politics of respectability, are ultimately aimed at the silencing of women, of the most visibly queer, of the blackest and of the poorest in bomba spaces.

As evidenced in many of the essays in this volume, women's participation in bomba has always been present and is increasingly marked with particular attention to the intersections of sexuality, class and race. The challenges to the historical gendering of bomba that we are currently witnessing have come from multiple sites, yet as discussed above, the Diaspora has played a significant role not just in terms of crossing gendered boundaries (e.g., women playing drums), or in disrupting the gendered binaries of movement vocabulary (e.g., women and men choosing to dance with or without skirts), but also, as a result of the above, contesting the gendered hierarchization of dancing versus drumming.[31] Once given the opportunity to learn to drum and to engage in the syncopated fast-paced footwork of minute steps and quick directional changes previously practiced almost exclusively by men dancers, women can access their dancing musically in distinct ways, just as they come to understand the drumming, particularly primo playing, through the experience of dancing. Music and dance thus cease to exist in a gendered hierarchy, but rather are revealed to be mutually constitutive.

Spaces dedicated to cultivating women's development as percussionists were key in bringing about these shifts. Opportunities for women to play drums, especially in regions with fewer drummers to begin with, also emerged from the need to have a sufficient amount of musicians. For instance, mayagüezana Norka Hernández Nadal would hold "Women Bomba Jam Sessions" on Sundays in the Bronx in the early 2000s. In the course of just a few years, an explosion of projects would emerge, one inspired and nurtured by the other. The first all-women's group to play bomba—together with Dominican palos—was Yaya, co-founded in New York in 2002 by Manuela Arciniegas and Raquel Z. Rivera. Later, in 2006 Arciniegas would develop the group Legacy Women which continues today. In 2006 Oxil Febles founded Grupo Nandí as the first all-women's ensemble in Puerto Rico, and shortly after in 2007, Denise Solis, Cynthia Renta and Sarazeta Ragazzi in the Bay Area created a performance *La Bomba es Nuestra*, inviting Febles and Hernández Nadal, Melanie Maldonado and today's leading virtuosic woman bomba percussionist Amarilys Ríos. This would lead to the creation of the all-women's ensemble Las Bomberas de la Bahia founded by AfroChicana Solis and co-directed with Ragazzi. In 2010, inspired by working on projects with Las Bomberas de la Bahía, Chi-Rican Ivelisse Díaz, a bombera since childhood in her uncle Eli Samuel Rodríguez's Grupo Yubá (1991), founded Las Bompleneras with Jessica Rodríguez, the daughter of Chicago bomba pioneer Evaristo Tito Rodríguez and director of AfriCaribe (2000). Finally, after collaborating on many of the above projects, Marién Torres López, director of Taller Tambuyé and trailblazer in today's generation of Puerto Rico bomberxs, founded the all-women's group Ausuba in 2012, which, as discussed here in Lladó Ortega's essay, is an ever-growing source of inspiration and politicization for women in Puerto Rico, especially as intersecting with the demands of La Colectiva Feminista en Construcción. Because of the collective work of these women, the support of the teachers who shared knowledges with them—especially virtuoso Víctor "Vitito" Emmanuelli—and shifting societal perceptions around different modes of bomba participation for women, hundreds of other women play bomba today.

Finally, the creation of women-centered bomba spaces and the empowerment experienced within them has also allowed for ever-present queer bodies, identities and experiences to become more normalized in bomba settings.

Moreover, following examples of directors like Isabel Albizu, women are increasingly taking active musical leadership and directorial roles in addition to the traditionally gendered organizational and choreographic ones they have played for some time. Having strong women primo drummers, modeled by pioneers Ríos, Solis, Arciniegas, Torres, Díaz, Mariela Solis and others, has also made a difference in placing women in key leadership roles, given their centrality to bomba's overall musical function. In the footsteps of elders such as Albizu, Maria Texidor, Las Villodas, María Cristina Alfonso Mangual, and Nellie J. Lebrón Robles whose singing styles have resisted the now almost ubiquitous rumba and salsa influences, women composers and singers today inscribe new narratives and subjectivities through original songs. A powerful example is the remake of Bobby Capó's intensely misogynistic song about gendered violence, "Si te cojo" (originally interpreted by Ismael Rivera), adapted by Tito Rodríguez (La R) with the all-women's group Ausuba and sung by master maraca artisan and singer Bárbara Pérez-Rodríguez. Other influential bomba singers doing this work include Chamir Bonano González, Amarilys Ríos, Ivelisse Díaz, Ángela Vázquez, Jamie Pérez, Sara Cristina Cruz Cepeda, Soreimi Bezares among many others. Finally, the creation of women-centered bomba spaces and the empowerment experienced within them has also allowed for ever-present queer bodies, identities and experiences to become more normalized in bomba settings. In 2015, Jesús Cepeda's daughter, bombera Julia Caridad Cepeda, granddaughter to Rafael Cepeda, married Denise Solis in one of the first same-sex marriages performed in Puerto Rico. Together, they now lead Taller Bombalele in the Bay Area.

It should be clear, however, that despite these inroads, in most bomba settings today women primarily sing and dance while the men play drums, and trans and queer identities are still barely finding space in the batey. That being said, women have taken on critical and creative roles as directors of dance classes, schools, and projects and in turn women have approached bomba dancing as a site of emotional and corporeal release and empowerment. In fact, the popularity and success of the bombazo movement can be in part credited to the many women eager for a chance to access the unique expressive capacities offered by bomba dance. Once given the basic movement vocabulary for entering a batey, dancers—of all genders, but in recent years especially women—will keep the bombazo going until the musicians tire or the location closes. As dancers learn the protocol of "only dancing once during a bombazo" that distinguishes the batey from other more free-for-all settings, they come to relish this opportunity to craft improvised movement phrases in relation to musicality, rhythmic specificity, and shifts in weight and posture, all with their own personal affective *sabor.* Particularly gifted dancers that have most influenced the dance styles commonly seen today through established dance programs in Puerto Rico include Brenda Cepeda, Margarita "Tata" Cepeda, Elia Cortés, Marién Torres López, and Jamie Pérez, and in the diaspora, Julia Gutíerrez, Ivelisse Díaz, and Shefali Shah. It should be noted that of these, the only black Puerto Ricans—here distinguished from *afrodescendiente*—are Tata and Brenda, both from the Cepeda family. This is not an indication of a lack of masterful and influential black bomba dancers and teachers—Jeanitza Áviles and loiceña Maritere Martínez being just a couple of examples—whose embodiments are emulated by many in the batey and in class settings, but rather more of a comment on the racialized circulations of capital and access when it comes to running a school. There are also other factors such as the concentration of resources in the metropolitan area over other less populated regions and, of course, the fact that for many black women of earlier generations, bomba knowledges were stigmatized and thus sought distance from, while non-black women were able to take on bomba projects without the same stakes involved. Finally, it should also be underscored that many of these women dancers draw inspiration from and directly study with and emulate virtuosic men dancers such Modesto Cepeda, Ángel Luis "Balancé" Reyes, Otoquí Reyes, José "Nuno" Calderón,

Manuel Carmona, Felipe "Junito" Febres, Omar "Pipo" Sánchez, Manuel Pérez Kenderish, Rafael Cepeda Rivera, Teo "Piro" López and countless others.

New and newly valued embodiments come to the batey, or—as in the case of the recent move by Marién Torres López and Proyecto Kokobalé to recuperate the no-longer practiced *cocobalé* "battle" danced between two people with sticks—come *back* to the batey. In doing so, they aim to address what many rightly decry as a loss of nuance, specificity and diversity of styles as bomba worlds have proliferated and overlapped. The batey itself has also taken bodies to different sites where their sounds and movements are activated for different purposes. Performance groups have for decades traveled with bomba across the world to Europe and Latin America. Yet in recent years, a new generation has mobilized bomba at the site of political activism. Some of these include: the 2010 University of Puerto Rico (UPR) student strike, Occupy protests in New York, Chicago, and in Madison, the Movement for Black Lives, deportation protests at the US-Mexico border, actions demanding the release of Oscar López Rivera, the PROMESA bill and fiscal control board protest in front of the capitol building, a "funeral" staged to "bury televisual blackface" in Puerto Rico once and for all, the Paro Internacional de Mujeres on International Women's Day, protest for budget cuts at the Conservatorio de Música, which stopped traffic on a principle thoroughfare in central San Juan, and just as this issue goes to print, the rumble of barriles on the street accompanies the #RenunciaRicky movement, as a betrayed people demand that the governor of Puerto Rico, Ricardo Roselló, resign. Finally, as a new anti-racist movement privileging the voices, bodies and experiences of black Puerto Ricans coalesces through a range of activist intellectual projects, bomba has and will be increasingly re-claimed from the convenient slippages of *mestizaje*. The creation of black-led and centered bomba projects that frame it as an expressly black practice to which black Puerto Ricans stand in unique relation —despite the many distinctly racialized bodies that have contributed to its growth and practice— will continue to inspire new terms of engagement, improved relational ethos of accountability, and ultimately, better practices of living for all who bring their bodies to the batey.

The Special Issue's New Scholarship on Bomba

The first essay in the issue is "Centro y periferia: Las identidades en el nuevo movimiento de la bomba puertorriqueña" by Barbara Idalissee Abadía-Rexach. Here, the author takes up the "syncopated identities" exhibited by what she terms the "Nuevo Movimiento de Bomba (NMB)" that has taken place from 1995 to the present. As an important voice in a new wave of critical work on the anti-black racism at the core of discourses of mestizaje, Abadía-Rexach brings a much-needed and oft-evaded conversation to the table: how has the NMB both created new ways of valuing and centering *negritud* while at the same time distancing bomba from black bodies and further rendering, black women's bodies specifically, hypervisible yet illegible? The essay begins with an ethnographic account of Glory Mar, a black bombera, dancing at a street bombazo in Old San Juan followed by an analysis of the variety of racial and national discourses used by those commenting on the video to both critique and defend her dancing. This account reveals the widespread ignorance that still exists about bomba amongst Puerto Ricans but also the lack of sufficiently complex frameworks for discussing race and racialization in Puerto Rico, especially concerning bomba. Using José Luis González, she discusses the *"cuatro pisos"* of bomba history signaling the simultaneity of currents of affirmation, appropriation, critique, confrontation and resistance that comprise the NMB and mark contemporary discourses on race, class and gender.

Following the critiques staked by Abadía-Rexach about the "old racisms" that persist in *"lo nuevo,"* Noel Allende-Goitía's essay offers an extensive historical analysis of primary and secondary texts about bomba, questioning the temporalities, more specifically the atemporality, in which bomba is typically framed, something he contends has led to the conflation of bomba with the totality of AfroBoricua musical expression and the subsequent reduction of "lo afropuertorriqueño" to bomba. In "Topografía social y cultural de las músicas africanas y afrodescendientes en el archipiélago puertorriqueño: La historia de las músicas afrodiaspóricas en Puerto Rico como antinomia de la historia folklorizada de la bomba" Allende-Goitía provides incisive reflections on how to consider bomba's past without mapping the many musical exchanges that have taken place between Puerto Rico and West Africa as linear and unidirectional, interrogating how the bomba present is imagined as an actualization of its past. Instead, he looks to the "metagenre" of bomba not as a singular practice but as one of multiple AfroBoricua musical products, valuable for what it tells us about music and dance-making but more importantly about the lives of the black people who gave it life. In so doing, he draws from theories such as Mikhail Bakhtin's "historical inversion," which questions how we look to the past in order to make our beliefs about the present true, Tricia Rose's "cultural priorities" which underscores how culture emerges not just in relationship to "traditions" but to the social conditions and technologies in which they exist, and finally, the author's own *"presiones evolutivas"* which he defines as the collective set of pressures that qualitatively change the social praxis that ultimately leads to a change in a cultural praxis. Engaging an impressive bibliography, this essay offers a historical framework for considering the creative vicissitudes we are currently witnessing in bomba's practice and as we look to its future.

The next two essays in the issue bring important new perspectives and original research centered on women and bomba, highlighting practices and strategies that women and queer identifying people have employed to disrupt the genre's gendered codes of comportment. Based on years of research as an ethnographer and a genealogist, Melanie Maldonado's essay "Suelta el Moño: The Herstories of Change Agents and Perpetuators of Bomba Culture" is a critical contribution to scholarship on bomba in two major ways. First, it brings detailed attention to bomba in the southern region of the island, including a mapping of the names, sites and practices of this tradition from the perspective of women. Second, Maldonado's focus on the material culture of the *enaguas* that women designed, created and donned for bomba dances in the early and mid 20th century—one woman bringing an entire suitcase of enaguas with her to a dance—models the type of research needed to recuperate an understanding of the micro and more meta ways that women asserted presence and agency in bomba's male-dominated spaces. Furthermore, these two contributions together underscore an important truism of the relationship between contemporary bomba and earlier histories—that the shift away from earlier traditions has caused the genre to lose much of its nuance. This is often discussed amongst bomberxs but usually in vague overarching terms and not in the specific ways she does. She ends by considering the important role that women in the diaspora have played in excavating and giving life to pre-folkloric bomba practices, ultimately linking the important gains that women have made in the space of the batey to these earlier "herstories" that paved the way. Replete with photographs and insightful first-person testimonials from the many elders she interviewed, this essay captures the kind of feminist scholarship long missing from the archive.

Mónica Lladó Ortega's "*Queering bomba*: Rupturas con lo heteronormativo en la bomba puertorriqueña" follows, bringing a much-needed queer lens to scholarship about 21st century bomba practice. Lladó Ortega does this both through a close reading of bomba artist Lionel (Lío) Villahermosa's prominent and purposeful use of the skirt as a masculine-presenting dancer, and by discussing other ways that bomberxs performatively invoke and reconfigure gender norms. This queering of bomba, she argues, is accomplished by making visible the restrictive bounds of normativity as they are crossed. In such a formulation, bomba and the community exchange it necessitates becomes available as a liberatory practice for other Puerto Rican bodies previously deemed unwelcome in the batey. Drawing on Carlos Alamo-Pastrana's earlier observations of how bomba dance offers opportunities of rupture for both men (through expressing emotionality) and women (agency), she documents bombera Marién Torres López's many feminist interventions, which range from song compositions that center self-confident women protagonists, to creating opportunities for women to drum, and an overarching framing of bomba as a site for both rupture and preservation. Torres López's accounts of the resistance she experienced to women learning to play drums and to being part of an all-women's group underscores the relative abruptness and recentness of this change, how heteropatriarchy has been couched in discourses of "protecting" bomba, and yet how in continuing to create these ruptures the bomba community at large benefits, including many of the men who initially did not support such projects. Importantly, with both Torres López and Villahermosa, their skill and long-term study as bomberxs has worked to justify and sanction the radical crossings they have achieved. Drawing on queer Latinx performance scholars Juana María Rodriguez and José Muñoz, Lladó Ortega ultimately asks important questions about the stakes of thinking through bomba queerly, queer here signaling both the non-normative as well as something that includes LGBTQ identities.

Continuing to examine bomba's uses as a liberatory praxis, the following essay is a sustained meditation on bomba's invocation of "the archival oceanic" and the potential for healing that stems from deep connection with ancestral memory. "'Water Overflows with Memory': Bomba, Healing, and the Archival Oceanic" by Ashley Coleman Taylor frames bomba as a product of the Middle Passage suspended in the liminal oceanic worlds that are simultaneously "groundless" and "transformational." As an ethnographer of religion, she brings an analysis that separates Africanness and blackness as they circulate in contemporary bomba worlds, drawing attention to how bomba indexes an "African interatlantic experience," while it simultaneously functions as a racial signifier on the island. This essay is an important contribution to this issue for its careful theorization of the frontiers between the secular and the sacred that many bomberxs experience in the batey and that remain difficult to name and signal. This has been the case both because many of the specific spiritual significations in the song/dance/drum have been lost to most practitioners even if still perceived, but also because of a discourse that separates bomba from "the spiritual" as an attempt to distance it from racist ideas about *brujería*, *santería* and other commonly practiced Afrodiasporic religions. Drawing on black feminist scholars such as Hortense Spillers and Jacqui Alexander and engaging with concepts such as the Kongo cosmogram, Coleman Taylor's rich prose makes a case for bomba being an ancestral gift archived in the oceanic that has now become a contemporary form of therapeutic engagement.

Juan Gudiño Cabrera's "La música como herramienta política de los *condenados*: un acercamiento a la bomba puertorriqueña" brings into focus other political valences of bomba by engaging with it as a praxis of decolonial resistance and subversion. In this exploratory essay, the author outlines how bomba's inscription into a state-sponsored racialized identity is an extension of what Aníbal Quijano calls "the coloniality of power." This move, he argues, extends a colonial rendering of bomba —and the bodies attached to it—as antimodern, without epistemological value, and ultimately, from which a distance must be sought out in order to achieve access to the ontology of "progress" and "liberation." Framing bomba as a knowledge-system/*cosmovisión*/cultural practice with its own set of logics and epistemological implications grounded in distinct conceptualizations of human existence and in relation to others and to the natural world, he traces how bomba and other related practices have been deemed "othered" through the discursive production of the modern Western subject. Delving into the historical and contemporary logics that enable this "othering," such as Cartesian binaries and the hierarchization of thought over embodiment, Gudiño Cabrera's essay offers an incisive critique of bomba's sublation into *la gran familia puertorriqueña* that, albeit not new in itself, reframes and nuances this claim through a deep engagement with decolonial studies and his own experiences in bomba worlds. He concludes by providing powerful examples of instances in which bomba has been activated—both in Puerto Rico and in Chicago with Bomba con Buya—as a tool of "*transresistencia,*" taking stances of resistance to dominant norms and the subjugation of subaltern populations, Puerto Ricans and otherwise, here *and* there.

The theme of "transresistencia" sets up the next piece which moves us to the diaspora and to practicing bomba alongside other Afrodiasporic traditions in order to access the particular "medicine" and wisdom they offer, both collectively and individually. In "The Bombazo-Fandango: An Interview with Hector Luis Rivera (aka HecOne, aka HecVortex)" by Jade Power-Sotomayor, Rivera narrates his experience as a Bronx Boricua who, after co-founding the group The Welfare Poets in New York and learning bomba in Chicago, moved to Southern California. Here, together with his wife and partner Melody González Chávez, he would create the Bombazo-Fandango, an event intended to bring together communities of bomba and AfroMexican *son jarocho* practice from Puerto Rico, Veracruz and across the US. As a composer perhaps best known for the yubá song "Me curé," Rivera recounts his journey with bomba and how the Bombazo-Fandango would ultimately be born out of the lived intimacies between bomba and son jarocho communities as well as the shared histories of the genres, despite an insistence on maintaining their separate integrity. This interview is a useful resource because it documents these exchanges and the labors involved in sustaining the Bombazo-Fandango for four years, but also because it extends bomba's map to the West Coast and to the many non-Puerto Ricans—here especially Mexican/Chicanx—that have contributed to its continued practice in the region, putting pressure on the normalizing forces of nationalism. Furthermore, as in the Bombazo-Fandango itself, looking at bomba and son jarocho alongside each other illuminates the critical work these genres respectively do for their diasporic communities in recuperating access to ancestral knowledges while also questioning best-practices for maintaining them at such a great distance from their source.

Extending bomba's trajectory even further to the Pacific Northwest, ethnomusicologist Shannon Dudley's "Bomba Goes to College – How's That Working Out" offers a valuable set of reflections on university engagements with bomba practice and teaching followed by well-theorized but practical suggestions for how to best facilitate and maximize these exchanges. Drawing on his experiences integrating "community musics" such as bomba and son jarocho into academic settings—specifically Music Department curriculum—Dudley first outlines the deeply-ingrained institutional cultures that make these exchanges challenging (and therefore all the more necessary) as they reveal logics that value individualism, virtuosity, and Eurocentricity over embodied pedagogies, process, and improvisation. Pointing to the 1990s history of "participatory action research" on bomba undertaken by CICRE in Puerto Rico, he focuses his analysis on how this work has been continued through Pablo Luis Rivera's trajectory as a "bomba activist," teaching and sharing bomba in diverse settings, most recently as a Community Artist in Residence at the University of Washington. Dudley's reflections on how Rivera and others impart critical knowledges that extend beyond technical expertise and products underscores the labor that bomba performs in spaces outside of Puerto Rico and outside popular sites of bomba practice. For students and faculty alike, these knowledges emphasize the importance of concepts such as piety towards elders and ancestors, embodiment, communication, and relationship building, the latter of which Dudley proposes as not just a route to research projects but ultimately the matrix that becomes the lasting product. As such, this essay calls on those in academia to think creatively about how bomba pedagogies and other "participatory arts" can be transformational to the university while also using their power to leverage institutional resources in support of artists and community projects.

The final piece in the issue is Pablo Luis Rivera's "Inventario de la Serie de Conversatorios Sobre la Bomba y la Cultura Puertorriqueña Instituidos por la Organización Restauración Cultural." Here Rivera discusses two decades of work with Restauración Cultural, the organization he co-founded in 1998 in order to broaden bomba education, investigation and the preservation of diverse knowledges about it. One of Restauración Cultural's most exceptional contributions has been the creation of a series of 44 public conversatorios about bomba between 2007-17. Organized around different themes, regional practices, and featuring presentations by elders, scholars, and over a hundred practitioners, these forums have created a space for deepening learning about bomba *alongside* the experiences in the batey. They were born out of an attempt to create a broader conversation that was simply absent in Puerto Rico's education system and has existed only in broad and often reductive strokes through other cultural institutions. In this essay, Rivera maps and catalogues the many bodies, voices and locations brought to life in these forums. As such, this document is incredibly valuable to the archive and the future of bomba research for it clearly lays out the different players, questions, and concerns involved in this era of bomba practice. Thus, the conversatorios have served the purpose of both consolidating a critical mass interested in engaging bomba more deeply, and in creating a lasting record. Although, the recordings of these forums have not yet found their way to a central archive—because there is no archive on bomba due to its perceived lack of archival value—this inventory marks a first step in making them visible and available to a broader public, one who may wish to one day sit and listen to the stories and teachings contained within the oral histories that have and will continue to sustain the genre.

Finally, we wish to mention other research on bomba that did not make it into this special issue, either because of timing or other circumstances, but that nonetheless signals other critical areas of interest not covered here. These include Manuela Arciniegas' work on women drummers in New York in relation to the historical racialization of gendered behavior, Micaela Díaz-Sánchez's engagement of bomba as a Queer Chicana, and Beth Colón-Pizzini's examination of the role of bomba recordings by reggaetón artists such as Tego Calderón and La Tribu de Abrante in bomba's recent repopularization as a space of Afro-centric identity formation. Other bomba research projects include Eileene Tejada's work on excavating the conditions for erasures of bomba in Arecibo, as well as José I. Fusté and Jade Power-Sotomayor's Bomba Wiki Project, an online digital archive in-progress. The sum of the above research and all that comes before is substantial and yet we still need much, much more as evidenced by the prevalence of miseducation and misconception about bomba popularly, within academic settings, and within Puerto Rican Studies. Some of the latent projects waiting to come to fruition, which will hopefully be seeded in some small form by the work contained herein include: historical archival research, compilation of oral histories, connections to other genres, multidisciplinary approaches to bomba's relationship with AfroCaribbean religions, attention to the political economy of bomba practice, the employment of bomba musicians in relationship to emigration and economic precarity, the various sites of bomba education and social justice projects, bomba as a practice of political subjecthood, the dynamics of commercial performance, elaboration of the diverse techniques and rhythms, the realization of commercially viable bomba recordings, and bomba on social media. For now, however, we note that the ability to linger with bomba here, in the specificities and complexities that distinguish it, as part of a call and response between scholar and practitioner, and in this newly-rendered precarious moment of Puerto Rican life, is nothing short of remarkable.

Coda: Re-picando

In addition to the many important projects not mentioned here due to spatial limitations, our own incomplete knowledges and the inevitable fallibility of memory, there are also many other intimate knowns and unknowns not alluded to here but that are, in many ways, more important: the people who make it all happen. Those who play the *buleadores* for classes, who sing the *coros*, who show up to events, who pay for the classes that employ artists, who listen deeply at the conversatorios, who bring their children so they may remember that this too is valued. The babysitters who care for the children so that the parents can experience the freedoms they seek in bomba. All the spaces that have collectively sustained these practices: the private homes that have served as rehearsal spaces, the neighbors that have varyingly tolerated and enjoyed loud music pouring out of windows into the streets, the cultural centers that have opened their halls and their stages, the businesses that have recognized the mutually beneficial relationship between bomba and selling food and drink even if they just break even. The people who design the flyers, post the events, record the videos, document with pictures, carry the drums, set up the sound. The people who sew the skirts and who iron them. The educators who have brought bomba into their classrooms. The folks who work with avid bomberxs in non-bomba related projects and who set aside their own time and resources. The people who apply for the grants, organize schedules via text, email and/or phone calls, who give rides, who bring food, who stay late to clean up, who bring the jokes and the *bochinches*. Those who keep it real and those who keep the peace. Those who forgo profit from a gig for the person who needs it more. The people who set aside their own egos so that others may shine. As with most communities created around artistic and cultural practices, bomba is a labor of love, carried out in a distinctly idiosyncratic Boricua style.

You're all a part of this story. ¡*Gracias!*

Gracias CENTRO Journal. Thank you for the space to bring works in both English and Spanish together, for nurturing scholarship from a variety of loci. An immense gratitude to Xavier Totti who, from the first suggestion, was supportive of the idea for this special issue and has patiently and expertly guided every step of this process, leading it to its fruition. A special thanks to José I. Fusté for helping initiate this vision and for adding his much-valued insight and meticulous attention to detail; for his work on the discography and for being a true collaborator on this project, in every aspect. Finally, we acknowledge the many people whose experientially-attained knowledges make such a project possible and are grateful to all who helped us verify, corroborating when possible, the many threads we have woven together here.

NOTES

[1] Pablo Luis Rivera uses "bombeador/a" to avoid the common confusion with the Spanish word for fireman "bombero." Here, writing in English, we have chosen the gender inclusive *bomberx* to describe a person who practices bomba.

[2] Batey was a word used by Taínos to denote the space used both for ceremonial *areitos* and as ball courts. It became a word used colloquially in Puerto Rico to describe a space free of obtrusive vegetation, adjacent to poor or working-class dwellings, usually of communal use (i.e., as opposed to a private yard or *patio*). In bomba it is the word used to describe the cipher-like space around which the drums, chorus and spectators congregate, and into which the dancers enter. "Batey" is also used interchangeably with "*soberao*" though the former is more common. In Castilian Spanish, "*soberado*" refers to a space that is architecturally not habitable, or useless. In Puerto Rico, "soberao" is used to describe the shared dirt floor space in a hut dwelling. In a discussion about African influences on Puerto Rican architecture, Arleen Pabón writes about this as a private-public space over which homeowners took much pride, signaling that "the soberao proves you have a space of your own (even if you are an *arrimao* and the land belongs to another person), that you possess your very own dwelling locus" (Pabón 2003). Bomba's batey/ soberao thus represents a claiming of space and a simultaneous distancing from the "outside world."

[3] Prolific artisans include Iván Dávila, Jesús Cepeda, Ángel "Papo" Del Valle, Jorge Martínez, Charlie Vega, Rafael Trinidad, Isaac Cruz, Jerry Finkelstein among a growing number of others. Most recently Bárbara Pérez-Rodríguez and Luis Ramos' Taller Kenuati has, by commission, created hundreds of individually designed maracas.

[4] According to New York-based bombero Alex LaSalle, the word "bámbula" which regularly appears in old bomba choruses and is also used as a name for a particular bomba sub-rhythm is derived from a similar word in the Ki-Kongo language that means "to remember a forgotten place." His sources for this explanation are Matu Kinzonsi, a Soukous musician as well as Dr. Fu-Kiau Bunseki and Dr. Robert Farris Thompson who are both scholars of Bantu-Kongo religions. LaSalle also states that in the Kongo-derived Palo practiced in the Hispanophone Caribbean, bámbula or similar words like Kimbamba or Kimbámbula denote the remembering of a "specific and powerful emotion found in the subconscious of a specific people" (LaSalle 2007, 14).

[5] For more on the necessity of addressing not just anti-blackness but white(r) privilege in Puerto Rico and amongst Puerto Ricans see (Fusté 2019). While there is no clear black/white binary in Puerto Rico and most Puerto Ricans, including bomberxs, have black ancestry, there remains a need to address how anti-black racism affects the most visibly black in the society.

[6] See the discography in the appendix. Additionally, virtuoso bombera Amarilys Ríos's group, Émina, has newly recorded bomba-inspired music.

[7] Pablo Luis Rivera also suggests that in this formulation plena effectively "softens" the "*africanía*" associated with bomba, thereby making bomba more broadly palatable and acceptable. (P.L. Rivera 2015).

[8] Traditional songs in today's repertoire come from diverse recordings, oral sources and recuperative projects; that said, a vast number of them come from Rafael Cepeda's meticulous collection of songs of the mid-20th century.

[9] A consensus view among bomba practitioners is that Kreyol and French lyrics evoke bomba's debt to the forced inter-Caribbean diaspora of slaves formerly enslaved in the colony of Saint-Domingue that were brought to Puerto Rico around the time of the Haitian Revolution. Because most planters from Saint-Domingue—and subsequent planter settlers from France,

Corsica, and from other francophone Caribbean islands—resettled mainly in the west of Puerto Rico, this may be the reason why Kreyol and French appears more frequently in songs associated with the Western Coast (Belmonte Postigo 2018; Camuñas Madera 1989; Galarza and Albino Pluguez n.d.). There are also songs composed during the 20th and 21st centuries that contain Kreyol in recognition of that partial ancestry.

[10] The *primo*, also referred to as the *subidor*, is the higher-pitched drum that takes the lead percussive voice and interprets the dancer's movements with different corresponding *golpes*, or hits. The other percussion instruments—*buleadores, cuá* and *maraca*—maintain the steady beat of the rhythm.

[11] In addition to works by these people cited elsewhere, see (López 2002; Maldonado 2008). Also, Maldonado has been organizing the biennial Bomba Research Conference at different sites since 2005 through the Puerto Rican Organization for the Performing Arts (PROPA).

[12] Examples include: Dufrasne-González (1994, 1985); Ramos (2011); Ferrao (2012); González García (2004); Álamo-Pastrana (2005); P. L. Rivera (2013); Ferreras (2005); Fernández Morales (1999); Adrover Barrios (2013); Viera Vargas (2008a); Peña Aguayo (2015); Berríos (2011); Quintero Rivera and Álvarez (2011); as well as unpublished oral historiographies by Nellie J. Lebrón Robles, José, Jorge and Víctor Emmanuelli Náter, and Víctor Vélez.

[13] Notably the first disc on the 2012 Rebuleadores de San Juan album *Tiempo al Tiempo* (see discography) memorializes the names of these historical bomberxs in new song compositions that have brought them into popular usage in contemporary bomba circles; whereas before they were not, as such demonstrating the power of song to repeatedly archive and reenact.

[14] In addition to long-standing projects such as Colectivo Ilé, see more recently the 2015 Primer Congreso de Afrodescendencia en Puerto Rico, the 2018 creation of *Revista Étnica*, the 2019 creation of the Black Latinas Know Collective featuring several AfroBoricua scholars as sites for activating critical black intellectual projects that in addition to black culture and arts, attend to politics, education, environmental justice, de-colonialism and historiography as intersecting with black life in Puerto Rico. See also: Godreau (2015); Lloréns, García-Quijano and Godreau (2017); Lloréns (2018). See also the work of La Colectiva Feminista en Construcción.

[15] The oldest primary source that we know of that mentions Puerto Rican bomba is a letter from the late 17th or possibly late 18th century that the mulato privateer, Miguel Enríquez (1674-1743) sent to his nephew, in which he mentions a type of drumming and dance performed at the time called "bomba" (López Cantos 1997, 38–9). Another early mention of bomba appears in the writings of the French naturalist, André Pierre Ledru, who visited Puerto Rico in 1797. In his book on his Caribbean travels, he recounts having visited an hacienda in Puerto Rico where he saw something resembling bomba, which in the French original he termed "bamboula" (Ledru 1810, 73–4, 1957). The mid-19th century *costumbrista* collection of poems titled *El gíbaro* (1849) also mentions bomba (Alonso 1849), and there are various mentions of it in early 20th century Puerto Rican literature. Bomba dances are also alluded to in Gov. Miguel de la Torre's revisions of local slave codes after various alleged slave conspiracies and attempted escapes between 1822-1826. Spanish officials feared that bomba gatherings were being used to hatch such plots. Various articles in the Reglamento de Esclavos of 1826 set explicit rules for recreational slave activities such as "sus bailes de bomba," making sure that they were held in open spaces within haciendas, under close supervision, and with strict separation between men and women, and only between 3pm and sunset, and only on Sundays or holidays (Baralt 1981, 67; Reglamento de Esclavos de 1826 2003).

[16] For example, in 1922, the Partido Unión's autonomist paper *La Democracia* printed a front-

page denunciation of a private bomba performance organized for a group of US Navy officers at the Union Club. They condemned the activity and its printed program for representing Puerto Ricans as dark-skinned primitive savages given their choice to invite bomberxs instead of lighter skinned performers of more European sounding music. Other newspaper articles about the incident noted that some criollo elite members of the Union Club protested the event because municipal ordinances of the time still banned bomba for being "detrimental to public morality" (Román 2003, 213–4; 256).

[17] For instance, the Emmanuelli brothers discussed elsewhere here, tell the story of having come to learn bomba via their own interests and in conducting research found that they were the grandchildren of the famed bombero Sergio Náter, memorialized in song. The family connection had been severed because their mother's generation had distanced themselves from bomba due to the fear of stigma.

[18] Her son Amaury Santiago Albizu now directs Bomba Iyá in Ponce and in 2012 he helped found the Escuela de Bomba y Plena Isabel Albizu with José Archeval Rodríguez.

[19] Calabó (Marie Ramos Rosado), Cimiento de Puerto Rico (Modesto Cepeda), Bombalele (Jesús Cepeda), Agueybaná (Ángel Luis Reyes), Tamboricua (Elia Cortés), La Escuela de Bomba y Plena de Caridad Brenes Cepeda (Margarita "Tata" Cepeda), Son del Batey (Omar "Pipo" Sánchez and Yván François), Restauración Cultural (Pablo Luis Rivera, Felipe "Junito" Febres and Rafael Maya), La Corporación Piñones se Integra/Majestad Negra – COPI (Maricruz Rivera Clemente, Marcos Peñaloza Pica) among others.

[20] Newer groups and projects in the 21st century not mentioned elsewhere have included Desde Cero (Rafael Maya), Rumbacuembé (Ricardo Soler and Miledys Santiago), Tambuyé (Marién Torres López) Los Rebuleadores de San Juan (Jerry Ferrao), Yubá Iré (Hector Calderón), Tambores Calientes (Marcos Peñaloza Pica), La Tribu de Abrante (Hiram Abrante), Bomba Evolución (Víctor Emmanuelli), Tendencias (Rafael Maya, Pablo Luis Rivera, Amaury Febres), Calle Cultura (Kily Vializ), El Cuarteto (Christian Galarza), La Raíz Bomba Mayagüez (Javier Muñiz and Christian Galarza), La Compañía Folclórica de Loíza (Marcos Peñaloza Pica), Taller de la Isla, (Randy Zorrilla), Los Gigantes de la Bomba Carolina (Felipe "Junito" Febres, Rafael Maya, Pablo Luis Rivera), AFROLegado (Pablo Luis Rivera and Yadilka Rodríguez), Junte Loiceño (Maribella Burgos), Bataklán (Xavier Rosario), and the youth group from Loíza Belelé (Lesvia Hernández/ Escuela Celso González Vaillant). Still others across the island have organized projects Bombalta in Cayey (Luis Sánchez), Bombae' in Luquillo (Jasmine Ocasio), Las ChamaKas del Buleo in Mayagüez (Jamie Pérez/Collective), Centro Cunyabe in Salinas (José Luis Baerga Aguirre), Colectivo Umoja in Guayama (Julie Laporte/Collective), as well as the long-standing and widely popular monthly bombazos in Hormigueros organized by Chayanne Martínez.

[21] For more on soberao see footnote 2.

[22] The late 17th-early 18th century letter that mentioned bomba referenced in a previous footnote was written by Miguel Enríquez, a wealthy privateer who lived in the old city of San Juan. The musicians and dancers he alluded to in the letter also lived in that area so we can presume that he had witnessed bomba around the San Juan area at that juncture. Also, in an interview, Rafael Cepeda mentions that bomba was played in various parts of the islet of San Juan—including within the old walled city—in the 1800s (Batista n.d.).

[23] Many dedicated individuals have labored to upload and curate countless bomba videos. Dennis Flores in New York was among the first to harness YouTube as a bomba resource in its early stages as a platform.

[24] Chicago's Bomba con Buya, whose members have family roots in Guayama, has also acti-

vated notable exchanges through events with bomberxs in Guayama in recent years, cultivating relationships with and celebrating elders such as Miguel Flores.

[25] Berta Jottar writes about a dynamic that existed in the 1970s in New York where Nuyoricans interested in celebrating their African heritage through learning bomba were denied study by Nationalist musicians from the island who deemed them not "authentic" enough for the "tradition" (Jottar 2011, 16).

[26] The Cepeda family first toured to the United States and Mexico in the 1970s performing a variety of *estampas* choreographed by daughter Petra Cepeda who would also sometimes lead informal "lecture/demonstrations." However, it wasn't until 1995, first as an experiment in New York and later more formally and across 25 states in 1998, that members of the Cepeda family—Roberto, Mario, Jesús, Luis "Chichito," Julia, José, Mandy Francesca, and on later tours Modesto, Gladys and Brenda—would officially teach through specific bomba and plena residencies and classes, at this point able to engage with a public interested in learning, not just being entertained. Integral to these tours were those who had been brought into bomba through their proximity to the family by living in Villa Palmera and Rafael Cepeda's recognition of the social value of teaching bomba to "*los muchachos del barrio*": Víctor Vélez, Ángel Luis "Balancé" Reyes, Juan Usera, Vilma Sastre, José "Nuno" Calderón, Mikey, Anthony and Ito Carrillo among others. Later visits from Paracumbé's Nellie J. Lebrón, in Chicago and Elia Cortés in California were also influential.

[27] Some key figures in laying the groundwork for and consolidating bomba practice in the diaspora not already mentioned elsewhere include Tito Cepeda, Jorge Vázquez, Mickey Sierra, Pedro "Único" Noguet, Papo Reyes, Tato Torres in New York. Myrna Rodríguez, Ángel Fuentes, Rubén Gerena, Roberto Pérez in Chicago, Héctor Lugo, María Elena García, Edwin Monclova, José Rodríguez, José I. Fusté in California, Ana María Tekina-eirú Maynard in Texas among others. Of the many groups and projects formed in the diaspora not mentioned elsewhere —though not all currently active— some have been Yerbabuena, Bámbula, Herencia Negra, Los Bomberos de Brooklyn, Bomba Yo, Redobles de Cultura, AfroInspira, Bombazo Dance Co., Ballet Folklorico de Celia Ayala, Borinbomba, Raíces Boricua, Cocobalé, Bembeteo, I'naru Chitown Bomberas, Grupo Paulé, Cacique y Kongo, Aguacero, Orgullo Boricua, Areito Borincano, Atabey, Bomba Liberté, Bomba E, Puerto Rican Folkloric Dance, Grupo Folklorico de Bomba y Plena Lanzo, Zona de Bomba, Semilla Cultural, Madre Tierra, Proyecto Piquete, Cukiara.

[28] It is important to note that the relationship to the "folkloric" costume codified in the 20th century by the Cepeda family is one that can be nuanced and complex to many bomberxs, especially women, taking great pride in wearing it, celebrating Caridad Cepeda de Brenes' visions and innovations as a designer, while also actively disidentifying with its stereotypifying effect. Furthermore, in attempts to challenge the individualism that has come with the development of the genre as a solo dance, some bomberxs have reintroduced "*bailes de pareja*," as a form of "re-socializing" the batey and have also subsequently attended to a recuperation of earlier practices without necessarily instantiating an enforcement of gendered identities.

[29] Their archive can be found at <http://segundaquimbamba.org/guiro-y-maraca-archive/>.

[30] Julia Gutierrez-Rivera, Personal communication. 27 October 2017.

[31] Lladó Ortega's essay discusses Lío Villahermosa's public use of a skirt for the first time at a bombazo in Puerto Rico in 2012. Yet, since 2003 José López, a bombero from Guayanilla living in San Diego, has been dancing publicly with skirts, as have other male-identifying bomberxs in the diaspora.

REFERENCES

Adrover Barrios, Itzaira E. 2013. Perspectiva antropográfica del baile de bomba en Guayama y Arroyo durante el siglo XIX. Ph.D. dissertation, University of Puerto Rico, Río Piedras.

Alamo-Pastrana, Carlos. 2005. Con el Eco de los barriles: Race, Gender, and the Bomba Imaginary in Puerto Rico. *Identities* 16(5), 573–600.

Alonso, Manuel A. 1849. *El gíbaro: cuadro de costumbres de la isla de Puerto Rico*. Barcelona: J. Oliveres.

Álvarez Nazario, Manuel. 1960. Historia de las denominaciones de los bailes de bomba. *Revista de Ciencias Sociales* 4(1), 59–63.

Aparicio, Frances R. 1998. *Listening to Salsa: Gender, Latin Popular Music, and Puerto Rican Cultures*. Hanover, NH: University Press of New England.

Baralt, Guillermo A. 1981. *Esclavos rebeldes: conspiraciones y sublevaciones de esclavos en Puerto Rico (1795-1873)*. Río Piedras, PR: Ediciones Huracán.

Barton, Halbert. 1995. The Drum Dance Challenge: An Anthropological Study of Gender, Race, and Class Marginalization of Bomba in Puerto Rico. Ph.D. dissertation, Cornell University.

________. 2004. A Challenge For Puerto Rican Music: How To Build A Soberao For Bomba. *CENTRO: Journal of the Center for Puerto Rican Studies* 16(1), 68–89.

Batista, Gustavo. n.d. Entrevista a Rafael Cepeda. Accessed 8 July 2019. <http://www.mymdpr.com/rafael-cepeda/>.

Belmonte Postigo, José Luis. 2018. Esclavitud, libertad y status social en Santo Domingo y Puerto Rico durante la diáspora de La Revolución Haitiana. In *Formas de Liberdade : Gratidão, Condicionalidade e Incertezas No Mundo Escravista Nas Américas, México, Cuba, Porto Rico, Santo Domingo, Caribe Francês, Brasil et Argentina*, eds. Jonis Freire and María Verónica Secreto. Rio de Janeiro: Mauad X.

Berríos, Raúl. 2011. *Bámbula: bomba puertorriqueña*. San Juan: n.p.

Cadilla de Martínez, María. 1933. *La poesía popular en Puerto Rico*. Madrid: Universidad de Madrid.

Camuñas Madera, Ricardo R. 1989. Los franceses en el oeste de Puerto Rico. *Caravelle* 53, 25–36.

Cartagena, Juan. 2004. When Bomba Becomes the National Music of the Puerto Rico Nation... *CENTRO: Journal of the Center for Puerto Rican Studies* 16(1), 15–35.

Dufrasne-González, Emanuel J. 1985. La homogeneidad de la música caribeña: sobre la música comercial y popular de Puerto Rico. Ph.D. Dissertation, University of California, Los Angeles.

________. 1994. *Puerto Rico también tiene... ¡tambó! Recopilación de artículos sobre la plena y la bomba*. Río Grande, PR: Paracumbé

Fernández Morales, José E. 1999. Análisis sobre cantos de bomba recogidos en Cataño. MA. thesis, Centro de Estudios Avanzados de Puerto Rico y el Caribe.

Ferrao, Jerry. 2012. *Ayeres de la bomba*. Documentary Film.

Ferreras, Salvador. 2005. Solo Drumming in the Puerto Rican Bomba: An Analysis of Musical Processes and Improvisational Strategies. Ph.D. dissertation, University of British Columbia.

Findlay, Eileen. 1999. *Imposing Decency: The Politics of Sexuality and Race in Puerto Rico, 1870-1920*. Durham, NC: Duke University Press.

Fiol-Matta, Licia. 2017. *The Great Woman Singer: Gender and Voice in Puerto Rican Music*. Durham, NC: Duke University Press.

Flores, Juan. 2000. *From Bomba to Hip-Hop: Puerto Rican Culture and Latino Identity*. New York: Columbia University Press.

———. 2009. *The Diaspora Strikes Back: Caribeño Tales of Learning and Turning*. New York: Routledge.

Fusté, José I. 2019. Residente en la blanquitud boricua. *80grados* 15 February. Accessed 13 July 2019. <http://www.80grados.net/residente-en-la-blanquitud-boricua/>.

Galarza, Alberto and Edwin Albino Pluguez. n.d. Bomba mayagüezana. <https://sites.google.com/site/bombaplenaymuchomas/bombamayag%C3%BCezana/>.

Glasser, Ruth. 1995. *My Music Is My Flag: Puerto Rican Musicians and Their New York Communities, 1917-1940*. Berkeley: University of California Press.

Godreau, Isar. 2015. *Scripts of Blackness: Race, Cultural Nationalism, and US. Colonialism in Puerto Rico*. Chicago: University of Illinois Press.

González García, Lydia Milagros. 2004. *Elogio de la bomba: homenaje a la tradición de Loíza*. Loíza, PR: La Mano Poderosa.

Jottar, Berta. 2011. Central Park Rumba: Nuyorican Identity and the Return to African Roots. *CENTRO: Journal of the Center for Puerto Rican Studies* 13(1), 5–29.

Kinsbruner, Jay. 1996. *Not of Pure Blood: The Free People of Color and Racial Prejudice in Nineteenth-Century Puerto Rico*. Durham, NC: Duke University Press.

LaSalle, Alex. 2007. Bambula. *Guiro y Maraca* Fall.

Ledru, André Pierre. 1810. *Voyage aux îles de Ténériffe, la Trinité, Saint-Thomas, Sainte-Croix et Porto Ricco : exécuté par ordre du gouvernement français, depuis le 30 septembre 1796 jusqu'au 7 juin 1798, sous la direction du capitaine Baudin, pour faire des recherches et des collections relatives à l'histoire naturelle ...* Translated by C. S. Sonnini. Paris: Chez Arthus Bertrand.

Ledru, André Pierre. 1957. *Viaje a la isla de Puerto Rico en el año 1797*. Translated by Julio L. de. Vizcarrondo. San Juan: Instituto de Cultura Puertorriqueña.

Lloréns, Hilda. 2018. Beyond Blanqueamiento: Black Affirmation in Contemporary Puerto Rico. *Latin American and Caribbean Ethnic Studies* 13(2), 157–78.

Lloréns, Hilda, Carlos G. García-Quijano and Isar Godreau. 2017. Racismo en Puerto Rico: ¿problema negado?" *80grados* 21 July. Accessed 13 July 2019. <http://www.80grados.net/racismo-en-puerto-rico-problema-negado/>.

López, Ramón. 2002. *La cultura popular puertorriqueña en los Estados Unidos*. San Juan: Instituto de Cultura Puertorriqueña.

López Cantos, Angel. 1997. *Mi tio, Miguel Enríquez*. San Juan: Instituto de Cultura Puertorriqueña.

López Cruz, Francisco. 1967. *La música folklórica de Puerto Rico*. Sharon, CT: Troutman Press.

Los Ayala-Bomba Puertorriqueña-Datos. 2001. Accessed 13 July 2019. <http://www.prfrogui.com/home/ayala-bomba.htm/>.

Maldonado, Melanie A. 2008. *Bomba Trigueña*: Diluted Culture and (Loss of) Female Agency in AfroPuerto Rican Music and Dance Performance. In *Caribbean Without Borders*, eds. Dorsia Smith, Raquel Puig and Ileana Cotés Santiago. 95–117. New Castle upon Tyne, UK: Cambridge Scholars Publishing.

Moten, Fred. 2003. *In the Break*. Minneapolis: University of Minnesota Press.

Muñoz, María Luisa. 1966. *La música en Puerto Rico: panorama histórico cultural*. Sharon, CT: Troutman Press.

Pabón, Arlene. 2003. Por la encendida calle antillana: African Impact on Puerto Rican Domestic Architecture. *Places of Cultural Memory: African Reflections on the American Landscape*. 140. National Parks Survey Conference Proceedings. Washington DC: National Center for Cultural Resources.

Peña Aguayo, José Javier. 2015. La bomba contemporánea en la cultura musical contemporánea. Ph.D. dissertation, Universidad de Valencia.

Power-Sotomayor, Jade. 2020. Corporeal Sounding: Listening to Bomba Dance, Listening to Puertorriqueñxs. *Performance Matters* 6(2): n.a.

Quintero Rivera, Ángel G. 2009. *Cuerpo y cultura: las músicas mulatas y la subversión del baile.* Madrid: Iberoamericana.

Quintero Rivera, Ángel G., and Luis Manuel Álvarez. 2011. Bambulaé sea allá, la bomba y la plena: compendio musical. SCRIBD. Accessed 13 July 2019. <https://www.scribd.com/document/176146880/bambula-sea-all-la-bomba-y-la-plena-compendio-histrico-social/>.

Ramos, Marie. 2011. *Destellos de la negritud: investigaciones caribeñas.* San Juan: Isla Negra.

Reglamento de Esclavos de 1826. 2003. Accessed 13 July 2019. <https://sites.rootsweb.com/~poncepr/reglamento.html/>.

Rivera, Pablo Luis. 2013. Orígenes culturales y desarrollo de la bomba puertorriqueña. Ph.D. dissertation, Centro de Estudios Avanzados de Puerto Rico y el Caribe.

________. 2015. El surgimiento de escuelas de bomba independientes ante la ausencia de enseñanza en el currículo oficial del sistema de educación en Puerto Rico. *Musiké* 4(1), 65–95.

Rivera, Raquel Z. 2003. *New York Ricans from the Hip Hop Zone.* New York: Palgrave Macmillan.

________. 2010. New York Bomba: Puerto Ricans, Dominicans, and a Bridge Called Haiti. In *Rhythms of the Afro-Atlantic World: Rituals and Remembrances,* eds. Mamadou Diouf and Ifeoma Kiddoe Nwankwo. Ann Arbor: University of Michigan Press.

________. 2012. New York Afro-Puerto Rican and Afro-Dominican Roots Music: Liberation Mythologies and Overlapping Diasporas. *Black Music Research Journal* 32(2), 3–24.

________. 2013. In Praise of New York Bomba: A Three-Part Series. *VOICES: The Journal of New York Folklore* 39(3–4), 22–6.

Rivera-Rideau, Petra R. 2015. *Remixing Reggaetón: The Cultural Politics of Race in Puerto Rico.* Durham, NC: Duke University Press.

Román, Reinaldo L. 2003. Scandalous Race: Garveyism, the Bomba, and the Discourse of Blackness in 1920s Puerto Rico. *Caribbean Studies* 31(1), 213–59.

Taylor, Diana. 2003. *The Archive and the Repertoire : Performing Cultural Memory in the Americas.* Durham, NC: Duke University Press.

Vega Druet, Hector. 1979. Historical and Ethological Survey on Probable African Origin of the Puertorrican Bomba: Including a Description of Santiago Apostol Festivalities at Loíza Aldea. Ph.D. dissertation, Wesleyan University.

Viera Vargas, Hugo René. 2008a. De-Centering Identities: Popular Music and the (Un)Making of Nation in Puerto Rico, 1898-1940. Ph.D. dissertation, Indiana University.

________. 2008b. La colección John Alden Mason: una documentación sonora para la historia de Puerto Rico. *Caribbean Studies* 36(2), 161–8.

APPENDIX

Bomba Filmography

Ballet Folklorico De Bomba y Plena Familia Cepeda. 1994. V&R Productions. DVD.

Borcherding, Eric, dir. 1986. *Don Rafael Cepeda: Patriarca de la Bomba y la Plena*. Instituto de Cultura Puertorriqueña. https://youtu.be/ms9Ov6Yu2GY.

Capeles Segarra, Ángela M., dir. 2017. *La Bomba: A Puerto Rican Tool of Resistance Through Creative Expression*. https://youtu.be/BYnMPeEqOIQ.

Ferrao, Jerry, dir. 2012. *Ayeres de la Bomba*. Independently produced. No DVD or online copies available.

García, Joaquín "Quino," dir. 1985. *Baquiné Para Un Maestro*. Taller de Cine La Red.

Hernández, Mario. 1977. *Mi Aventura en Puerto Rico*, feat. Antonio Aguilar, the Cepeda Family.

James, Ashley, dir. 2000. *Bomba, Dancing the Drum*. Roberta Singer, Familia Cepeda (Musical group), Searchlight Films., City Lore. https://vimeo.com/198901090.

Maldonado, Melanie. 2005. *Bomba Research Conference*. 12 part DVD.

Nazario, Papo, dir. 2012. *Un Belém Pa' Rafael: El Documental*. Jesus Cepeda, Instituto de Cultura Puertorriqueña., National Endowment for the Arts. DVD.

Restauración Cultural. 2008. *Documento Educativo Para Aprender a Bailar Bomba, Básico*. DVD.

———. 2008. *Documento Educativo Para Aprender a Tocar Bomba, Básico Bomba*. DVD.

Richeport-Hayley, Madeline, dir. 2008. *Puerto Rican Bomba: In Search of Our Roots*. Triangle Productions., Filmmakers Library, inc. DVD.

Sanchez, William Q, dir. 2002. *La Bomba*. NJN Public Television, Trenton, NJ. DVD.

Suau, Paloma, dir. 2001. *Raíces*. Ángel Peña, Banco Popular de Puerto Rico., Paradiso Films. https://youtu.be/mvTX6YA30Lc.

Tirado, Amílcar, dir. 1966. *La Plena*. División de Educación a la Comunidad (DIVEDCO). https://archive.org/details/LaPlena.

Torres, Oscar, dir. 1955. *Nenén De La Ruta Mora*. División de Educación a la Comunidad (DIVEDCO). https://youtu.be/Ch-0fKT6SbA.

Vissepó, Mario, dir. 1983. *La Herencia De Un Tambor*. Cinetel. Part 1: https://youtu.be/VhcgmehknuE, Part 2: https://youtu.be/rcTtuuhWRCA.

Bomba Discography

Albizu, Isabel. 2010. *Isabel Albizu: La Matriarca de la Bomba y su Ballet Folklórico Bambalué*. Casabe Records, CD, MP3.

Alduén, Félix. 2006. *Candela*. Casabe Records, CD, MP3.

Alma Moyó. 2010. *No Hay Sábado Sin Sol*. Independent production, CD, MP3.

Areyto: Ballet Folklórico Nacional de Puerto Rico. 1977. *La Música del Areyto*. Independent production, LP.

Atabal. 1991. *Voces y Tambores*. Taller Estudio TE790, CD.

———. 1993. *Música Morena*. Saravá Records ATABAL93, CD.

Barez, Héctor "Coco." 2017. *El Laberinto del Coco*. Obi Musica, CD, MP3.

Bomba con Buya. 2015. *Buya (Live)*. Independent Production, CD, MP3.

———. 2019. *Southern Sessions*. Independent Production, CD, MP3.

Bomba Con Trovadores. 2015. *Juntos Sonamos Mejor*. CD. Taller Palenque Inc. 889211472802, CD, MP3.

Bomba Siglo XXI. 2014. *Pal' Marunguey*. CD. Jose E. Pizarro, Independent production, 888174683232, CD, MP3.

Bomba y Plena. 2009. *Pal' Mundo*. Diamond Music & Mini Diamond, CD, MP3.
Boria, Juan. 1992. ¡Que Negrota! *Declama Juan Boria, el faraón del verso negro con Rafael Cepeda y sus Bomberos*. Disco Hit, CD.
__________. 2017. *Majestad Negra*. Instituto de Cultura Puertorriqueña, CD, MP3.
Calderón, Tego. 2003. *El Abayarde*. White Lion Music. WL004, CD, MP3.
__________. 2006. *El Underdog*. Jiggiri Records, CD, MP3.
__________. 2015. *El Que Sabe Sabe*. Jiggiri Records, CD, MP3.
Compañía Folclórica de Loíza. 2010. *Bombas de Mi Batey*. Independent Production, CD.
Cepeda, Jesús. Y su Grupo ABC. 1988. *Pa' los Maestros*. High Yield Records 01, LP.
__________. 2011. *De la raíz a la salsa*. AudioLab and Mas Studio 884501565264, CD, MP3.
Cepeda, Luis "Chichito." 2003. *Dancing the Drum*. Bembé 602303202824, CD, MP3.
Cepeda, Modesto. 1992. *Encuentro de bomba y plena*, Independent Production, CD.
__________. 1995. *Raíces de bomba y plena*, Independent Production, CD.
__________. 1997. *Legado de bomba y plena*, Independent Production, CD.
__________. 2000. *Antología*, CD.
__________. 2003. *De la bomba al bolero*. Bombazo music 862247612, CD.
Cepeda, Rafael. 1977. *Patriarca de la Bomba*. Cangrejo 664829197, LP.
__________. 1996. *El Roble Mayor*. Bombale Records HC010CD, CD.
__________. 2017. *In Spirit: 20 Years After His Death*. Bombale Records 8829567935, CD.
Cepeda, William. 1998. *My Roots and Beyond*. Blue Jacket Records BJAC 5028-2, CD.
__________. 2000. *Expandiendo Raíces*. Blue Jacket Records BJAC 5037, CD.
__________. 2008. *Ando Vacilando*. Casabe records. CD
__________. 2017. *Bomba Jazz*. Casabe Records, CD, MP3.
Cortijo, Rafael. 1977. *Caballero de Hierro*. Coco Records MPCDP-6223, CD.
Cortijo y Kako 1970. *Ritmos y Cantos Callejeros*. Ansonia HGCD 1477, CD.
Cortijo y su Combo, con Ismael Rivera. 1958. *Baile con Cortijo y su Combo*. Seeco Records SCCD-9130, CD, MP3.
__________. 1958. *El Alma de Un Pueblo*. SCLP 9326, CD, MP3.
__________. 1959. *Cortijo en Nueva York*. Gema Records LPG-1115, CD, MP3.
__________. 1959. *Quítate de la Vía Perico*. Gema Records LPG 1148, CD, MP3.
__________. 1960. *Fiesta Boricua*. Gema Records LPG-1119, CD, MP3.
El Gran Combo 1973. *Bombas, Bombas, Bombas*. Gema Records LP-3044, CD, MP3.
Desde Cero 2012. *Semilla de Identidad*. Independent production, CD, MP3.
García, Fernando. 2013. *Subidor*. Montalvo Records, CD, MP3.
__________. 2018. *Guasábara Puerto Rico*. Zoho Music, CD, MP3.
Grupo Afroboricua. *Bombazo*. Blue Jackel Entertainment BJAC 5027-2, CD, MP3.
Grupo Yubá. 2005. *Chicago Sabe a Bomba y Plena*. Independent production, CD.
Hermanos Ayala. 2002. *Bomba de Loíza*. Casabe 727 CD, MP3.
La Sista. 2006. *Majestad Negroide*. Machete Music, CD, MP3.
La Tribu de Abrante. 2016. *Otro Formato de Música*. The Last Latin Records, CD, MP3.
Los Pleneros de la 21. Conjunto Melodía Tropical. 1990. *Para Todos Ustedes*. Shanachie Globetrotters Series 65001, CD, MP3.
__________. 1996. *Somos Boricuas/ We Are Puerto Rican*. Henry Street, CD, MP3.
__________. 1997. *Puerto Rico Tropical*. Lattitudes LAT50608, CD.
__________. 2005. *Para Todos Ustedes*. Smithsonian Folkways SFW40519, CD, MP3.
__________. 2018. *Live at Pregones*. Truth Revolution Recording Collective 0931139372, CD, MP3.

Los Pleneros de la 23 abajo. 2005. *Bembe en la 21.* Independently Produced 888295543309, CD, MP3.
Los Rebuleadores de San Juan. 2012. *Tiempo al Tiempo.* Independent Production 684557461523. CD, MP3.
Marcial Reyes y sus Pleneros and Cuerdas de Borinquen. *Puerto Rico in Washington.* Smithsonian Folkways SFW40460, CD, MP3.
Martínez, Leró. 2015. *Sacao' d el horno.* Independent production, CD.
_________. 2016. *Boricua Soy.* Independent production, CD.
Nuestro Tambó. 2010. *Otras Historias de Elena.* Independent production 884501268677, CD, MP3.
Paracumbé. 1987. *Bomba y Plena.* Independent production, LP (available on youtube).
_________. 1997. *Tambó.* Independent production, CD, MP3.
Puertorican Folkloric Jazz. 2008. *Barriles De Bomba.* Jorge D. Rodriguez 684557517220, CD.
Rivera, Ismael. Rafael Cortijo. 1977. *Llaves de la Tradición.* Tico Records LPS 99.028, CD.
Segunda Quimbamba. 2010. *Aquí También.* SQFC Records 884502361643, CD, MP3.
_________. 2015. *Experimental y Tradicional.* SQFC Records 888295300575, CD, MP3.
Tambuyé. 2013. *Tambuyé.* Independent production B00FL5O87K, CD, MP3.
Torruellas, Ángel Luis. N.d. *Plenas y bombas.* Borinquen DG-1092, LP.
_________. 2005. *A Gozar de la Plena y la Bomba.* Disco Hit DHCD-2130, CD, MP3.
Various Artists. 1971. *Folk Songs of Puerto Rico.* Smithsonian Folkways Recordings, CD, MP3.
_________. 1977. *Caliente = Hot.* New World Records NW 244, CD.
_________. 1999. *Bombas y Plenas Bailables de Puerto Rico.* Disco Hit DHCD 8201, CD.
_________. 2001. *Raíces.* Banco Popular de Puerto Rico, CD.
_________. 2010. *Así bailaba Puerto Rico al son de la bomba y plena.* West Side Latino Records WSCD 4449, CD.
_________. 2012. *Saoco!* The Bomba and Plena Explosion in Puerto Rico. Vampisoul, CD, MP3.
_________. 2013. *Saoco!* Bomba, Plena and the Roots of Salsa in Puerto Rico 1955-1967Vampisoul, CD, MP3.
_________. 2016. *De Puerto Rico al Mundo.* Banco Popular de Puerto Rico, CD, MP3.
_________. 2017. *Plenas y bombas de Puerto Rico.* Mambo Music, CD, MP3.
_________. 2018. *Más de un Siglo.* Banco Popular de Puerto Rico, CD, MP3.
Vázquez, Jorge. 2013. *Cuando La Bomba Te Llama, Vol. 1.* Jorge Vázquez 884501985314, CD, MP3.
Viento de Agua. 1998. *De Puerto Rico Al Mundo.* Qbadisc/Agogo B0047R4F26, CD, MP3.
_________. 2004. *Viento De Agua Unplugged: Materia Prima.* Smithsonian Folkways Recordings B000V8YS9U, CD, MP3.
_________. 2009. *Fruta Madura.* Independent production B002ZYVBLQ, CD, MP3.
_________. 2013. *Opus IV.* Independent production B00GTB4EGA, CD, MP3.
_________. 2015. *Sonidos Primarios.* Independent production 888295325981, CD, MP3.
Yubá Iré. 2007. ¡Esta es mi rumba! Independent production 885767826458, CD, MP3.
_________. 2011. ¡Ya está! ¡Se formó! Independent production 885767912342, CD, MP3.
_________. 2018. ¡Baila Conmigo! Independent production 192914227342, CD, MP3.
Zona de Bomba. 2015. *Zona De Bomba.* CD. Independent production 190394028701, CD, MP3.

VOLUME XXXI • NUMBER II • SUMMER 2019

Centro y periferia: las identidades en el nuevo movimiento de la bomba puertorriqueña

BÁRBARA IDALISSEE ABADÍA-REXACH

ABSTRACT

The new Puerto Rican *bomba* movement (NMB), a period I define from 1995 until today, proposes new ways of seeing and analyzing contemporary bomba. The spread of bomba groups and the uses applied to the rhythm are proof of how Puerto Rican identities are reconfigured. From bomba aerobics, baby bomba, bomba workshops, and *bombazos*, syncopated identities are interwoven on Puerto Rican race, nationality, culture, gender, and class. On one hand, a rhetoric of miscegenation that overlaps the essence of blackness in bomba stands out. This blackness is also negotiated under the light of the discourse of bomba as a purely cultural manifestation. In this article, from an ethnographic point of view, I describe NMB as a setting that showcases the reconfigurations of blackness. In NMB, blackness is positioned in relation to the idea of the democratization of bomba. [Keywords: Puerto Rican bomba, racialization, identities, race, miscegenation, Puerto Rico]

The author (barbara.abadiarexach@gmail.com) is communicator and social anthropologist. She obtained her bachelor's and master's degrees in Communication from the University of Puerto Rico. Later on, she completed a doctorate in Sociocultural Anthropology at the University of Texas at Austin. She is the author of the book *Musicalizando la raza. La racialización en Puerto Rico a través de la música* (Ediciones Puerto, 2012). She is currently an adjunct assistant professor at the University of Puerto Rico, Río Piedras Campus.

Introducción

Puerto Rico es una nación racializada en la que el mito de la democracia racial —la gran familia puertorriqueña— se manifiesta en los discursos nacionales, raciales, culturales, de clase y de género. Se ha institucionalizado la idea de que en el país no existe racismo. Los dichos populares "¿Y tu agüela a'onde ejtá?" y "Porque aquí el que no tiene de dinga tiene de mandinga" se utilizan para enfatizar el mestizaje desde lo que bien puede entenderse como multiculturalismo neoliberal. Sin duda, son formas de obliterar las discusiones sobre la raza en el país; inclusive, se anula la existencia de la inequidad racial que opera desde distintos frentes en el archipiélago.

En este artículo, utilizo la bomba puertorriqueña contemporánea, un escenario fértil para explorar los discursos sobre la raza en Puerto Rico, como herramienta de análisis. El género musical de raigambre africana, tal como pervive hoy día, permite problematizar y visibilizar las complejidades que definen la raza en el país. ¿Cómo se constituye el discurso racial en Puerto Rico? ¿Cómo opera la raza en Puerto Rico? Estas son solo algunas de las preguntas que busco responder a la luz de la bomba puertorriqueña contemporánea. Particularmente, busco exponer cómo las paradojas sobre el discurso racial en Puerto Rico abonan a perpetuar prácticas de discriminación y prejuicio racial. Bajo la premisa de que la bomba es un espacio democrático para hacer cultura, permean prácticas indiscutiblemente racistas, que anulan el reclamo por la equidad racial en el país y perpetúan la folclorización de la Negritud.

La bomba adoquinada

En enero de 2015, vi en Facebook el enlace de un vídeo[1] que me llamó la atención. El vídeo se grabó durante las Fiestas de la Calle San Sebastián.[2] Las fiestas de la Calle San Sebastián nacieron en la década de 1950, cuando un párroco católico quiso recaudar fondos para restaurar la conocida calle, pero al ser trasladado a otra parroquia, cesó la celebración. Posteriormente, para los años 70, el fenecido arqueólogo e historiador Ricardo Alegría[3] retomó la idea de celebrar las fiestas, en las que se exhiben elementos de la cultura puertorriqueña. Los días que duran las fiestas, la música y las artesanías tienen un espacio primordial.

Históricamente, los organizadores de las Fiestas de la Calle San Sebastián han incluido la bomba en la oferta musical. Al menos, dentro del programa vespertino, los tradicionales *ballets* folclóricos de bomba no han estado excluidos de las fiestas típicas. Sin embargo, no fue hasta finales de los años 90 que la bomba comenzó a escucharse persistentemente en el Viejo San Juan. Grupos como Son del Batey y Los Rebuleadores de San Juan fueron pioneros en tocar semanalmente en locales hoy extintos como Nuyorican Café y Café Seda. Más recientemente, la plaza Colón y el callejón de la Tanca sirven de escenario para la bomba durante los fines de semana, algo que no se veía en el Viejo San Juan hacía 20 años.

En la edición número 45 de las Fiestas de la Calle San Sebastián, celebradas en el Viejo San Juan del 15 al 18 de enero de 2015, hubo varios grupos de bomba que tocaron por las calles de la zona histórica de la capital puertorriqueña. Además, el

Café Cuatro Sombras, localizado en la calle Recinto Sur, invitó al grupo Tendencias a tocar bomba frente al local, en la calle, con motivo de su cuarto aniversario.

Ante los sonoros repiques de los músicos de Tendencias —Pablo Luis Rivera, Rafael Maya, Amauro Febres y Gregory Palos—, la joven Glory Mar González-Mejías entró al batey a hacer sus piquetes. Cientos de personas, locales y turistas, que se aglomeraron en la calle observaron la escena, la grabaron en vídeo y la publicaron en la red social Facebook. Como cuestión de hecho, más de 400,000 personas vieron el vídeo *amateur* en Facebook y más de 14,500 lo compartieron.

Gloriann Sacha Antonetty Lebrón revivió detalladamente los 50 segundos de duración del vídeo en una entrada publicada del blog *Afrofémina*. La reseña/reflexión crítica escrita por Antonetty Lebrón se titula "Sublevación de una mujer afroboricua":

> Eran las Fiestas de la Calle San Sebastián y la mujer hizo el paseo de la mano de un caballero con una camiseta de Súper Man. El batey, los adoquines de la ciudad amurallada del Viejo San Juan. Suena de los barriles, el cuá y las maracas un Seis Corrido. La mujer vestida de tonos violetas, le hace la reverencia acostumbrada al tocador en el primo. De inmediato da cinco piquetes con una mano en su cintura y la otra aguantando su falda invisible. Mueve sus pies en avanzada provocando el movimiento de sus caderas. Hace una pausa con un piquete fuerte de hombros descansando sus puños nuevamente en las caderas. Su seriedad lo dice todo. Actitud de concentración y fortaleza en sus movimientos, en el reto al tocador. La multitud grita con cada paso firme que da. Continúa con el piquete acercándose cada vez más al tocador, creando un ritmo constante. Cruza sus piernas y avanza. Sigue con los puños cerrados apostados en su cintura, repite seis veces el piquete. Abre las manos y menea sus hombros y sus senos demostrando que no le teme a nada, que es dueña de su todo y del batey. El tocador no falla y recoge cada movimiento. Ella se inclina un poco, poniendo sus nalgas en alzada y moviendo en pasos pequeños hacia atrás todo su cuerpo. Vuelve a coger de manera simulada la falda y pide el toque. Se sacude todo con su saya. La mueve a los lados cada vez más cerca al tocador. Vuelve a dar su piquete favorito, arraigando sus puños a la cintura, agita los hombros y termina su baile. Vuelve a hacer reverencia al tambor y sale del batey sabiendo que dominó cada paso. Los aplausos de la gente lo confirman. (Antonetty Lebrón 2015)

A la par del vídeo original, se publicó un breve metraje en el que se manipuló la velocidad de los movimientos corporales de Glory Mar. Se ridiculizaron su sobrepeso, voluminosas caderas, los contundentes movimientos de su busto y su trasero. Ese metraje alterado provocó críticas negativas con respecto a la ejecución de la mujer. Se decía que Glory Mar estaba ebria y que estaba haciendo el ridículo. En Puerto Rico, el acoso y la burla hacia las personas obesas son muy comunes. Si a ese hecho se le añade el desconocimiento insular sobre cómo se baila la bomba, no causa sorpresa que Glory Mar haya sido víctima de manifestaciones producidas por la ignorancia. Lo que comenzó, quizás, como una broma, cobró importancia al confirmar cuál es la visión de un sector de la sociedad al ver a una mujer bailando bomba en la calle.[4] Glory Mar, en total control de su cuerpo, reflejó seguridad y se apoderó de la calle. Sorprendió el poder que ejerció con su cuerpo, que atrajo la atención de los espectadores y que demostró la dinámica del baile entre la bailadora y el tocador del tambor. Sobre todo, se ratificó la noción de que la bomba puede interpretarse como una música popular poco relevante, carente de valor, calidad y significación.

La reacción de Glory Mar, publicada en su perfil de Facebook el 19 de enero, se hizo pública en varios medios también:

Entonces veo que se publica un breve video, de la mano de muchos otros alusivos al desmadre y las cosas negativas ocurridas en las Fiestas de la Calle San Sebastián, en el que salgo bailando bomba puertorriqueña; gente inculta reacciona, no cuestiona, ni se inmuta en averiguar pero emiten comentarios soeces sobre los movimientos como si tuvieran pleno conocimiento de lo que allí pasó...pero sabes que, te voy explicando:

Soy una mujer afropuertorriqueña que pertenece a un núcleo de personas que sacan la cara por ti y los tuyos en cuestión al arte, la música y la cultura de tu país; tanto yo como muchos otros no tenemos inseguridades de nuestra identidad y tenemos sumamente claro lo que nos define como pueblo, que llevamos en nuestra sangre, de dónde venimos y hacia dónde queremos llegar como país.
Nos educamos e informamos de los orígenes de la bomba puertorriqueña y como se debe entrar a un "batey", repicar frente a un tambor "primo" o "subidor" para retarle y como movernos y disfrutamos de ello sanamente sin prejuicios y teniendo en mente que es para el gozo de todos los boricuas.
Para nada me siento aludida en relación a comentarios inoportunos, más bien siento lástima de quienes desconocen de sus riquezas culturales; sobre todo con un ritmo como el seis corrido que es uno de los más arraigados a su pueblo de Loíza. Si para ti es una ofensa que yo, tanto como otros excelentes músicos, bailadores y seguidores de este género, disfrutemos de la bomba en un evento cultural... mejor no le llegues, porque esto SÍ es de aquí, es mucho más antiguo que tú y hay mucha gente que se esfuerza por preservar nuestras raíces.

Edúcate e infórmate sobre tu cultura, es clave para el éxito... dicho sea de paso, dejo el video completo para que deguste quien quiera, en este Facebook se respeta la liberta de expresión.

PD: gracias a ese corillo de gente, de otras escuelas y proyectos, que sacaron metralletas de sabiduría y opacaron al ignorante... ¡más que agradecida!

El músico Pablo Luis Rivera (2015) asimismo reseñó el momento en su página de Facebook, y manifestó:

Tal y como sucede en estas ocasiones algunas personas, (que se convierten en la nota discordante), trataron de subir un video donde una dama (Glory Mar González Mejías) que disfrutaba de su cultura bailando bomba con (el grupo) "Tendencias", utilizando su cuerpo como instrumento, ejecutando sus piquetes para que el tocador del primo o subidor marcara sus pasos simultáneamente, fuera tomado para tratar de ridiculizar la escena y a la persona en cuestión. La energía de la presentación, el ritmo que se ejecutaba en ese momento, (seis corrido de Loíza), la euforia del público en la calle escuchando las voces y canciones, los tambores, barriles de bomba, el cuá, los distintos sones, ritmos y seises, provocaron que todas las personas bailaran con una fuerza y emoción inigualable. Sin embargo, las personas que subieron el mencionado vídeo, y muchos de los que comentaron, no conocen lo que es la música tradicional de su país y peor aún, tienen un prejuicio muy grande, especialmente contra los elementos negros, demostraron una gran distorsión en su conocimiento, demostraron que lamentablemente desconocían de que se trataba la presentación, y se trataron de mofar de las personas que ejecutaron y bailaron, y de los componentes de raíz africana en nuestra nación presentados en este espacio, lo que también demuestra muchos otros prejuicios y odios que no abonan a una mejor sociedad y demuestras una gran falta de educación en nuestro país reflejado en la voces de algunas de estas personas.

La popularidad del vídeo y la acogida de las manifestaciones de Glory Mar han sido tales que la versión digital del periódico *Metro* publicó una nota titulada "Joven defiende la cultura afropuertorriqueña de las críticas" (Joven defiende 2015). Por su parte, el portal en línea *TuNoticiaPR* tituló su reseña "Mujer saca la cara por la tradición en las Fiestas de la Calle San Sebastián" (Vídeo: mujer saca la cara 2015). Finalmente, en el programa de televisión *Día a Día*, contaron con la presencia de Glory Mar, y dedicaron el segmento, titulado "Bailarina de bomba de la SanSe saca la cara por la tradición puertorriqueña" (Bailarina de bomba de la SanSe 2015), a platicar con ella sobre qué ocurrió y por qué reaccionó públicamente. Glory Mar, acompañada de dos mujeres tocadoras del tambor, hizo una breve demostración de cómo se baila la bomba puertorriqueña. Incluso, enfatizó que la bomba es parte de la cultura e identidad puertorriqueñas.

La escena que se originó en una calle adoquinada del Viejo San Juan trascendió y recorrió las redes sociales y los medios de comunicación del país. La participación espontánea de Glory Mar González-Mejías, una mujer de 28 años nacida en el pueblo de Ponce y que se autoidentifica racialmente como Negra, provocó un debate mediático sobre la bomba puertorriqueña. Glory Mar es bailadora de bomba desde hace más de un lustro. Además, toma clases de percusión y forma parte del grupo folclórico Gracimá, dirigido por Tata Cepeda, una de las bombeadoras más reconocidas del país. Resulta interesante que, a pesar de la brevedad del vídeo, se ponen de manifiesto los contrastes entre la bomba tradicional y la bomba contemporánea.

Así que ver al grupo de bomba Tendencias tocando en la calle Recinto Sur, un nuevo espacio, como parte de la celebración del cuarto aniversario del Café Cuatro

Sombras y en la coyuntura de las Fiestas de la Calle San Sebastián es novedoso. Por ello, de entrada, llama la atención que el suceso se produjo en una de las principales calles del Viejo San Juan y no en uno de los establecimientos antes mencionados, plazas, callejones o en un batey de Loíza o Ponce, por mencionar dos de los pueblos donde la bomba tiene mayor arraigo en Puerto Rico. Hoy día, la bomba puertorriqueña tiene una presencia notable en la capital.

La bomba contemporánea exhibe nuevos actores que escenifican una integración racial.

Otro hecho atípico, que salta a la vista en el vídeo de Glory Mar, es que dos de los integrantes de Tendencias, Rafael Maya y Gregory Palos, no son fenotípicamente Negros, como solían ser los bombeadores tradicionales. La bomba contemporánea exhibe nuevos actores que escenifican una integración racial. Este hecho representa un cambio. Ver grupos de bomba integrados por personas no Negras significa que la bomba ha logrado impactar otros sectores de la sociedad puertorriqueña en los últimos 20 años.

Es evidente que Glory Mar, una experta ejecutante de la bomba, bailó espontáneamente. Glory Mar salió a bailar el seis corrido sin una falda como típicamente bailaban las mujeres bombeadoras. Por eso, son más preclaros los movimientos rítmicos que ejecuta con su cuerpo. A mi juicio, la proliferación de grupos de bomba, el aumento de espacios donde se pueden ver grupos de bomba tocando y la aparición de nuevos actores, la mayoría jóvenes, ha provocado que la rigurosidad de la práctica tradicional del baile de bomba se haya tornado laxa. Hoy día, el ajuar típico de la bailadora de bomba es prescindible. Por un lado, esa práctica es atrayente; por el otro, para los observadores, la falta del traje puede prestarse a malinterpretaciones. En el caso de Glory Mar, ver los movimientos tan marcados y al descubierto puso en duda el significado de lo que ella estaba haciendo en la calle al son de los repiques de Tendencias.

A pesar de la proliferación de talleres y grupos de bomba en la zona metropolitana de Puerto Rico, la escena durante las Fiestas de la Calle San Sebastián ha dado voz a quienes se consideran "hacedores de la cultura puertorriqueña"[5] y a las personas que muestran interés por la bomba, y aseguran que hay mucha ignorancia sobre esa tradición. De los comentarios que ha recibido Glory Mar, hay un consenso por llamar la bomba puertorriqueña como un elemento tradicional, cultural y nacional. Se asume que la bomba es un símbolo inalienable de la identidad puertorriqueña. De ese discurso se desprende que la identidad puertorriqueña es unificadora. Glory Mar insta a los puertorriqueños a aprender sobre sus raíces y su cultura, lo que implica aprender sobre la bomba y conocer el porqué de los movimientos que se emplean al bailarla. Por ello, el *performance* de la bomba cumple con los roles de entretener, atraer y educar. En este sentido, se reconfiguran los discursos de los que se agenciaba la bomba tradicional y se percibe como una bomba democrática, inclusiva y abierta que opera desde las identidades nacionales y culturales y prescinde del elemento racial.

La bomba racializada

El nuevo movimiento de la bomba puertorriqueña (NMB)[6] sirve de instrumento para explorar, principalmente, cómo se reconstruyen las identidades raciales que se vinculan a la puertorriqueñidad —desde el centro—[7] y el género musical de la bomba. Examino las instancias en las que el diálogo sobre la identidad racial se pone de manifiesto en la bomba puertorriqueña. Desde la observación presencial y virtual, identifico las paradojas sobre la Negritud[8] que se distancian de la bomba tradicional y sobrepasan la periferia[9] del soberao.[10] En fin, se trata de estudiar la polifonía del NMB y su relación con las identidades puertorriqueñas.

La historia oficial de los puertorriqueños enfatiza en su fenotipo y constitución racialmente mixta, aunque la tendencia al autoidentificarse racialmente sea dicotómica: blanco o Negro. Desde pequeños, se les enseña a los niños mediante los textos escolares que la "gran familia puertorriqueña" es una fusión heterogénea de tres razas: del indígena Taíno, del europeo (particularmente, español) y del Negro africano. Esta mezcla se celebra cada 19 de noviembre en conmemoración del Día del Descubrimiento de Puerto Rico. El "Día de la Puertorriqueñidad", como comúnmente se le llama, la mayoría de los niños que asisten a las escuelas públicas del país visten el tradicional disfraz de jíbaros, con el machete, que simboliza la identidad nacional, autenticidad y herencia blanca de los antepasados conquistadores españoles. A esta estampa se añaden niñas vestidas como Pocahontas y niños que parecen emular a los indios *cherokee* de Estados Unidos.

Una parte fundamental de la celebración consiste en las caracterizaciones de los niños bailando al ritmo de las tradicionales bomba y plena. Para el baile, visten muy similar a los jíbaros, pero les añaden colorido a sus pintorescos ajuares; los niños llevan un pañuelo en el cuello y las niñas usan pañuelos en la cabeza al estilo de la antigua imagen de "Aunt Jemima". Estos son los Negros que representan los antepasados africanos, de manera que la herencia africana se representa únicamente en el baile en estas manifestaciones artísticas. Según Godreau (2008), se reduce la Negritud a la esclavitud, y al elemento africano, como lo extranjero.

En estas celebraciones, la referencia a la brutalidad de la trata de esclavos se borra; en su lugar, se celebra la herencia como un fenómeno aislado con cabida para todos los puertorriqueños. De esta forma, el mestizaje sirve para encubrir y despolitizar la historia. El pasado multirracial se entiende como el origen de una población nacional que es mezclada. Por otra parte, esta naturaleza mixta es asumida por muchos puertorriqueños como la razón para la ausencia de racismo en la nación (Godreau 2008). En otras palabras, las narrativas puertorriqueñas oficiales afirman que el hecho de la mezcla racial ha dado como resultado una nación con una democracia racial. Este hecho se puede explicar desde la racialización como plataforma teórica.

La racialización es un concepto teórico que afirma que la raza es el eje central para cualquier práctica social y cultural. Refiere a la función estructurante de la raza "... el uso de "raza" en la estructuración de las relaciones sociales" (Oboler y Dzidzienyo 2005, 3). En Puerto Rico, no es tan evidente el binomio blanco-Negro como lo es en

Estados Unidos; sin embargo, la raza posee un carácter estructurante. El discurso cultural dominante de las tres razas y las prácticas generalizadas de mestizaje suscriben una visión de que la raza no importa en el fondo, pues "todos somos puertorriqueños".

De una parte, Puerto Rico es un país racializado donde el discurso sobre la raza organiza cognitivamente a los individuos y sus acciones. De otra parte, la música sirve como un mecanismo para negociar o enfrentar el discurso sobre la raza impuesto por los sistemas sociales. Por ejemplo, canciones como "Loíza" (2002), de Tego Calderón, y "Raza" (2014), de Welmo Romero Joseph, ponen de manifiesto la desigualdad racial. Sendas canciones enumeran ejemplos concretos de prejuicio racial y critican las prácticas discriminatorias. Históricamente, los músicos Negros y los géneros musicales que practicaban estaban subyugados, y la música de la corriente dominante (*mainstream*) era la danza que se tocaba y bailaba en los salones de baile acaparados por gente evidentemente blanca. Rafael Cortijo, un músico Afroboricua, decía que aceptaba que lo discriminaran si recibía la oportunidad de entretener a otras personas con su música (Quintero 2002). Es *vox pópuli* que los músicos Negros en Puerto Rico no podían utilizar la misma entrada que las personas interpeladas como blancas. Estos ejemplos de discriminación son evidencia de cómo opera la racialización en Puerto Rico a través de la música, entre ellos los bombeadores.[11]

La bomba en cuatro pisos

Siguiendo el modelo de los cuatro pisos de José Luis González (1980), identifico el origen de la bomba puertorriqueña durante la colonización española y demarcó su desarrollo desde la invasión estadounidense hasta hoy día. Vale la pena señalar que es imperativo pensar en el sótano y la azotea de la bomba, pero, para fines de este escrito, me circunscribo a la metáfora de los cuatro pisos para articular la idea del desarrollo histórico-racial del género musical. Para González, Puerto Rico constaba de cuatro pisos: el primer piso estaba definido por la cultura popular Afroantillana; el segundo piso se caracterizó por la presencia europea en la isla durante el siglo XIX; entretanto, el tercer piso alude a la llegada de los estadounidenses en 1898; y finalmente, el cuarto piso exhibe la modernización de Puerto Rico desde la década de 1940 y la fundación del Estado Libre Asociado en 1952 en adelante. En *El país de cuatro pisos*, González rechaza la asimilación del puertorriqueño ante cualquier presencia externa; manifiesta que los Afrocriollos fueron los precursores del nacionalismo puertorriqueño. Al dividir la sociedad entre opresores y oprimidos, define la cultura nacional como la de los opresores y dominantes versus la cultura popular constituida por los oprimidos. Por ello, contradice la idea de que la intervención de Estados Unidos trastornó la cultura puertorriqueña y creó una norteamericanización en la isla.

La bomba puertorriqueña nació en la isla en el siglo XVI, con la llegada de los Negros. Durante esa etapa de colonización española y posteriormente ante la presencia estadounidense en la isla, logró sobrevivir pese a la prohibición a la que fue sometida. En el siglo XX, empezó a despuntar como un elemento de la identidad cultural y nacional puertorriqueña. Hoy, en el siglo XXI, la bomba puertorriqueña exhibe nuevas formas de resistencia. Por lo tanto, los cuatro pisos de la bomba puertorriqueña revelan dinámicas asociadas a la Negritud y a la nacionalidad puertorriqueñas, y sirven para explicar la racialización en Puerto Rico desde la cultura popular.

Para la doctora Marie Ramos Rosado:

> **La bomba es muestra de la herencia africana en la música típica puertorriqueña. Antes de terminar el primer cuarto de siglo XVI, llegaron a nuestras costas los primeros grupos de la raza negra, traídos como esclavos con el objetivo de trabajar en la caña. Éstos no pudieron traerse sus tambores, pero en Puerto Rico y el Caribe los construyeron con los barriles de ron y tocino para dar nacimiento al barril de bomba... (2011, 37)**

La bomba "es principalmente una tradición de danza, con canto de llamada y respuesta..." (Brill 2011, 147). Los instrumentos que se utilizan para tocar bomba son el barril[12] buleador (o segundo), el barril primo (o subidor), dos palos de madera a los que llaman *cuá* y una maraca. El buleador mantiene el ritmo; entretanto, el primo dialoga con los danzantes produciendo patrones rítmicos, o improvisa si no hay nadie bailando.

Puntualiza Ramos: "La melodía puede ser interpretada por hombres y mujeres en el área norte, pero en el sur, sólo cantan las mujeres" (2011, 38). La bomba se divide entre dos ritmos: sones (son en el sur) y seises (seis en el norte). Algunos tipos son balancé, bambulaé, belén, calindá, cocobalé, congo, corvé, cuembé, cunyá, danué, gracimá, güembé, holandé, leró, mariandá, paulé, rulé, seis corrido, sicá, yubá o anaízo.

Hay una relación directa entre la bomba y la tumba francesa de Cuba, el rara de Haití y el gagá de la República Dominicana.

Estas variaciones dependen de cómo la mano golpee el tambor y qué parte del tambor se toque. Los timbres que se logran constituyen las variaciones de sonidos. Raquel Z. Rivera (2010a) recalca la influencia francesa en la bomba y la relación del ritmo con otras músicas Negras del Caribe. Por ejemplo, leró proviene de *les roses*, "las rosas" en francés. Hay una relación directa entre la bomba y la tumba francesa de Cuba, el rara de Haití y el gagá de la República Dominicana. Muchos de estos ritmos se atravesaron en las rutas caribeñas luego de la Revolución haitiana (1804) y las migraciones que entraron por el pueblo de Mayagüez, Puerto Rico. Hoy día, se juntan esas tradiciones en la diáspora Afrocaribeña en Nueva York, según asegura Raquel Z. Rivera (2010b).

Sobre el baile, del ritmo traído por los esclavos Ashanti de Ghana, añade Ramos: "Es un baile que puede ser cantado o no. Generalmente, lo baila una pareja, de forma muy dramatizada, desarrollándose una "conversación no verbal" o controversia entre (la) o el bailarín (a) y el tocador... Este baile tiene su razón de ser, pues era el medio de liberación que tenían estos seres humanos negros frente al blanco explotador o colonizador" (2011, 37). Brill describe el baile de bomba de la siguiente manera:

> En el corazón de la bomba, está el doble diálogo entre el cantante y el coro, por un lado, y los bailarines y percusionistas por el otro. Al igual que en algunas tradiciones de las islas caribeñas de habla francesa, los bailarines dictan los ritmos de los tambores. Uno de los bailarines desafía al subidor, bailando una secuencia de pasos llamados piquetes. El tocador debe responder al desafío improvisando su respuesta —el repiqueo— que tiene como objetivo transmitir e imitar los movimientos de los bailarines. Otros desafíos, cada uno más rápido y más vivo que el anterior, mantiene el nivel de energía en un punto álgido. Las canciones normalmente contienen pocas letras, con el solista improvisando variaciones cortas en una idea principal —normalmente comentando eventos de la comunidad— y el coro responde después de cada variación. (2011, 147)

Pablo Luis Rivera agrega:

> Típicamente, una bomba comienza con una solista, que canta una frase que evoca una llamada ancestral. El coro hace una respuesta a esta llamada mientras los músicos tocan instrumentos de percusión. Por supuesto, el canto es uno de los elementos importantes que definen esta música de raíz africana... Mientras tanto, los bailadores proceden con sus movimientos, en pares y sin contacto a la hora de improvisar. Si entran en pareja pueden entrar uno al lado del otro solo teniendo contacto con la mano y luego de efectuar el paseo o desplazamiento por el área de baile, la dama baila primero y el caballero baila después. El tambor afinado más agudo marca los pasos de la persona que improvisa. También se puede entrar a bailar individualmente. (2013, 89–90)

De ese ritual musical desarrollado por los Negros en Puerto Rico durante la colonización española se destaca su poder de resistencia. A pesar de que carecían de una lengua común, la bomba les sirvió de idioma unificador. El tambor se convirtió en una herramienta de comunicación que sembraba el terror entre los amos de las plantaciones (Rivera 2010). Aunque eran vigilados, no se les permitía tener contacto con Negros libres ni de otras plantaciones, y se les restringía sus tiempos de ocio para que no planificaran rebeliones y continuaran transformando el trabajo esclavo por el libre, mantuvieron una práctica que se niega a desaparecer.

En el escenario de la bomba, emergen diversas representaciones sobre la Negritud. A través de las letras y el baile, se dotan de significado las situaciones y los hechos que se intercambian social y culturalmente. Estos significados permanecen o se modifican en los imaginarios de los individuos de una generación a otra y viabilizan que los receptores de estos textos se identifiquen con ellos y que sus emisores adquieran visibilidad. Por medio del uso de la representación como categoría de análisis, puedo constatar o evidenciar cómo "... ese racismo implícito en lo que podría llamarse 'la folclorización de la negritud' tiene efectos particularmente insidiosos sobre la representación del cuerpo de la mujer negra" (Godreau 2003), pues la participación de la mujer Negra en el NMB es relevante.

En efecto, "representaciones populares de 'diferencia' racial... [énfasis] la condición de subordinación y 'pereza innata' de los negros —para la que nacen equipados naturalmente— la servidumbre, pero, al mismo tiempo, tercamente dispuestos a trabajar de acuerdo a su naturaleza y rentabilidad para sus amos..." (Hall 1997, 244).

Utilizo la bomba como un mecanismo para explicar cómo opera la racialización en el país. Inclusive, el NMB, como denomino al período que comprende el último lustro del siglo XX hasta hoy, permite explorar los procesos transnacionales y Afrodiaspóricos de formación de identidad que, de hecho, no son esencialistas. Obviamente, hay muchas maneras a través de las cuales se puede abordar el tema de la raza y su vínculo con el discurso de identidad nacional. No obstante, la bomba constituye un cosmos heterogéneo, con múltiples interseccionalidades que provocan innumerables interrogantes. Sobre todo, cuestiona cómo se (re)construye el discurso sobre la identidad racial de las personas puertorriqueñas. En la teoría, el discurso nacional unifica; en la práctica, categoriza, jerarquiza, margina y subvalora.

La bomba, un género musical Afropuertorriqueño de indudable raigambre africana, es un escenario en el que emergen mecanismos de construcción de identidades, valores y utopías. A su vez, el NMB sirve para discernir lo que el consenso sociocultural adjudica como Negro y no Negro en Puerto Rico. En la bomba, se escenifican prácticas simultáneas de afirmación, apropiación, crítica, enfrentamiento y resistencia. Los músicos, bailarines y el público que sigue la bomba en Puerto Rico calibran la Negritud desde sus experiencias ligadas a la marginación, exclusión y subestimación de habilidades intelectuales y talentos musicales.

Las diferencias que he identificado entre la bomba puertorriqueña de hoy día versus las etapas anteriores demuestran que, a la par, están ocurriendo transformaciones importantes con relación a la identidad nacional puertorriqueña y el lugar que ocupa la Negritud dentro de ese discurso de la nación. Ya sea desde la retórica del mestizaje o desde el blanqueamiento, la tendencia en la práctica del NMB es a alejarse de la Negritud. La bomba ha sido tradicionalmente un signo del primitivismo y la alteridad racial-cultural. El NMB como movimiento cultural está evolucionando hacia una noción multicultural que se ha ido expandiendo y que incluye lo Negro. Sin embargo, la apropiación de la bomba por parte de puertorriqueños no Negros y como signo de nacionalismo no ha cambiado significativamente las jerarquías raciales de la sociedad.

La bomba contemporánea

Al examinar la bomba de hoy, salen a relucir múltiples escenarios y formas de agenciarse del género musical de raigambre africana. Es por ello que se valida referirse a las dinámicas contemporáneas de la bomba como un nuevo movimiento. Para Ricardo Pons:

Hoy en día se toca mucha más bomba que hace un par de generaciones. Esto se debe, en gran medida, a que la generación de los 90's se apoderó de la tradición, se acercaron a aprender las diferentes regiones tanto en música como en baile y, al aprender, hicieron suya su misión de la bomba. Se desbancaron los gurúes de la tradición como únicos proponentes del género y se ha hecho accesible a cualquiera que demuestre interés. El lado negativo de esta proliferación de la bomba en la actualidad es que se está homogeneizando; las sutilezas que marcan los regionalismos están desapareciendo poco a poco. (2012, 246-7)

Es curioso que, a pesar de que el número y la variedad de grupos está en aumento y posee innegable diversidad, hay un consenso paralelo sobre algunos asuntos inherentes a la bomba. Al hablar con personas de distintas generaciones, hombres y mujeres, de grupos de bomba diferentes, que llegaron a la bomba a través de circunstancias diversas, resuena el tema de la cultura.

Las bombeadoras y los bombeadores se enorgullecen al proclamar que están haciendo cultura. Para la mayoría, el mero hecho de continuar desarrollando y promoviendo el ritmo de la bomba —a través de la creación de grupos, la apertura de escuelas, las presentaciones públicas, las charlas que proveen, etc.— es una forma clara de que están cumpliendo con un deber ministerial. Asumen con gallardía su responsabilidad no solo de ejecutar y bailar el ritmo, sino de enseñarlo a futuras generaciones.

Gran parte del NMB está compuesto por jóvenes adultos menores de 40 años. En su mayoría, fueron universitarios para finales de la década de los noventa. En esa época, combinaban sus estudios con actividades sociales en el área metropolitana del país. Algunos comenzaron a tomar clases de bomba y, posteriormente, pertenecieron a agrupaciones dirigidas por maestras y maestros educados por los "mayores" (personas vinculadas a las familias tradicionales de la bomba en Puerto Rico). En esos eventos, pueden trazar su evolución dentro del género, cómo fueron despuntando poco a poco hasta llegar a ser lo que son hoy en el mundo de la bomba puertorriqueña.

Dentro del NMB, por el contexto histórico en el que se originan, se destacan agrupaciones como Son del Batey (1998), que comenzó a tocar en *pubs* y discotecas en Mayagüez y San Juan; y, paralelamente, Restauración Cultural (1998). Ambas agrupaciones incursionaron también en el ámbito de la educación sobre la bomba; por ejemplo, Restauración Cultural ofrece talleres a maestros de escuela intermedia del Departamento de Educación, a la población de edad avanzada, fuera de la isla como parte del Proyecto Unión (organización que aglutina grupos de bomba de la isla y la diáspora y promueve sus eventos) y abrió la Escuela y Centro Especializado de Restauración Cultural en 2011. Desde 2016, su gestor, Pablo Luis Rivera, continúa la labor educativa y cultural desde el proyecto AfroLegado. Otros grupos de bomba destacados son Majestad Negra (Loíza, 2000), Tambuyé (2003), Gracimá (2003) y Desde Cero (2004). Vale destacar que Desde Cero está compuesto por hombres y mujeres que intercambian sus roles de bailadores, cantadores y tocadores en escena. Tanto Tambuyé como Desde Cero publicaron sus primeros discos en 2013: *Tambuyé* y *Semillas de identidad*, respectivamente.

El músico Afropuertorriqueño Jorge Emmanuelli-Náter divide la bomba en cuatro eras: señala que la primera etapa de la bomba remite a la época de la esclavitud. A su juicio, la segunda era transcurrió de 1873 a 1960 con el desarrollo de la bomba comunitaria a cargo de los descendientes de los Negros. Luego, surgen los grupos folclóricos en la tercera era. Posteriormente, para 1994, Emmanuelli-Náter y sus hermanos crearon los "bombazos" y volvieron a llevar la bomba a la calle. Esta última era es la que sigue en constante desarrollo y evolución, y se ha diseminado por toda la isla y sus diásporas en Estados Unidos.

Posteriormente, para 1994, Emmanuelli-Náter y sus hermanos crearon los "bombazos" y volvieron a llevar la bomba a la calle.

A pesar de que no existe un discurso político que explique la razón por la cual la bomba está adquiriendo mayor visibilidad en Puerto Rico y sus diásporas, es evidente su crecimiento vertiginoso; la proliferación de escuelas, talleres y grupos del ritmo Afropuertorriqueño es innegable.

Está ocurriendo el reavivamiento de un género que tuvo un lapsus de silencio, reprimido, pero no desaparecido. Prohibiciones, persecuciones y prácticas íntimas conocidas solo por los asistentes a las actividades y las personas aledañas mantuvieron a la bomba en un anonimato que caducó por el esfuerzo de organizaciones que decidieron difundirla, experimentar y transformar la exposición que hasta el momento del surgimiento de estos grupos no existía. (Rivera 2013, 147)

Indudablemente, el reavivamiento de la bomba visibiliza el ritmo musical Negro, pero invisibiliza las discusiones sobre la Negritud en Puerto Rico.

La bomba sincopa identidades

El NMB se encuentra en plena ebullición tanto en Puerto Rico como en sus diásporas en Estados Unidos. Se reconocen muchos éxitos y logros, pero falta mucho por hacer, según reconocen los gestores culturales que protagonizan el espacio de la bomba en Puerto Rico. Siguen surgiendo escuelas que enseñan historia; baile básico, intermedio y avanzado; y percusión a hombres y mujeres desde los seis meses de edad en adelante. También, se abren nuevos escenarios para la ejecución de la bomba, pero siguen siendo espacios populares asociados con ciertas clases sociales.

Hay quien afirma que "el nuevo movimiento aportó a crear interés en nuevas generaciones. La gente que uno impactó va a impactar a otros"; "Tengo el ánimo de que to' el mundo lo asuma como propio. Yo tuve la herramienta de tener a unos viejos vivos. Me pregunto, ¿cuándo llegará el día que una llegue a un bombazo y no conozcas a nadie? Siempre somos los mismos. Todos nos conocemos". También, es un hecho que "muchos integrantes están en varios grupos a la vez porque hubo una etapa en la que éramos muy pocos. Con las escuelas, eso cambiará, pues hay nuevas perspectivas de cómo ejecutar". Pablo Luis Rivera afirma que "surgen grupos que ya no ven la bomba como regional y local. Se empiezan a rescatar los ritmos y se incorporan a los repertorios de los grupos".

Una bailadora y percusionista explica que "hay que reconocer que la bomba ha sufrido cambios, se ha fusionado a otros ritmos, pero no ha perdido su esencia, su fundamento". Por su parte, Rivera enfatiza: "La música se va adaptando a la época, va evolucionando. Tengo que ver cómo sigo enamorando a la gente para que conozca el fundamento y después desarrolle y haga lo que quiera hacer. Lo que hará que la bomba se siga enriqueciendo y expandiendo es que las personas oigan letras nuevas y se identifiquen con esas letras". Rivera exhorta a que las personas interesadas en la bomba hagan autogestión; ahí le ve un futuro prometedor al nuevo movimiento de la bomba.

Sin duda, los cambios que van ocurriendo en el NMB, desde las fusiones con otros estilos y otros ritmos y las canciones nuevas, entre otras modificaciones, dan cuenta de que el tema racial sigue desplazándose a la periferia. Se buscan formas de atraer nuevos rostros, y sí se habla de la historia de la bomba y su vínculo inherente con la Negritud en los talleres, pero desde ciertos cuerpos privilegiados. Es decir, el NMB todavía no representa un movimiento político de educación antirracista en Puerto Rico. La Negritud que se celebra en el NMB está supeditada a un discurso colonial racializado y folclorizado que continúa devaluando los cuerpos Negros.

Apuntes finales

La escena de Glory Mar González-Mejías es solo un ejemplo de cómo el NMB es un terreno fértil para visibilizar la Negritud. Sin embargo, esa visibilización opera desde una apropiación cultural de parte de sujetos no Negros que explica la contradicción entre el desplazamiento y la aceptación de la bomba versus la marginalización de lo Negro en Puerto Rico. En el proceso de hacer cultura, como denominan los bombeadores a la práctica de mantener la bomba activa, se perpetúa la folclorización de la Negritud. Y es que en el NMB, la bomba posee un carácter inconfundible de supeditación, que se refleja en los aspectos menos tangibles de la Negritud.

Por ejemplo, los signos de género están subordinados a las señales de la Negritud, como quedó explícito con el cuerpo de Glory Mar violentado a través de los insultos y las burlas. Por ello, el género no es una mera adición en el análisis por razón de raza. Paralelamente, la bomba modula y modifica las narrativas discursivas sobre el género. Hay un vínculo innegable entre los roles de género asignados a los ejecutantes a partir de su adscripción racial. Sin embargo, a pesar de los avances que se han alcanzado en cómo se representa la Negritud y en las resignificaciones de género en la bomba, aún se jerarquiza desde esa óptica en el NMB. Los remanentes de las feminidades y masculinidades (por ejemplo, el exotismo y la hipersexualización) en la representación de la Negritud de la bomba tradicional siguen presentes en la puesta en escena del NMB. Nuevamente, se percibe en la bomba, como espacio micro, un reflejo del Puerto Rico en general.

Por otra parte, el NMB visibiliza y reclama una Negritud que permanece justamente porque ha evolucionado. El NMB ratifica la jerarquización en la sociedad puertorriqueña en tanto las nociones del Puerto Rico mezclado, asumidas desde el discurso nacional, y las nociones de la Negritud, que traspasan la fenotipia, están cambiando. Es decir, las mediaciones y representaciones que ocurren en la bomba denotan una transformación de la tradición; en ocasiones, el ritmo transmuta en un elemento de reafirmación étnica. Pero al mismo tiempo, la bomba demuestra que la democracia racial en Puerto Rico es un mito. Por un lado, se rompe con lo primitivo; se crea un movimiento alterno. Por el otro, no se desasocia lo Negro, pero hay una apropiación de lo Negro desde lo no Negro.

El ritmo musical, que en algún momento delimitó las geografías de la Negritud, ha logrado trazar nuevos mapas culturales que extienden la idea de la puertorriqueñidad (o bien, puertorriqueñidades) en múltiples diásporas puertorriqueñas.

La bomba también ha funcionado como un instrumento para construir las rutas de lo puertorriqueño. El ritmo musical, que en algún momento delimitó las geografías de la Negritud, ha logrado trazar nuevos mapas culturales que extienden la idea de la puertorriqueñidad (o bien, puertorriqueñidades) en múltiples diásporas puertorriqueñas. La bomba —y las identidades puertorriqueñas— transitan de ida y vuelta del centro a la periferia.

En fin, en la bomba puertorriqueña, emergen intersecciones intrínsecamente relacionadas a las cambiantes identidades raciales, nacionales, culturales, de clase y género de los Afropuertorriqueños. Hoy día, el NMB no es únicamente un proyecto contestatario ante la supremacía blanca; es, a su vez, un espacio para agenciar visibilidad en un país que aparenta celebrar su mestizaje y alardea de exhibir institucionalmente una democracia racial a la par que degrada lo Negro como elemento constitutivo. El impacto en la isla de estas dinámicas persistentes, entre la lucha de lo Negro versus las sistemáticas acciones antiNegritud, merece seguir estudiándose por las complejidades que representa.

NOTES

[1] Ver <https://www.youtube.com/watch?v=sOM_gps1XHA/>.

[2] En 2014, la alcaldesa de San Juan, Carmen Yulín Cruz-Soto, les cambió el nombre a "Fiestas de la Calle", pues alegó que las fiestas se celebran más allá de la calle San Sebastián. Las fiestas se han tornado en un espacio disputado por ciertos sectores dentro del ELA. Ver Cambian el nombre (2014).

[3] Ricardo Alegría Gallardo (1921-2011) completó su bachillerato en Arqueología en la Universidad de Puerto Rico y, posteriormente, hizo una maestría en Antropología e Historia en la Universidad de Chicago y un doctorado en Antropología en la Universidad de Harvard. Dirigió el Instituto de Cultura Puertorriqueña y fundó el Centro de Estudios Avanzados de Puerto Rico y el Caribe. Entre sus temas de interés académico se encontraban el mestizaje en Puerto Rico y la noción de la puertorriqueñidad para definir la identidad nacional de los puertorriqueños.

[4] El 8 de diciembre de 2014, se encontró a dos mujeres de 38 y 47 años de edad asesinadas en una carretera del municipio de Arecibo. Las mujeres, que eran primas, acostumbraban a salir a ejercitarse a las 6:00 a.m. Se las halló desnudas, y sus cuerpos presentaban varios impactos de bala. Dos meses después, el 8 de febrero de 2015, un conductor arrolló a la cantautora Ivania Zayas y se dio a la fuga. La discusión de los trágicos sucesos reveló que los cuerpos de las víctimas se convirtieron en victimarios. A las mujeres asesinadas se les considera provocadoras y seductoras; se cuestiona la presencia del cuerpo femenino en los espacios públicos. Hay una insistencia recurrente por controlar los espacios y los cuerpos (Martínez-Vergne 1999).

[5] Los bombeadores se hacen llamar hacedores y gestores de la cultura puertorriqueña. Para ellos, producir bomba es un claro ejemplo de cómo mantienen vivas las tradiciones culturales de la isla.

[6] En este texto, utilizo las siglas NMB para referirme al concepto "nuevo movimiento de la bomba puertorriqueña". El Nuevo Movimiento de la Bomba Puertorriqueña es un término empleado por Bárbara Abadía-Rexach (2015) en su disertación doctoral. Abadía-Rexach se refiere a la proliferación de grupos y talleres de bomba en la zona metropolitana de San Juan, Puerto Rico, a partir de 1995 en adelante.

[7] Propongo el centro como el discurso nacional inclusivo y unificador, es decir, la "historia oficial" con respecto a la identidad nacional unilateral producto de la tríada indígena-español-africano.

[8] Es una prerrogativa de la autora escribir Negra(s), Negro(s), Negritud y Afro con N y A mayúsculas en todo el texto. En principio, es un acto político de visibilización. Por otro lado, en este texto, utilizo Negra(o) y Afropuertorriqueña(o) como sinónimos cuando me refiero a la fenotipia de personas evidentemente Negras, que se autoidentifican y son interpeladas como tal en Puerto Rico.

[9] Utilizo *periferia* para referirme a los márgenes, las negociaciones y los entramados que son alternos al discurso identitario del "centro".

[10] Soberao, dentro del léxico de la bomba, es un sinónimo de batey; es el espacio en el que se toca y se baila bomba.

[11] Adopté el término bombeador/a, acuñado por Pablo Luis Rivera (2013), para referirme a la persona que practica la bomba. Comúnmente, se le llama bomber/a, pero se confunde con la persona que se dedica a extinguir fuegos.

[12] "El instrumento africano primario, por supuesto, era el tambor, que, con sus complejas prácticas

rítmicas, apoyó una cultura que anhelaba volver a conectar con la comodidad de la patria africana. Uno de los usos del tambor era como un medio de comunicación, y por esta razón, algunos europeos por temor a la rebelión a menudo reprimida o prohibió su uso, aunque incluso en estos casos, las tradiciones de tambores a menudo continuaron creciendo clandestinamente. Por el contrario, en otras islas, tambores se creía para que los esclavos trabajen más duro, y por lo tanto se les permitió e incluso animó. Como resultado, los tambores caribeños desarrollan de diferentes maneras en diferentes islas, y aparecen en una gran diversidad de formas y tamaños, con técnicas de interpretación innumerables y funciones" (Brill 2011, 117).

OBRAS CITADAS

Abadía-Rexach, Bárbara I. 2015. ¡Saludando al tambor! El nuevo movimiento de la bomba puertorriqueña. Tesis doctoral, University of Texas at Austin.

Álvarez, Luis Manuel. s.f. La presencia negra en la música puertorriqueña. Recuperado el 3 de octubre de 2002. <http://musica.uprrp.edu/lalvarez/Articulos/presenciaNegra/presencia.html/>.

Antonetty Lebrón, Gloriann Sacha. 2015. Sublevación de una mujer afroboricua. *Afroféminas,* 29 de enero. <https://afrofeminas.com/2015/01/29/sublevacion-de-una-mujer-afroboricua/>.

Bailarina de bomba de la SanSe saca la cara por la tradición puertorriqueña. *Día a Día.* <http://www.telemundopr.com/programas/dia-a-dia/videos/Bailarina-de-bomba-de-la-SanSe-saca-la-cara-por-la-tradicion-puertorriquena-289349301.html/>.

Brill, Mark. 2011. *Music of Latin America and the Caribbean.* New York: Routledge.

Cambian el nombre de las Fiestas de la Calle San Sebastián. 2014. *El Nuevo Día,* 26 de noviembre. <https://www.elnuevodia.com/noticias/politica/nota/cambianelnombredelasfiestasdelacallesansebastian-1900181/>.

Costa-Vargas, João. 2006. *Catching Hell in the City of Angels. Life and Meanings of Blackness in South Central Los Angeles.* Minneapolis: University of Minnesota Press.

Dzidzienyo, Anani y Suzanne Oboler, eds. 2005. *Neither Enemies Nor Friends. Latinos, Blacks, Afro-Latinos.* New York: Palgrave Macmillan.

Godreau, Isar P. 2003. Dinámicas de género en la representación del folclor puertorriqueño negro. Manuscrito no publicado. Universidad de Puerto Rico, Recinto de Cayey.

Godreau, Isar P., Mariolga Reyes Cruz, Mariluz Franco Ortiz y Sherry Cuadrado. 2008. The Lessons of Slavery: Discourses of Slavery, *Mestizaje,* and *Blanqueamiento* in an Elementary School in Puerto Rico. *American Ethnologist* 35(1), 115–35 .

González, José Luis. 1980. *El país de cuatro pisos.* Río Piedras, PR: Ediciones Huracán.

Hall, Stuart, ed. 1997. *Representation: Cultural Representations and Signifying Practices.* Thousand Oaks, CA: Sage Publications.

Joven defiende la cultura afropuertorriqueña de las críticas. 2015. *Metro,* 20 de enero. <http://www.metro.pr/locales/joven-defiende-la-cultura-afropuertorriquena-de-las-criticas/pGXoat!N8gq5RmdEiQk/>.

Martínez-Vergne, Teresita. 1999. *Shaping the Discourse on Space: Charity and Its Wards in Nineteenth-Century San Juan, Puerto Rico.* Austin: University of Texas Press.

Pons, Ricardo. 2012. Evolución musical de la bomba puertorriqueña. En *Bomba que rumba. Memorias del primer simposio sobre la bomba y la rumba.* 243–56. San Juam: Fundación Puertorriqueña de las Humanidades.

Ramos-Rosado, Marie. 2011. *Destellos de la negritud. Investigaciones caribeñas.* San Juan: Isla Negra Editores.

Rivera, Pablo Luis. 2013. Orígenes culturales y desarrollo de la bomba puertorriqueña. Tesis doctoral, Centro de Estudios Avanzados de Puerto Rico y el Caribe, San Juan, Puerto Rico.

———. 2015. Un género que supera los prejuicios. *Facebook,* 20 de enero. <https://www.facebook.com/pablo.l.rivera.7/posts/10155075294600322/>.

Rivera, Raquel Z. 2010a. New York Bomba: Puerto Ricans, Dominicans and a Bridge Called Haiti. En *Rhythms of the Afro-Atlantic World,* eds. Ifeoma C.K. Nwanko y D. Mamadou. Ann Arbor: University of Michigan Press.

———. 2010b. Bomba puertorriqueña y palos dominicanos en Nueva York: de diásporas y mitologías de la liberación. *Boletín Música: Revista de Música Latinaomericana y Caribeña* 26, 3–26.

Video: mujer saca la cara por la tradición en las Fiestas de la Calle San Sebastián. *Tu Noticia PR,* 19 de enero de 2015. <http://www.tunoticiapr.com/puerto-rico-pa-lante/1516285556-Video:-Mujer-Saca-la-Cara-por-la-tradici%C3%B3n-en-las-Fiestas-de-la-Calle-San-Sebasti%C3%A1n-/.>

von Vacano, Diego A. 2012. *The Color of Citizenship, Race, Modernity and Latin American/Hispanic Political Thought.* New York: Oxford University Press.

VOLUME XXXI • NUMBER II • SUMMER 2019

Topografía social y cultural de las músicas africanas y afrodescendientes en el archipiélago puertorriqueño: la historia de las músicas afrodiaspóricas en Puerto Rico como antinomia de la historia folklorizada de la bomba

NOEL ALLENDE-GOITÍA

ABSTRACT

This essay engages the historical memory of the Puerto Rican Afrodiasporic metagenera today known a *bomba*, from a historiographical perspective. In Puerto Rico, during and since the 19th century, a memory of music making is created and developed, which reduced afro-Puerto Rican identity to the practice of bomba. Here, I criticize this type of memory, which includes an exploration of the elements of "historic hyperbaton" in its historical discourse: I propose that, when talking about bomba, more often than not, and unwittingly, we project our present into its past, as if its present was an inevitable destiny, determined by some original conditions as if "the present" of bomba is some kind of actualization of its past. [Key words: bomba, Puerto Rico, Afrodiasporic, historical memory, historical discourses, floklorization]

The author (allendegoitia@gmail.com) is an associate professor of Music at the Metropolitan Campus of the Interamerican University of Puerto Rico. He has published books, articles, and book reviews on Puerto Rican music's social and cultural history, music instruction, and music historiography. His works in Music/Culture Social History have been presented at national and international conferences in Puerto Rico, the Dominican Republic, Cuba, Jamaica, Brazil, Uruguay, Spain, Peru, the United States, Mexico, and Ghana.

> [...] ... conócense además algunos de los de Africa, introducidos por los negros de aquellas regiones, pero que nunca se han generalizado, llamándoseles *bailes de bomba*, por el instrumento que sirve de música.
>
> ...
>
> [...] ... los bailes de los negros de Africa y los de los criollos de Curazao no merecen incluirse bajo el título de esta escena; pues aunque se ven en Puerto-Rico, nunca se han generalizado: con todo, hago mención de ellos porque siendo muchos, aumentan la grande variedad de danzas que un estranjero puede ver en sola una isla, y hasta sin moverse de una población.
>
> Manuel Alonso (1849, 58, 67)

> [...] La memoria no es "histórica" en virtud del contenido particular (político o social, por ejemplo) de los recuerdos. Lo es, en cambio, en cuanto *facultad* que distingue la existencia singular. Las estructuras y procedimientos de esta facultad procuran, en efecto, una vía de acceso a la historicidad de la experiencia, de cualquier experiencia, de la experiencia en general. La memoria, que siempre es memoria del individuo, constituye, sin embargo, una especie de "recapitulación ontogénica" de los diversos modos del ser histórico, como también la matriz formal de las categorías historiográficas. Precisamente, tan sólo allí reside su valor suprapersonal, su índole pública.
>
> Paolo Virno (2003 [1999], 12-13)

1. Introducción

Este artículo aborda, desde la historiografía, el tema de la memoria histórica del metagénero afropuertorriqueño hoy día conocido como *bomba*. Desde el siglo XIX, se ha creado y desarrollado una memoria del "hacer" musical isleño que reduce lo afropuetorriqueño a la bomba. La crítica que aquí hago a este tipo de memoria explora los elementos de "hipérbaton histórico" en su recuento histórico: propongo que cuando hablamos de la bomba generalmente lo hacemos, en ocasiones, sin percatarnos, proyectándonos del presente hacia el pasado, como si el presente de la bomba fuese un destino inevitable, determinado por unas condiciones originales, como si "el presente" de la bomba fuese un tipo de actualización del pasado.

¿En qué cambiaría la narración histórica de los eventos de la fiesta campestre que describe Pierre Ledrú en 1797; los bailes callejeros de las fiestas celebradas en 1830, 1831 y 1832; las descripciones en memorias personales; los cuentos de costumbres; y las leyes de policía y regulación de las actividades humanas en la vida cotidiana si las abordamos como actividades afropuertorriqueñas en general y no como anotaciones al calce de la historia de la bomba? O sea, ¿cómo hablaríamos de la bomba contemporánea si habláramos de ella como uno de los elementos de las músicas afrodiaspóricas en el archipiélago puertorriqueño? Este artículo responde, provisionalmente, a esta pregunta con la propuesta de una topografía [un estudio de superficie] social y cultural de las músicas africanas y afrodescendientes en el archipiélago puertorriqueño.

A lo largo de este escrito se usarán tres términos que se utilizarán como categorías de análisis: "hipérbaton histórico", "prioridades culturales" y "presiones evolutivas". El primero es un préstamo teórico a Mijaíl Mijáilovich Bajtín (1895-1975). Este identifica esta categoría de análisis con un recurso discursivo de las narraciones mitológicas y las fábulas: la inversión histórica [hipérbaton histórico] (M. Bajtín 1981), dice:

> La esencia de ese hipérbaton [inversión] se reduce al hecho de que el pensamiento mitológico y artístico ubique en el pasado categorías tales como meta, ideal, justicia, perfección, estado de armonía del hombre con la sociedad, etc. Los mitos acerca del Paraíso, la Edad de oro, el siglo heroico, la verdad antigua, las representaciones más tardías del estado natural, los derechos naturales innatos, etc. son expresiones de ese hipérbaton histórico. Definiéndolo de una manera un tanto más simplificada, podemos decir que consiste en representar como existente en el pasado lo que, de hecho, solo puede o debe ser realizado en el futuro; lo que, en esencia, constituye una meta, un imperativo, y, en ningún caso, la realidad del pasado. (1981, 147; 1989 [1975], 299)

Esta idea de inversión temporal guarda relación con lo que David Lowenthal llama al pasado: "El pasado es un país extraño cuyas características están configuradas de acuerdo con las predilecciones actuales; su rareza está domesticada por las formas en que conservamos sus vestigios" (1998, 8). Iris M. Zavala (1991), comentando sobre el trabajo de Bajtín, arguye que el ejercicio de la inversión histórica se muestra en prácticas sociales que intentan domesticar el pasado en espacio y tiempo. Esta categoría analítica resulta muy útil en la revisión de la literatura que construye una memoria sobre el metagénero de la bomba como historia musical de lo afropuertorriqueño.

Los próximos dos términos pertenecen una familia conceptual: "prioridades culturales" y "presiones evolutivas". El concepto "prioridades culturales" lo podemos encontrar en el libro de Tricia Rose *Black Noise* (1994). Respondiendo a la pregunta: "¿Qué motiva el nacimiento del hip hop?", ella desarrolla un argumento teórico en el cual usa el concepto "prioridades culturales". Leamos, en una larga cita, la constelación de variantes en juego que utilizo de base teórica a lo largo de este ensayo. Ella dice:

> Few answers to questions as broadly defined as, "what motivated the emergence of hip hop" could comprehensively account for all the factors that contribute to the multiple, related, and sometimes coincidental events that bring cultural forms into being. Keeping this in mind, this exploration has been organized around limited aspects of the relationship between cultural forms and the contexts within which they emerge.

More specifically, it has attended to the ways in which artistic practice is shaped by cultural traditions, related current and previous practice, *and* by the ways in which practice shaped by technology, economic forces, and race, gender, and class relations. These relationships between form, context, and cultural priority demonstrate that hip hop shares a number of traits with, and yet revises, long-standing Afrodiasporic practices; that male dominance in hip hop is, in part, a by-product of sexism and that active process of women's marginalization in cultural production; that hip hop's form is fundamentally linked to technological changes and social, urban space parameters; that hip hop's anger is produced by contemporary racism, gender, and class oppression; and finally, that a great deal of pleasure in hip hop is derived from subverting these forces and affirming Afrodiasporic histories and identities. (1994, 61)

En este párrafo Rose subraya la necesidad de partir de las condiciones propias de los hechos existenciales humanos que se investigan. Sin embargo, para esta autora esas condiciones locales están conectadas con condiciones globales [i. e.: la tecnología] que, por una parte, las conecta, con resultados insospechados, a las corrientes mundiales de mercado, pero que, por otro lado, añade colores particulares a condiciones específicas. Esta trinidad conceptual —forma, contexto y prioridades culturales— la reduzco al concepto de "prioridades culturales". Este destilado conceptual lo proceso a través de las lecturas de autores como Fernand Braudel (1987 [1949]), Eric Wolf (1982) y Gary Tomlinson (2007, 2015). Es a partir de dicha síntesis que defino "prioridades culturales" como el conjunto de características del campo de acción de las sociedades humanas que explican la transformación de su entorno natural y de sus relaciones, mediadas y comprendidas, en el contexto inmediato de sus propias condiciones de vida; no en comparación inconmensurable con sociedades, en ocasiones, ajenas a dichas condiciones. Así, la vida cotidiana en general, y la vida musical en particular, de los grupos humanos que querramos examinar, hay que estudiarlas a partir de la dinámica de sus propias prioridades culturales.

A través del concepto de prioridades culturales, por ejemplo, se puede caracterizar la africanía de la cultura del archipiélago de Borikén como un hecho humano que se lleva a cabo en una geografía específica. Este hecho humano se da como procesos sociales que hacen posible que africanos y afrodescendientes sean parte constitutiva de la población y demografía que habita dicha geografía. Por ejemplo, africanos y afrodescendientes fueron protagonistas de los primeros mestizajes:

1. como conquistadores [i. e.: Francisco Piñón (Tanodi 2010, 24) y Juan Garrido (Alegría 2009c, 573–84)];
2. como trabajadores libres y esclavos [i. e.: Duarte, esclavo, arriero de la Hacienda del Rey (2010, 44), y Juan Ortiz, negro ladino (52, 54)];
3. como empleados de la Iglesia católica cristiana [i. e.: en 1528, autorizan al señor obispo, Alonso Manso, a entrar "catorce negros" esclavizados (Alegría 2009c, 9) y, en 1532, Juan Cea, Chantre, desembarca dos africanos esclavizados (Tanodi 2009, 440)];

4. y su participación en los procesos de mestizaje que se dieron entre la población nativa —los taínos— y los africanos esclavizados escapados, cimarrones [i. e.: reporte de "negros alzados" en 1515 (Alegría 2009a, 568) y de "negros e indios alzados", en 1525 y 1527 (Alegría 2009b, 529, 637)].

Estas condiciones culturales son particulares al archipiélago de las Antillas en general, y al de Puerto Rico en particular. A partir de estas y otras condiciones particulares, o prioridades culturales dadas, se dieron eventos que crearon dinámicas de relaciones humanas que llamo *presiones evolutivas.*

Defino presión evolutiva como el conjunto de causalidades que hacen posible unos cambios cualitativos en la praxis social que resultan, a su vez, en praxis culturales observables. Esta definición es una adaptación de un término tomado de la biología evolutiva: "presión selectiva" [*selective pressure*], definida como "el conjunto [*set*] de circunstancias que hacen posible que los rasgos característicos adaptativos que se hacen visibles en términos de un crecimiento de su progenie, y un grado razonable de variabilidad tiene que estar presente, para que dichos rasgos puedan ser seleccionados un grado de variabilidad genética" (Bickerton 1999, 156). Esta perspectiva desde la biología evolutiva la comparten, y la problematizan, estudiosos de la música como François-Berbabd Mâche (1999), Ian Cross (2006; 2011) y Gary Tomlinson (2015), entre otros.

Quiere decir que, de 1508 en adelante, la presencia de los africanos y afrodescendientes fue un ingrediente ingénito de las condiciones de vida que cambiaron radicalmente la existencia de los pobladores de Borikén.

¿Qué cosas cualificarían como un conjunto de circunstancias que hacen posible unos cambios cualitativos en la praxis social que resultan, a su vez, en praxis culturales observables? En el caso de este ensayo, la praxis social, que produce praxis culturales observables, se refiere a la mezcla y coexistencia de "haceres" musicales específicos. Por ejemplo, el paisaje sonoro del archipiélago borinqueño entre 1508 y 1530 estaba compuesto por, primero, las músicas africanas y mulatas provenientes del al-Ándalus [Andalucía]: i. e.: el guineo, el ye-ye, el zarambeque, el canario y el paracumbé (García de León Griego 2002; Bejarano Pellecer 2015, 222); segundo, los sonidos generados por las cada vez más escasas celebraciones públicas de la población aborigen (Tomlinson 2007): los ecos lejanos de las ceremonias celebradas en enclaves taínos fuera del alcance de una reducida, pero creciente población europea; y tercero, el musicar de los africanos escapados, cimarrones, que "alzados" [en la terminología del conquistador (Alegría 2009c, 305–29)], empezaron a colonizar y a mestizarse con la población nativa. Quiere decir que, de 1508 en adelante, la presencia de los africanos y afrodescendientes fue un ingrediente ingénito de las condiciones de vida que cambiaron radicalmente la existencia de los pobladores de Borikén. Por lo tanto, se tienen que considerar las prácticas musicales afrodiaspóricas como consustanciales a las "prioridades culturales" fundacionales de la nueva sociedad colonial que se creó en el siglo XVI (González 1987).

Mediante estos tres conceptos, trato de problematizar el tema de este trabajo, el cual se aborda en tres partes: primero, ante el planteamiento de una memoria histórica del metagénero de la bomba como una historia cultural de un "hacer" musical particular de lo afropuertorriqueño. Propongo una mirada a dicho metagénero como parte de un conjunto de sistemas culturales; de prácticas músico-danzarias que comprenden una galaxia compleja-dinámica-adaptativa de la cultura afropuertorriqueña en general y que es consustancial al universo de la cultura musical del archipiélago. En segunda instancia, la actividad de la población humana que se dan dentro del entorno geográfico del archipiélago es lo que crea las condiciones originarias de las "prioridades culturales". Estas condiciones, a su vez, fundamentan el génesis y desarrollo de unos "haceres" afrodiaspóricos, a los que hay que considerar parte del "hacer" cultura de la totalidad de la población. De esta forma, abordaremos unos casos particulares que nos mostrarán cómo el musicar y el bailar los diferentes bailes afropuertorriqueños con bombas son solo parte de una constelación de prácticas afrodiaspóricas que tienen fuerza formativa en le criollización de los "haceres" musicales en general. En tercer lugar, la comprensión de esas "prioridades culturales" nos ayudarán a identificar eventos que, en la corta y mediana duración, nos indicarán las "presiones evolutivas" que impulsan los cambios —que en la mayoría de los casos no son únicos, sino plurales; que son múltiples, pero, en ocasiones, simultáneos—. A su vez, argüiré que dichos cambios crean nuevas condiciones que establecen nuevas prioridades con sus pequeñas tormentas de presiones evolutivas. Los momentos de choque, o dialécticos, ocurren, es mi contención, en la coexistencia de procesos. Estos procesos pueden aparecer, simultáneamente, como en estados de no-cambio, u homeostasis, por la lentitud de su desarrollo, y como eventos de cambios acelerados, en estado de *flux* constante, o alostático.

En fin, este ensayo topográfico es una aproximación crítica a los discursos históricos que han creado y fomentado [y todavía crean y fomentan] una memoria histórica folklorizada de dicho metagénero. La proposición central de esta crítica es: si las músicas afrodiaspóricas isleñas son el resultado de "prioridades culturales" específicas en tiempo y espacio, entonces las "presiones evolutivas" que componen los cambios particulares de estas son una serie de formas de musicar que no son "destino", sino momentos eventuales en el continuo proceso de crear la cultura musical en el hábitat humano en que existimos.

2. La construcción de una memoria de la bomba como lo afropuertorriqueño

En esta sección vuelvo a hacer una lectura a las muy conocidas y leídas palabras de Manuel Antonio Alonso Pacheco (1822-1889) en su libro *El Gíbaro* (1849), sobre el metagénero de la bomba. Analizo el texto de Alonso a través de los lentes conceptuales de los trabajos de Mijaíl Mijáilovich Bajtín (1989 [1975]) y de Paolo Virno (2003 [1999]). Con ello, quiero establecer el perfil de una genealogía ideológica que ha sido recurrente en nuestra historia intelectual y mostrar la conexión y el funcionamiento mnésico, o de memoria histórica, con los abordajes posteriores.

Para mediados del siglo XIX, a sus 27 años, Alonso narra su memoria de los bailes "de negros" en Puerto Rico de la siguiente manera:

> **[. . .] . . . conócense además algunos de los de Africa, introducidos por los negros de aquellas regiones, pero que nunca se han generalizado, llamándoseles *bailes de bomba*, por el instrumento que sirve de música.**
>
> . . .
>
> **[. . .] . . . los bailes de los negros de Africa y los de los criollos de Curazao no merecen incluirse bajo el título de esta escena; pues aunque se ven en Puerto-Rico, nunca se han generalizado: con todo, hago mención de ellos porque siendo muchos, aumentan la grande variedad de danzas que un estranjero puede ver en sola una isla, y hasta sin moverse de una población. (1849, 58, 67)**

Vamos a "desempacar" [*unpack*] —o en puertorriqueño, "desempaquetar"— estos párrafos. Quiero llamar la atención a cuatro puntos que son centrales para este ensayo. Primero, en trabajos anteriores he llamado la atención a la imaginación geográfica de la primera declaración; los "bailes de bomba", como él los llama, quedan excluidos de la geografía insular: son de África, son de Curaçao, no son nativos, se consideran una presencia extranjera, no vernácula (Allende Goitía 2008-2009; 2013a; 2013b). Segundo, en una forma explícita, evita su descripción destallada; para él son una mera presencia que hay que nombrar porque, sencillamente, están ahí, alguien los va a ver. En contraste, los bailes de sociedad y de garabato, como él los denomina, aparecen en la narración con denominación de origen —son de España, son indígenas, son criollos— e identificados como activos culturales. En tercer lugar, su discurso traiciona el intento burgués-criollo de construcción de una memoria de lo vernáculo, de lo constitutivo de la "puertorriqueñidad". La contradicción aparece, yo arguyo, cuando, después de establecer la extranjería y lo que él identifica como la poca generalización de los bailes, él mismo observa: "hago mención de ellos porque siendo muchos, aumentan la grande variedad de danzas que un estranjero puede ver en sola una isla, y hasta sin moverse de una población". Se advierte en estas líneas una percepción de superficie, topografía, de la presencia y distribución de estas prácticas musicales afropuertorriqueñas. Esta topografía es humana: es social y es cultural. Su actuación no solo cubre una particular topografía, sino que también es un conjunto de espacios topológicos. Esto nos debe llamar la atención, es mi argumento, porque es el fundamento de su tipo de memoria: fíjense en que él establece el plural, primero, en la denominación del metagénero: *bailes de bomba*; luego señala que son muchos y se pueden ver a lo largo Puerto Rico. Así, leyendo entre líneas a Alonso, podemos entender que el plural de bailes que usan bomba [tambor] no son solo variados a lo largo del archipiélago, sino variados en los límites de un poblado.

El cuarto elemento es la subversión de la temporalidad y, por lo tanto, de la memoria. El subtexto de los géneros bailables asociados a la conquista española y las tradiciones aborígenes apuntan a una temporalidad enmarcada en el calendario europeo con la conquista como horizonte eventual. Sin embargo, al hablar de los bailes de bomba, cambia a una referencia geográfica, totalmente atemporal. Aun así, su confesión, aunque vacilante, de una variedad de bailes a lo largo de la topografía isleña, traiciona su intención de borrar y de desautenticar como puertorriqueños dichos bailes. Más aun, la topografía implicada en su declaración apunta a una topología cultural de estos bailes, pues su radio de acción cultural implica convergencia, conectividad, continuidad y vecindad. Entonces, ¿por qué esta cita ha alimentado, ya por varios siglos, la idea de que solo habla del metagénero de la bomba como la observamos hoy día? Aquí Alonso sienta las bases para la creación de un discurso del recordar que trata lo afropuertorriqueño en general y lo afromusical en particular, como lo diría Paolo Virno, en un "[r]ecordar el presente que significa considerar el 'ahora' como un 'entonces'". (2003 [1999], 67).

Esta reversión temporal, o hipérbaton histórico (M. M. Bajtín 1989 [1975]), implicado en el texto de Manuel Alonso (1849), toma forma en un *meme* (Dawkins 2006 [1976]; Blackmore 1999) que se establece como memoria histórica oficial. Por ejemplo, Melanie A. Maldonado (2008), Edgardo Díaz Díaz (2014) y Bárbara Idalissee Abadía-Rexach (2015) llevan la memoria atemporal de Alonso a un tipo de memoria omniteporal. Por ejemplo, la primera declara sumariamente: "Bomba is one of the two genres of AfroPuerto Rican music and approximately 400 hundred years old" (Maldonado 2008). En su disertación doctoral, Abadía-Rexach es mucho más específica al establecer el cronotopo de este metagénero: "La bomba puertorriqueña nació en la isla en el siglo XVI con la llegada de los Negros" (2015, 62). Para el mismo año, Jade Y. Power Sotomayor, en el *Oxford Handbook of Dance and Theater* (2015), replica el *meme* al decirle a la audiencia anglo-lectora que: "*Bomba* music and dance was first created by enslaved Africans and their descendants in the sugarcane plantations of Puerto Rico as early as the sixteenth century" (2015, 706). Este sistema memético reduce la totalidad de las músicas afropuertorriqueñas al metagénero de la bomba; establece como año cero de las músicas afrodiaspóricas el 1508; y, más específicamente, lo circunscribe a los seres humanos raptados y esclavizados en África Occidental que comenzaron a llegar después de esa fecha a nuestras costas.

Los trabajos de Ángel G. Quintero Rivera (1998, 2009) y Salvador Ferreras (2005) traen una visión menos explícita y no problematizada de la distinción que hemos estado haciendo entre lo afrodiaspórico como una generalización de lo afropuertorriqueño y el metagénero de la bomba como una parte de las expresiones de esta. Ambos desarrollan sus particulares temas asumiendo como dado que la bomba, en su sentido más estricto y presentista, se origina y se desarrolla exclusivamente a partir de la trata de seres humanos esclavizados. Por ejemplo, Quintero Rivera afirma, hablando de los tropos rítmicos de los seises con décimas y los de aguinaldo, que "[n]adie que no viviera esos ritmos podía realmente imaginar que la música jíbara estaba colmada de bomba" (1998, 251). Igualmente, Ferreras resume tres siglos de historia de la siguiente forma: "During this period of settlement and expansion of the slave trade circumstantial evidence in the way of anecdotes, drawings and stories indicate that certain forms of recreational dance and song emerged within the slave population" (2005, 32). Aun, en su libro *Cuerpo y cultura*, Quintero Rivera desarrolla todo un análisis de datos, muy provocador y rico, basado en la presunción de la constante histórica de la bomba como práctica de canto y rítmica encarnada [corporeizada], cuya fuerza metafórica, trópica, antitética a las propuestas burguesas eurocentristas, se encarnan en el repique —el tambor— y el piquete —el bailador—. Pero la inmutabilidad del género, su existencia en un continuo presente, es una inferencia base no solo de Quintero Rivera, sino de los autores anteriormente discutidos y los que los utilizan como fuentes secundarias de referencia.

En Puerto Rico, al historiar y crear una memoria del metagénero de la bomba, se ha dependido de trabajos de autores como María Cadilla Martínez (1938), María Teresa Babín (1951), María Luisa Muñoz (1966), Cesáreo Rosa Nieves (1967), Manuel Álvarez Nazario (1974) y Héctor Campos Parsi (1976). La enjundiosa labor investigativa de estos letrados se caracteriza por una aproximación atemporal al objeto de estudio. Por ejemplo, en los trabajos de María Luisa Muñoz (1966) y de Héctor Campos Parsi (1976), el tiempo previo al siglo XIX se racializa; las categorías de indígena, español y africano, o negro, se usan en sustitución de un cronotopo explicativo: los índices de sus trabajos reducen tres siglos de procesos humanos complejos, dinámicos y adaptativos a un proceso único de aportes, cuyo único elemento de agencia radica en qué se mantiene, qué se abandona y qué se absorbe. Autores como María Teresa Babín (1958) y Cesáreo Rosa Nieves (1967) aplican este mismo paradigma atemporal en sus trabajos de análisis y crítica cultural. María Cadilla Martínez (1938) y Manuel Álvarez Nazario (1974), entre estos autores, adoptan un acercamiento global al tema de los bailes de bomba. La inamovilidad geográfica sustituye lo temporal como proceso. Esta inmanencia geográfica sitúa la bomba como trasplante unidireccional a través de la trata humana desde las costas de África Occidental a las nuestras (Malavet Vega 1992). Esta narrativa se convierte en fundamento de un mito de los orígenes, el cual propone que esta es "la única música genuinamente africana" (Campos Parsi 1976, 47) en nuestro archipiélago y que, por virtud de dicha transposición espacial, se dio el fenómeno, según esta generación de letrados, de que estos "conservaran su cultura en un estado de genuina pureza, libre de adulteraciones" (Muñoz 1966, 79).

María Teresa Babín resume el trabajo de sus compañeros letrados en un tipo de explicación en la que la praxis humana en el tiempo es sustituida por una visión estática de geografía poblacional. Su obra más leída, *Panorama de la cultura puertorriqueña* (1958), impone un meme ideográfico que perdura hasta hoy. Los eventos que ocurren a lo largo de los siglos XVI, XVII y XVIII se interpretan usando una visión estática de lo social y reduce procesos completos a la mera categorización demográfica de tres elementos, en sus propias palabras: el indio, el blanco y el negro (Babín 1958). Más aun, esta síntesis tiene unas profundas raíces en las mentalidades blancas-criollas de las sociedades insulares durante el siglo XIX. Ella, y su generación, hereda de esas mentalidades del siglo XIX la construcción de una particular visión de lo puertorriqueño, desde la cual se construye la memoria de la bomba como un "hipérbaton histórico". Primero, su historia se reduce al "ahora" del tambor, la bomba. Segundo, el nombre del instrumento se convierte en tropo tópico de la totalidad de la praxis, del "hacer", canto-músico-danzario y de su índole. Tercero, la bomba como un referente, en su más profundo sentido semiótico, subsume todo conocimiento de las prácticas musicales de los afropuertorriqueños.

Ella, y su generación, hereda de esas mentalidades del siglo XIX la construcción de una particular visión de lo puertorriqueño, desde la cual se construye la memoria de la bomba como un "hipérbaton histórico".

Además del ya citado Manuel Alonso, los trabajos de Fernando Callejo Ferrer (1915), Salvador Brau (1882) y Julio Vizcarrondo (1866) resumen la visión de Alonso respecto a subsumir lo negro a lo rítmico y, por ende, lo único puramente afropuertorriqueño. Para Callejo eso significa que, a pesar de hablar de las celebraciones de los afropuertorriqueños de San Juan y Cangrejos como "las diversas tribus de negros", su existencia como agentes de cultura se reducía a "grotescos bailes y canturías" acompañados de instrumentos "denominados *bombas* y *maracas*" (2015 [1915], 453). La bomba, como música y baile de negros, como exclusiva manifestación afropuertorriqueña, se caracteriza como una especie invasora de la cultura criolla blanca puertorriqueña y se *solidifica* como una praxis que debe, en el peor de los casos, minimizarse o, en el mejor de los casos, eliminarse (Brau 1971 [1882]; Dueño Colón 1973 [1913]). La traducción que hace Julio L. de Vizcarrondo (1863; 1957 [1863]) del informe que hace el científico francés André Pierre Ledru, titulada *Voyage aux iles de Tériffe, la Trinité, Saint-Thomas, Sainte-Croix et Porto-Rico* (A.-P. Ledru 1810), ha quedado para muchos como el trabajo que establece el nombre del tambor, *bomba*, como el nombre del metagénero. Tenemos que entender que, para la década de 1860, Vizcarrondo ya había leído a Alonso y la voz *bomba* estaba normalizada en su praxis lingüística cotidiana. A pesar de su conocimiento del francés, no puede evitar traducir el vocablo *bambula* por bomba, aunque haya traducido muy bien la palabra *tambourin* por *tamboril*. El término usado por Ledru es un préstamo que hace de su propia cultura musical, pues se está apropiando de lo que él conoce: el término *tambourin* se refiere a un tambor provenzal largo y estrecho. Es a ese tipo de tambor que Ledru llama genéricamente *bamboula*, al cual caracteriza como vulgar por ser de una construcción poco refinada, pero que, también, implica que era de uso común (A. P. Ledru 1863; P. A. Ledru 2013 [1810, 1863]; Allende Goitía 2012).

Sin embargo, el enlace de esta larga tradición letrada y el presente se hace a través del trabajo de investigación de Héctor Vega Drouet (1979). Basada en su trabajo de campo en Ghana y una revisión de la literatura disponible, principalmente los trabajos pioneros de Joseph Hanson Kwabena Nketia (1974), su disertación doctoral se ha convertido en la obra más citada y utilizada como fuente secundaria —en ocasiones como primaria— para todo trabajo sobre la bomba (Campos Parsi 1976; Malavet Vega 1992; Ferreras 2005; Quintero Rivera 2009; Ferrao 2012; Abadía-Rexach 2015). Lo que esta investigación hace es reafirmar una narrativa atemporal de la historia africana en general y de la afropuertorriqueña en particular. Su obsesividad por una esencia originaria unívoca desde el África Occidental ha dejado un rastro eurocentrista de estricar del discurso musicológico todo sentido de agencia temporal, o sea, establece las bases para caracterizar la bomba del presente, de alguna forma, como una actualización de una bomba primigenia. Pero esta práctica retórica-discursiva de su narrativa es heredada de escritos fundacionales como el de Kwabena Nketía. El trabajo de Kwabena Nketía está construido, igualmente, a base de elementos retóricos atemporales muy cónsonos con la visión folklorista del final del siglo XIX y el siglo XX, en la que se estudia la cultura, llamada tradicional como una producción humana más o menos inmutable, o con cambios mínimos (Bartók 1985 [1948]; Ortiz 1981 [1951]). ¿Qué ocurre, como ya mencioné en la introducción, cuando se abandona este paradigma a la hora de reabordar, o recaracterizar, el metagénero de la bomba no como centro, sino como parte de una praxis musical afropuertorriqueña más a tono con las dinámicas humanas en el África Subshariana y la banda occidental llamada por los europeos Guinea?

3. "Las prioridades culturales": lo "afrodiaspórico" en la construcción de las sociedades del archipiélago puertorriqueño

La memoria histórica de las músicas afropuertorriqueñas, como todas las pertenecientes a los procesos afrodiaspóricos a nivel mundial, yo arguyo, debe reflejar en mayor o menor grado los niveles de complejidad, dinamismo y adaptabilidad de las músicas en el continente africano, o sea, las prioridades culturales particulares estas. ¿Cuáles son algunas de estas prioridades culturales relevantes al génesis y desarrollo de las músicas en las islas borincanas? Primero, tenemos que comenzar con el trasiego comercial entre Europa y la costa norte de África, donde llegaban las caravanas de mercancías que cruzaban el Sahara. Segundo, el creciente número de personas que sobrevivieron a un largo proceso de esclavización que comenzó con su rapto, siguió con su sobrevivencia al cruce del Sahara como del Atlántico, lo cual incluía procesos de despersonalizar su identidad. En la bibliografía fundacional puertorriqueña sobre este tema, los autores ya citados —Luis Díaz Soler (1981

[1953]), Manuel Álvarez Nazario (1974) y Vega Drouet (1979)– resumen una vasta literatura que nos enfrenta a la magnitud territorial de esta región [la costa norte del continente, el Sahara y la inmensa región al sur del río Níger, entre el río Senegal y el río Ogooue, hoy Gabón]. Pero estas no eran regiones vacías, suspendidas en el tiempo, ni, mucho menos, desconectadas de las dinámicas de mundialización de su época. Entre los años 400 y 1591 de nuestra era, los imperios de Ghana, Kanem-Bornu, Takrur, Shongai, Mali, más los Estados Hausa, Fulani, Yoruba, Dahomey y Ashante, formaron, y fueron formados, dentro de una red comercial que conectaba la costa de Guinea con los reinos cristianos de Europa, el Imperio bizantino y los califatos islámicos, desde la península Ibérica hasta la misma península arábica (Davidson 1991; Conrad 2009; Newitt 2010).

El actual metagénero de la bomba, entonces, es el producto de unas prioridades culturales dentro de las cuales se dan las prácticas musicales afropuertorriqueñas. O sea, que deberíamos considerarlas como parte del proceso de génesis y formación de los géneros musicales afrodiaspóricos del gran Caribe y las Américas. Esta sección trata de arrojar luz sobre la denominación del metagénero como lo conocemos hoy día a través de una recaracterización de su memoria histórica: dentro de las músicas afropuertorriqueñas existen unas prácticas músico-danzarias que se ejecutan con bombas [tambores]. Por lo tanto, hoy día, la Bomba resulta ser un meta-género afropuertorriqueño bailable, constituido por una constelación de varias y diversas prácticas danzarias que emergieron a lo largo del tiempo. Como sucedía en las regiones de donde procedían los seres humanos esclavizados, el tambor no era el único instrumento que era marca de identidad. Sin embargo, cuando eran utilizadas, las bombas aparecían en las calles, en las plazas de centros urbanos y los "soberaos" de las haciendas y plantaciones, donde grandes contingentes de seres humanos esclavizados, junto con sus contrapartes libres, actuaban y encarnaban sonoramente su humanidad. Quiere decir que, cuando en la actualidad se habla de los seises de bomba, o los ritmos de bomba (Álvarez Nazario 1960, 1974; Barton 2004; Ferreras 2005), se refiere a los nombres propios de bailes en sí: *candungué, sicá, paulé, holándes, yubá, güembé, leró, gracimá, holandé, calindá, yubá, belén, cunyá, seis corrido* y *mariandá*.

¿Cómo, a pesar del hipérbaton histórico que hemos discutido anteriormente, podemos seguirle la huella a datos que evidencian unas prioridades culturales de lo afropuertorriqueño? Podemos comenzar, por ejemplo, con reflexiones intuitivas, fruto de lecturas de documentos o artículos de posición sobre la bomba. Por ejemplo, en un corto ensayo, Christian Rodríguez, barrilero y director del grupo de bomba Calindá, nos invita a:

> [R]econocer la riqueza de unos orígenes emergentes, fragmentados, efervescentes, asincrónicos y dinámicos, acaecidos en el devenir histórico puertorriqueño. Más allá de corregir perspectivas tradicionales o empuñar una propuesta redentora, este escrito es una apuesta por la diversidad en la composición histórica puertorriqueña y por lo que pudo haber ocurrido, aunque de inmediato no haya evidencias. (Rodríguez n.d.)

Aunque Rodríguez no cuestiona lo extraño que resulta la existencia de un género musical que no se llame de otra forma o haya existido sin aparentes cambios, sus preguntas son acertadas y su intuición lo dirige a cuestionar las respuestas que se han dado hasta el momento. Este ejercicio se puede reconocer en el trabajo de Cadilla de Martínez. En 1945, ella publicó un cuento de costumbre basado en sus memorias de niña sobre su nana, llamada Tate. Esta era una mujer que había sido esclavizada y que, después de 1873, trabajó como nodriza y sirvienta en la casa de Cadilla. La importancia de este relato es que es uno de los pocos casos donde se registra a una afroboricua identificando su práctica músico-danzaria. Cadilla registra a Tate hablando de que ella bailaba candungué en los guateques [celebraciones] y se da como entendido que se bailaba al son de bombas, de tambores. La narración es clara en hablar del candungué como un baile diferente de otros bailados con bombas. Me parece claro que la historia, como la narra Cadilla, sugiere que hablemos no de bailes *de* bombas, sino de bailes *con* bomba (1945).

Ya al final de la década de 1930, María Cadilla de Martínez nos ofrece evidencia de que la información y la data que maneja sobre los bailes *con* bombas hace referencia a diferentes prácticas músico-danzarias. Lo primero que llama la atención de sus escritos es que nunca usa la palabra *bomba* como denominación de baile. Dice:

> En los ingenios, particularmente durante el período de la esclavitud, y aún pasada aquella, también, en los parajes donde se concentraban los negros para vivir, celebrábanse (sic) bailes, especialmente los domingos u otros días festivos. Ellos duraban todo el día y una noche. Bailábanse (sic) los siguientes bailes: la mariyandá, acentuado en compases y como de saltos; el guateque que era de música alborotada, bulliciosa y alegre. En él las parejas gesticulaban y saltaban con abundantes risas y gritos; el mariangola, que era cadencioso, acompasado, de vueltas lánguidas; el curiquingue, que se bailaba en ruedas e hileras con una pareja central que extremaba el movimiento; el candungo o condungué, graciosamente vivo y sensual. De este último baile proceden muchos otros que están de moda. Sus similares de Argentina y Uruguay se llama candombe y candumbé; aristocratizado, llámase tango. En Cuba la rumba es un derivado que acentúa su parte sensual, viva. En la América del Norte tiene estos descendientes el Charleston, el cake walk y el shimany. Probablemente y como diremos adelante, algo tiene nuestra plena de este baile. Todos los derivados del candungué son cantados. (Cadilla de Martínez 1938, 45–6)

Quiero llamar la atención a cuatro puntos que podemos extraer de este párrafo: 1) cada baile tiene una coreografía particular: "como de saltos", de parejas, de "vueltas lánguidas", ruedas e hileras con una pareja en el centro, etc.; 2) en la nota al calce sobre el baile llamado *guateque*, ella escribe que "así llamaron luego los jíbaros a sus bailes y fiestas bulliciosas", en una década cuando se concretiza una ideología que establece de facto que los jíbaros son la población blanca antigua de la isla; 3) no aparece la palabra *bomba*, Cadilla da por sentado que estos géneros se bailan *con* bombas; y 4) en una década cuando la ideología emergente es una insularista, en la que se aísla al archipiélago de Puerto Rico de un Caribe que se percibe como muy negro, ella arguye que estos bailes pertenecen a una familia de prácticas afrodiaspóricas a lo largo de las Américas en general y las Antillas en particular.

Aunque en el presente la práctica más vista es la de un solo bailador frente al tambor, la historia nos señala otra cosa. Como lo indica la cita anterior, existieron bailes *con* bombas de pareja e incluso para géneros específicos como el *cocobalé*, un baile de artes marciales con palos, que es solo para varones. Igual con la organología [instrumentación] de este metagénero. Hoy día la componen dos tambores llamados "el buleador", o tambor primo (primero); "el seguidor", o segundo tambor; una maraca, usualmente utilizada por la persona que canta; y el cuá, construido en ocasiones de bambú o de un barril pequeño que se sabe que se tocaba en el costado de uno de los tambores. Sin embargo, la lectura de documentos de los siglos XVIII y XIX parece indicar que las bombas de diferentes tamaños coexistían en conjuntos que incorporaban guitarras, guitarrillos, güiros y calabazos (Daubón 1904; Diaz Soler 1981 [1953]).

Este fenómeno humano se combinó con la creación de "políticas culturales" durante la década de 1950, que no fue otra cosa que la creación de prioridades culturales desde la esfera gubernamental.

A mediados del siglo XX se dan dos eventos que forman una combinación de prioridades culturales. La primera corresponde a la movilidad poblacional y el asentamiento de las poblaciones afrodescendientes. La segunda corresponde a la creación de instituciones gubernamentales de implementación de política cultural pública. Sobre la primera, geográficamente hablando, la memoria de las formas bailables actuales se circunscribe a las tradiciones bailables de las comunidades de Loíza, Santurce, San Juan (barrio La Perla) y Cataño. A esta se le están añadiendo las prácticas danzarias y "performativas" de las comunidades afrodescendientes de Mayagüez, Ponce, Guayama e Isabela. Sin embargo, dicha memoria no incluye la gran migración interna que se da a nivel isla al final de la década de 1940 (Zelinsky 1949, 215). Este fenómeno humano se combinó con la creación de "políticas culturales" durante la década de 1950, que no fue otra cosa que la creación de prioridades culturales desde la esfera gubernamental. Estas políticas culturales se implementaron a través de instituciones gubernamentales, como el Instituto de Cultura Puertorriqueña, el Departamento de Instrucción Pública y la División de Educación a la Comunidad. Los programas de patrocinio a artesanos, grupos musicales y artistas dieron paso a unos procesos de folklorización cuyo resultado fue la agrupación del conjunto de prácticas danzarias afropuertorriqueñas, como prácticas genéricas discretas, bajo el nombre del instrumento acompañante: bomba (Rodríguez Cancel 2007; Allende Goitia 2008-2009, 2010).

Durante el siglo XIX, las prácticas musicales afropuertorriqueñas *con* bombas no se limitaban al contexto social al que hoy día estamos acostumbrados. Una de las "prioridades culturales" determinantes en el génesis y desarrollo de las prácticas musico-danzarias de los africanos y afrodescendientes durante el siglo XIX puertorriqueño se dio en la cotidianidad del goce popular: por un lado, las demostraciones públicas de unas formas de expresión de una sensibilidad músico-danzaria y, por el otro lado, el programa gubernamental de control y apropiación de dichas manifestaciones. Por ejemplo, en 1843, Francisco Vasallo narró un recuerdo de navidades, para él, de antaño: "las trullas de los negros con sus bombas y banderas, ataviados con fajas de todos colores, sombreros de tres picos con plumas, y mil adornos raros con que les gusta engalanarse para pedir el Aguinaldo en un lenguaje especial" (VVAA 1843). Esta narración, que antecede al texto de Alonso, sugiere una tradición de parrandas de aguinaldo que tenían el mismo carácter celebratorio que los carnavales, fiestas de Santiago y de los Santos Inocentes [28 de diciembre] dentro del recinto murado de San Juan, con unas bombas [tambores] transportables, sugiriendo la existencia de otros tipos de membráfonos. Este mismo tipo de observaciones sugerentes pueden extraerse de documentos que no hacen referencia directa a descripciones de festividades.

La historia de los bailes con bombas sigue muy de cerca la historia del ejercicio del control político y social de la población africana y afrodescendiente. Un ejemplo de ello es el cuerpo de normativas de vigilancia y policía del comportamiento cotidiano de los afropuertorriqueños, tanto los esclavizados como los considerados libres. Estas normas se publican originalmente en 1814 y se reimprimen en varios bandos hasta 1868. Estas no solo nos informan sobre prácticas específicas y sus contextos cotidianos, sino que también nos marcan el desarrollo de los mecanismos de control de esta población, como el Bando contra la raza africana (PARES 1848-1855). En los Bandos de policía y buen gobierno, de 1824 al 1868, encontramos los bailes de "negros bozales" [africanos esclavizados llegados recientemente], extremadamente reglamentados. Para los afropuertorriqueños en general los bailes y toques de sus músicas estaban permitidas solo en las fiestas de los Santos Reyes, San Miguel, San Juan, San Pedro, Santiago, Santa Rosa, Cruz de Mayo y Corpus Cristi [Día del Santísimo Sacramento]. Las músicas y bailes de sus naciones estaban prohibidas en velorios de párvulos [niños], en las casas de los difuntos y en las marchas fúnebres al cementerio (Gobierno de Puerto Rico 1849, 1862, 1868). Estas normativas estaban en vigor para las fiestas conmemorativas del nacimiento de María Isabel, Princesa de Asturias, en 1852 (Gobierno de Puerto Rico 1852), y en las que celebraban el natalicio de Don Alfonso, en 1858 (Gobierno de Puerto Rico 1858). Otro factor, o prioridad cultural, es nuestra condición de isla en el archipiélago de las Antillas. También, la entrada continua de africanos y afrodescendientes —algunos como parte de los cargamentos nuevos de esclavos provenientes de África Occidental, luego de puertos intermediarios como Curaçao, Haití y Jamaica; y otros como parte de la continua inmigración procedente de las islas de habla inglesa, danesa, francesa y holandesa—. Estos factores —represión estructural e inmigración— añaden un factor de cambio, renovación e iniciación de procesos de fertilización cruzada que hay que tomar en cuenta a la hora de hablar del metagénero de la bomba (Morales Carrión 1974 [1952]; Díaz Soler 1981 [1953]; Álvarez Nazario 1974).

Durante la década de 1860, el cronista del Ayuntamiento de San Juan, con motivo de las celebraciones de su Santo Patrón, describe de la siguiente manera la intervención de los llamados "congos finos":

> Llegados que hubieron ante los balcones del Palacio de su S.S.E.E. cantaron y bailaron largo rato á usanza de su país, siguiendo el compás marcado por los especiales instrumentos que constituyen las orquestas en el mismo; y despues de los vivas de costumbre, marcharon á recorrer la Ciudad, seguidos de un numeroso pueblo, para terminar su alborada con un bailecito que tenían preparado en la casa de uno de los cabezas. (Gobierno de Puerto Rico 1864)

La manifestación de prácticas músico-danzarias dentro y fuera de las murallas de San Juan no fue algo particular de esta década. Encontramos que en las fiestas celebradas en 1830 se reportaron "reuniones de pueblo, con bombas y otros instrumentos propios en los bailes de morenos" (Gobierno de Puerto Rico 1830), además de que, en 1844 y 1846 (Gobierno de Puerto Rico 1844, 1846), las crónicas de las celebraciones hablan de bailes con bombas en la Cruz de Santa Bárbara (Gobierno de Puerto Rico 1844). Las celebraciones de africanos y afrodescendientes en los días de fiestas designados eran días que marcaban momentos significativos para dicha comunidad. En 1840, Ciriaco Sabat, autoidentificándose como "Rey de los Negros Congos" de San Juan, le dicta a un escribiente una carta dirigida al Gobernador Santiago Méndez Vigo pidiéndole que autorice una celebración de estos en el día de San Miguel Arcángel [29 de septiembre] y la Señora del Santo Rosario, que se llevaría a cabo en la plaza del mercado (Daubón 1904; Díaz Soler 1981 [1953]).

Después de las Leyes de Emancipación de Esclavos de 1873, la población de afropuertorriqueños esclavizados se integraron a una vida libre de tan infame institución, pero tratados, junto al resto de afroboricuas considerados legalmente libres, con el mismo sentido de condescendencia y prejuicio de siempre. Durante las primeras décadas del siglo XX, José Antonio Daubón (1840-1922), Ángel Rivero Méndez (1862-1930) y María Cadilla de Martínez (1884-1951) ofrecen una muestra, en diferentes formatos narrativos, de cómo, por un lado, la población autoidentificada como blanca percibía la cultura musical afrodescendiente vernácula y, por el otro lado, cómo los africanos y afrodescendientes criollos actuaban y se expresaban de su propia práctica cultural.

Daubón describe un baile con bombas en las cercanías de la plaza de mercado de San Juan. El baile es parte de las celebraciones del día de San Miguel Arcángel. Ese día se coronaban el rey y la reina de "los negros congos". El baile que describe es uno de varones en el que un bailarín "seguía otro no menos esforzado ni menos ligero; y a cada golpe de timbal entraba en el círculo un nuevo combatiente". Pero llama la atención la descripción de las bombas que acompañaban este baile: "constituida por timbales de dos metros de longitud [cerca de 78.7 pulgadas, unos 6.5 pies] y [otros] tambores de construcción primitiva" (Daubón 1904). Por su parte, la descripción que nos ofrece Rivero Méndez de un baile con bombas celebrado en la finca El Alto, en Sabana Llana, es diferente. Rivero nació en el barrio Cacao de Sabana Llana, y estaba familiarizado con las prácticas músico-danzarias afroboricuas. Recordando a "el negro Simón" dice que:

Le vi por última vez en la Piedra Blanca, una noche de hermosa luna en que yo andaba de caza de yaguasas. Simón, bien metido en juerga y en *romo colorao*, repicaba con sus manos sabias el pellejo de una bomba; varias morenas y morenos sudorosos movían con movimientos helicoidales sus redondeces traseras, en baile acompasado, lúbrico y bullanguero. (*El Imparcial*, 18 de octubre de 1924 en Rivero Méndez 2008 [1924-1927])

Note que se habla de un baile de grupo en que se sugiere, que cada participante mantenía sus propios movimientos. La mirada racializada es notable, pues es consistente con la visión decimonónica que equipara el baile rítmico con tambor como primitivo.

Una visión que nunca se estudia en las músicas bailes con bomba es la percepción que de estas tienen de las personas que vienen de afuera del archipiélago puertorriqueño. En 1831, Edward Bliss Emerson le escribió a su hermano William:

[I] saw collection of negroes assembled on the ramparts for a dance, with the instruments of music peculiar to their nations — two large & long buoy-shaped drums of which the one end rests on the ground while the other is covered with parchment & is beaten with rapid strokes. On the side I observed the word Congo painted;— & I hear that the Congos consider themselves as the most eminent here, & claim some little prerogatives on the day of St Michael. (inquire) Others of the negroes had rattles made of calabash & called in English "shake shake" a name excellently descriptive of the music; there are two other instruments in use among the blacks & their dances. They separate themselves into the four or five nations to which they pretend to belong. A boisterous singing & violent jumping joined to the clatter make out the merry ball, which must stop at 8 P.M after which I suppose they are permitted to dance within doors. (Rigau Pérez 2003, 87)

Pero estas diversiones citadinas no estaban restringidas a fiestas oficiales, porque el domingo 26 de junio, en las vísperas de las festividades de San Pedro, escribió en su diario:

Walked tonight, saw a band of negroes dancing to drum & shake shake & congo upon the ramparts, singing a simple tune with I should think not more than three different notes, & perhaps no meaning — & moving backwards & forwards from within a circle with a step about as uniform as the song, & such as it needs no Monsieur to teach; I noticed three or four houses also on the way where similar music & jumping was going on within doors.— Labouring as they do perforce they seem indefatigable in their diversions. (2003, 100)

Emerson nos llama la atención a los instrumentos utilizados y da una descripción muy vaga del baile. También se refiere a lo cotidiano de los eventos y cómo dentro del recinto murado de San Juan las músicas afropuertorriqueñas eran parte del paisaje sonoro. Lo más importante es la relación de dicho baile con la celebración de los días de los santos Pedro y Miguel Arcángel.

Setenta y dos años más tarde, en 1903, otro extranjero, Joseph B. Seabury, escribe un libro sobre su viaje a Puerto Rico y trata de describir el baile de los afropuertorriqueños de esta manera:

> The negroes are very boisterous in their antics. They romp and caper and contort their bodies into all sorts of shapes. The "cake walk" is a mild performance compared with the pranks of these people. Their gayety lasts for several days, and ceases only when the participants have exhausted all new forms of amusement and are completely tired out. (1903, 53)

Aunque no hace ninguna mención de instrumentos, coreografía o letras de canciones, sí hace una comparación entre el baile de afrodescendientes que observa en Puerto Rico con aquellos de los afroestadounidenses: el *cake walk*. O sea, tanto los puertorriqueños como los extranjeros visitantes podían observar una similitud y unas correspondencias entre las prácticas danzarias afropuertorriqueñas y aquellas afrodiaspóricas de la región caribeña y del hemisferio de las Américas.

4. Las "presiones evolutivas", los debates de identidad y las políticas de la folklorización cultural de las músicas puertorriqueñas

Las "presiones evolutivas" que hacen posibles cambios en las prácticas culturales se dan tanto en el ámbito del "hacer" musical como en el acto de construcción de una memoria de dicho "hacer". Durante los primeros años del siglo XX comienza a definirse cada vez más la reducción de todo baile *con* tambor como baile de bomba. Durante las décadas comprendidas entre 1921 y 1939, los registros sobre los bailes con bombas nos ofrecen datos sobre lo generalizado de estas prácticas músico-danzarias a lo largo del archipiélago, pero también podemos leer una movida ideológica dirigida a domesticar discursivamente lo que se observaba. Por ejemplo, la académica María Teresa Babín (1910-1989) relata unos recuerdos de adolescencia de esta forma:

> La fiesta de fin de zafra en las haciendas de caña del sur de Puerto Rico se celebraba no hace tantos años con el baile de bomba de los negros de la bajura. En la hacienda de la Florida en Santa Isabel, donde mi padre trabajaba de mayordomo entre los años 1924 al 1928, recuerdo estos pintorescos bailes en que las mujeres lucían varias enaguas profusamente adornadas con encajes y tiras bordadas, ostentándolas al levantar la falda discretamente al compás de la danza rítmica y monótona al son del bombo. (1958, 97–8)

Nos debe interesar la mención del pueblo de Santa Isabel, pues no es parte de los "pueblos" que hoy día se cuentan como que poseen una tradición de bombas. A este podemos añadir pueblos como Isabela, Aguadilla e incluso pueblos de la montaña como Utuado y Lares, que durante los siglos XVII y XVIII tenían una población afrodescendiente significativa. También, nos debe llamar la atención cómo relaciona la práctica danzaria con celebraciones de la vida cotidiana de estos afropuertorriqueños, y que los presente en una versión del siglo XX de algo que venía celebrándose desde el siglo XIX, cuando eran legalmente esclavos.

Años más tarde, María Luisa Muñoz Siaca (1905-2000) comparte un recuerdo de su juventud y nos habla del famoso bailador identificado solo como Dominguito. Para la década de 1930, este era un famoso bailador natural de Cataño. Aquí Muñoz Siaca establece inequívocamente la bomba como lo negro que ha sobrevivido en la cultura puertorriqueña. Las descripciones que hace son más cerca de lo que observamos hoy día. Como testigo, ella nos describe el baile de esta forma:

> Yo recuerdo haber visto a Dominguito bailando esta antigua danza y no se me puede olvidar la elegancia de los movimientos exigidos en la interpretación del baile que, posiblemente, había sido ya pigmentado con el color de las aristocráticas contradanzas europeas. (1966, 84)

Nos establece a Cataño como un conocido pueblo donde vivían bomberos y bailadores. Ofrece una lista de nombres que se están rescatando del olvido (Ferrao 2012): Bailadores de Guayama, Salinas, Ponce y Arroyo como Modesta Amaro, Isabelita Navarro, Pablo Lind, Bruno Cora, Narcisa Godineaux, Amalia Villodas y Damasia Alonso (Muñoz 1966, 83–4). A esta descripción, Muñoz añade una transcripción del testimonio de Candita, hija de Dominguito, que, a mi entender, se comienza a usar como un molde conceptual a través del cual se establece la forma de bailar bomba. Ambas citas son excelentes ejemplos de cómo las presiones evolutivas se dan tanto en el ámbito de la práctica danzaria como en el plano de la construcción ideológica: Muñoz Siaca pertenece a un grupo de letrados, como María Teresa Babín, Jack Delano, y Manrique Cabrera, que conocen, visitan, entrevistan y fotografían a Dominguito en Cataño. Estos letrados son protagonistas en los procesos de domesticación de prácticas culturales populares a través de inventar una nueva memoria, oficializada por el estado. Aparte de eso, la descripción de Candita es cautivante:

> Los domingos, desde la una de la tarde, comenzaban a llegar los bailadores. Se utilizaban dos barriles forrados con un cuero al que llamábamos bomba; en uno de ellos, el cuero estaba más tenso que en el otro. Usaban también dos maracas y dos palitos que se tocaban sobre un banco de madera. Había un cantador y el coro que se componía de los espectadores.
>
> El hombre comenzaba a bailar y la mujer le seguía. Para comenzar, el bailador marcaba el paso, y el tocador de bomba tocaba el ritmo de acuerdo con lo pedido por el

bailador. Al cabo de un rato, la mujer pasaba al frente y el hombre le seguía; ella era entonces quien indicaba los pasos y el ritmo que había de repiquetear el tocador de bomba. (1966, 84)

El valor intrínseco de este testimonio radica en el momento etnológico, o sea, la descripción de un "hacer" en un tiempo y espacio particular. El observador, los letrados, son testigos de una práctica afropuertorriqueña que está cambiando en tiempo real con los cambios demográficos y los procesos de marginalización urbana. Lo observado, o los seres humanos observados, activamente están actuando su identidad musical en medio de unos cambios sociales y económicos que cada vez más niegan su relevancia como auténtica cultura vernácula. Sin embargo, para 1966, este "hacer" cultural se estaba informando como recuerdo. Dicho recuerdo se establece como una memoria que, por un lado, comienza a utilizarse como un entonces —como medida y norma de una práctica actualizada del pasado— y que, por el otro lado, se usa como objeto folklórico.

Aparte de los tambores —atabales o bombas—, todo instrumento melódico armónico se utiliza como evidencia de las músicas europeas o europeo-descendientes no como instrumentos enculturados por los africanos o afrodescendientes.

Estas descripciones muestran la intersección de eventos que funcionan como presiones evolutivas que, a su vez en su conjunto, son parte de procesos humanos que componen prioridades culturales y que ayudan a entender el pasado como una inversión temporal. Por ejemplo, diez años después, Héctor Campos Parsi reforzó el tipo de memoria que confunde el presente de los bailes *con* bombas con su entonces: en su libro se establece la convención de que esta es una práctica exclusiva de soberao, tierra apisonada, de espacio abierto; la organología se estandariza a dos tambores (buleador y subidor); el canto responsorial; y se establece un canon, o repertorio, que comienza a primar tradiciones creoles por el tipo de cantos y de referencias al Caribe francés, creando así el mito del origen haitiano de las prácticas contemporáneas (Campos Parsi 1976, 50–3). Esto se entiende cuando descubrimos que Campos Parsi está dependiendo totalmente, y acríticamente, del trabajo de Héctor Vega Drouet (1979), como Muñoz Siaca dependió del trabajo de Luis Díaz Soler (1981 [1953]) y Arturo Morales Carrión (1974 [1952]). Esta dependencia de fuentes secundarias para apoyar aserciones, o construcciones explicativas, ha creado, a mi entender, una comprensión lineal, unidireccional y atemporal de los intercambios musicales entre nuestro archipiélago y las regiones de África Occidental; además de una cultura generalizada de recirculación de supuestos históricos cuestionables.

Por ejemplo, maestros de apreciación musical y educadores musicales insertados en la corriente general del sistema de educación pública han utilizado los trabajos de Cesáreo Rosa Nieves (1967) y Francisco López Cruz (1967) para informar sus clases (Departamento de Educación 2007). El resultado de este tipo de apropiación académica ha producido un menoscabo en las importantes aportaciones de estos pioneros de los estudios musicales puertorriqueños, pues en lugar de utilizarlos como puntos de partida para nuevas preguntas e hipótesis de trabajo, se manejan como una suerte de fuentes primarias que guardan un conocimiento inmutable. El mismo trabajo del Departamento de Educación *Estableciendo conexiones a través de la música* (2007) mantiene prácticas afropuertorriqueñas como la bomba, la plena, el seis y el jazz como fenómenos musicales separados, sin percatarse de que siguen un paradigma establecido durante la década de 1930 y que, además, reafirman dispositivos de implementación de política pública por parte del estado que ha establecido la bomba como lo único directamente afrodiaspórico. Aparte de los tambores —atabales o bombas—, todo instrumento melódico armónico se utiliza como evidencia de las músicas europeas o europeo-descendientes no como instrumentos enculturados por los africanos o afrodescendientes. Poco se habla de la marímbula; la larga tradición de violinistas afrodescendiaentes, tanto de entrenamiento formal y de tradición oral —que durante el siglo XIX también fungían como bastoneros en las contradanzas inglesas y francesas—; el arpa; y el piano, todos instrumentos descartados como no negros. La larga historia del ud [la-ud] sudanés, sahariano y andaluz cierra un circuito afrodiaspórico con el desarrollo de instrumentos de cuerdas en Europa que producen la vihuela y la guitarra. Los rabeles de los reinos de Shongai, Ghana y más tarde de los estados Ashanti, Dahomey y Hausa tienen una vida global en el rebec europeo y la gestación de las familias de instrumentos de cuerda frotada (Wetzel 2012). La minusvaloración de los seres humanos esclavizados creó en las Américas una cultura de prejuicio racial tan destructiva que despropia al africano capturado de sus capacidades creativas y de adaptabilidad a los nuevos elementos y condiciones de vida (Fraginals 1978; Waterman 1999; Alvarado 2014). En el caso de Puerto Rico, ¿qué ocurre durante el largo siglo XIX y durante los primeros cincuenta años del siglo XX, que una rica tradición de tambores, marímbulas, calabazos y guitarrillos son reducidos a una práctica musical, que siendo rica en sí misma, tiene solo dos tambores y que, mientras más pasa el tiempo, se han estandarizado? Parte del problema está en la implicación de que una vez dicha tradición se ha cristalizado en su versión de la segunda mitad del siglo XX, se pelea y se resiste cada prospecto de aprovechar las nuevas "prioridades culturales" y fluir con las "presiones evolutivas" y dar fruto a nuevas [en plural] tradiciones de tambor con otros tipos de tambores creados en el proceso mismo de crear cultura.

Es sobre esta reducción de las prácticas afropuertorriqueñas al metagénero de la bomba que trabajan los investigadores posteriores a la década de 1970. Las teorizaciones, muy pertinentes, de Ángel Quintero Rivera (1998, 2009) sobre la corporeización de la cultura, en el musicar en el cuerpo, parten de dicha meseta cognitiva. Sin embargo, dichos trabajos, a pesar de partir de una memoria folklorizada del metagénero de la bomba, ofrecen visiones frescas que pueden replantearse en una recaracterización de esta. Si leemos otra vez el testimonio de Candita, como lo transcribe Muñoz Siaca, este ofrece un buen contraste con los bombazos y la resemantización de las prácticas del metagénero en el siglo XXI (Barton 2004; Ferreras 2005; Abadía-Rexach 2015). En su documental *Ayeres de la bomba*, Jerry Ferrao hace una excelente recopilación de testimonios que devuelven las tradiciones bombísticas de Cataño a un cronotopo [en espacio y lugar] más humano. Sitúa, históricamente, las prácticas bailables negras no como un evento excepcional, sino como evidencia de un circuito de prácticas musicales *con* bombas que se extiende hasta Bayamón, el valle del Toa y Dorado, por la banda costera del norte, que se conectaba con las comunidades afrodescendiente, a través de la bahía de San Juan, San Mateo de Cangrejos y Loíza. Pero este meme no es exclusivamente vernáculo. Los trabajos de académicos fuera de Puerto Rico también comparten esta misma apropiación creativa de una tradición músico-danzaria-cantada presentada en un presente continuo y, aparentemente, inamovible, como lo son los escritos de Peter Manuel (2012), Robin Moore (2010) y el ya mencionado Halbert Barton (2004).

5. Cierre: con repique, piquete... ¿y *perreo*...?

En su libro fundacional *From Bomba to Hip-Hop: Puerto Rican Culture and the Latino Identity* (2000), Juan Flores confronta la visión estática de la cultura folklorizada haciendo una invitación a los lectores de las comunidades puertorriqueñas y de las Américas hispanoparlantes a considerar que existe un *continuum* entre la bomba como metagénero afropuertorriqueño y el *hip-hop* como un producto emergente afrodiaspórico de las comunidades jamaiquina, afroestadounidense y puertorriqueña —una metaidentidad afroneoyorquina—. Esta experiencia de la diáspora es fundamental, pues, a mi entender, ha forzado a prácticas musicales puertorriqueñas folklorizadas como la bomba fuera de su ámbito cerrado de práctica. Linda Valli Morales Martínez (2003) evidencia el desplazamiento de los géneros bailables salseros a la bomba y la plena como marcas de identidad en las comunidades puertorriqueñas a través de Estados Unidos. En este trabajo de tesis, Morales Martínez nos presenta cómo el perfil de las prácticas bomberas cede a las nuevas "prioridades culturales" en que dichas comunidades se encuentran y enfrentan. De Orlando, Florida; Jersey City, New Jersey; Chicago, Illinois; hasta Austin, Texas, las músicas puertorriqueñas en general y las afropuertorriqueñas en particular entran en las dinámicas de nuevas "presiones evolutivas" que ejercen fuerzas formativas que las moldean. En estos lugares, los bailes con bombas se enculturan en la vida cotidiana de estas ciudades y de las dinámicas culturales y de políticas de identidad de los Estados Unidos. En estas comunidades se practica de forma abierta la bomba como marca de identidad de comunidad y de autoidentificación genérica, como cuestionamiento a las ideologías patriarcales en general y como actuación de identidades sexuales y de géneros alternos (Alamo-Pastrana 2009; Abadía-Rexach 2014). Pero a pesar de estos cuestionamientos, todavía queda la visión ahistórica y atemporal de la bomba como un metagénero afrodiaspórico puertorriqueño (Abadía-Rexach 2015).

¿Por qué la propuesta estético-cultura de Rafael Cortijo e Ismael Rivera enfrentó la crítica y la oposición de aquellos que protestaron en contra de lo que ellos estimaban que era la comercialización de la bomba?

El reposicionar el metagénero de la bomba dentro de un cronotopo discursivo nos devolvería una memoria histórica de los seres humanos que son la base de esa forma de musicar. Las visiones folklorizadas del performance musical vacían al ser humano de su capacidad de agenciar su existencia y se cambia el acento a la práctica descarnada que usa como referencia de autenticidad unas convenciones abstractas inventadas en las refriegas de los debates de identidad. ¿Por qué la propuesta estético-cultura de Rafael Cortijo e Ismael Rivera enfrentó la crítica y la oposición de aquellos que protestaron en contra de lo que ellos estimaban que era la comercialización de la bomba? Curiosamente, esa crítica no incluyó a la plena, pues desde muy temprano en el siglo veinte pasó por los mecanismos formativos, primero, del consumo popular comercial; segundo, por la apropiación de consumo suntuario de la élite puertorriqueña y turistas en los clubes nocturnos de la industria hotelera; y, tercero, sometida los procesos transformadores de la industria cultural de la grabación. Es mi contención que una vez la bomba se devuelva al conjunto general de las músicas afropuertorriqueñas, sus practicantes podrán abordar procesos creativos que, a partir de las músicas con bombas, se renueven y se creen nuevas familias de tambores, nuevos géneros afropuertorriqueños que den inicio, y continuidad, a la historia que no se ha vivido todavía.

OBRAS CITADAS

Álvarez Nazario, Manuel. 1960. Historia de las denominaciones de los bailes de bomba. *Revista de Ciencias Sociales* 4(1), 59–73.

______. 1974. *El elemento afronegroide en el español de Puerto Rico: contribución al estudio del negro en América*. San Juan: Instituto de Cultura Puertorriqueña.

Abadía-Rexach, Bárbara Idalissee. 2014. De aquí pa'llá y de allá pa'cá: los" toques" de la migración en la bomba puertorriqueña/From Here to There, and From There to Here: The "Pitches" of Migration in Puerto Rican Bomba. *Relaciones Internacionales* (25), 123–41.

______. 2015. ¡Saludando al tambor!: el nuevo movimiento de la bomba puertorriqueña. Tesis doctoral, The University of Texas, Austin.

______. 2015. Repiques y piquetes: bomba y racialización en Puerto Rico. En *Caribbean Without Borders: Beyond the Can(n)on's Range*, ed. María del Carmen Quintero Aguiló, Gabriel Jiménez Fuentes, Marisol Joseph Haynes, Gabriel Mejía González y Diana Ursulin Mopsus. 54–67. Newcastle upon Tyne: Cambridge Scholars Publishing.

Alamo-Pastrana, Carlos. 2009. Con el eco de los barriles: Race, Gender and the Bomba Imaginary in Puerto Rico. *Identities: Global Studies in Culture and Power* 16(5), 573–600.

Alegría, Ricardo E., ed. 2009a. *Documentos históricos de Puerto Rico, Volumen I 1493-1516*. San Juan: Centro de Estudios Avanzados de Puerto Rico y el Caribe.

_______, ed. 2009b. *Documentos históricos de Puerto Rico, Volumen II 1517-1527.* San Juan: Centro de Estudios Avanzados de Puerto Rico y el Caribe.

_______, ed. 2009c. *Documentos históricos de Puerto Rico, Volumen III 1528-1544.* San Juan: Centro de Estudios Avanzados de Puerto Rico y el Caribe.

Allende Goitía, Noel. 2008-2009. The Geographical Imagination: The Ontology of Race, Memory, and Place in the Identity Debate in Puerto Rico, 1849-1950 (An interpretative Essay). *Kálathos* (Universidad Interamericana de Puerto Rico) 4.

_______. 2010. Las músicas otras: La africanía de las músicas puertorriqueñas en las prácticas de la vida cotidiana. *La Página* 83/84/85.

_______. 2010. *De Margarita a El Cumbanchero: vida musical, imaginación racial y discurso histórico en la sociedad puertorriqueña (1898 -1940).* San Juan: Ediciones Puerto.

_______. 2012. Mare Clausum, Mare Musicum: las músicas afrodiaspóricas y Puerto Rico and the Non-Hispanic Caribbean. In *Arturo Morales Carrión: Dimensiones del gran diplomático puertorriqueño*, ed. Luis Héctor Acevedo. San Juan: Universidad Interamericana de Puerto Rico.

_______. 2013a. Danza y resistencia: bailes afropuertorriqueños y conflicto social en el Puerto Rico del siglo XIX. En *El Caribe y sus relaciones con España: políticas y sociedades en transformación (siglos XIX y XX)*, ed. Jesús Raúl Hernández Palomo, José Jesús Navarro García, Ángel Luis Vélez Oyola y Rafael Luis Cabrera Collazo. San Juan: Universidad Interamericana de Puerto Rico.

_______. 2013b. Del criollismo "Ilustrado" al nacionalismo musical "Romántico": cultura musical, vida cotidiana y el ámbito público del ejercicio del poder político y social en Puerto Rico (1747-1849). *La Habana Elegante (2ª Época)* <http://www.habanaelegante.com/Fall_Winter_2013/Dossier_Antillano_AllendeGoitia.html>/, 54.

Alonso, Manuel A. 2007 [1849]. *El gíbaro: cuadro de costumbres de la isla de Puerto Rico. Edición crítica.* Editado por Eduardo Forastieri-Braschi. San Juan: Academia Puertorriqueña de la Lengua Española.

_______. 1849. *El gíbaro: cuadro de costumbres de la isla de Puerto-Rico.* Barcelona: D. Juan Oliver, Impresor de S. M.

Babín, María Teresa. 1958. *Panorama de la cultura puertorriqueña.* Vol. II. Biblioteca Puertorriqueña. Prólogo de Andrés Iduarte. New York: Las Americas Publishing Co.

Bajtín, Mijaíl Mijáilovich. 1981. *The Dialogic Imagination.* Editado por Michael Holquist. Traducido por Caryl Emerson y Michael Holquist. Austin: University of Texas.

_______. 1989 [1975]. *Teoría y estética de la novela: trabajos de investigación.* Traducido por Helena E. Kriukova y Vicente Cazcarra. Madrid: Taurus.

Barton, Halbert. 2004. A Challenge for Puerto Rican Music: How to Built a Soberao for Bomba. *CENTRO: Journal of the Center for Puerto Rican Studies* 16(1), 69–89.

Bartók, Béla. 1985 [1948]. *Escritos sobre música popular.* 3ª edición. Traducido por Roberto V. Raschella. México, D.F.: Siglo Veintiuno Editores.

Bejarano Pellecer, Clara. 2015. Las danzas en la representación cultural española de América y África: mestizaje musical en Sevilla en los siglos XVI y XVII. *Baetica. Estudios de Arte, Geografía e Historia* 35/36, 205–34.

Bickerton, Derek. 1999. Can Biomusicology Learn from Language Evolution Studies?. En *The Origins of Music*, editores Nils L. Wallin, Björn Merker y Steven Brown. Cambridge: The MIT Press.

Blackmore, Susan. 1999. *The Meme Machine.* New York: Oxford University Press.

Brau, Salvador. 1971. *Ensayos: disquisiciones sociológicas.* Río Piedras, PR: Editorial Edil, Inc.

Braudel, Fernand. 1987 [1949]. *El Mediterráneo y el mundo mediterráneo en la época de Felipe II.* Vols. I y II. México, D.F.: Fondo de Cultura Económica.

Cadilla de Martínez, María. 1938. *Costumbres y tradicionalismos de mi tierra.* San Juan: María Cadilla de Martínez.

________. 1945. *Hitos de la raza: cuentos tradicionales y folklóricos.* San Juan: publicado por la autora.

Callejo Ferrer, Fernando. 1915. *Música y músicos puertorriqueños.* San Juan: Tipografía Cantero Fernández, Co.

________. 2015 [1915]. *Música y músicos puertorriqueños.* Edición conmemorativa de su centenario. Ensayos, notas y documentos anejos de Noel Allende Goitía. San Juan: Ediciones Clara Luz.

Campos Parsi, Héctor. 1976. *La música en Puerto Rico.* Volumen 7, Música, de *La gran enciclopedia de Puerto Rico.* Madrid: Ediciones R.

Conrad, David C. 2009. *Empires of Medieval West Africa: Ghana, Mali, and Songhay.* Revised edition. n.p.: Chelsea House Publications.

Cross, Ian. 2006. Four Issues in the Study of Music in Evolution. *The World of Music* 48(3), 55–63.

________. 2011. Music and Biocultural Evolution. En *The Cultural Study of Music: A Critical Introduction,* editado por M. Clayton, T. Herbert y R. Middleton. 17–27. Londrés: Routledge.

Daubón, José Antonio. 1904. *Cosas de Puerto Rico.* San Juan: Tipografía la Correspondencia.

Davidson, Basil. 1991. *Africa in History: Themes and Outlines.* Revised and expanded edition. New York: Simon and Schuster.

Dawkins, Richard. 2006 [1976]. *The Selfish Gene.* Oxford: Oxford University Press.

Departamento de Educación. 2007. *Estableciendo conexiones a través de la música.* San Juan: Departamento de Educación del Estado Libre Asociado de Puerto Rico.

Díaz Díaz, Edgardo. 2014. Bomba. Vol. I, de *Latin Music: Musicians, Generes, and Themes,* de Ilan Stavans et al. 77–9. Santa Barbara: Greenwood.

Díaz Soler, Luis. 1981 [1953]. *Historia de la esclavitud negra en Puerto Rico.* Río Piedras: Editorial Universitaria de la Universidad de Puerto Rico.

Dueño Colón, Braulio. 1913. Estudio sobre la danza puertorriqueña. Premio del Ateneo de Puerto Rico. Archivo General de Puerto Rico.

________. 1973 [1913]. Estudio sobre la danza puertorriqueña. *Revista Educación* (Departamento de Educación de Puerto Rico) 37, 113–23.

Duverger, Christian. 2007. *El primer mestizaje: la clave para entender el pasado mesoamericano.* México, D.F.: Consejo Nacional para la Cultura y las Artes, Instituto Nacional de Antropología e Historia, Taurus, Universidad Nacional Autónoma de México.

Emerson, Edward Bliss. 2013 [1831-1834]. *The Caribbean Journal and Letters, 1831-1834.* San Juan: José G. Rigau-Pérez, edición y transcripción de los manuscritos.

Ferrao, Jerry. 2012. *Ayeres de la bomba (Documental).* Dirigido por Jerry Ferrao.

Ferreras, Salvador E. 2005. Solo Drumming in the Puerto Rican Bomba: An Analysis of Musical Processes and Improvisational Strategies. Tesis doctoral, The University of British Columbia.

Flores, Juan. 2000. *From Bomba to Hip-Hop: Puerto Rican Culture and the Latino Identity.* New York: Columbia University Press.

García de León Griego, Antonio. 2002. *El mar de los deseos: el Caribe hispano musical: historia y contrapunto.* México, D.F.: Siglo Veintiuno Editores.

Gobierno de Puerto Rico. 1830. *Relación de las fiestas públicas verificadas en esta capital, y mayor número de los pueblos de esta Isla, con el plaucible motivo del enlace de su amado soberano el Señor Fernando VII con la serenísima Princesa de Nápoles Doña María Cristina de Borbón.* San Juan: Oficina de Gobierno a cargo de D. Valeriano Sanmillán.

———. 1832. *Relación exacta de las fiestas que se han practicado en esta plaza, con motivo de la instalación de la real Audiencia y entrada del real Sello.* San Juan: Imprenta del Gobierno a cargo de D. Valeriano de Sanmillán.

———. 1844. *Descripción de las fiestas y regocijos públicos con que esta ciudad de Puerto-Rico ha celebrado el juramento prestado el 10 de febrero de 1844 a S. M. la Reina de las Españas Doña Isabel II, declarada mayor de edad por las Cortes del Reino.* San Juan: Imprenta de Gimbernat.

———. 1846. *Programa de las fiestas reales y regocijos públicos con que la capital de Puerto Rico va a celebrar los rejios enlaces de S. M. la Reina Nuestra Señora Doña Isabel II, (D.G.), con su excelso primo el Infante Don Francisco de Asís, y de la serenísima Infanta Doña María Luisa Fernanda, su augusta hermana, con el Príncipe francés Duque de Montpernsier.* San Juan: Imprenta del Gobierno.

———. 1848. Celebridad del cumpleaños de la serenísima Señora Infanta Doña María Luisa Fernanda. *Gaceta de Puerto Rico* 17(14), 1-2.

———. 1849. *Bando de policía y buen gobierno de la isla de Puerto Rico.* San Juan: Imprenta del Gobierno.

———. 1852. *Programa de los festejos que han de verificarse en la Capital de esta Isla, con motivo del nacimiento de la Princesa de Asturias.* Puerto-Rico: Imprenta Márquez.

———. 1858. *Descripción de las Fiestas Reales que celebró la muy Noble y Leal ciudad de San Juan de Puerto-Rico con motivo del fausto natalicio del Serenísimo Príncipe de Asturias Don Alfonso.* Puerto-Rico: Imprenta Acosta.

———. 1862. *Bando de policía y buen gobierno de la isla de Puerto Rico.* Reimpresión. San Juan: Imprenta del Gobierno.

———. 1864. *Crónica de San Juan o sea Descripción de las Fiestas con que la ciudad de Puerto-Rico ha celebrado á su Santo Patrón en el año de 1864.* Puerto-Rico: Imprenta del Comercio.

———. 1868. *Bando de policía y buen gobierno de la isla de Puerto Rico.* San Juan: Imprenta del Gobierno.

González, José Luis. 1987. *El país de cuatro pisos y otros ensayos.* 6ª edición. Río Piedras: Ediciones Huracán.

Kwabena Nketia, Joseph Hanson. 1974. *The Music of Africa.* New York: W. W. Norton & Company.

Ledru, André-Pierre. 1810. *Voyage aux Iles de Ténériffe, la Trinité, Saint-Thomas, Saint-Croix et Porto-Rico.* París: Chez Arthus Bertrand.

———. 1863. *Viage a la isla de Puerto Rico en el año 1797.* Translated by Julio L. de Vizcarrondo. Puerto Rico: Imprenta Militar de J. González.

Ledru, Pierre André. 2013 [1810, 1863]. *Viaje a la isla de Puerto Rico.* Nueva traducción basada en la de Julio de Vizcarrondo de 1863. Estudio introductorio de Libia M. González López. Editado por Manuel A. Domenech Ball. Traducido por Manuel A. Domenech Ball, Henry Gadiel Rivera Flores y Luis Armando Rodríguez García. San Juan: Oficina del Historiador Oficial de Puerto Rico.

Lowenthal, David. 1998. *El pasado es un país extraño.* Traducido por Pedro Pedras Monroy. Madrid: Edición Akal.

López Cruz, Francisco. 1967. *La música folklórica de Puerto Rico.* Prólogo de Walter F. Starkei, dibujo por Antonio Martorell, diseño y adornos por Elaine Sherer y Antonio Salcedo Carpas, copista musical. Sharon: Troutman Press.

Mâche, François-Berbabd. 1999. The Necessity of and Problem with a Universal Musicology. En *The origin of Music*, editado por Nils L. Wallin, Björn Merker y Steven Brown. Cambridge: The MIT Press.

Malavet Vega, Pedro. 1992. *Historia de la canción popular en Puerto Rico (1493-1898)*. Ponce, PR: Editora Corripio.

Maldonado, Melanie A. 2008. Bomba Trigueña: Diluted Culture and (Loss of) Female Agency in AfroPuerto Rican Music and Dance Performance. En *Caribbean Without Borders: Literature, Language and Culture*, editado por Doris Smith, Raquel Puig y Ileana Cortés Santiago. 95–117. Newcastle upon Tyne: Cambridge Scholars Publishing.

Manuel, Peter, Kenneth Bilby y Michael Largey. 2012. *Caribbean Currents: Caribbean Music from Rumba to Reggae*. Filadelfia: Temple University Press.

Moore, Robin. 2010. *Music in the Hispanic Caribbean: Experiencing Music, Expressing Culture*. New York: Oxford University Press.

Morales Carrión, Arturo. 1974 [1952]. *Puerto Rico and the Non Hispanic Caribbean: A Study in the Decline of Spanish Exclusivism*. Río Piedras: University of Puerto Rico Press.

_______. 2004 [1978]. *Auge y decadencia de la trata negrera en Puerto Rico, 1820-1860*. Edited by Ricardo E. Alegría. San Juan: Centro de Estudios Avanzados de Puerto Rico y el Caribe.

Morales Martínez, Linda Valli. 2013. Bomba: vivencia e identidad cultural en la diáspora. Tesis de maestría, Centro de Estudios Avanzados de Puerto Rico y el Caribe.

Moreno Fraginals, Manuel. 1978. *El ingenio: complejo económico social cubano del azúcar.* Vol. 1. La Habana: Editorial de Ciencias Sociales.

Muñoz, María Luisa. 1966. *La música en Puerto Rico: panorama histórico*. No. 3 de la serie *Puerto Rico: Realidad y anhelo*. Dibujos de J. A. Torres Martinó. Sharon: Troutman Press.

Navarro Alvarado, Guillermo Antonio. 2014. Alienación y diáspora. La colonización ontológica del negro y su búsqueda. *II Congreso de Estudios Poscoloniales, III Jornada de Feminismo Poscolonial*.

Newitt, Malyn, ed. 2010. *The Portuguese in West Africa, 1415-1670: A Documentary History*. New York: Cambridge University Press.

Ortiz, Fernando. 1981 [1951]. *Los bailes y el teatro de los negros en el folklore de Cuba*. La Habana: Editorial Letras Cubanas.

PARES. 1848-1855. *Medidas del gobernador Prim contra negros libres y esclavos*. Archivo Histórico Nacional, ULTRAMAR, 5069, Exp. 3, 4, 5 y 6. Madrid: Portal de Archivos Españoles. URL: http://pares.mcu.es.

Power-Sotomayor, Jade Y. 2015. From Soberao to Stage: Afro-Puerto Rican Bomba and the Speaking Body. En *The Oxford Handbook of Dance and Theater*, editado por Nadine George-Graves. 706–28. New York: Oxford University Press.

Prim, Juan. 1848. El Bando contra la Raza Africana. *Gaceta del Gobierno de Puerto Rico* 67.

Quintero Rivera, Ángel G. 1998. *¡Salsa, sabor y control!: sociología de la música "tropical"*. México, D.F.: Siglo Veintiuno Editores.

_______. 2009. *Cuerpo y cultura: las músicas "mulatas" y la subversión del baile*. Madrid: Iberoamericana.

Rigau Pérez, José, ed. 2003. *Edward Bliss Emerson: The Caribbean Journal and Letters, 1831- 1834*. Transcripción expandida y anotada de manuscritos Am 1280.235 (349) y Am 1280.235

(333) (páginas selectas) en la biblioteca Houghton, Harvard University, y cartas a la familia. Houghton Library y Emerson Family Papers en Massachusetts Historical Society.

Rivero Méndez, Ángel. 2008 [1924-1927]. *Remigio, historia de un hombre: las memorias de Ángel Rivero Méndez*. Editado por María de los Ángeles Castro Arroyo. San Juan: Centro de de Investigaciones Históricas de la Universiad de Puerto Rico/Academia Puertorriqueña de la Historia/Editorial de la Universidad de Puerto Rico.

Rodríguez Cancel, Jaime L. 2007. *La Guerra Fría y el sexenio de la puertorriqueñidad: afirmación nacional y políticas culturales*. San Juan: Ediciones Puerto.

Rodríguez, Christian. s.f. La Bomba: la diversidad sobre el origen. *Cruce: crítica socio-cultural contemporánea*. Humanidades y Comunicaciones, Escuela de Ciencias Sociales. Último acceso: 26 de febrero de 2017. <http://revistacruce.com/artes/item/1628-la-bomba-la-diversidad-sobre-el-origen/>.

Rosa Nieves, Cesáreo. 1967. *La voz folklórica de Puerto Rico*. No. 6 de la serie *Puerto Rico: realidad y anhelo*. Prólogo de Walter F. Starkie. Sharon: Troutman Press.

Rose, Tricia. 1994. *Black Noise: Rap Music and Black Culture in Contemporary America*. Hanover: Wesleyan University Press.

Seabury, Joseph B. 1903. *Porto Rico: The Land of the Port Rich*. Book XII The World and Its People. New York: Silver, Burdett and Company.

Tanodi, Aurelio, ed. 2009. *Documentos de la Real Hacienda de Puerto Rico, Volumen II, 1510-1545*. Edición corregida y aumentada por José Cruz de Arrigoitía, Josué Caamaño-Dones, Amarilis Cintrón López y Frank Cosme Arroyo. San Juan: Centro de Investigaciones Históricas.

_______, ed. 2010. *Documentos de la Real Hacienda de Puerto Rico, Volumen I, 1510-1519*. 2ª edición. San Juan: Centro de Investigaciones Históricas y la Academia Puertoriqueña de la Historia.

Tomlinson, Gary. 2007. *The Singing of the New World: Indigenous Voice in the Era of European Contact*. New York: Cambridge University Press.

_______. 2015. *A Million Years of Music: The Emergence of Human Modernity*. Brooklyn: Zone Books.

Vega Drouet, Héctor. 1979. Historical and Ethnological Survey on Probable African Origins of the Puerto Rican Bomba, Including a Description of Santiago Apostol Festivities at Loiza Aldea. Tesis doctoral, Wesleyian University.

Virno, Paolo. 2003 [1999]. *El recuerdo del presente: ensayo sobre el tiempo histórico*. Traducido por Eduardo Sadier, Yolanda Daffunchio y Luis Argüello. Buenos Aires: Paidós.

VVAA. 1843. *Aguinaldo Puerto-riqueño: colección de producciones orijinal en prosa y verso*. San Juan: Imprenta de Ginbernat y Dalmau.

Waterman, Richard Alan. 1999. African Influence on the Music of the Americas. En *Write Me a Few of Our Lines: A Blues Reader*, editado por Steven C. Tracy. 17–27. Amherst: University of Massachusetts Press.

Wetzel, Richard D. 2012. *The Globalization of Music History*. Londrés: Routledge.

Wolf, Eric R. 1982. *Europe and the People without History*. Berkeley: University of California Press.

Zavala, Iris M. 1991. *La posmodernidad y Mijail Bajtin*. Madrid: Colección Austral, Editorial Espasa Calpe.

Zelinsky, Wilbur. 1949. The Historical Geography of the Negro Population of Latin America. *Journal of Negro History* 34(2), 153–221.

VOLUME XXXI • NUMBER II • SUMMER 2019

Suelta el Moño: The Herstories of Change Agents and Perpetuators of Bomba Culture

MELANIE MALDONADO

ABSTRACT

This monograph gives voice to generations of women who live on through the many performers and culture bearers who represent bomba today. Excerpts of more than twenty-five interviews and personal communications with artists, practitioners, eyewitnesses and descendants of bomberxs will help detail different roles women have taken in both bomba practice and performance over the last 100 years. This text draws on ethnographic and genealogical research to provide insights into place making, inclusion rituals, the use of the *enagua* in traditional 20th century bomba dance, the roles of families in perpetuating this practice, knowledge transmission and challenges to male-dominated representations. It also draws attention to the diaspora and some of the ways women outside the Island are working to stay connected to bomba history and performance. [Key words: Bomba, women, petticoats, Villodas, Bomberas, Ponchinela, Mason]

The author (propa2003@gmail.com) is a bombera and artivist. She is the founder and director of PROPA: the Puerto Rican Organization for the Performing Arts and its biennial Bomba Research Conference. Melanie is committed to creating access and building community. Her work in bomba analyzes contributions of women, importance of textiles, genealogy, lineages of learning, songs, historic spaces, and other topics. She completed doctoral coursework in Performance Studies at Northwestern University and is an alumnus of the Smithsonian's Latino Museum Studies Program.

The community knowledge that has survived in regard to the AfroPuerto Rican traditional music and dance of bomba holds that, historically, it was a male-dominated genre—from those who played the primary instrument by the same name to those who created music through stylized gestures and other movements. While both men and women have enjoyed a fairly equal representation in songs that have survived to the present, the role of women is remembered as mostly ornamental throughout the early- to mid-1900s. This paper attempts to unpack the lesser-known contributions of women and help create space for them in the archives by reviewing how they created and nurtured spaces that continue to be identified with bomba practice. Thus, this essay is meant to consider how petticoat (*enagua*) fashion became an unregulated realm where women could experiment and dictate their own participation, as well as examine the legacies of women whose names continue to circulate because of their contribution and others who are unknown outside of their families or communities. More recent herstories help illuminate lesser-known contributions to the perpetuation of traditional practice and shifts in contemporary performance. This paper will reveal the names of *bomberas* that have otherwise been lost to the recorded history and will illuminate the specific contributions of women who have been identified in archival sources with passing mention or should be recorded for posterity's sake.

As a result of the folklorization of bomba during the mid-twentieth century and the representation of this new performance style by specific families, there is a mythology surrounding families as the gatekeepers of knowledge, history, and tradition. However, history indicates the genre was preserved by the community at large—from the individuals whose home spaces and properties hosted *bailes de bomba* to the *barrios* where the everyday life reflected in bomba songs manifested. As a result, many families often had multiple members engaged in bomba practice, but there was also widespread participation by individuals for whom there is little or no existing evidence of a family tradition.

The repositories of bomba history tell us that men organized the community bailes in the mid-1900s. Presbiterio Cepeda Ayala (1895–1988) in Las Carreras, Mediania Alta, Loiza (Dufrasne 1985); Ricardo "Chato" Candelario López (1913–2009) in Puerto de Jobos, Guayama (PROPA 2008); and Domingo "Dominguito" Sanchez Cora (1898–1974) in Las Palmas, Arroyo (Rosario Rivera 2013), among many others. Missing from those archives are the names of women who helped facilitate such activities. As early as the mid- to late-1800s, we find whispers of women's contributions to Bomba. Nineteenth-century newspapers reporting on crimes committed at social events identify both men and women as facilitators of community gatherings through bomba dances. In an 1870 issue of the state-sponsored paper *Gaceta de Puerto Rico*, we find a quick mention of a baile de bomba in a San Juan home: "en la causa que se instruye contra Manuel Andino, por hurto, se cita y llama a Juan de los Angeles y a un tal Tomas que la vispera de Reyes estuvieron tocando en un baile de bomba en la Marina en casa de Concepción Dueño" (Guerra 1870). While the name Concepción may denote the host was a woman, a more direct identification of a woman is found on the west coast of the Island, where we learn of someone referred to as "doña" in 1885 who may have been elderly or recognized as such because of her economic means or other elevated stature in her community: "llamo y emplazo a los individuos que en la noche del día veinte y tres de febrero último concurrieron en un baile de bomba en la casa de Doña Nicomedes González, vecina de Añasco" (De Jesús Font and Vázquez 1885).

Women were also the nameless teachers of tradition and practice through song composition and transmission. Celia Ayala Carrasquillo (the eldest sibling of the Hermanos Ayala of Loiza and living in Greater Boston for more than a half century) relied on elders in her community to teach her traditional bomba. Those who did so included her maternal grandmother Quintina Ortiz Calcaño (c. 1884–1976), who served as one of her primary sources for learning songs such as "Aurelia, Aurelia, dile al conde que suba" (Ayala Carrasquillo 2006). Nelie Lebrón Robles refers to bomberas who created songs as protagonists. They took a center position in the execution of bomba through lyrical composition and subject matter that served as social commentary on the happenings of their communities. Isabel Albizu Dávila (1937–2012) remembered learning the art of singing bomba from her mother Teresa Dávila (1901–1987) and provided a clue as to the importance of content by indicating that it was nuanced (Albizu Dávila 2005).

Cuando yo me criaba, mi mamá se pasaba en la orilla del río. Yo me iba con mi mamá a la orilla del río a lavar...y me iba y ella se empezaba cantando coplas y cantando cosas de la bomba. Mamá cantaba, "Dile ese hombre que no me mande ese papel, dile ese hombre que no me mande ese papel."[1]

All of these bomberas have connection to at least one other woman remembered for bomba practice in her respective community. One family represented bomba in their town, throughout the Island, in the diaspora, and in the pages of history—the Villodas of Guayama. This southern town is one of the widely regarded epicenters of historical bomba practice. In early 2008, I met and interviewed Evangelia Díaz Villodas about the legacy of her family in both the town of Guayama and the practice of bomba. The bomberas known as the Villodas trace their lineage back to an enslaved woman they identify as Mamá Candó. Their family's oral history recalls that her daughter Nicolasa Villodas Anes (1862 – 1906) was given land by the Villodas family of enslavers in the area known as Puerto de Jobos on the coast of Guayama. Throughout the mid- to late-1900s, this barrio was repeatedly documented as the center of bomba practice in Guayama. More than 100 years later, generations of Nicolasa's family continue to live on this land.

Nicolasa's oldest daughter, Salomé Villodas Vázquez (1874–1970), was a bomba singer and dancer who appears in the one Bomba scene of Amilcar Tirado's 1957 film *La Plena* (1957). Salomé is shown dancing along with a group of other practitioners that included Flora Texidor (another dancer from Guayama), among others. Doña Salomé is spoken of fondly in the interviews I have conducted with three of her granddaughters: Evangelia Díaz Villodas, Luz María Rosado Villodas, and Marta Almodóvar Clavell. They tell stories of her rule in the small neighborhood established on the land her mother inherited and of her disdain for Spaniards, but it is her elaborate preparation for bomba dances that is memorable.

Salomé is one of the most remarkable examples of how important enaguas were to a woman's feeling of empowerment at a Bomba dance.

Bomberas of the early 1900s engaged younger generations in becoming behind-the-scenes agents who helped facilitate the liminal spaces where women could not only fully participate but also dominate execution. The grand preparation and adornment of enaguas helped create a display space just underneath the skirt that a woman controlled by when and for how long she displayed it. Her enagua wowed and tantalized, taunted and inspired. Salomé is one of the most remarkable examples of how important enaguas were to a woman's feeling of empowerment at a Bomba dance. Marta Almodóvar Clavell is Salomé's more-than-eighty-year-old granddaughter through her youngest daughter Julia Ernesta Clavell Villodas (1914–2001). Doña Marta was raised in her grandmother's home and remembers helping Salomé prepare for Bomba dances by ironing her petticoats (Almodovar Clavel 2013).

Figure 1: Salomé's Irons. Personal photograph of author.

MMD: *Y hablando de la bailadora, ¿usted se recuerda algo de la enagua...?*
MAC: *Yo aprendí a coser para hacerle la enagua a mi abuela.*
MMD: *¿A tu abuela Salomé?*
MAC: *A Salomé.*
MMD: *¿Sí? ¿Para lo' baile' de bomba?*
MAC: *Porque ella cuando salía, ella iba con una maleta. Ella iba con tre' o cuato enagua.*
MMD: *¿Sí? ¿A un baile de bomba?*
MAC: *A un baile de bomba. Porque...el lujo del baile era la enagua. Aquí, el traje era bien sencillo, no e'cotado. E'te, y a vece' ha'ta con su manguita' larga'. Pero, entonce', la, la falda tenía vuelo porque ahí era, de'bajo estaba la enagua.*
MMD: *¿Y llevaba su maleta?*
MAC: *Ella llevaba su maleta con tre' y cuatro enagua' para un baile. Ah, y en, en el próximo, ella no iba con la' mi'ma. Ella siempre iba con su' enagua' nueva'.*
JEN: *Y entonce', ¿cómo la' adornaba?*
MAC: *Ah, con encaje, cinta, eh, con...*
JEN: *¿Se ponían cinta alrededor, o, o...?*
MAC: *Se le hacía, casi siempre se hacía la enagua...con una tabletita aquí y una fajita, y una fajita. Entonce' se le ponían uno' volante'. Cue'tion que, cuando ella' se levantaban el traje, ella' lo que exhibian era esa enagua, la enagua. Eso era el lujo del baile, la enagua.*

Julia Ernesta Clavell Villodas is remembered by her family as a bomba dancer and singer. She was interviewed by the daily newspaper *El Nuevo Día* in 1996 and also appeared in the 1995 film *La Tercera Raíz* (González and Malavé 1995), under her middle and maternal last name, Ernesta Villodas, There she speaks about her mother Salome and grandmother Nicolasa (Clavel Villodas 1992).

Salomé's oldest daughter, Amalia Villodas Madera (1895–1991), was a distinguished bomba dancer who appears in video footage sometimes colloquially referred to within the bomba community as *The Oppenheimer Video* (*Bomba del Sur de Puerto Rico* n.d.). She was prolific enough in her time to be named in María Luisa Muñoz's (1966, 83–4) cultural survey as one of the best bomba dancers in southern Puerto Rico. Here, she is documented by photographer Hiram Maristany in 1971 or 1972 while dancing at a baile de bomba in Bélgica, Ponce.

Two of Amalia's daughters were also bomba practitioners. Candelaria "Pusa" Díaz Villodas (1920–2009) was a singer and composer, and Luz María Rosado Villodas (2008) (1932–2013) was a dancer. Per doña Luz, she was the last in their Villodas line to represent the traditional methods of bomba practice. Her older sister Eva echoed these sentiments: "La tradición está acabando en la familia. No hay una próxima generación después de Candelaria y Luz María" (Díaz Villoda 2008).

In 2008, PROPA (Puerto Rican Organization for the Performing Arts) organized an event in Lakeland, Florida that celebrated the contributions of the Villodas family to the practice of bomba. Luz María was the honored guest and shared numerous stories about her mother Amalia and grandmother Salomé. She also demonstrated

Figure 2: Amalia Villodas. Photograph by Hiram Maristany. Reprinted by permission.

how bomberas traditionally held their skirt and how they created a *figura* (or elegant pose) while dancing. During the event, doña Luz used one of her mother's scarves to demonstrate how the women in her family tied their *pañuelos* (scarves) around their head (tied in the back or behind the ear) and donated the scarf to this work to document her family. When she passed in 2013, her daughter Cuca donated all of Luz María's enaguas to this project and the excavation of their family history.

Salomé's legacy continues to be celebrated through her great-grandson José "Ñeco" Flores Díaz (2011), who composed and still sings the song "Salomé" in her honor. Her legacy has also been celebrated in print and in the Diaspora. In 2014, the Austin, Texas, performance ensemble Puerto Rican Folkloric Dance (PRFDance) organized their annual event "Celebrando." The director Ana María Tekina-eirú Maynard expressed interest in this effort to document the contributions of the Villodas family and agreed to a cross-collaboration that involved using commissioned work by poet and Guayamesa Nora Cruz Roque. Nora's poem "Salomé Villodas" inspired PRFDance's *Baila Salomé* number calling upon the chorus of Ñeco's song, which is incorporated into that poem.

PROPA's relationships with the Villodas descendants in Barrio Puerto de Jobos, with other cultural workers in greater Guayama, and bomba performers in the Diaspora have ensured that this family's legacy of female participation within the practice of bomba is re-membered and shared with current artists, practitioners, and enthusiasts of this tradition. Other female dancers and singers are lesser known within the bomba community or have otherwise been forgotten.

Bomba lore holds a whisper that there may have been a group of women called Las Ponchinelas.

The first time this author met Luz María Rosado Villodas, she, like every other older bomba practitioner I have interviewed—was quick to list off the people from whom she learned and those she admired. One of these was Julia Saunion Scrimony (1887–1957), a singer from Puerto de Jobos, Guayama, and mother to one of the dancers remembered with great fondness in that community, Pascual "Mano Gasón" Saunion Pica (1905–1984) (Flores López 2008). Other women whose stories are more obscure or yet unknown include Luisa Villodas Pillot (another of Nicolasa Villodas Anes' daughters), Enriqueta Rivera (singer from Guayama), María Magí (of Guayama), Cicí (of Arroyo), Tamba (of Guayama), Narcisa "doña Cisa" Godineau and Damiana Alonso (the latter two, dancers mentioned in Muñoz), and countless others (Muñoz 1966, 83–4). Names excavated by Fernández Morales (1999) include La Santomeña (6), Teresa Maíz Mangual (54), Emilia Canales Rivera (*bailadora*) (79), Paula Rivera Nieves (*cantadora*) (167), Paula Resí (cantadora y bailadora) (167), La Ñeña (171), Nunú (171), Julia "La Guayamera" Curet (cantadora y bailadora) (171), La Brasileña (172), La Conguita (179), María Bultrón (bailadora) (182), and La Machén (bailadora y cantadora) (182). Women who have a near mythological presence in bomba and also require greater study include Petronila Gilbee and La Ponchinela. *Ponceña* Petronila Gilbee[2] was a dancer who frequented the batey of Domingo "Dominguito" Negrón Matías (1877–1955) in Cataño (Fernández Morales 1999, 180), and is memorialized in a bomba song composed as a yubá that calls on her name: "Petronila Guilbe, yo no declaré." La Ponchinela is perhaps the most elusive woman of Bomba history. Researchers and other writers have attempted to include her in the archives with great inconsistency. She is documented as Carmen La Pulchinela (Dufrasne 1985), as Gloria Ramos (Fernández Morales 1999), and as Carmen María Ortíz Sadmons (Alegría y bomba e' 2015). María del Carmen Ortiz Salomón (1898–1981) was a *Santurcina* from birth to death. Her great nephew and godson Carlos Haddock Rivera (2018) informs that within her family, she was referred to as Ponchinela, Ponchi, La Madama, and La Madamita; the social memory of the bomba community has elevated her to a unique stature, adding "La" to her family's principal nickname for her and remembers her as the quintessential female bomba dancer. Bomba lore holds

Figure 3: Gladys la Henana. Reprinted by permission from José M. Cepeda.

a whisper that there may have been a group of women called Las Ponchinelas. While there is no known evidence to support this, this author proposes this was a reference to the Salomón sisters (not all were fathered by Ortiz). Per the oral history of La Ponchinela's family, she and her sisters danced bomba together. Ponchi's great niece Esmeralda Santiago Rivera (Valcárcel 2018) recounts that her grandmother Lucía Ortiz Salomón (1902–1967) shared that she and her sisters (which include La Ponchinela) danced bomba for a U.S. president. Among other associations, Ponchinela is popularly credited as initiating *piquetes* (call through movement for drum slaps) for women—and therefore responsible for the fact that women in modern bomba performance and practice interact directly with the drum and have an ample and ever-growing dance vocabulary with which to do so.

The woman credited with advancing this initial dialogue with the drum is Caridad Brenes Caballero (1914–1994); her evolution of the dance vocabulary for women was carried on through her daughter Petra Cepeda Brenes (1945–2018) and, in more recent decades, through her granddaughter Margarita "Tata" Sánchez Cepeda. This family has a legacy of bomba performance that pre-dates the formation of the Instituto de Cultura Puertorriqueña and state-sponsored cultural representations in Puerto Rico. For the purposes of this monograph, it is also important to highlight this family's creation of a costume for female bomba performers (an early version of which was used as early as 1960) that remains the standard for folklorized representations of this ancestral tradition throughout the Island and its U.S.-based diaspora (Sánchez Cepeda 2018).

While the oral tradition has provided women with a measure of credit for their contributions, the archives have provided less meaningful documentation of women's participation. In the last twenty-five or so years, bomba has experienced a renaissance of practice, performance, and documentation. In that time, there have been a growing number of doctoral dissertations, academic articles, book chapters, and conference papers exploring the history and practice of bomba over its projected history (with some sources situating it as part of criollo cultural practices as early as the 1600s [Vega Drouet 2000, 138–9]). The widespread elision of Black cultural product in Puerto Rico over the centuries has contributed to superficial knowledge of many traditions that have been erased from social memory and the collective national narrative. Particularly absent from these records are the names of individual contributors. One example of erasure comes from field recordings conducted by anthropologist John Alden Mason from 1914–1915. If one engages in a cursory analysis of his methods used to document songs, it is clear that he demonstrated preferential treatment within the folklore Franz Boas urged him to record. This is evident in how the more European-derived styles are identified by genre and singer; however, the same audio research tag is absent from many of the recordings of bomba and *baquiné*—both genres being Black cultural product. In his article touting the importance of these recordings, Hugo Viera Vargas notes, "El doctor Mason, al igual que otros investigadores norteamericanos que llegaron a la isla luego de 1898, construyó una imagen de lo puertorriqueño basada en los lineamientos antropológicos y prejuicios raciales de su época" (2009, 164). Most of Mason's field recordings of bomba begin immediately with the singing of the song but include no identification of the singer. Listening to these recordings, it is apparent that women participated in this massive research project, yet they are mostly erased from the record by lack of identification. We may never know the names of the bombera(s) whose knowledge and execution were captured on these wax cylinders through songs such as "Con lo' rile'" and "La resina."

The contribution of women to Bomba has been nominally portrayed in the growing body of literature as primarily limited to dancing and singing; however, it is important to consider the many other ways in which women shaped and facilitated practice. The overwhelming majority of people I interviewed who were raised in a community in which they were able to witness pre-folkloric bomba throughout their childhood have shared with me that bomba was a tradition of the older folks, and as such, children were not generally allowed to participate. This may be a result of a tradition that was already in decline across the Island by the mid-1900s and that was not being carried forth by the younger generation. Alternatively, this may have been an echo of a more ancient root of the tradition than remains unknown or unarticulated by modern researchers and practitioners. While 95-year-old Ana Luisa Tirado Lopes (2013) remembered sneaking to the main plaza of Arroyo in the late 1920s and early 1930s to observe bailes de bomba with her friends, she is quick to report that these social activities were only for the older folks. Don Miguel Flores López (2008) has also shared that although he witnessed bomba as a child, he did not participate until he was fifteen years old. He recalls very clearly that one of the premier dancers of his community approached him during a baile de bomba and invited him to dance with her. This gesture marked his entrance into the world of bomba as a sanctioned practitioner, and he is quick to relate that story and honor not only the person, but also the moment he was allowed to cross over from the isolated position of observer into the ephemeral space of active community practice. The person who extended an invitation into the intimate society of pre-folkloric bomba was a woman and the very person who would soon become his mother-in-law, famed dancer Amalia Villodas Madera. Unfortunately, when interviewed in 1996 by Fátima Seda (1996, 7), don Miguel's relationship to doña Amalia was ill recorded and later reported as grandson and grandmother. A decade later it is misrepresented again as he is mistakenly identified as don José Miguel Flores Villodas (instead of Miguel Flores López), and having "no relation" to the previously named (Amalia) Villodas; this is the most common last name in the area" (Ferreras 2005, 81). This perpetuation of misinformation contributes to the erasure of bomberas from the historical record and the indelible marks they made upon bomba. While the written word has repeatedly failed bomberas, oral histories preserve remnants of memories related to the importance of textiles for female practitioners.

Many witnesses of traditional bomba from the early to the mid-1900s reference a fashion subculture that served as an important space in which women were active agents of expression. Witnesses, descendants, and culture bearers alike refer to the care and attention made by women to their clothing, particularly their petticoat. Lidia Ortiz (2017) remembers watching bomba dances as a child during the mid-1940s at the annual *fiestas patronales* of Patillas. She has vivid recollections of watching Eustropia Sánchez Sánchez (1903–1971) and her mother Josefina Sánchez Cintrón (1879–c. 1966) lift their skirts to the waist showing beautifully adorned enaguas. Doña Lidia (like several other interviewees) referred to this as *pavonear* or to strut in full display and beauty like the (male) peacock. This *patillense* remembers bows of different colors (particularly blue and green), ruffles, and small decorative flowers on white, cotton fabric. She comments that attendees and participants of the bailes de bomba were more interested in the enaguas than the dresses worn over them. As a fourth-generation seamstress, this 80+ year-old holds special memories about the detail and beauty of the enaguas she saw during her childhood.

Like doña Lidia's own grandmother—dancer Teresa Sánchez Baerda (1887–1977), Nelie Lebrón Robles' *abuela* Olimpia de León Cora (1906–1986) was also a seamstress:

> One of the things that was very important was the petticoat or enagua. That was basically where women would put all of their money, whatever funds they had, because the petticoat was, you know, it was a garment.
>
> When you would go out to dance Bomba and you knew there was a Bomba dance, you would go to a local seamstress that was, she was kind of an expert in making enaguas. And, whatever funds you had, she would be very resourceful in adorning your enagua, in making it pretty so that when you had to lift your dress to dance—and you would lift it so you won't step on it or to make more space—so they would see your shoes or your feet, so that what was covering your legs would be beautiful.
>
> I've spoken to many seamstresses, among them my grandmother, who was a very known seamstress in Guayama, and she was trained. She would make bridal dresses, quinceñera dresses. I mean she was a really good, good, good seamstress, and she would tell me that when women would come to her when there would be a Bomba dance in the future or a few weeks later, they would ask her to be as resourceful as she could with the monies they gave her but also to not make their enagua look like any other. So it is also kind of a personal touch to be able go to your seamstress who knew your style, who knew you from your community and make an enagua that was unique, that was exclusive so that when you would go into the Bomba dance, yours would stick out because it was lovely, it was beautiful. (Lebrón Robles 2005).

Marta Amaro Navarro speaks lovingly about her aunt Isabel Lind Navarro (1901–1955), who helped raise her. According to doña Marta, Isabelita was among the best dressed at bomba dances due to the beautiful enaguas made by her seamstress Dominga Lind (Amaro Navarro 2013). Isabel was the beloved daughter of the famed bomba drummer Juan Pablo "Pablito" Lind Pirela (1874–1960). Isabel, her father, and her maternal aunt Modesta Amaro Navarro (c. 1892– 1972) were documented for posterity by Muñoz (1966, 83–4).

María Luisa Vázquez Texidor attended bailes de bomba in the early 1960s with her grandmother, the legendary singer from Guayama—Ana María Texidor Santiago, known simply as María Texidor (c. 1885–1971). Doña María Luisa easily recalls her grandmother's intricate enaguas that she sewed herself, adding *volantes* (ruffles), *puntilla* (lace edging), and flowers among other decorations. According to her granddaughter, this singer's home was the gathering place for female dancers before a baile de bomba and thereby became a space in which this enagua tradition was shared among generations (Vázquez Texidor 2017). One of the most classic displays of the enagua in a recording of a bomba dance is found in the 1957 documentary *La Plena*'s only bomba scene, which highlights María Texidor's daughter / María Luisa's mother Florentina "Flora" Texidor Texidor (1920–1963) through languid pans of her dancing at the beginning of the *estampa* (a contrived baile de bomba staged for the film). The camera moves slowly downward showing Flora lifting her skirt to reveal her petticoat while dancing to the *yubá* rhythm played for the song "Cachón dice Elena."

Doña María Luisa easily recalls her grandmother's intricate enaguas that she sewed herself, adding volantes *(ruffles),* puntilla *(lace edging), and flowers among other decorations.*

Men also participated in the admiration of enaguas in bailes de bomba. Ricardo Candelario López (1913–2009) recalled the following about what he witnessed when he organized and hosted bailes de bomba from his *cafetín* in Barrio Puerto de Jobos, Guayama during the 1950s:

> Venían mucha', mucha', mucha' mujere'. Por ese tiempo, este, la mujere' se podían mirar, se podían ver, porque venían bien vestida'.
>
> Mucha' de esa' mujere', ella' tenieron, como se llama, e'te, la ropa interior, bien bonita, bien buena...y traje' bueno.
>
> En el tiempo era una, e'te, era una cue'tion bien buena verla porque valía la pena. Ella' mujere' con, con un, como eh, como un, esa negra con un, traje. Y a la' baile de bomba, venían bien vestida', con traje' de, bien serio. No como, como ahora. Ya, no eh lo mi'mo. Candelario López 2008)

These memories become important to reconstructing the ways in which women asserted agency within the male-dominated world of pre-folkloric bomba. From the information that has been collected about contributions to bomba practice by women, the oral histories and documentation are fairly consistent in portraying women as lead singers, members of the chorus, and dancers. However, there is nominal discussion of their roles within the dance and how they shaped an exclusive opportunity for themselves within a practice that imposed restrictions on their participation. During the known history related to the pre-folkloric era of bomba, dancing by women was limited to the adornment of the men. Dancers always entered the *batey* or *soberao* (Barton 2004) as a male and female couple or, less commonly, as a trio – one man with a woman on either side of him.[3] The man led his chosen partner into the soberao and engaged in a *paseo* (a promenade) with her, displaying themselves and defining their dance space. He would then twirl her around before they began dancing. His dance was marked by sudden movements that employed a range of dance vocabulary from shaking of the upper body, twists made with the foot, backward shuffles, and figures made with the arms calling upon the subidor (lead drum) to respond. Dissimilarly, her dance, which also took place in the soberao and within his periphery did not directly engage the subidor. When referring to bomba in Mayagüez, Diane Millán Alduén (2005) shared that "la costumbre era que los hombres bailaban." This reference comes from a lifetime in a community known as "la cuna de la Bomba" and membership in a storied family of practitioners. Her immediate and extended family include the following bomberxs: maternal grandfather Félix Venancio Alduén Caballeri (1926–2003); and his older sisters Soledad Alduén Caballeri (1915–1951) and Rosario Alduén Caballeri (1913–1982);

Figure 4: Bambalue. Personal photograph of author.

and her great, great aunt, the renowned singer María Asunción "Mamá Tontón" Caballeri Caballeri) (1876–1978),[4] and her daughters Cecilia Quiñones Caballeri (1907–1989) and María Luisa "Wichín" Ruiz Caballeri (1918–2000); and granddaughter Rosa María Mangual Quiñones (1914–1983), among others.

Consensus of older interviewees informs us that during the early to mid-twentieth century, a female dancer's movement was never sudden and quite limited to alternating poses or fairly static figuras that never created a piquete. Most often, the woman would lift her skirt to display a petticoat by putting one hand on her waist and holding the edge of her skirt away from her body at varying distances. She would then move near or around the man while he interacted with the main drummer. I observed this live for the first time in 2004 when I saw Isabel Albizu Dávila's group perform at BomPlenazo at Hostos College. Having been exposed to contemporary bomba performance at that point for approximately four years, I remember feeling disappointed by what seemed to be a purposeful limitation on female dancers during the numbers performed by her group Bambalue. In their routines, the man and woman approached the drum together, but only the man interacted with the drum. The woman moved her skirt and twirled at the periphery of the soberao but did not call for a piquete. Little did I know that I was witnessing a vestige of the older, traditional style of bomba Isabel Albizu Dávila was surrounded by as a child.

Cuando fui niña, que mi papá a los dies años me llevaba a bailar bomba. Nos llevaba a bailar bomba a los sitios que el creía que nosotros podíamo' ir a bailar bomba. Porque en todo' lo' sitios no se permitía bailar bomba. En todo' lo' sitio' no podían ir jovenes. Iban lo' adulto'. Porque allí se bebía mucho ron. Allí se bebía pitorro y el pitorro siempre ha sido prohibido. Siempre. Pues mira, aquí en Ponce había uno' sitio', que no voy a decir nombre, que hoy en día son escuela', que eran lo' sitio' de bailar bomba. Pues mi papá, tío Juan, mi mamá que era cantaora de bomba, mi abuela que era bailaora de bomba, mis tías que eran cantaora' y bailaora' de bomba pues decían, "las muchachas pueden ir." Y como digo, lo que teníamos que hacer era caminar a pie' porque no habían carro..." Ello' van cerca. Y aquí van a estar y estan de esta hora." Mi papá bebía muchísimo ron pero cuando andaba con nosotras parecía un pincel. No lo torcía nadie porque eramos las nenas y el nos velaba mucho... Y nos llevaba a bailar. Nos llevaba a bailar de cierta hora a cierta hora. Y a cierta hora "Vamo' pa' casa, a dormir." Y el viraba pa'tra'. (Albizu Dávila 2005)

Doña Isabel inherited this tradition and her talents from many family members, including her father, drummer Domingo Albizu Alvarado (1905–1949); her paternal grandmother Rosa Delpín Alvarado (1885–1959), dancer and first cousin of Juan "Balao" Alvarado (1895–1983), who gave Isabel his drums so that she could found her group Bambalue in the late 1970s (Santiago 2017); and her mother Teresa Dávila (1901–1987).

These family and community memories come together to inform both practice and performance for women like Luz María Rosado Villodas, Isabel Albizu Dávila, Nelie

Lebrón Robles, and Diane Millán Alduén. They use(d) the social memory they inherited combined with their own lived experiences to shape how they interpret(ed) bomba for modern audiences. Although doña Luz lived through the decades when petticoats were still worn as a societally required component of everyday women's fashion, and her own grandmother was known to take multiple, uniquely designed enaguas to bomba dances, she too was influenced by the move of the genre from practice to performance for the sake of consumption and entertainment. This is most clear in her prized enagua, one onto which she sewed Puerto Rican flags, which was the first item she showed me during our initial visit in February 2008. Isabel also hailed from a family deeply embedded in the practice of this traditional music, but her bomba fashion was reflective of a more folkloric, Victorian-era costume and not the clothing she would have seen worn by her mother, aunts, and grandmother. She too was quick to show me a new costume of this kind that she had recently added to her repertoire when I interviewed her in 2005. Nelie chose to allow practice to inform her performance, which is why she shared that she values dressing nicely for bomba dances as a nod to the tradition (Lebrón Robles 2005).

During the mid-twentieth century, the shift from practice motivated by tradition and shared experience to performance for celebration and audience consumption caused the genre to lose many of its nuances. Bomba began to evolve quickly through folkloric representations, which drew on uniformity for costumes and created a presentation style that interrupted organic practices reflecting everyday life (including clothing styles) and time-honored traditions (such as participation primarily limited to adults).

In the early 2000s, Nyree Feliciano's website BombaBoricua.com was a portal for those who had never had contact with pre-folkloric bomba connecting visitors to a bygone time.

Since that time, the community of bomba performers has grown exponentially, and the efforts of women in the diaspora have made significant contributions to that boom. In the early 2000s, Nyree Feliciano's website BombaBoricua.com was a portal for those who had never had contact with pre-folkloric bomba connecting visitors to a bygone time. The landing page featured a picture of bomberxs from Arroyo, Puerto Rico, including dancer and singer Felícita "Fela Atiles" de la Cruz Andino (1918–2001) (Colón Díaz 2008), that had been given to Justo Echevarría Figueroa (2013) by her family for use in his annual almanac of Arroyo. As the most well-remembered bomba dancer from Arroyo, Fela Atiles became a female symbol of traditional bomba for the Diaspora through Nyree's website.

Another significant effort by a woman in the Diaspora to digitally connect people to representations of bomba is found in the work of Ana María Tekina-eirú Maynard through her website prfdance.org, which as early as the late 1990s provided users of the internet images of her troupe performing folkloric representations of Puerto

Rico's traditional music and dance genres. This website was a critical tool for people in the diaspora looking for a way to connect with Puerto Rico's traditional cultural forms—particularly before social media facilitated the ease of information sharing.

These and other efforts from the diaspora have resonated in Puerto Rico. In 2013, a week after her signature event—Encuentro de Tambores (the largest gathering of bomba drums on the Island)—Norma Salazar Rivera (2013) (1943–2014) invited several of her closest collaborators and other guests (including this author) to her home for a debriefing and celebration of that year's event, during which she made a statement that included admiration for the conservation work of bomba conducted in the diaspora. In response to this author's dance of pre-folkloric bomba, she witnessed as part of the Guayama contingent's participation in her event, she exclaimed:

> Ella venía bailando aquello lo que yo vi cuando yo tenía veinte años, por eso lloré. ¡De la diáspora! ¡De la diáspora! ¿y cómo esa nena...? ¿Dónde diantre aprendío esa nena? ¿Dónde lo vio? Sabe, porque era otra cosa lo que ella estaba... Sabe, yo dije ¡Dios! Entonces, lo que yo quiero decir con esto es que no le podemos cerrar la puerta a la diáspora porque ellos traen lo suyo y ellos han conservado...

Bomberas in the Diaspora share that bomba is a critical tool of resistance in their efforts to maintain culture, celebrate traditions, and share history in their spaces of dislocation from the Island. Shefali Shah is the first generation in her Indian family to be born and raised in Puerto Rico; she currently lives in the San Francisco Bay Area.

> I really believe that you can't just learn, a basic step (of bomba) without knowing the meaning of the art or cultural form. Bomba to me is, is more than just, an art form. It's tradition, history, and it involves so much, so much more than just the basic step or just the piquete. It's, it's resistance, really, in my mind.
>
> One of the things that I know, from learning about history and learning about my own history as an Indian woman and as a Puerto Rican woman as well is that, our, our art forms are a way for us to grow and develop in so many ways and strengthen our communities. Through the process of colonialism... folks have tried to take our art forms from us, our culture away from us, and so bomba, as well as, maintaining, maintaining [*sic*] and helping evolve and continue, my Indian culture is definitely a form of resistance. We, we need to, to really resist, and we need to really fight to maintain our culture.
>
> We're here playing Puerto Rican music, dancing bomba, playing bomba, and teaching it to others, but why is it our responsibility? Why do we take on this responsibility? It is because others have fought. The struggle for Puerto Rican independence, the struggle for self-determination is a struggle to maintain culture. It's a struggle of resistance, and it's a struggle to be able to *mantener lo que, lo que es nuestro*, and that's what it's all about.

Bomba, right now, continues to be a form of resistance... This is part of, part of who we are, and we're not going to, we're not going to let go of it. We're going to keep it! (Shah 2006)

Lydia Pérez (2005)—born in Canóvanas but living and performing *cultura* in Rhode Island—shares these sentiments and feels strongly that "donde hay bomba, hay resistencia." These acts of resistance by women are contrary to the strict gender-defined roles that historically limited opportunities for participation. When describing why men dance with a pañuelo, Wilfredo "Ito" Santiago (2017) shared that it was a way of signaling interest in dancing with a woman. If a man shook his pañuelo in the direction of a woman or near her, he was simultaneously indicating intent to dance with her and asking permission of her husband or (male) partner to dance with her. If agreeable, the husband / partner would take the woman over to the other male dancer and put the dangling end of the pañuelo in her hand so that she was now paired with the solicitor.[5] They did not hold hands; instead, they were paired and connected through the pañuelo.[6] Per this witness memory of pre-folkloric bomba, the degree to which a woman may have desired to dance a particular rhythm, her favorite *seis* (compositional song style), or with the man requesting her participation, the implication was the same. She needed at least one but possibly two degrees of approval in order to participate in bomba through dance: 1) the identification of the woman as a desired dance partner followed by an invitation to couple in movement; and 2) the permission of her husband / partner to accept the petition. Her prescribed gender role as ornamental accompaniment was controlled by the degrees of permission socially required to grant her access to that dance space. Once she entered the soberao, she was then restricted to peripheral dancing.

Women found their own subversive ways to claim space within the genre in order to assert agency and create more opportunities for active participation. Nelie Lebrón Robles highlights composition as a realm in which women could move freely within the practice of this tradition. Composing allowed women to create lyrics that were reflective or responsive to daily life occurrences. A version of a traditional song first sung to me by ponceña doña Isabel draws attention to this practice through a chorus alluding to a controversy: "Mi enemiga no tiene pelo, mi enemiga no tiene pelo, mi enemiga no tiene pelo, vete a la plaza y compra un pañuelo." *Loizeña* doña Celia Ayala Carrasquillo recorded a slightly different version with "Pela no tiene pelo, Pela no tiene pelo, Pela no tiene pelo, vete a la plaza y compra un pañuelo." Women lyricists could engage in social commentary or *indirectas* with few repercussions, unlike the regulated way in which they participated through dance.

The 2015 Bomba Research Conference took participants on a historical site visit to the Concordia, Arroyo, home of long forgotten bombera María Inés Ramos Claussell (1887–1964), who in addition to being the mother of one of the bomberos in the photograph featured on the now defunct website BombaBoricua.com—dancer, Erasmo Ramos Claussell (1907–2000)—was also the dance partner of Pablo Lind. During that 2015 visit, participants heard from her family and other community members.

Figure 5: Ramos Clausell House Visit. Personal photograph of author.

Conference attendees learned that while her home was not remembered as a gathering place of bomba, it had a trunk in which her favorite enaguas were stored (Ramos Ramos 2013). Her home had become the last connection the community had to her participation in the tradition of bomba and the subculture of creating and parading enaguas. The disappearance of that trunk and its contents becomes an allegory for how women's contributions to bomba have been lost and disregarded over time. I have heard similar stories from bombero Víctor Vélez (2008) about visiting a descendant of La Ponchinela in Santurce, who reported her ancestor's enaguas had been discarded within a relatively short period before that visit and María Luisa Vázquez Texidor, who lamented that the trunk with her abuela María Texidor's enaguas had also been lost over the years.

These and other stories about the significance of the enagua within the practice of bomba inspired the Competencia de Enaguas, which has been part of several of the Bomba Research Conferences (2011, 2013, and 2015). The intent behind the competition was to stimulate community inquiry into this practice and set people on individual research missions to create their best petticoat entry. Bomberxs of any level of knowledge or experience could equally participate alongside community members with no bomba knowledge, history of practice, or performance experience. Its purpose was to serve as a neutral opportunity for people to engage with bomba in a way that honored

PROPA ha establecido tres categorías para la Competencia de Enaguas:

- **Enagua Tradicional** – Esta enagua fue muy común durante los 1900s específicamente entre la década de los 20 hasta los 60. La misma se asentaba alrededor del área de la rodilla y eran confeccionadas por lo general en colores blanco o crema. Las damas que practicaban el baile de Bomba durante esa época acostumbraban poner adornos tales como encajes, cintas, lazos, botones y lentejas.
- **Enagua Folklorizada (década de los 60 hasta el presente)** – De la enagua tradicional surge otra versión folklorizada específicamente para propósitos artístico-comerciales y diseñada para la tarima. Esta nueva versión por lo general es color blanco y se extiende hasta los tobillos adornada con volantes, encajes y lazos en colores solidos. Esta enagua debe ser confeccionada utilizando una combinación de dos colores diferentes – un color para la enagua y otro color para los lazos y las cintas.
- **Enagua Creativa** – En esta categoría la creación de la enagua para bailar Bomba será expresada de manera libre y abierta a la imaginación y la creatividad de su creador. La misma debe caracterizarse por su concepto artístico derivado de ideas originales. Cada participante deberá presentar una pieza completamente funcional y única.

Para oportunidades de auspicio o más información:
787.902.3520 • PROPA2003@gmail.com

Auspiciado por:

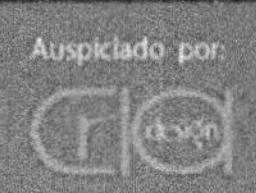

Figure 6: Image Competencia de Enaguas. Personal photograph of author.

Figure 7: Doña Marta and Brenda. Personal photograph of author.

the practice but also created room for contemporary interpretations. The 2013 winner, Chicago-based Puerto Rican visual artist Brenda Torres Figueroa, called upon remembrances of the enaguas her grandmother used daily as part of her design and fused them with her mother's artisanal practices of making *muñecas de trapo*. Her enagua reflected history and tradition, family, and artisanry. Her participation and that of all the other entrants of the competition honored the memories of the bomberas discussed here and those whose names and stories are yet unknown.

The contributions of women to bomba practice and performance have been historically relegated to singing and dancing. However, this text provides evidence that there were other, more meaningful ways in which women of the early- to mid-1900s *soltaron sus moños* to serve as active agents of knowledge transmission and practice, even carving out their own subculture in which they could exert creativity and dominance. The shift from practice motivated by tradition and shared experience to performance for celebration and audience consumption caused the genre to lose many of its nuances. Bomba began to evolve quickly through folkloric representations that drew on uniformity for costumes and created a presentational style that interrupted organic practices reflecting everyday life (including clothing styles) and time-honored traditions (such as participation primarily limited to adults). This essay creates opportunities for future research and study of these and other contributions to bomba by women in order to help excavate, reconstruct, and preserve the knowledge regarding their historical participation in this traditional music and dance. Areas for continued inquiry include the subject matter and historicity of songs composed by women; the transition of bomba dance for women from peripheral, ornamental participation within the practice to the broad piquete vocabulary of contemporary performance bomba; all-women performance ensembles (including Yaya, Bomberas de la Bahía, Nandí, Las BomPleneras and Ausuba); female drummers, particularly those who play the *subidor* or lead drum (such as Denise Solis and Amarilys Ríos, among others); and trends of the last two decades in bomba fashion, which include the use of shawls and scarves and diverse skirt designs. The contributions of women to bomba as both practice and performance are significant and deserve a more equitable representation in the archives and the collective narrative of remembrance.

ACKNOWLEDGMENTS

This research was funded in part by a 2005-2006 Diaspora Grant from the Center for Puerto Rican Studies at Hunter College, CUNY.

NOTES

[1] A song credited to Mamá Tonton by her granddaughter Isabel García Quiñones and student Ramón "Papo" Alers.

[2] A five-year-old Petronila is found in the 1872 Registro Central de Esclavos as enslaved to the señores Marich y Gilbee in Capitanejo, Ponce.

[3] This latter representation of bomba dancing will not be discussed in this text and deserves greater study.

[4] Per her own report on April 6, 1898, when registering her daughter María Gabriela Quiñones Caballeri's birth, she was born three years after institutional slavery legally ended in Puerto Rico in 1873. This is in direct conflict with popular narratives that claim she had been enslaved. The documented and published oral histories inform us of bomba practitioners who were born during the mid- to late 1800s, with very few named participants being born before the abolition of slavery.

[5] This may be what Rafael Cepeda described as the dance used for gracimá: "Eso es un baile con pañuelos, es muy elegante y se coge la pareja y se baila y se da vuelta y se ponen a bailar... se guarda el pañuelo y se saca el pañuelo, es una cosa muy linda."

[6] A similar experience is captured by Fernández Morales: "Chipichá — Bailador de bomba... Sacaba a bailar a La Ponchinela. Él no la tocaba con las manos. Tenía un pañuelo blanco entre sus dedo y la tocaba con el pañuelo" (1999, 181).

References

Albizu Dávila, Isabel. 2004. Interviewed by author. Ponce, Puerto Rico. 1 March.

Alegría y bomba e' en la placita de Santurce. 2015. *Primera Hora* 26 June. Accessed 26 June 2015. <http://www.primerahora.com/entretenimiento/musica/nota/alegriaybombaeenlaplacitadesanturce-1091402/>.

Almodóvar Clavell, Marta. 2013. Interviewed by author and Jorge Emmanuelli Náter. Guayama, PR. 6 February.

Amaro Navarro, Marta. 2013. Personal communication. 30 June.

Ayala Carrasquillo, Celia. 2006. Interviewed by author. Roxbury, Massachusetts. 31 March.

Barton, Halbert. 2004. A Challenge for Puerto Rican Music: How to Build a Soberao for Bomba. *CENTRO: Journal of the Center for Puerto Rican Studies* 16(1), 68–89.

Bomba del Sur de Puerto Rico. n.d. YouTube. <https://youtu.be/XXk0XxPpyg8/>.

Candelario López, Ricardo. 2008. Interviewed by Jorge Emmanuelli Náter and author. Guayama, PR. 7 February.

Cepeda, Rafael. 1983. Interview by Gustavo Batista. Santurce, Puerto Rico. Accessed 12 March 2014. <http://www.mymdpr.com/rafael-cepeda/>.

Clavell Villodas, Julia Ernesta. 1992. *Ernesta Villodas*. YouTube. <https://youtu.be/Q6k-4mNllmgk/>.

Colón Díaz, Daniel. 2008. Personal communication. 24 July.

De Jesús Font, José and José S. Vázquez. 1885. Lcdo José de Jesús Font, Juez de 1ª Instancia de la Ciudad de Mayagüez y su partido. *Gaceta de Puerto Rico* (San Juan) 2 June. Accessed 28 February 2017. <http://chroniclingamerica.loc.gov/lccn/2013201074/issues/>.

Díaz Villodas, Eva. 2008. Interviewed by author. Guayama, PR. 7 February.

Dufrasne Gonzalez, J. Emanuel. 1985. La homogeneidad de la música caribeña: sobre la música comercial y popular de Puerto Rico. Ph.D. dissertation, University of California, Los Angeles.

Echevarría Figueroa, Justo. 2013. Personal communication. 4 June.

Fernández Morales, José E. 1999. Análisis Sobre Cantos de Bomba Recojidos en Cataño (1918 – 1965): Datos y Comentarios Sobre la Ejecución del Género. Master's thesis, Centro de Estudios Avanzados de Puerto Rico y el Caribe.

Ferreras, Salvador E. 2005. Solo Drumming in the Puerto Rican Bomba: an Analaysis of Musical Processes and Improvisational Strategies. Ph.D. dissertation, University of British Colombia.

Flores Díaz, Miguel "Ñeco". 2011. Personal communication. 2 September.

Flores López, Miguel. 2008. Personal communication. 11 April.

Galarza Ramos, Alberto and Edwin Albino Plugues. 2004. *La bomba y la plena mayagüezana.* Mayagüez, PR: n.p.

Guerra, Mauricio. 1870. Escribanía Pública. *Gaceta de Puerto Rico* (San Juan) 3 March. Accessed 27 March 2015. <http://chroniclingamerica.loc.gov/lccn/2013201074/issues/>.

González, Lydia Milagros and Carlos H. Malavé. 1995. *La tercera raíz: presencia africana en Puerto Rico.* YouTube video. Directed by Carlos H. Malavé. Río Piedras: Centro de Estudios de la Realidad Puertorriqueña.

Haddock Rivera, Carlos. 2018. Personal communication. 18 March.

La Plena. 1957. Directed by Amílcar Tirado. YouTube. San Juan: Departamento de Instrucción Pública, División de Educación de la Comunidad.

Lebrón Robles, Nelie. 2005. Interviewed by author. Río Piedras, PR. 20 February.

Maldonado, Melanie. 2008. Bomba Trigueña: Diluted Culture and (loss of) Female Agency in AfroPuerto Rican Music and Dance Performance. In *Caribbean Without Borders: Literature, Language and Culture,* eds. Ileana Cortés Santiago, Raquel Puig, and Dorsia Smith. 95–117. Newcastle: Cambridge Scholars Publishing.

Millán Alduén, Diane. 2005. Interviewed by author. Mayagüez, PR. 26 February.

Montano, Fernando J. 2016. Setenta y siete años bailando la bomba puertorriqueña. *El Laurel Sureño* 20 May – 2 June. Accessed 25 March 2017. <https://www.facebook.com/fernandojmontano/posts/10154271812081942:0/>.

Muñoz, María Luisa. 1966. *La música en Puerto Rico: panorama histórico-cultural.* Sharon, CT: Troutman Press.

Ortiz, Lidia. 2017. Personal communication. 8 March.

Pérez, Lydia. Interviewed by author. Warwick, Rhode Island. 15 December.

PROPA. 2008. Don Chato. *YouTube Video.* Posted August 2011. <https://youtu.be/PXE2hyiJTS4/>.

Ramos Ramos, Jorge. 2013. Interviewed by Jorge Emmanuelli Náter and author. Arroyo, PR. 6 February.

Rosado Villoda, Luz María. 2008. Personal communication. February.

Rosario Rivera, Aníbal. 2013. Personal communication. 7 February.

Salazar, Norma. 2013. De la diáspora. Debrief and celebration of 2013 Encuentro de Tambores, Norma Salazar's home, 7 September.

Sánchez Cepeda, Margarita "Tata". 2018. Personal communication. 5 September.

Santiago, Wilfredo. 2017. Personal communication. 14 March.

Seda, Fátima. 1996. La última bomba. *El Nuevo Día* 4 February.

Shah, Shefali. 2006. Interviewed by author. Oakland, California. 11 June.

Tirado Lopes, Ana Luisa. 2013. Personal communication. 25 August.

Valcárcel, Hope. 2018. Personal communication. 20 March.

Vázquez Texidor, María Luisa. 2017. Personal communication. 14 March.

Vega Drouet, Héctor. 2000. Puerto Rico. In *The Garland Handbook of Latin American Music*, eds. Dale A. Olsen and Daniel E. Sheehy. New York: Garland Publishing, Inc.

Vélez. Víctor. 2008. Personal communication. 24 February.

Viera Vargas, Hugo. 2009. La colección John Alden Mason: una documentación sonora para la historia de Puerto Rico. *Caribbean Studies* 36(2), 161–8.

VOLUME XXXI • NUMBER II • SUMMER 2019

Queering bomba: rupturas con lo heteronormativo en la bomba puertorriqueña

MÓNICA CELESTE LLADÓ ORTEGA

ABSTRACT

This article explores several instances that challenge the heteronormative aspects of bomba in Puerto Rico, in which traditional gender-based roles are subverted and questioned. Breaks and continuities with the traditional Puerto Rican bomba are analyzed with emphasis on the participation of women and members of the LGBT community. It is proposed that bomba, as a music and dance of liberation, becomes a fertile vehicle for problematizing traditional gender roles in both the traditional structure of the genre and in society as well. From the body in movement, the male/female binary is questioned revealing its performative character, while proposing new approaches that open spaces of inclusion and close gaps of marginalization, to create a queer bomba open to the participation of all. [Keywords: bomba; Puerto Rican, queer, heteronormative, gender, liberation]

The author (monica.llado@upr.edu) is a professor in the Department of Spanish at the University of Puerto Rico, Carolina. She holds a B.A. in Hispanic Studies from the University of Puerto Rico, Rio Piedras, and an M.A. and Ph.D. in Hispanic Literature from the University of Michigan, Ann Arbor. She has presented her research in conferences and in several publications. *Detox: Venenos y remedios* (Trabalis, 2018) is her first book of poetry.

Figure 1: Grupo Ausuba en el Festival de Claridad, 2017.

I. "Honrando a nuestros mayores reafirmo mi identidad, piqueteando en el batey mi bomba no morirá".[1]

Tal como afirman estos versos, la bomba continúa siendo una expresión afropuertorriqueña vinculada a la identidad y a la tradición en Puerto Rico. En el presente ensayo me propongo ponderar instancias de rupturas con lo heteronormativo en la bomba del siglo XXI en Puerto Rico. El interés surgió cuando vi el documental *El hijo de Ruby*, de Gisela Rosario Ramos (2014). Me interesó cómo en su narrativa inserta rupturas con aspectos heteronormativos de la bomba y propone implícitamente que es un catalítico para la liberación personal. El protagonista, Lío Villahermosa, transgrede roles tradicionales a base de género al bailar con falda. Para propósito del presente artículo defino lo heteronormativo como la práctica de diversas instituciones —educativas, políticas y sociales— de privilegiar lo heterosexual para organizar los roles sociales a base del binario de género: hombre/mujer. Esto impone una lógica de binario heterosexual como la norma y exige a los individuos comportamientos sociales y sexuales conforme a esta. Por tanto, romper con lo heteronormativo en la bomba implica no dejarse imponer un rol de participación a base de género. Además de Villahermosa, estaré explorando otras instancias de ruptura con roles heteronormativos protagonizadas por mujeres que tocan barril o bailan en pantalones con movimientos tradicionalmente asignados a los hombres.

Propongo que la bomba puertorriqueña, como género musical de liberación desde sus inicios, produce un espacio fértil para estas rupturas con lo heteronormativo, tanto en la estructura tradicional de la bomba como en la sociedad per se. Exploraré cómo, desde varias instancias de ruptura con los roles tradicionales de género, en la bomba se proponen nuevos acercamientos que abren espacios de inclusión y cierran brechas de marginación en la bomba en Puerto Rico. Estas rupturas producen un efecto de *queering*, donde la bomba transita nuevas coordenadas identitarias pluralizadas que paradójicamente reproducen elementos de la tradición mientras simultáneamente los reconfiguran. Conforme a David Halperin, lo queer "does not name some natural kind or refer to some determinate object; it acquires its meaning from its oppositional relation to the norm. Queer is by definition whatever is at odds with the normal, the legitimate, the dominant" (1995, 62). Desde esta definición propongo que las rupturas que exploraré producen una bomba *queer* que se opone a lo heteronormativo de roles prescritos a base de género mientras inscribe nuevas formas de rearticular la participación al flexibilizar las normas de "lo auténtico" sin perder la tradición. En mi uso del término queer, no lo limito a instancias de rupturas que involucren sexualidades LGBTQ solamente, sino que lo aplico incluso para rupturas a base de género, independientemente de si quien las ejecuta se identifica como gay, lesbiana o trans. Mi interés es en resaltar esa cualidad paradójica que tiene lo queer de retar mientras inscribe, de revelar los límites de lo heteronormativo mientras los subvierte.

A modo de contexto, se podría afirmar que la bomba es de las más antiguas expresiones musicales de Puerto Rico. Sabido es que la bomba, en su origen, fue instrumento de liberación, para denunciar y resistir el régimen esclavista en Puerto Rico desde el siglo XVI (Ramos Rosado 2011, 37). Hoy día, en Puerto Rico la bomba se celebra como parte de nuestro riquísimo repertorio de expresiones musicales autóctonas. Ahora bien, como tema de estudio, no ha recibido tanta atención como otros géneros musicales caribeños debido a su origen afropuertorriqueño y la marginación provocada por el racismo (Abadía-Rexach 2014, 127; Barton 1995, 11; Cartagena 2004, 20).

Desde las primeras expresiones literarias puertorriqueñas del siglo XIX, se inserta la música como tema vinculado a lo literario y a la identidad nacional que se comenzaba a fraguar, la cual privilegiaba esas expresiones criollas más cercanas a la cultura española. Desde sus títulos, las primeras expresiones literarias puertorriqueñas —*El aguinaldo puertorriqueño* (1843) y *El cancionero de Borinquén* (1846)— se identificaron con la música como una expresión cultural vinculada a la literatura y a la formación de una identidad criolla que se erguía en contraposición a la peninsular o española.[2] Manuel Alonso, en *El jíbaro* (1849), menciona los bailes de bomba en "Escena V. Bailes de Puerto Rico"; no obstante, alega que "no merecen incluirse bajo el título de esta escena; pues aunque se ven en Puerto Rico, nunca se han generalizado" (1983, 81). Este comentario refleja el racismo que relegó la bomba a la esfera del folclore por muchos años.[3]

Así como en el siglo XIX los criollos bajo el régimen colonial español construían una identidad cultural propia, más centrada en las producciones culturales que privilegiaban lo europeo, en el siglo XX la bomba, como música y baile, fue fraguando una identidad afropuertorriqueña como resistencia a la marginación y al discrimen sufrido por el racismo.

Durante la década de 1930, en el ámbito de la literatura, fueron Luis Palés Matos y Fortunato Vizcarrondo quienes contribuyeron a la revalorización de nuestra herencia africana desde los ritmos, sabores y colores que insertan en sus obras poéticas *Tuntún de pasa y grifería* (1937) y *Dinga y mandinga* (1942), respectivamente.[4] Luego, Francisco Arriví, con su obra de teatro *Vejigantes* (1958), elevó la bomba, implícitamente, a música nacional, en su propuesta de afirmar nuestra herencia africana.[5] En las siguientes décadas, la música siguió presente en nuestras letras, pero privilegiando otros géneros musicales. Por su parte, la crónica de Edgardo Rodríguez Juliá *El entierro de Cortijo* (1983) afirma la importancia y el impacto social de nuestra música afropuertorriqueña (Cartagena 2004, 19).

Fue a partir de 1955, con la fundación del Instituto de Cultura Puertorriqueña (ICP), que el Estado comienza a organizar su apoyo a las artes autóctonas puertorriqueñas. No obstante, el apoyo a las producciones cultures afropuertorriqueñas siempre fue menor al que recibían las vinculadas a la herencia española e incluso a la herencia taína, por racismo de considerar la aportación africana menor a las otras (Barton 1995, 29; Dávila 1997, 68; Duany 2005, 182). A través de ese apoyo formal se fue armando el concepto de autenticidad folclorista prescrito y determinado por el ICP. Es el mito de mestizaje de las tres raíces (española, taína y africana) el que facilita marginar y subyugar las expresiones culturales puertorriqueñas a un conjunto de parámetros para, por un lado, comprobar su autenticidad y por el otro, mantener bajo control todo género que se perciba como oposicional con el pretexto de evitar que se "contamine" con influencias musicales extranjeras (Dávila 1997, 68–9). Al insertarlo, al ámbito estático del folclore se corre el peligro de limitar su desarrollo y coartar su renovación (Alamo-Pastrana 2009, 579–80).

Los medios de comunicación masiva como la radio, televisión y redes sociales han sido instrumentales en la difusión de la bomba en y fuera de Puerto Rico.

Según Arlene Dávila, no fue hasta las décadas de 1970 y 1980 que realmente se aumentó el apoyo del ICP a la bomba, en gran medida gracias a la radio, que había popularizado la música de Rafael Cortijo, entre otros (1997, 68). Los medios de comunicación masiva como la radio, televisión y redes sociales han sido instrumentales en la difusión de la bomba en y fuera de Puerto Rico. Por ejemplo, el documental *La herencia del tambor: homenaje a Rafael Cortijo* (1983) dio valor al rol de la bomba no solo como producción cultural afropuertorriqueña, sino como expresión identitaria afroboricua vinculada a la liberación de negros esclavizados, a la vez que destaca su importancia como expresión de la herencia africana en el contexto de las fiestas de Santiago Apóstol en Loíza. (Dávila 1997; Dufrasne 1985).[6]

Fue mediante el apoyo del ICP que se formalizaron escuelas de bomba, entre ellas la de la familia Cepeda de Santurce, que producirían espectáculos para los hoteles y otros lugares urbanos donde se expondrá lo que Hal Barton ha llamado "stage bomba", o bomba de tarima, que es más coreografiada que improvisada, con vestimenta tradicional, en la que el público no participa, sino que es espectador pasivo

(1995, 126). Esto, por un lado, privilegia a algunas familias sobre otras agrupaciones de bomba y produce un distanciamiento de la bomba del público que reduce el acceso a las generaciones más jóvenes, quienes, en respuesta a ello, desarrollan grupos juveniles que bajan la bomba "del escenario a la calle" (Alamo-Pastrana 2009, 580; Barton 1995).

Desde la década de 1990 al presente, ha aumentado la presencia de la bomba tanto en la isla como en la diáspora, con una marcada participación de los jóvenes (Barton 1995; Flores 2000). Este resurgimiento de la bomba se caracteriza por una mayor participación del público, en particular de jóvenes, y una simultánea "renovación" y "reafirmación" del género como un legado musical afropuertorriqueño (Alamo-Pastrana 2009; Cartagena 2004, 27–9; Rivera 2005).[7] Como afirma Pablo Rivera: "Podemos decir que en la transformación de sus contextos, la bomba ha logrado diseminarse y está más generalizada en Puerto Rico que nunca antes en su historia. Gran parte de los puertorriqueños y puertorriqueñas reconocen su valor artístico-cultural, y cada día más jóvenes están aprendiendo a bailarla y a tocarla" (2015, 67–8).

En 2001, el especial del Banco Popular se tituló *Raíces* y fue una validación de la bomba y de la plena como manifestaciones de la "tercera raíz" y sus aportaciones significativas a la cultura puertorriqueña (Arroyo 2010; Cartagena 2004). Además, el filme reconocía la influencia de la bomba en otros géneros musicales como el reggae y el hip hop, y los artistas invitados en su mayoría eran jóvenes. Por otra parte, la reacción al filme fue mixta: algunos criticaron la inclusión del hip hop y el reggae con discursos de autenticidad, señalando posturas prejuiciadas que no reconocían el valor social de dichos géneros musicales y los asociaban a lo extranjero (Arroyo 2010, 197). Jossianna Arroyo afirma que estas reacciones mixtas, tanto de personas en Puerto Rico como en la diáspora, responden a la racialización de estos géneros musicales y la vinculación de la bomba en particular a los discursos de identidad nacional, en los que muchos puertorriqueños prefieren adherirse al discurso de mestizaje para invisibilizar la negritud y otros, asumen la negritud como coordenada identitaria que les abre espacio de agenciamiento social (2010, 197–8). En la diáspora, esta conflación de múltiples coordenadas étnicas y raciales fomenta alianzas con grupos de otros orígenes nacionales a la vez que reitera visiones positivas de negritud que trascienden los discursos nacionalistas limitantes y excluyentes (Arroyo 2010; Cartagena 2004; Flores 2000). De hecho, es la presencia de los ritmos de bomba en otros géneros musicales contemporáneos como el jazz, el hip hop y el reggaetón lo que la validan como influencia importante afropuertorriqueña que trasciende barreras culturales y nacionales (Arroyo 2010; Cartagena 2004; Flores 2000).

En las últimas décadas, las manifestaciones contemporáneas de la bomba, gestadas muchas veces por los jóvenes, la renuevan y reafirman como legado y expresión cultural afropuertorriqueña (Alamo-Pastrana 2009; Cartagena 2004; Flores 2000; Rivera 2015). La bomba como fusión de música y baile siempre ha sido fértil para resistir y denunciar injusticias y navegar contradicciones. En su origen, denuncia el deplorable e inhumano régimen esclavista; luego, la desigualdad social y el discrimen racial; y ahora, como veremos en este artículo, desde nuevas voces y nuevos cuerpos, se gestan rupturas con el machismo y la reproducción de discursos de género heteronormativos en su expresión tradicional.[8]

Me refiero, en particular, a las transformaciones y los tránsitos que inscriben tanto mujeres como hombres al transgredir roles basados en el binario de género hombre/mujer, femenino/masculino, dentro de la estructura tradicional de la música y el baile de la bomba. Me concentraré en varias instancias de estas rupturas en Puerto Rico para proponer que por su historia de liberación la bomba provee el terreno perfecto para estas renovaciones. Estas instancias de ruptura reafirman la bomba como baile afrocaribeño subversivo que fomenta transformaciones internas y externas, tanto en su estructura como en su expresión. Por tanto, es desde la bomba misma como música y baile de liberación que emerge esa innovación y ruptura con lo heteronormativo, ese *queering*, que la abre a nuevas expresiones liberadoras.

II. "Fuimos luchadoras por la libertad, somos luchadoras por la igualdad".[9]

Estos versos de la canción "Nací mujer", de Chabali González, afirman la bomba no solo como herramienta de lucha por la libertad en el pasado, sino que aseveran que la lucha ahora es por la igualdad en el presente. En particular la letra alude a la lucha por los derechos de las mujeres. Como veremos en esta sección, la bomba, como música y baile de liberación, ha sido instrumento para retar el racismo y los roles de género heteronormativos y estereotipados del hombre macho y la mujer sumisa o hipersexualizada (Alamo-Pastrana 2009, 576). Según afirma Álamo-Pastrana, la bomba para los hombres representa un espacio de expresión de emociones (negada a ellos por el machismo), y para las mujeres, participar del baile brinda acceso al poder de dictarle al primo los piquetes, produciendo así "alternative masculine discourses of affectivity and dialogue while female practitioners impart notions of agency that both challenge and rearticulate gendered forms of popular knowledge on the island" (2009, 577). Como afirma Álamo-Pastrana: "There is no doubt that performance, either corporeal and/or musical, constitutes a key site for reexamining the ways gendered performances are articulated in Puerto Rico" (2009, 594). Por tanto, se podría afirmar que el baile de bomba reta ciertas nociones de lo femenino y masculino mientras simultáneamente reproduce otras.

Esta división de participación a base de género reproduce discursos heteronormativos en los cuales al hombre se le negaba ciertas participaciones o pasos considerados femeninos, mientras a la mujer se le negaba acceso a la percusión, designada exclusivamente a los hombres.

En su manifestación tradicional, la bomba asigna roles particulares de participación a base de género, con leves variaciones dependiendo de la región: Santurce (Cangrejera), Cataño, Loíza, Sur (Ponce, Patillas, Arroyo, Guayama) y Mayagüez. Por ejemplo, los barriles los tocaban solamente los hombres en cualquier región,[10] aunque los bailadores podían ser hombres o mujeres y los cantadores también, variando por región: "la melodía puede ser interpretada por hombres y mujeres en el área norte, pero en el sur, sólo cantan las mujeres" (Ramos Rosado 2011, 38). Esta división de participación a base de género reproduce discursos heteronormativos en los cuales al hombre se le negaba ciertas participaciones o pasos considerados femeninos, mientras a la mujer se le negaba acceso a la percusión, designada exclusivamente a los hombres. Según afirma Bárbara Idalissee Abadía-Rexach: "El racismo, la homofobia, la explotación económica, el colonialismo, no actúan de manera independiente sino en infinitos arreglos de opresión que dan lugar, a su vez, a formas múltiples de discriminación y, como es el caso de la bomba puertorriqueña, dan lugar a representaciones plurales, complejas, en las que se refuerzan estereotipos y autodegradaciones; se opacan ciertas dominaciones o se subsumen a otros relatos de identidad" (2014, 131). Según Abadía-Rexach "en el performance de la bomba se hacen eco las prácticas de inequidad de género que predominan en Puerto Rico", porque además de dividir a base de género los elementos de la interpretación de la música y el baile, algunas letras de bomba incluso reforzaban el machismo (2014, 134). Esto señala a una de las paradojas de la bomba, que se ha ido transformando desde los participantes mismos, principalmente los jóvenes (Alamo-Pastrana 2009, 582). Fue en la década de 1990 que la participación de mujeres y hombres jóvenes se convirtió en un elemento transformativo, que hace que, por un lado, se celebre y aprecie la bomba como un legado histórico vital afropuertorriqueño y, por el otro, se expandan y evolucionen los aspectos tradicionales para ser más inclusivos. Conforme Pablo Rivera, fueron los grupos y las escuelas de bomba surgidos a finales de la década de 1990 los que rompían con varios aspectos de la tradición, incluyendo la vestimenta. Por ejemplo, Bombazo de Puerto Rico buscaba:

> **...llevar los bailes de bomba a escenarios que por lo regular no eran tradicionales [...]. El proceso de cambio fue bastante impactante por llevar la bomba directamente de la tarima al batey o suelo. [...] Cabe aclarar que los bailes de bomba ya se realizaban, pero la estructura atrevida (vista por algunos como 'irreverente') atrajo a muchas personas porque le quitaba las 'barreras'. (Rivera 2015, 76)**

Estas barreras que se iban quitando tenían que ver con el acceso del público espectador a la bomba, el cual se fue convirtiendo en público partícipe, y cada vez más jóvenes se le sumaban. A estos jóvenes se les llamaría "la generación bombazo". Fueron estas nuevas generaciones de bomberos y bomberas quienes abrieron espacio no solo para cambios estructurales al retar lo heteronormativo de la bomba, sino para enriquecerla con nuevas letras de temáticas "atemperadas a nuestra realidad histórica" y social (Rivera 2015, 88; Sefranek Potter y Cruz Mejías 2016).

Pablo Rivera, por su parte, reconoce que las mujeres han asumido un rol mucho más activo gracias al surgimiento de nuevas escuelas de bomba en la isla como en la diáspora; afirma que su participación "ya no se limita a que solamente canten o bailen en las actividades, se han integrado más equitativamente en la ejecución y desempeño y le han inyectado elementos edificantes" (2016, 88-9). Una de las pioneras en gestar mayor participación de las mujeres en la bomba fue Marién Torres López, como veremos en la próxima sección.

III. "Dueña de tu cuerpo
nunca permitas que nadie exija,
controlar tu ser,
controlar tu vida.
Eres de ti misma".[11]

Estos versos de la canción "Mujer boricua", de Marién Torres López, resumen su postura de gestar equidad de género a través de la bomba puertorriqueña. Marién Torres López se unió al grupo Bombazo de Puerto Rico a los 18 años. Luego, se unió a Plenibom, grupo de Norma Salazar, una de las primeras mujeres en dirigir un grupo de bomba en Puerto Rico. Desde entonces, incursionó en una travesía de aprendizaje

Figure 2: Grupo Ausuba.

autodidacta nutrida por la tradición oral que sostiene el género de la bomba en la isla: "Me fui a Loíza y me metía en los bateyes en 'La 23'".[12] Dentro del estilo de Loíza, sus maestros fueron miembros del grupo Los Hermanos Ayala y otros ejecutantes loiceños que no necesariamente participaban de algún grupo profesional. Allí, por ser un estilo tan distinto al cangrejero, ella tuvo que aprender desde cero la bomba, pero su perseverancia la convirtió en "la hija adoptiva de Loíza". Al mismo tiempo, viajaba a Mayagüez a toques de bomba y actividades familiares y de barrio. Así llegó al hogar de la familia Alduén, pilares de la bomba mayagüezana. De forma similar, conoció la bomba sureña, nutriéndose de nuevos ritmos y dinámicas dentro del batey. Sostuvo largas conversaciones con Doña Isabela Albizu, directora del grupo Bambalué, de Ponce, las cuales enriquecieron su desarrollo y conocimiento de la bomba. También aprendió sobre la bomba de Cataño, la cual se desarrolló en su origen más entre hombres porque estaba relacionada al trabajo en los puertos, y de la cual sobresalía la familia Negrón. Marién explica que:

> **Me hubiese gustado tener mayor inquietud y madurez para poder hacer preguntas más dirigidas al saber de la bomba, pero era una adolescente y mis prioridades eran otras. En la medida que enseño los diversos estilos de bomba en el Taller Tambuyé, me doy cuenta de toda la información que aprendí, que no la leí, sino que la aprendí en mi compartir con los maestros y ahora, comparto lo aprendido con todos, porque es un legado del pueblo.**

Así conoció todas las regiones históricas de la bomba en Puerto Rico, aprendiendo las variaciones en el baile, canto y ritmo de cada una. Esta experiencia enriquecedora de aprender observando y en la praxis misma fue la que la llevo a decidirse por ser educadora de bomba. Ella añade que "la bomba no es solo una destreza motora, es involucrarse en un lenguaje musical, cultural y social. Es más que bailar, hay que estar entre la gente que practica ese lenguaje, así es que lo aprendes". Por eso, fundó Taller Tambuyé en 2003, como un espacio para compartir ese conocimiento.

"Me senté en un barril, empecé a tocar pero sin saber cómo traducir el sonido a mis manos, y entonces, un bombero compañero queridísimo, mi amigo, me bajó con un discurso paternalista sobre cómo me veo más bonita bailando y que se me van a dañar las manos".

La ruptura con lo heteronormativo de Marién Torres López ocurrió antes de fundar Taller Tambuyé, cuando intentó romper la barrera de género del tambor. Cuenta que su primera experiencia tocando el barril fue en 1999, en un bombazo que convocó en protesta de la presencia de la marina estadounidense en Vieques: "Me senté en un barril, empecé a tocar pero sin saber cómo traducir el sonido a mis manos, y entonces, un bombero compañero queridísimo, mi amigo, me bajó con un discurso paternalista sobre cómo me veo más bonita bailando y que se me van a dañar las manos". Pasarían varios años antes de que Marién volviera a tocar el barril.

Fue cuando fundó Taller Tambuyé que comprendió que tenía que saber tocar barril: "Si quería llevar un proyecto en la comunidad, un proyecto cultural y social, no podía depender de nadie más. Tenía que estar completa. Si iba a dar un taller, tenía que poder, de ser necesario, ir yo sola y darlo". Recuerda que siempre había querido tocar desde que comenzó a bailar por primera vez la bomba. Desarrolló un oído fiel a como tenía que sonar un tambor. Tanto así que fue ella quien le enseñó a tocar primo a sus primeros tocadores de Taller Tambuyé, dictándoles con la voz como debía sonar: "Sin darme cuenta tenía esa comprensión del lenguaje del tambor más allá de la interacción del baile, sabía cómo tenía que sonar. Les enseñé de forma oral como tocar y seguir al bailador".

Su deseo de abrir la bomba a mayor participación de mujeres la llevó a fundar, junto a Oxil Febres, otra reconocida bailadora de bomba, el grupo Nandí. Marién cuenta que su deseo era crear un taller de mujeres para luego fundar un grupo. Pero resultó que en vez de taller se creó un grupo desde sus inicios. En los primeros años de Nandí, Marién fue cantadora y bailadora. Comenta que la resistencia de que las mujeres tocaran los barriles era muchísima, y el grupo no fue aceptado de entrada por toda la comunidad de bomberos en Puerto Rico y algunos en la diáspora:

Al comienzo cuando salíamos como grupo profesional hubo una explosión de críticas en las redes sociales de bomberos en la isla y en la diáspora. A pesar de que en la diáspora ya habían grupos de mujeres tocando barril, como Las Yayas en Nueva York y Las Bomberas de la Bahía en San Francisco, había mucha resistencia. Recuerdo que llegaron una serie de comentarios hasta citando cosas históricas para justificar por qué una mujer no se podía sentar al barril, diciendo que era una falta de respeto al género de la bomba. Que ese no era su rol. Eran unas cosas bien cuadrás. Nada que ver con la bomba, que no es cuadrá, el género de la bomba no puede ser cuadra'o, porque es un género de liberación desde sus inicios. Yo pienso que eso, en vez de disuadirnos, nos dio más fuerza.

Se podría afirmar que Nandí fue una agrupación queer en el sentido de que retó la estructura del binario según reproducida en la bomba tradicional, en la cual se le reservaba a los hombres la percusión por considerarla masculina e "inapropiada" para las mujeres. La resistencia inicial a este queering de la bomba gestado por Nandí les "dio más fuerza" y provocó que Marién decidiera participar también como tocadora. Luego, una estrategia que ideó Oxil Febres fue traer a un tocador experimentado una vez al mes a ofrecerles un taller a las barrileras de Nandí. Esto les ayudó a aprender y, a su vez, poco a poco, a ganar la aceptación de los demás:

Porque cuando hacíamos presentaciones en público, esos que nos habían ofrecido los talleres ahora nos apoyaban. Así los hacíamos parte de nuestro crecimiento, ellos se sentían partícipes del grupo en el sentido de que ellos fueron parte del proceso educativo y eso causó que la resistencia a que las mujeres tocaran y tuvieran sus

propios grupos mermara y fuimos ganando apoyo. Los que antes decían que las mujeres no podían tocar ahora nos apoyaban. Fue a través de establecer una relación recíproca que se transformó la etapa de la resistencia varonil.

Nandí como agrupación duró como 5 o 6 años, hasta 2010. Fue entonces que Marién decidió fundar el taller de mujeres Ausuba: "Yo quise crear en vez de un grupo, un taller de mujeres sin importar lo mucho o poco que supieran de bomba, para que se compartiera lo que sabíamos entre nosotras, y entonces, ahí convoqué abiertamente a las mujeres a entrar al taller para aprender". Eran más de 30 mujeres de todas las edades; la mayor tenía 93 años. Era un colectivo de diferentes procedencias, niveles educativos, y clases sociales: "El propósito era compartir todo lo que sabíamos, hasta que todas llegáramos a un mismo nivel. Hicimos lo mismo que en Nandí. Llamamos a los compañeros bomberos a dar talleres de cuas, de buleador y de primo. De ahí nace el grupo de mujeres Ausuba".

En los pasados 15 años, la bomba fue creciendo en su desarrollo, y ahora hay más acceso a los barriles: "Muchas mujeres se compraron sus barriles. Entonces, en un bombazo abierto llega la mujer con su propio barril y no la pueden sacar". Gracias a la lucha que dieron estas mujeres al exigir equidad de género en la bomba, la cantidad de grupos de mujeres en la isla y la diáspora incrementó:

Figure 3: Marién tocando con el Taller.

> **Ahora es normal e incluso puedes ver más mujeres que hombres. Nuestra generación fue la que luchó contra muchas cosas y en apenas 15 años ha tenido fruto, mucho más rápido de lo que yo pensaba. Por ejemplo, esas mismas personas que resistían tanto a que las mujeres participáramos, luego cambiaron y fueron los maestros de las mujeres en Puerto Rico y en la diáspora. Eso es lo hermoso, de cómo la bomba como género musical se transforma a sí mismo, y así contribuye a la transformación a nivel social. Pues, seguimos tocando el fundamento, no tiene nada que ver el género de la persona.**

Por otra parte, Ausuba incluso creó un repertorio de canciones que representan a la mujer y hablan sobre sus diferentes inquietudes: "cuando es una presentación de Ausuba, nos quedamos en el repertorio de la voz de la mujer, porque eso es lo que traemos a la bomba, lo que queremos decir a través de nuestra bomba".

Marién Torres López también compuso y grabó un disco de canciones de bomba con el mismo título de su taller: *Tambuyé* (2013). La producción incorpora temas de la actualidad, algunos centrados en la mujer, como, por ejemplo, "Mujer boricua", "Juanita" y "Ruperta". Además, es la primera producción de bomba en Puerto Rico y la diáspora dirigida por una mujer.

Según se afirmó en el programa del evento, "estas mujeres abrieron el camino para que otras continuáramos su legado, su filosofía de vida y, sobre todo, su liberación de roles de género y ruptura de estereotipos impuestos por una sociedad patriarcal".

Desde entonces se ha dedicado a dirigir y producir todo tipo de espectáculos e intercambios culturales internacionales con Taller Tambuyé y Ausuba. Alineado a la postura de Marién de continuar la lucha por la equidad y su compromiso con abrir espacio para las mujeres en Puerto Rico a través de la bomba, el espectáculo anual de Tambuyé de 2017, *Perspectivas*, fue un homenaje a mujeres puertorriqueñas que destacan por sus aportaciones culturales y políticas al pueblo de Puerto Rico. Las seis mujeres homenajeadas fueron Lola Rodríguez de Tió, Anjelamaría Dávila, Julia de Burgos, Pura Belpré, Luisa Capetillo y Lolita Lebrón. Según se afirmó en el programa del evento, "estas mujeres abrieron el camino para que otras continuáramos su legado, su filosofía de vida y, sobre todo, su liberación de roles de género y ruptura de estereotipos impuestos por una sociedad patriarcal". En 2018, Taller Tambuyé celebró el espectáculo *Trayectoria*, el cual conmemoró los 15 años de su fundación y su gesta de lucha por la equidad y la reafirmación de la bomba como música y baile de liberación. Sin duda, Marién Torres López ha contribuido grandemente a aumentar la participación de mujeres en la bomba al retar lo heteronormativo. Por ello, otras mujeres bomberas en Puerto Rico continúan transformando la bomba, como veremos en la próxima sección, que explora rupturas gestadas desde Mayagüez.

IV. "En los barriles, empoderadas. Cargo la rabia, la rebeldía, cargo la fuerza de mis ancestras, pa' reafirmarme día tras día".[13]

Estos versos de la canción "Las mujeres andamos armás", de Coraly Cruz Mejías, afirman la bomba como espacio de empoderamiento. Así como Marién Torres López gesta rupturas con lo heteronormativo en San Juan, en Mayagüez también se van dando varios retos a lo heteronormativo en la bomba de esa región, como explican las bomberas Mary Sefranek Potter y Zoralyz I. Cruz Mejías en su ponencia titulada "Hacia una bomba queer: desafiando los binarios de género en la bomba mayagüezana" (2016).[14] Explican que, aunque en la enseñanza de baile y percusión en la bomba de Mayagüez generalmente se reproducen los binarios de género, han surgido instancias de rupturas.

Por ejemplo, María Cristina Alfonso Mangual es considerada por muchos una de las pioneras en romper con lo heternormativo en la bomba de Mayagüez, ya que ella baila sin falda. Ella es miembro de una de las familias de bomberos más reconocidas en Mayagüez y, tal vez por ello, por el respeto a esa familia, se le abrió ese espacio de ruptura con lo tradicional.

Por otra parte, hace unos años hubo un grupo de mujeres, Los Lirios Rojos, integrado por estudiantes y maestras de la Escuela de Bomba Municipal de Mayagüez. Pero no pudo mantenerse: "no se le dio continuidad" por "limitaciones de tiempo" de las participantes, quienes asumían "dobles y triples jornadas" al ser "profesionales, madres, activistas, compañeras" (Sefranek y Cruz 2016).

En el documental *Con sabor a Mayagüez* (2011), de Ruperto Chaparro Serrano, se toca el tema de género en la bomba mayagüezana en la entrevista a Liz Saira Nadal, quien comenta: "Sí, he sentido un poco de discrimen en cuestión de tocar, verdad, porque siempre quise aprender a tocar. [...] Mi tío, Juan Nadal, me decía que no, que las mujeres estaban nada más que para bailar".[15] Una vez falleció su tío, ella comenzó a dedicarse a tocar el barril. Sefranek y Cruz afirman que en Mayagüez "Las mujeres mayormente han tenido que autogestionarse para ser incluidas, han tenido que rehusarse a bailar para poder participar como percusionistas" (2016).

En 2015, ocurrió otra instancia de ruptura, un queering de la bomba, cuando en el concierto de la Escuela de Bomba Municipal de Mayagüez, dos mujeres abiertamente lesbianas bailaron en pareja como parte del espectáculo. Esto fue significativo no solo por tratarse de dos mujeres, lo cual rompe con la estructura tradicional heteronormativa de que la pareja de baile sea una mujer y un hombre, sino además por su vestimenta, ya que una llevaba pantalones y marcaba piquetes tradicionalmente asignados a hombres.

Por lo general, en el baile las mujeres que bailan sin falda y asumen movimientos considerados tradicionalmente masculinos reciben menos rechazo que hombres

Figure 4: Baile en pareja, Escuela de Bomba Municipal de Mayagüez.

que hacen lo opuesto. La imposición de lo heteronormativo también impacta a los hombres, como señalan Sefranek y Cruz: "un compañero joven, nos menciona el caso de ser corregido en el batey de bomba por hacer movimientos femeninos" (2016). Por su parte, Marién Torres López comenta al respecto:

> Hay otras compañeras, mujeres que bailan como hombre. Pero, no es tan impactante, no las rechazan tanto como un hombre bailando con falda. Que un hombre baile como mujer o una mujer baile como hombre es algo que no debemos juzgar de manera conservadora. [...] A pesar de que al yo sentarme en el barril hubo toda una tesis de improperios de parte de muchos bomberos para justificar el por qué una mujer no podía sentarse en un barril de bomba, eso realmente respondía a prejuicios sociales basados en el machismo y realmente no tenía nada que ver con el género de la bomba en sí.

Como afirma Torres López, ciertas posturas que limitan la participación de las personas a base de género responden más al machismo que a la bomba en sí. Por tanto, el rechazo más marcado contra hombres que asumen movimientos femeninos o incluso que usan falda —como es el caso de Lío Villahermosa— responde a la construcción de género en Puerto Rico en la cual la masculinidad heteronormativa se prescribe desde el machismo que refuerza el binario y el patriarcado al reducir al hombre a su falo y su capacidad de penetrar como acceso al ámbito del poder y la dominación social (Ramírez 1999, Barradas 2006).[16] Desde la perspectiva del travestismo de un hombre que baila bomba en falda, la ruptura con lo heteronormativo es más drástica que la de mujeres al tambor o incluso en pantalones, porque en estas instancias no necesariamente están poniendo en duda las categorías mismas de género, sino que están subvirtiendo los roles tradicionales asignados a estas. No obstante, el travestismo o *drag* provoca cuestionar las categorías mismas de género al revelar su carácter performativo y abrirlas a una "tercera" posibilidad de articulación que reta de raíz lo binario (Butler 1990; Garber 1992).

Según Hal Barton estas rupturas con las categorías de género en la bomba se aceptan solamente cuando se dan en Loíza en el contexto carnavalesco de las fiestas patronales de Santiago Apóstol y a través del personaje de "la loca" (1995, 120).[17] La percepción de Barton sobre el rol de "la loca" dentro del contexto de las fiestas de Loíza y su reto a la masculinidad heteronormativa apunta a una paradójica representación que desestabiliza las categorías de género binarias e incluso abre espacios temporales de representación a personas de identidades queer (1995, 121). Aunque el personaje de "la loca" es aceptado en el contexto de las fiestas de Loíza, un hombre que baila bomba en falda es una ruptura con los roles de género dentro de la tradición heteronormativa de la bomba que no es aceptada fácilmente en la cultura patriarcal de Puerto Rico. No obstante, en la siguiente sección veremos una instancia de ruptura de esta índole, protagonizada por Lío Villahermosa, que logró aceptación.

V. "Un gay, un gay, lo llevaron ante la ley, por ponerse una falda pa' bailar bomba en el batey".[18]

Estos versos de la canción "El gay", de Jerry Ferrao, inscriben una postura homofóbica en la que se denuncia al hombre por bailar en falda en el batey —"lo llevaron ante la ley"— a la vez que se tilda de gay por dicho acto.[19] Por su parte, Lío Villahermosa recalca que bailar en falda no te hace gay.[20] Tal vez por eso no estaba completamente de acuerdo con Jerry Ferrao, fundador del grupo Los Rebuleadores de San Juan, quien compuso la canción sobre la primera vez que Lío bailó con falda en público. Jerry invitó a Lío a bailar la canción en una presentación del grupo en El Boricua, un negocio nocturno en Río Piedras. Lío cuenta que estaba encontrado con la idea porque no estaba completamente de acuerdo con la letra de la canción. Explica que la letra tiene sus contradicciones porque, aunque defiende al bailador con falda, también critica a quienes no lo aceptaron y lo tildaron de gay ("pluma, pluma, pluma"), como si eso fuese un insulto, lo cual le resta y contradice la supuesta crítica que buscaba hacer. El vídeo de YouTube *El gay en El Boricua* (2012) que subió Jerry Ferrao del performance tuvo una reacción mixta; no obstante, según Lío, hubo más aceptación que rechazo.[21]

Figure 5: Lío bailando con falda.

Tal vez, lo que más incomodó a Lío fue el título de la canción, "El gay", y ese estribillo que automáticamente asocia el acto de ruptura con lo heteronormativo de un hombre que baila en falda como indicativo de que es gay. Además, al ser la mirada masculina heteronormativa la que está nombrando o identificando al sujeto aquí, ocurre un *labeling* que incomodaba a Lío en ese entonces por el hecho de que fuera otro quien articulara su *coming out* y no él mismo, en sus propios términos.

Por su parte, Lío Villahermosa recalca que bailar en falda no te hace gay

La primera vez que Lío bailó en falda en público fue en 2012 en un bombazo frente al local Ashé, en Santurce. Él entró al batey con su amiga, quien ya conocía que, entre amigos, Lío bailaba bomba en falda. Ella lo retó en medio del batey, se quitó su falda y se la entregó. Lío aceptó el reto y comenzó a bailar con la falda puesta. Esto provocó una reacción mixta entre el público. Según cuenta Lío, sintió que hubo más aprobación que rechazo, que la mayoría de la gente lo veía como algo positivo, mientras que a otros no les sentó muy bien, algunos de ellos de la vieja guardia de la escuela de los Cepeda, donde Lío comenzó a estudiar bomba desde joven.

Al recordar ese momento, Villahermosa consideró que esa reacción más positiva que negativa se debió, en parte, al hecho de ser respetado entre la comunidad de bomberos por ser estudiante de los Cepeda, por llevar muchos años en la bomba y por ser el hijo de Ruby. Quienes conocieron a su padre afirman que fue uno de los mejores bailadores que ha visto la bomba. De él haber sido otro, es decir, un principiante, una persona considerada ignorante del legado que representa la bomba, tal vez la reacción habría sido otra. De hecho, algunos pensaron que era una broma, ya que en ese entonces él no estaba fuera del clóset.

Este evento provocó que él usara la bomba como medio de expresión y exploración de su proceso de hacer pública su orientación sexual, y desarrolló un performance (monólogo y baile) titulado "Con la falda bien puesta". En este, lo visitaba Sylvia Rexach y le cantaba su canción "Alma adentro"; entonces él se iba vistiendo con elementos femeninos, mientras conservaba los masculinos, construyendo su identidad en vaivén entre ambos polos. Así como las mujeres han logrado romper con lo heteronormativo en la bomba, en ese performance Lío manifestaba un reto mayor, ya que en sus performances cuestiona las categorías mismas del binario masculino/femenino, hombre/mujer. Esto produce un queering de la bomba, ya que las categorías se han retado al grado de revelar su carácter performativo. Según Judith Butler ha propuesto, tanto la identidad de género como la sexual son constructos sociales; no hay una esencia de lo femenino o masculino (2006). Butler afirma que, al entrar en lo social y en el lenguaje, se le asigna el sexo desde el cuerpo, pero es en el asumir o no ese sexo que nace el género, y el género es una cosa fluida, una interpretación, un performance de entrada mediado por construcciones sociales y culturales (1999).

Figure 6: Foto del cartel "Con falda bien puesta".

Por su parte Marjorie Garber propone que la función del travestismo como "modo de articular" un espacio de posibilidades es descentrar el concepto de binarios al "reconfigurar la relación" entre los polos (1992).

Cuando le preguntamos a Lío Villahermosa qué lo motivó a propulsar este estilo de baile en vaivén entre los polos del binario, cuenta que fue el deseo de tener la experiencia de sentir y bailar la bomba en la falda: "fue un impulso, una necesidad, una urgencia". No surgió como un *statement* ni un deseo de hacer crítica social o activismo en ese momento. Surgió de un lugar muy interno en su búsqueda individual de expresarse. Reconoce que al principio salía con miedo al batey, con temor al rechazo por la homofobia, algo que ha superado por completo:

> **El batey no es fácil, siempre da nervios por más experimentado que uno sea en la bomba. Hay una responsabilidad. Una conexión. Es algo serio, es sagrado. Y es desde el respeto que se tiene a la bomba y su historia como legado de expresión cultural de liberación, lo que permite que sea ese espacio de ruptura y preservación simultáneo.**

Por otra parte, desde su perspectiva, lo que él hace tampoco es una reafirmación de lo masculino, como algunos han criticado, sino al contrario, es un modo de retar y abrir ese binario y revelarlo como un performance.

Por ello, en todos sus bailes en el batey él lleva elementos que representan lo masculino y lo femenino a la vez, y mezcla pasos que en la bomba tradicional se reservan a cada género. Lío cuenta que tiene apego a su barba, un elemento que siempre está presente cuando baila. En su muy particular expresión de bomba, Lío construye y deconstruye, rompe con la tradición a la vez que la preserva. Hoy día ya no es "el que baila con falda", sino "el que no baila sin falda", es decir, ya se ha convertido en su forma de expresarse en el batey.

Propongo que estas rearticulaciones de la bomba pueden leerse desde una óptica de performance queer en las que producen un paradójico espacio de tránsitos y pluralizaciones de género, en el que conservan e interpelan elementos tradicionales mientras simultáneamente se retan y rearticulan para abrir espacios de inclusión y expresión de identidades otras. Según afirma Juana María Rodríguez, para personas queer que manejan múltiples espacios identitarios, sexuales, raciales, étnicos y nacionales, las prácticas discursivas que los subyugan, marginan e incluso hieren pueden resignificarse mediante prácticas identitarias de autorepresentación que incorporan y reorganizan elementos heteronormativos para producir espacios paradójicos de simultaneidad discursiva (2003, 50–4). Por su parte, José Esteban Muñoz propone esta práctica como la "desidentificación" que define como "a performative mode of tactical recognition that various minoritarian subjects employ in an effort to resist the oppressive and normalizing discourse in dominant ideology. [...] It is a reformatting of self within the social. It is a third term that resists the binary identification and counteridentification" (2013, location 2083-2087, Kindle). Propongo que esta teoría de la desidentificación aplica a la bomba según la rearticulan participantes como Lío y otros, quienes al mezclar elementos performativos tradicionales de lo masculino y lo femenino, la abren para incluir nuevas expresiones identitarias no binarias. Por tanto, las personas que rompen con estos roles tradicionales a base de género y los reorganizan en nuevas combinaciones que integran los piquetes que se asignan a mujeres con los asignados a hombres producen una desidentificación de género que abre la bomba a otras identidades queer y a participaciones pluralizadas que no se limitan al género del bailador o bailadora.

Por otra parte, Lío Villahermosa reconoce que él y otros de la llamada generación del bombazo, en particular las mujeres, han innovado la bomba, pero que esto lo hacen con el mayor respeto y con la intención de preservar a la vez que renuevan. En nuestra conversación, mientras Lío afirmaba esta función doble de preservar e innovar, me provocaba pensar en las artes plásticas como disciplina —él también es un artista plástico— y la importancia de conocer los fundamentos antes de romper con ellos e innovar. Por otra parte, desde una perspectiva lingüística, un idioma está vivo conforme haya hablantes que lo utilicen para expresarse. Y es precisamente en esa expresión cotidiana del hablante, en particular la de los jóvenes, que se renueva tanto su grafía (escritura) como su léxico. De forma similar, el baile de bomba es un lenguaje lleno de entendidos y códigos que se comunican en claves musicales y gestos rítmicos. Por eso, dice Lío, cuando bailan, el público los anima a "hablar": "¡Habla, habla!". Entonces, no debe sorprender que sean, precisamente, los jóvenes de la generación del bombazo y las nuevas generaciones quienes provocan la innovación a la vez que respetan y preservan la tradición.

En nuestra conversación, mientras Lío afirmaba esta función doble de preservar e innovar, me provocaba pensar en las artes plásticas como disciplina —él también es un artista plástico— y la importancia de conocer los fundamentos antes de romper con ellos e innovar.

Figure 7: Foto del cartel El hijo de Ruby.

Para Lío, bailar bomba es contar una historia que muchas veces será dictada por el ritmo. Y así como un cuento tiene su desarrollo, punto culminante y desenlace, la bomba también tiene su estructura expresiva: "todos los ritmos tienen una carga o energía que facilitan la expresión de vivencias y sentires". En el documental *El hijo de Ruby*, de la cineasta puertorriqueña Gisela Rosario Ramos, se ve más claramente a qué se refiere Lío con esta analogía entre bailar bomba y contar. En el filme se narra cómo Lío, a través de la bomba, encuentra un espacio de expresión y búsqueda no solo para conocerse a sí mismo, sino para descubrir el legado que su padre fenecido le había regalado sin saberlo.

En el filme, Rosario Ramos se centra en ofrecer la perspectiva en torno a la bomba de Lío, el hijo de Ruby, en varios niveles de narración. Por un lado, se cuenta, desde la imagen propia del cine, el reencuentro simbólico a través de la bomba, de Lío con su padre, ausente desde su niñez a causa de la drogadicción. Este vínculo entre ambos se presenta como un legado, como una herencia filial y a su vez cultural. Este reencuentro ocurre póstumamente, es decir, ya el padre había fallecido y él lo va conociendo mediante anécdotas que le cuentan los bomberos en los bateyes, desde sus 17 años, gracias a su hermano mayor, quien fue el primero en insertarse en la bomba. La narración nos lleva de forma fragmentada a través de un proceso de transformación de Lío, es decir, de encontrarse a sí mismo a través de encontrarse con su padre. El documental registra diversos ritmos dentro de la bomba, los cuales van marcando emociones y etapas en su transformación interior, hasta manifestarse las rupturas con lo tradicional en varios sentidos: primero, con su padre (rol masculino tradicional); luego, con la bomba como género musical tradicionalmente heteronormativo; y finalmente, con las nociones de género binarias. Al concluir, se nos presenta a Lío bailando bomba, con su barba, camisilla sin mangas y su falda.

En su performance, va mezclando pasos, piquetes y movimientos tradicionalmente reservados al rol del bailador con los que se reservan a la bailadora, y así traza un tránsito entre los polos, lo que el propio Lío ha llamado el espacio de "medianía", o estar entremedio de ambos. En este performance, él crea un gesto completamente nuevo como resultado de su encuentro simbólico con su padre y consigo mismo, el cual produce una obra de arte y una subjetividad en tránsito. Es un gesto de renovación dentro de la bomba, un queering, que la vuelve fluida y que reta lo heteronormativo al inscribir su tránsito desde el agite de volantes de su falda y su cuerpo que dibuja movimientos femeninos y masculinos en vaivén constante, como inscripción del nuevo orden que suaviza y agita, a la vez, que abre la bomba a nuevos horizontes estéticos y a la participación e inclusión de identidades otras. Se podría afirmar que, desde la narrativa del documental de Gisela Rosario Ramos, se propone que la bomba proporciona un espacio de liberación, de sanación, de transformación de ausencias, y que fomenta la libertad de expresión individual. A modo de cierre, en la siguiente sección exploraré esta cualidad de la bomba que muchos bomberos y bomberas afirman.

VI. "No, no, no, no te quedes con na' por dentro. Sí, sí, sí, que la bomba te va a curar".[22]

Desde este estribillo de una canción de Marién Torres y Ricardo Pons, se propone que la bomba es mucho más que una música o un baile; es un instrumento de transformación social e individual. Alineados a esta visión trasformativa de la bomba, Ángel Quintero ha señalado el carácter subversivo del baile afrocaribeño y Carlos Álamo-Pastrana ha identificado la bomba como espacio que "permite una reconsideración de los discursos masculinos afectivos", como lugar para expresar "masculinidades alternativas" (Alamo-Pastrana 2009, 577; Quintero Rivera 2009).[23] Como hemos visto, Lío Villahermosa añade en su estilo de bomba otra dimensión al retar lo heteronormativo desde el cuerpo y el baile. Pero sin duda las mujeres fueron las pioneras en su ruptura con lo tradicional, lo cual abrió el espacio para otras expresiones queer dentro de la bomba puertorriqueña. Estas simultáneas rupturas y renovaciones de la bomba no deben sorprendernos, ya que, como afirma Lío, "el batey en la bomba, desde su origen, fue un espacio de liberación y lo sigue siendo. Nació de tanto sufrimiento y opresión que a través de la bomba se transformaba en algo bello. Hoy, sigue siendo un espacio de liberación, sanación, creación y celebración".

Figure 8: Taller Tambuyé.

Por su parte, Marién compartió varias anécdotas de sus estudiantes, quienes a través de la bomba encontraron la valentía de expresarse dentro y fuera del batey. Es decir, al vivir la liberación de la bomba dentro del batey pudieron aplicar esa expresión liberadora aprendida a situaciones en sus propias vidas, sus relaciones de pareja, filiales y sociales. Esto apunta al poder de liberación, sanación emocional y autogestión que provoca la bomba. Como reitera Marién Torres:

> **He tenido estudiantes por montones que sienten el empoderamiento que nace de la bomba. La bomba fue el catalítico para muchas estudiantes para salir de relaciones dañinas de pareja o salvar una relación que estaba en problemas. Ha ayudado a mujeres a salir de sus prisiones internas. Es el género de la bomba el que carga con esto, promueve esos espacios de liberación, provoca que te abras y bregues con tus monstruos internos.**

De hecho, una de las primeras experiencias de Marién Torres con el poder de liberación de la bomba fue en Crearte, la escuela comunitaria para jóvenes en comunidades de alto riesgo. Comenta Marién que jamás olvidará cuando una de sus jóvenes estudiantes fue entrevistada para una tarea especial creativa por un compañero de la clase de arte, quien le preguntó: "¿Qué sientes cuando bailas bomba?", a lo que ella respondió: "¡Libertad!". Así fue como supo que quería dedicarse a la enseñanza de la bomba: "Con las experiencias que viví en Crearte entendí que este es el mejor trabajo de base que puedo hacer por mi país".

Gracias a las instancias de rupturas previas gestadas por mujeres y hombres en Puerto Rico, en 2016 surgió un nuevo movimiento de mujeres bomberas llamado

Figure 8: Círculo Barrileras de Mayagüez.

Círculo de Barrileras de Mayagüez, que tiene como propósito apoyar actividades educativas en defensa de la equidad de género y otras luchas sociales. Por ejemplo, recientemente participaron en una actividad de Proyecto Siempre Vivas, una organización sin fines de lucro de apoyo a mujeres y sus hijos. También participaron en las protestas en contra de los depósitos de cenizas tóxicas en Peñuelas y continúan participando en otras protestas que defienden los derechos del pueblo ante injusticias del gobierno local y estadounidense. Del mismo modo, Marién Torres López participa como bombera en diversas protestas que buscan defender las mujeres o el pueblo de atropellos del patriarcado y del colonialismo. En Puerto Rico, la bomba continúa siendo una herramienta de lucha por libertades y derechos, mientras simultáneamente denuncia injusticias.

Esta bomba queer se opone a lo heteronormativo de roles prescritos a base de género mientras inscribe nuevas formas de rearticular la participación al flexibilizar las normas de "lo auténtico" sin perder la tradición.

La innovación y apertura en la bomba que han provocado las nuevas generaciones ha renovado y expandido su música y baile. El afán simultáneo de preservar e innovar, que ellos proponen tanto en la teoría como en la práctica, le da vida a la bomba y continúa su legado. Por tanto, es desde la bomba misma como música y baile de liberación que emerge esa innovación y ruptura con lo heteronormativo, ese queering, que la abre a nuevas expresiones liberadoras. Esta bomba queer se opone a lo heteronormativo de roles prescritos a base de género mientras inscribe nuevas formas de rearticular la participación al flexibilizar las normas de "lo auténtico" sin perder la tradición. Tal como afirma Ángel Quintero, la música y el baile "mulato", como él lo denomina para incluir otros géneros además de la bomba, libera lo suprimido, ya sean sentimientos o identidades, desde el cuerpo como espacio creativo de innovación (2009, 52–8).[24] Precisamente es desde el cuerpo que se construye el binario de género; por ende, es en el baile que se expresa su carácter performativo.

Aunque actualmente en Puerto Rico la enseñanza de la bomba continúa la división de pasos de baile por género, se hace en pos de preservar. A la hora de bailar, el batey se abre a la expresión libre de esa tradición, en la cual, como si se tratara de una obra plástica, el bailador o bailadora dibuja desde su cuerpo en movimiento su propio gesto para contar su historia. En el batey les abraza el ritmo y las voces de la comunidad de bomberos y bomberas, que alientan con su coro a que cada cual se exprese a su manera con la consciencia y el respeto que el legado de la bomba puertorriqueña amerita.

NOTES

[1] Versos de la canción "Tambuyé" (2013), de Ricardo Pons y Marién Torres.

[2] Estas dos publicaciones, junto a Álbum Puertorriqueño (1844), fueron producto de esfuerzos colectivos de escritores criollos que buscaban plasmar en verso y prosa las costumbres de Puerto Rico con las características generales del Romanticismo español de la época. Se consideran las primeras manifestaciones literarias propiamente puertorriqueñas.

[3] Según explica Juan Cartagena (2004), varios estudiosos atribuyen esa "invisibilidad" de la bomba ante otros géneros musicales a la noción racista que prevaleció de que no "merecía" estudiarse, la cual, en el fondo, se debía a su herencia marcadamente africana. Entre ellos se encuentran Halbert Barton, Emanuel Dufrasne González y Juan Flores, entre otros.

[4] Ambos autores eran contemporáneos de Antonio S. Pedreira, quien en *Insularismo* (1934) privilegia la danza como música representativa de lo nacional, en otra instancia de menosprecio a las expresiones culturales afropuertorriqueñas. Por su parte, el también contemporáneo Tomás Blanco, aunque dedica su ensayo "Elogio a la plena" (1935) a la música afropuertorriqueña de la plena, no logra soltarse de los vestigios del racismo en sus discursos.

[5] Esta obra de Arriví forma parte de una trilogía de dramas que el autor denominó *Máscara puertorriqueña*. En ella, explora la diversidad cultural de los puertorriqueños. Las otras obras que conforman la trilogía son *Bolero y plena* (1955) y *Sirena* (1959).

[6] El documental fue escrito por Lydia Milagros González y dirigido por Mario Vissepó. Contó con el auspicio de la Fundación Puertorriqueña de las Humanidades y el Instituto de Cultura Puertorriqueña. Ver vídeo *La herencia del tambor: Homenaje a Rafael Cortijo* en el siguiente enlace: <https://youtu.be/VhcgmehknuE/>.

[7] Como afirma Cartagena, "bomba today is much more fully expressive than in the Cortijo era, both in the commercial recordings market and in live presentations. And in many ways is closer to its roots [...] bomba as it enters the millennium, is not a proxy for Puerto Rico's past but, with increasing acceptance among Puerto Rican youth, is instead a dynamic modality for contemporary expression" (2004, 27–8).

[8] Por cuestiones de tiempo, me limitaré a explorar varias instancias de rupturas con lo heteronormativo en Puerto Rico. Reconozco que mi aportación será limitada y que hace falta profundizar y documentar otras instancias en otras regiones de la bomba en Puerto Rico y la diáspora.

[9] Versos de la canción "Nací mujer", de Chabali González (2015).

[10] Según Hal Barton (1995), aunque algunas mujeres sabían tocar barril en los bombazos tanto de tarima como de la calle, eran los hombres los únicos que tocaban los barriles.

[11] Versos de la canción "Mujer Boricua", de Marién Torres López (2013).

[12] Todas las citas de Marién Torres López incluidas en este ensayo son de una entrevista que le realicé en su Taller Tambuyé el jueves, 9 de febrero de 2017.

[13] Versos de la canción "Las mujeres andamos armás", de Coraly Cruz Mejía (2016).

[14] Esta ponencia se presentó en el 6º Coloquio Del Otro La'o, en la Universidad de Puerto Rico, Recinto de Mayagüez, en marzo de 2016.

[15] Según citado por Sefranek y Cruz (2016) en su ponencia ya citada.

[16] En su ensayo "El macho como travesti: Propuesta para una historia del machismo en Puerto Rico", Efraín Barradas explora el machismo como una forma de travestismo en la que se exageran comportamientos considerados masculinos, del mismo modo que "el barroquismo esencial [...] sirve de base al travesti" (2006, 149).

[17] Barton afirma que la loca "temporarily disrupts and/or suspends the organization of gender roles. [...] She trips up gender codes by offering liminal space between two genders for rein-

vention and recasting of gender dynamics within the space of bomba" (1995, 120).
[18] Versos de la canción "El gay", de Jerry Ferrao (2012).
[19] Jerry Ferrao, considerado miembro de la generación del bombazo, tiene dos producciones discográficas, y en 2012 dirigió el documental *Ayeres de la bomba*. Estos proyectos forman parte de la aportación de la juventud puertorriqueña a la renovación y preservación de la bomba en Puerto Rico.
[20] Las anécdotas y citas que incluyo en esta sección son producto de la entrevista que le hice a Lío Villahermosa el miércoles, 8 de febrero de 2017 en Santurce.
[21] Para ver el vídeo, vaya al siguiente enlace: <https://www.youtube.com/watch?v=yqiCevRVA4k/>.
[22] Versos de la canción "Tambuyé", de Ricardo Pons y Marién Torres.
[23] Traducciones mías del original en inglés (Alamo-Pastrana 2009, 577).
[24] En su libro, Ángel Quintero afirma que la fuerza subversiva de la música y los bailes "mulatos", o de herencia africana (bomba, salsa, danza, hip hop y reggeatón, entre otros), radica en su oposición a "la radical separación —cartesiana— entre mente-civilización y cuerpo-naturaleza, que la creatividad expresiva del cuerpo danzante pone en tela de juicio" (2009, 357). Es decir, el cuerpo y la mente se juntan para concienzudamente crear espacios de liberación.

OBRAS CITADAS

Abadía-Rexach, Bárbara Idalissee. 2014. De aquí pa'llá y de allá pa'cá : los "toques" de la migración en la bomba puertorriqueña. *Relaciones Internacionales* 25, 123–41. <http://www.relacionesinternacionales.info/ojs/article/view/496/376.html/>.

Alamo-Pastrana, Carlos. 2009. Con el eco de los barriles: Race, Gender and the Bomba Imaginary in Puerto Rico. *Identities: Global Studies in Culture and Power* 16, 573–600.

Alonso, Manuel. 1983 [1849]. *El jíbaro*. Río Piedras, PR: Ediciones Edil.

Arriví, Francisco. 1970 [1958]. *Vejigantes*. Río Piedras, PR: Editorial Cultural.

________. 1971 [1959]. *Sirena*. Río Piedras, PR: Editorial Cultural.

________. 1975 [1955]. *Bolero y plena*. Río Piedras, PR: Editorial Cultural.

Arroyo, Jossianna. 2010. "Roots" or the Virtualities of Racial Imaginaries in Puerto Rico and the Diáspora. *Latino Studies Journal* 8(2), 195–219.

Barton, Halbert. 1995. The Drum-Dance Challenge: An Anthropological Study of Gender, Race and Class Marginalization of Bomba in Puerto Rico. Tesis Doctoral. Cornell University.

Barradas, Efraín. 2006. El macho como travesti: Propuesta para una historia del machismo en Puerto Rico. *Fuentes Humanísticas* 33, 141–50.

Blanco, Tomás. 2004 [1935]. Elogio a la plena. En *Literatura puertorriqueña del siglo XX: Antología*, ed. Mercedes López Baralt. 50–8. Río Piedras: Editorial de la Universidad de Puerto Rico.

Butler, Judith. 1999 [1990]. *Gender Trouble: Feminism and the Subversion of Identity*. New York: Routledge.

________. 2006. *Deshacer el género* (*Undoing Gender*). Traducido por Patricia Soley Beltrán. Barcelona: Paidós.

Cartagena, Juan. 2004. When Bomba becomes the National Music of Puerto Rico. *CENTRO: Journal of the Center for Puerto Rican Studies* 16(1), 15–35.

Chaparro Serrano, Ruperto. 2011. *Con sabor a Mayagüez: perpetuando la herencia plenera y bombera mayagüezana*. Mayagüez: Sea Grant Puerto Rico. DVD

Cruz Mejías, Zoralyz I. y Mary Sefranek Potter. 2016. Hacia una bomba queer: desafiando los binarios de género en la bomba mayagüezana. Ponencia presentada en 6º Coloquio Del Otro La'o: Perspectivas Sobre Sexualidades Queer, Universidad de Puerto Rico, Recinto de Mayagüez, 1–3 de marzo.

Dávila, Arlene M. 1997. *Sponsored Identities: Cultural Politics in Puerto Rico*. Philadelphia: Temple University Press.

Duany, Jorge. 2005. The Rough Edges of Puerto Rican Identity: Gender, Race and Transnationalism. *Latin American Research Review* 40(3), 177–90.

Flores, Juan. 2000. *From Bomba to Hip Hop: Puerto Rican Culture in Latino Identity*. New York: Columbia University Press.

Garber, Marjorie. 1992. *Vested Interests: Cross-Dressing and Cultural Anxiety*. New York: Routledge.

Halperin, David. 1995. *Saint-Foucault: Towards a Gay Hagiography*. New York: Oxford University Press.

Muñoz, José Esteban. 2013. *Disidentification: Queers of Color and the Performance of Politics*. Minneapolis: University of Minnesota Press.

Palés Matos. Luis. 1994 [1937]. *Tuntún de pasa y grifería*. Río Piedras: Editorial Universidad de Puerto Rico.

Pedreira, Antonio S. 1992 [1932]. *Insularismo*. Río Piedras, PR: Editorial Edil.

Quintero Rivera, Ángel G. 2009. *Cuerpo y cultura: las músicas "mulatas" y la subversión del baile*. Frankfurt: Iberoamericana, Vervuert.

Ramírez, Rafael L. 1999. *What It Means to Be a Man: Reflections on Puerto Rican Masculinity*. New Brunswick, NJ: Rutgers University Press.

Ramos Rosado, Marie. 2011. *Destellos de la negritud: investigaciones caribeñas*. San Juan/Santo Domingo: Isla Negra Editores.

Rivera Rivera, Pablo Luis. 2015. El surgimiento de escuelas de bomba independientes ante la ausencia de enseñanza en el currículo oficial del sistema de educación en Puerto Rico. *Musiké: Revista del Conservatorio de Música de Puerto Rico* 4(1), 65–95.

Rodríguez, Juana María. 2003. *Queer Latinidad: Identity Practices, Discursive Spaces*. New York: New York University Press.

Rodríguez Juliá, Edgardo. 1983. *El entierro de Cortijo*. Río Piedras, PR: Ediciones Huracán.

Rosario Rosado. Gisela. 2014. *El hijo de Ruby*. Producciones Cine Luz Negra. Documental.

Torres López, Marién. 2013. *Tambuyé*. San Juan. Producciones Awóniyé. CD.

Vizcarrondo, Fortunato. 1983 [1942]. *Dinga y mandinga*. San Juan: Editorial Instituto de Cultura Puertorriqueña.

VOLUME XXXI • NUMBER II • SUMMER 2019

"Water Overflows with Memory": Bomba, Healing, and the Archival Oceanic

ASHLEY COLEMAN TAYLOR

ABSTRACT

Once used as a method for enslaved Africans to plan rebellions and socialize, contemporary bomba participants report experiences of healing, self-expression, and stress relief as they honor Puerto Rico's African history through embodied movements and musicality. After centering the batey as a site through which Africanness and Blackness resist erasure and marginalization, I explore the ways that the transcaribbean Afro-Puerto Rican art form promotes healing through ancestral memory by theorizing what I name the *archival oceanic*. Here, memory is rendered as a source of both survival and healing. This article explores how a theory of the archival oceanic (grounded in ancestral memory and healing) might expand our understanding of *bomba* and its relationship to other African diasporic cultural practices. I ask, what roles do ancestral memory and healing play in the lives of *bomba* practitioners? What other possibilities lie in its practice? [Key Words: Race, Blackness, Healing, Religion, Archives, Africanness]

The author (AshleyColemanTaylor@austin.utexas.edu) is an interdisciplinary ethnographer who specializes in the intersecting lived experiences of black embodiment, black genders and sexualities, and African diaspora religious experience. She will begin a position as an Assistant Professor of Religious Studies and Women's and Gender Studies at the University of Texas at Austin in Fall 2019. She was previously a Visiting Fellow at the James Weldon Johnson Institute at Emory University. Her book project, *Majestad Negra: Race, Class, Gender and Religious Experience in the Puerto Rican Imaginary* is an intersectional black feminist approach to racialized embodiment in Puerto Rico. Her current research project employs queer oral history methods to explore the lived experiences of Atlanta-based LGBT activists.

1. Introduction

I begin and end with the ocean, allowing its waters to inform a conceptualization of Puerto Rican *bomba* characterized by fluidity, dynamism, and healing potential through ancestral memory. I am interested in the deep figurative unknown: the site of black trauma in the rupturing experience of the transatlantic slave trade where black bodies were converted into capital for the sake of economic robustness and growth, as well as the elective and resistive processes of self-making through African diasporic subjectivity. The mid-Atlantic Ocean waters are troubled, and "the Middle Passage...is a loaded concept" (Davies 2013, 85). Not only does the Middle Passage conjure up "difficult, pain-filled journeys across ocean space...dismemberment...the economic trade and exchange in goods in which Africans were the capital, deterritorialization...and the parallel disenfranchisement," but also "the necessary constitution of new identities in passage and on after arrival" (Davies 2013, 85). As a site of disrupture, deculturation, and dehumanization, the ocean's troubled waters are a key image in the transatlantic saga that continues in the New World.

Deep within the oceanic darkness are nuanced, rich metaphors of divinity, maternity, creative potential, and restorative power. That place where Africans in passage exchanged "country marks" was, subsequently, the site of remaking; it birthed a type of resistance through re-identification and a new, composite, nation on the sea's surface (Gomez 1998, 1). In *Civilization and its Discontents,* Freud describes an exchange he had in which his dear friend had described the "oceanic feeling" associated with religious experience. Freud gestures toward a "limitless, unbounded" "sensation of eternity," which he had never felt firsthand (Freud 1962, 11). Inspired by this notion, in "Mama's Baby, Papa's Maybe," Hortense Spillers describes the liminal oceanic Atlantic and the ungendering process undergone by black bodies that traversed its vastness on slave vessels. As a site of "undifferentiated identity" where African subjects were "removed from indigenous land" and still "not yet American" or, as Spillers puts it, "culturally unmade," Spillers points out that "those African persons in 'Middle Passage' were literally suspended in the oceanic, in movement across the Atlantic, but they were also nowhere at all" (Spillers 1987, 72). In middle passage, the "human-as-cargo stand for a wild and unclaimed richness of possibility" as they were "thrown in the midst of a figurative darkness" (Spillers 1987, 72). The oceanic itself thus becomes a spatial site of groundlessness and nationlessness, an absence of borderlands but yet of transformation as African persons were forced into the throes of deterritorialization and loss of home. The oceanic waters, in their fluidity, were destined to disrupt the process of objectification and subsequent commodification superimposed by European captors. The "oceanic" gave way to reformed ontologies. Inspired by the "oceanic" that Spillers describes, and its relationship to black bodies, I employ what I name the *archival oceanic* to describe the complex, nuanced role of bomba in Puerto Rico and countless sites of diasporic creative cultural enterprise in the Americas.

Two characteristics of the archival oceanic are important to note here. The first part of the term, the "archival," represents a fluid site of ancestral memory. This term is informed by one of the constitutive elements of African diaspora religion, the revered ancestors—those who have died yet continue to live amongst humans and represent a dynamic realm of being (Stewart 2005). The presence of the ancestral community mirrors the subjectivity of the human community involved in the praxes of making and remaking identities. An *archive*, as I refer to it here, is not merely a collection of material culture in a library or museum special collection. Instead, a community and an individual can be an archive. The archive can carry and maintain the stories and experiences of the ancestors who have transitioned beyond the material realm. Thus, as a site of human/ancestral convergence, in this archive one can feel the spirits of those who have passed, carry their memories, and at times become them, "nonindividuated" (Alexander 2015, 300). In this sense, the immaterial materializes, and the intangible is made tangible. As metaphor, the archival oceanic reminds us that the living diaspora's reified and emergent cosmological systems are "marked by anything but stasis," and instead demonstrate the dynamism of the African interatlantic experience (Alexander 2015, 292).

Specifically, I'm interested in bomba's "richness of possibility" and new ways of engaging ancestral memory and healing alongside other African diasporic cultural forms.

Second, the archival oceanic offers a hermeneutic for healing rooted in the practices of the African diasporic culture. The "oceanic" part of this term operationalizes what Spillers calls "unclaimed richness for possibility" and points to a sense of transcendence, interconnectedness, and potential for healing that is found in the experience of ancestral memory (Spillers 1987, 72). This healing answers the call for the liberation of confined peoples, and ancestral memory becomes a vital element in the healing arts. As M. Jacqui Alexander reminds us in the line that inspired the title of this work, "Water overflows with memory. Emotional memory. Bodily memory. Sacred memory" (Alexander 2015, 290). Although the site of the oceanic in the transatlantic journey is contested space, healing exists in memory because the past shapes the present and our orientation for the future. In other words, at the watery crossroads where ancestral memory, the oceanic, and healing intersect, we are reminded that communities, cultures, and the legacies of the African diaspora are complex, multidimensional, dynamic, and fluid. To be sure, across the diaspora ritual cultural practices elicit ecstaticism, or as one of my research participants names them, "tranciness." Healing often takes place during these moments, providing recourse to the violence inflicted upon black flesh and a method for reclaiming fractured selves in diasporic discursive life. Although black bodies often carry the legacies of ancestral trauma reified through a climate of anti-Blackness in places like Puerto Rico, the archival oceanic offers a method for survival and reclamation of selfhood, rooted in the lived experience of African diasporic communities (Sharpe 2016). I question how a theory of the archival oceanic (grounded in ancestral memory and healing) might expand our understanding of bomba and its relationship to other African diasporic cultural practices? What role do ancestral memory and healing play in the lives of bomba practitioners? What possibilities lie in its practice?

In the context of Puerto Rico, I employ a theory of the archival oceanic, including its associated properties, to understand what bomba participants may experience in the *bombazo*. Specifically, I'm interested in bomba's "richness of possibility" and new ways of engaging ancestral memory and healing alongside other African diasporic cultural forms. In this article, I will focus on bomba as a place where the archival oceanic manifests, and memory is rendered as a source of both survival and healing. My work critiques the fixed ideologies and stereotypes of Blackness and Africanness as exotic and separate from true Puerto Rican identity—which serves to distance them from "modern" culture, treating them as folkloric figures of the past with fixed identifying characteristics.

What grounds the archival oceanic in the context of bomba is its ability to reject what anthropologist Isar Godreau calls the "politics of erasure" that govern ideologies surrounding Africanness and Blackness in the Puerto Rican imaginary (Godreau 2015, 69). The politics of erasure that impact black/African derived cultural elements depends upon their relegation to the past or to specific areas, deemed as static, and understood as incapable of nuance or change. Engaging the archival oceanic approach to bomba resists the politics of erasure by making tangible Blackness and Africanness in material form, fostering healing through ancestral memory, reminding us that dynamism is key, and centering marginal cultural elements within the Puerto Rican imaginary. The power of bomba, I demonstrate, is related to its archival oceanic properties. Through the fluid praxes of making and remaking identities, bomba is reinforced by an African diasporic link between ancestral memory and waterscapes of interatlantic traversals of crossing water and being transformed in the process. Its connection to religiocultural dance forms, percussive music, performance arts, and symbolism of memorial waters enliven bomba and continue to render it a site of transformation and political discourse. But bomba is not only ancestral, bomba is not only folklore; bomba is a contemporary site of therapeutic engagement, it is a form of resistance to a legacy that colonizes Puerto Rican bodies and lands deemed as commodifiable and controllable through imperialist eyes. The archival oceanic reminds us that as a fluid and dynamic cultural art form, much of bomba's power is in its ancestral memory and healing potential.

In this article I will first discuss the ways that bomba's presence in Puerto Rico may combat the politics of erasure that impact Africanness and Blackness. Second, I situate bomba within the larger body of Kongo-inspired art forms that are connected to living communities instead of to a static history. Third, I articulate the ways that Blackness becomes embodied in bomba. Oftentimes, Blackness in Puerto Rico is erased, hidden, or localized to certain areas. Yet, bomba serves as a site where Blackness maintains a dominant presence; thus, it cannot be erased. I will explore how

Africanness and Blackness are made both tangible and visible through the embodiment of the Cepeda and Ayala bomba families. Fourth, while participants deny the religious nature of bomba, I found that there are significant overlaps between bomba and religious experience. Lastly, I posit the *batey* as a site with the potential for healing through ancestral memory.

2. On Blackness and Africanness in the Puerto Rican Imaginary

Documented as early as 1797, Puerto Rican bomba is believed to have developed initially in the batey (from the Taíno word of the same name), a gathering place of sociopolitical engagement, communalism, and entertainment for enslaved black communities. While there are documented accounts of its use to plan rebellions in the southern parts of the island, enslaved Africans employed bomba as a means of communication, liberation, and interconnection (Álamo-Pastrana 2009). In present-day iterations, bomba participants report experiences of healing, self-expression, and stress relief as they celebrate the embodiment of Puerto Rico's African history through movement. The singer, the solo dancer emerging from the audience, the lead drummer, those who hold the drum rhythms, and the watching members of the community form the oceanic space of possibility, creative imagination, and fluid engagement. To be sure, while a large part of Puerto Rican culture is known to be racist or anti-African, I found that a unique intimacy exists within the diverse community of individuals in the bomba circle who use the Afro-Puerto Rican art form as a source of community empowerment. I am particularly interested in the evolving role of bomba in Puerto Rican culture, its ability to heal and transform individuals and communities, as well as the art form's role in the construction and endurance of black identity and African cultural legacies participants have kept alive beyond the batey.

I approach this work as an ethnographer of religion with Afro-Puerto Rican and circum-Caribbean ancestry, as well as a life-long relationship with dance. My work results from 12 months of interviews, informal conversations, pop culture analyses, and participant observation, revealing the different ways that Blackness and Africanness operate as cultural notions in the larger Puerto Rican popular imaginary. Punctuating my ethnographic data is the information I gathered from interviews with two leaders in the bomba community, for whom I use pseudonyms.[1] The first, Caridad, was in her early thirties at the time of our interview and is pale complexioned with long, straight, black hair. She is Puerto Rican and Peruvian, describes her race as mixed, and is the founder of two prominent bomba groups in the San Juan area. The second, Raúl, was in his early thirties and is pale complexioned with short straight hair. He also describes himself as racially mixed and leads several groups. Like Caridad, Raúl travels internationally to teach and perform bomba. I focused in these two participants because of their embeddedness in the bomba community and the ways that their personal experiences and cultural knowledge punctuated their own involvement in bomba.

During my fieldwork, I discovered that both participants and nonparticipants are aware of bomba as an African-descended drum and dance form performed by enslaved communities in their batey. In addition, I found a prevalent familiarity with the "revered apex"; in bomba, this event is found in the intercommunication between the lead drummer and the solo dancer who emerges from the audience (Daniel 2011, 143). Waves of high and low intensity energy fill the circular batey as the drummer mimics the hand, foot, and hip movements of the dancer. The mark of a great dancer is the ability to create a rhythmic song appealing to even novice bomba participants. A great drummer, likewise, has the ability to follow the rhythm of the dancer with almost perfect syncopation, marking each step and hand gesture with the appropriate drum sound.

My everyday conversations during fieldwork also point to larger conceptual understandings of racial ideologies in Puerto Rico; recited scripts of blended mixed-race heritages are meant to serve as proof that there is no racism in Latin American nations like that of the racially stratified United States (Godreau 2015). This particular discourse on race, however, reflects a transnational narrative in Latin America in which views of Blackness and African heritage are masked by the mythical concept and false ideology of racial utopianism, or *mestizaje*, through the perfect blend of cultures and races (Dulitzky 2005).

In fact, in Puerto Rico, mestizaje was state-institutionalized through a nationalizing initiative led by Governor Luis Muñoz Marín in the middle of the twentieth century.

The *mestizaje* ideal silences and erases racial differences, prejudices, and social inequities in favor of a unified nationalist image of racial harmony through centuries of intermarriage. In fact, in Puerto Rico, mestizaje was state-institutionalized through a nationalizing initiative led by Governor Luis Muñoz Marín in the middle of the twentieth century. The initiative sought to define the culture of Puerto Rico and purported an evenly blended triadic cultural legacy consisting of African, Taino, and Spanish, which consequently shaped the national narrative surrounding both Africanness and Blackness. The founding of the Instituto de Cultura Puertorriqueña in the 1950s solidified the institutionalization of Puerto Rico's mestizaje ideal, prizing Spanish heritage while honorably historicizing Taíno culture and folkloricizing the African (Godreau 2016).

Those with whom I spoke would often express a scripted understanding of race and ancestry. I noticed two common refrains: One, when I would talk about race more broadly, I would hear the explanatory, "You know, Puerto Ricans are a mixture of Spanish, Taino, and African." This emphasis on the mestizaje without the critical context of racial hierarchy erroneously depicts a racial utopia through the disappearance of the consequences of racial difference and the absence of racism. Two, when I would mention that I wanted to study the lives of black people in Puerto Rico, specifically, I would often hear the suggestive comment, "You should go to Loíza, there are black people in Loíza"—as if Blackness is situated and localized contemporarily in geographic sites, but contained within rigid defined boundaries of racialized property. These findings reflect what Isar Godreuau names "scripts of Blackness," or the processes of everyday speech which reveal the popular epistemologies of race in the Puerto Rican imaginary. Since the publication of José Luis González's ground-breaking text, *El país de cuatro pisos*, scholars have explored race in Puerto Rico through television and media (Rivero 2005), religious experience (Hernández Hiraldo 2006), residential segregation (Dinzey-Flores 2013), medicalization (Briggs 2002), colonialism and nationalization projects (Rodríguez-Silva 2012), sexuality (Findley 2000, and popular music (Rivera-Rideau 2015). Guided by my fieldwork, my research departs from other scholars who study race in Puerto Rico because I separate Africanness and Blackness in my analysis.

On the one hand, African elements in present day Puerto Rican life remain part of a distant, historical folklore. Africanness in Puerto Rico, as part of the mestizaje script, is intrinsically manifested as living deep in one's veins, residing in the historic blood which pumps through the Puerto Rican body, underneath the skin and often ignored because it often goes unseen. Africanness is the historical legacy, the folkloric manifestation of the enslaved persons who toiled sugar cane fields and coffee plantations some 300 persons deep. Complicit with the findings of other scholars, many participants treated "*lo africano*" as a static folkloric element with its roots in enslavement. To this day, the national script imagines Africa as a one-dimensional, distant land associated with the dark-skinned people of Puerto Rico's past. In a conversation, Caridad—one of the participants whose reflections deeply influence this article—even told me, "Africa is seen as a country, but Africa is a continent with distinct ethnic groups, cultures and languages. And it was very rich—and here... [People assume] Africa is black, nothing else." This "nothing else" points to the narrow range of characteristics of Africanness, which propagates the politics of erasure by disallowing Africanness to be "something more," beyond those characteristics associated solely with a past of enslavement. In the construction of Puerto Rico's nationalist discourse, bomba became the folkloric performative representation of the African aspect of the island's three-part historical legacy. In the larger Puerto Rican imaginary, therefore, bomba is simply "African," devoid of complexity, associated with fixed characteristics informed by the era of enslavement, and incapable of being a contemporary living art form.

Blackness, on the other hand, exists contemporarily and is relegated to certain parts of the island like towns, neighborhoods, and certain dark-skinned persons. Blackness is readily visible, living and breathing in the present, yet not existing in the mainstream, dominant Puerto Rican cultural landscape. Blackness exists "over there," outside of non-black bodies, communities, and cultural imaginary (Godreau 2015). Blackness is made tangible through embodied lived experiences of darker individuals on the island, represented phenotypically in characteristics like kinky hair (*pelo grifo*), dark skin, a wide nose, and full lips. Further, as Godreau writes, "Dominant discourses of cultural nationalism often locate 'authentic' products of Blackness in specific geographic areas (i.e., the coast), in towns (i.e., Loíza), or in communities (San Antón)....” (Godreau 2015, 16). Blackness, and its rigidly affixed stereotypes and characteristics, is embedded, or situated and localized in specific sites (Rivera-Rideau 2015). As I studied bomba and its complex and resistive history in Puerto Rico, I began to deeply understand the genre's role in constructed sites of Blackness as localized and situated into fixed areas on the island and the specific role of Africanness in constructing a mythic norm of idealized racial mixture.

3. Afro-Caribbean Roots

Examining the resilience of Kongo presence in Puerto Rico, particularly through religious and artistic avenues, helps us expand beyond the Ashanti and Yoruba origin story and elucidates the interconnections among diverse living African diasporic practices in the Caribbean, thereby rescuing “lo africano” from its designation of “folkloric” and anachronistic. While direct connection to one's ancestors may not be the goal as it is in other African diasporic practices, each execution of bomba has the ability to crystallize ancestral memory in the movements and methods of dancing, drumming, and singing. As if it is a gift from the enslaved Africans who first performed its steps and rhythms, bomba's enduring presence in Puerto Rico and its ability to evolve to serve the needs of the participants, mirrors the fluidity of the archival oceanic. Assessing bomba through a Kongo lens opens new possibilities for understanding its power and potentiality in the Puerto Rican cultural landscape as a site for healing through ancestral memory.

By situating bomba as a Cariglobal art form with both Kongo and French-Caribbean influences, our understanding of “lo africano” in Puerto Rico can expand beyond previous discourses as we approach the complexities of the vibrant, dynamic, and evolving African diaspora with more nuance.

Bomba as an art form is the result of an intercultural flow between central African Kongo and Afro-Caribbean populations in Puerto Rico. The 19th century saw an influx of inter-island cultural exchange on Puerto Rican soil and the dynamic evolution of bomba. Performing bomba not only connects its participants to a larger African diasporic community, but through its evolution bomba also reifies this connection to Afro-Puerto Rican cultural praxis, both tangiblizing and modernizing its image. Through bomba, dominant narratives of “lo africano” as folkloric, static, and erasable are rejected and redefined. In the bombazo Africanness lives, breathes, and is remembered as a dynamic connection to a history with contemporary relevance and intra-Caribbean cultural connections. In this framework, bomba is no longer stagnant and monolithic as Caridad described earlier but is a part of an expansive, fluid body of performance art. Exploring bomba's Afro-Caribbean and Central African roots asserts that "Africanness" is not only an everyday lived heritage and performative cultural element, but also a nuanced, Cariglobal phenomenon with multiple streams of influence.

In lieu of a transnational approach that centers those who have the economic means and access to travel to the global North, a Cariglobal approach to cultural analysis is also "concerned with people or phenomena that remain in and/or travel to the Caribbean. [It] is pan-Caribbean; it recognizes and takes seriously the linguistic, ethnic, racial, cultural, political, and economic differences within these areas, yet remains convinced that there is enough history and experience among Caribbean people to warrant an inclusive approach" (King 2014, 3–5). By situating bomba as a Cariglobal art form with both Kongo and French-Caribbean influences, our understanding of "lo africano" in Puerto Rico can expand beyond previous discourses as we approach the complexities of the vibrant, dynamic, and evolving African diaspora with more nuance. Further, despite the fixed definitions and characteristics ascribed to Africanness within the mestizaje ideal, bomba's historical branches reach beyond the geographic confines of the island and further back than the period of enslavement, reflecting an ideology of the archival oceanic process in which history and the present flow together to create the diasporic art form.

Marta Moreno Vega's work demonstrates the Kongo influence on religious practices in Puerto Rico in her article, "Espiritismo in the Puerto Rican Community: A New World Recreation with the Elements of Ancestor Worship." Moreno Vega explains that the last waves of enslaved Africans were brought to Puerto Rico from Central Africa: "Some of the names recorded [in the archives in Puerto Rico] include the following: Longo, Congo, Lingongo, Linga, Lambe, Liguelo and Dingongo..." signaling the ships' sites of origin (Moreno Vega 1999, 326). She goes on to articulate the intersections between Kongo religiosity and *Espiritismo* ancestor veneration practices and beliefs in Puerto Rican communities. Alongside direct Kongo population renewal that likely influenced bomba's origins, bomba's history features radical cultural processes and intra-Caribbean influences that have shaped its structure.

As I attended bomba performances and spoke to participants about bomba's specific African origins, I began to learn about the Kongo influence in Puerto Rico's cultural landscape more broadly. Since anthropologist Hal Barton published his work over 20 years ago, the academic study of bomba has begun to explore its central African Kongo roots, in contrast to bomba's previously assumed West African Ashanti roots (Barton 1995). A deeper examination of transcaribbean dance practices reveals significant similarities between bomba and other Kongo-derived dances in the region, further hinting at its roots. Nathaniel Hamilton Crowell, Jr. notes: "In Puerto Rican bomba and Martinican *bele lino* and *calenda ticano*, as is common in the Congo, the dancer leads the chief drummer in setting the rhythm" (Crowell 2002, 12). Additionally, in Martinican dance, the spectators who often become participants form a circle around the dancing individuals or partners, and the steps are similar to those of *bele* in Trinidad and *bomba* in Puerto Rico (Cyrille 2002). The Kongo-derived dances in Guadeloupe also have strong similarities; the *gwoka* in Guadeloupe, where the drummer follows the dancer, is believed to have been present in Kongo secret societies. The Kongo rite in Haiti and *Palo Mayombe*, a secret society in Cuba, also shares elements with other Kongo-derived dances across the Caribbean.

In a personal communication with Alex LaSalle, a renowned Puerto Rican scholar, bomba dancer, and founder and director of the Alma Moyó Afro-Puerto Rican bomba group in New York, he confirmed that bomba has several Kongo carry-overs. As a practitioner of a Kongo-derived Afro-Cuban initiation system, he is fluent in Kikongo and knowledgeable about the dances and customs of the culture. Many of the songs in bomba, he told me, are in Kikongo and about the Kongo region, not in French Creole as many people assume. Yet, dances and linguistics traces of the French Caribbean have informed bomba and its evolution.

In an interview I conducted with Caridad, she explained:

...it was after the revolution in Haiti. Bomba was influenced by the French people who fled Haiti for New Orleans and the rest of the Caribbean. Many came here too. Bomba is greatly influenced by the slaves and masters who mixed with other black people from here. And they practiced the drums, so many of our songs are in [French] creole. [Caridad]

Many participants in the bomba community understood that bomba had Caribbean influences, and they did not use "Africa" as a reductionist term to describe its place of origin. Raúl, another teacher and leader in the community, describes the intercultural flow of French creole influences within bomba of the 19th century:

There's theories that from Africa it went to Haiti and from Haiti off to the other islands which is a theory that kind of makes a little more sense to me because of the Afro-French influence. That's real deep in bomba... Because first of all the rhythms, all the names of the rhythms are all in Creole, like they're not in Spanish. And those Creole rhythms are actually the same names; you can find them all over the island, so all the way up to New Orleans where you find yubá. And it comes from that same root. And there's a lot of the French-speaking Africans in New Orleans, as you know. So it's real interesting how that migration went around that whole area oblivious to what was going on. [Raúl]

Caridad and Raúl name specific islands to elucidate the Cariglobal cultural connections between Puerto Rican bomba and other art forms in the area. The archival oceanic leads us to reflect on the ancestral legacies of the art form alongside its potential to transform itself in varying contexts to serve the populations who use the rhythms, songs, and dancing to engage African diasporic legacies of survival. The archival oceanic frames bomba as an art form enriched with ancestral memory and legacy through multiple cultural streams of influence and debunks the deeply entrenched myth of unidimensional Africanness in Puerto Rico's historical legacy.

4. Performance and Memory

The Cepeda family of Santurce, an area of San Juan, is well known for public performances of bomba. Families like this one reflect an archival oceanic praxis because, as careful culture-bearers, they keep alive ancestral memory through maintenance of the form in Puerto Rico. As a result, bomba has become a well-known component of Puerto Rican history, as well as a site of visible and tangible Africanness. Appearing on televisions and stages around the island and the U.S., the Cepedas have become a representation of the historic "lo africano" in Puerto Rico when erasure and racism sought to ignore African residuals on the islands. At the urging of the Instituto de Cultura Puertorriqueña (ICPR), the Cepeda family became the face of Puerto Rican bomba. Caridad described the formation of the Puerto Rican ideology of race through the ICPR's government-designed campaign of the 1950s:

> This image of Puerto Rico from 1952 onward reflected what was packaged [and distributed] through the Institute of Culture. They wanted to represent and strengthen this propaganda. As colonized people, we questioned where we came from. This is the big turning point between how we were before and how we are today. [Caridad]

Caridad's explanation demonstrates the ICPR's need to crystallize Puerto Rican identity as an ideal mix of three racial groups, a notion that remains in the psyche of Puerto Ricans today. The inclusion of bomba as part of the national racial discourse, with the help of the Cepeda family, led to the performance of bomba as a folkloric dance form instead of a site of improvisation and liberation that bomba had been in the past. The hypervisibility of bomba and Africanness and the Cepeda's shift to the main stage are not necessarily negative, however. It was actually important to the present state of bomba as a representation of Puerto Rican culture. As Caridad explained:

> That was the first time bomba began to be practiced for the Other, for the enjoyment of the Other. For another to see you sitting and dancing. But they don't understand what is happening there. [They say] "Look at the pretty skirts!" But, I consider that perspective to be racist and superficial. I'm not saying it's wrong that the Cepeda family paid for it and it's something negative, no. For me, the Cepeda family was very important. And the fact that bomba is practiced the way it is practiced today, they no doubt had a hand in that. [Caridad]

Performing Africanness

Transitioning from a social pastime for enslaved Africans and means for enjoyment, bomba became one of the folkloric art forms that would signify Puerto Rico's African heritage in festivals and performances not only for other Puerto Ricans, but also monied tourists who sought to "experience" the culture. It should be noted that bomba families were instrumental in the survival of the art form when it fell from national popularity before the middle of the century. The history of the Cepeda family as the public-facing culture-bearers (unlike the more insular Ayala family, which I will discuss later) has shaped its role in the San Juan bomba community. Bomba schools run by members of the famous family educate a racially and economically diverse group of Puerto Ricans about their African heritage, using performance as a tool for keeping the legacy alive. Many of the participants would not identify as black, yet they honor an African heritage as part of the historical legacy of Puerto Rican identity. Performing Africanness thus becomes a way to celebrate part of the one's distant history, "lo africano" that lives deep within one's blood and is brought to the forefront to emerge in the batey. At a bombazo hosted inside the dance school of Tata Cepeda of the famous Cepeda family, I observed the typical posturing and movement of those who dance bomba in the Santurce area—this style is more formal than in Loíza. Having visited the school earlier, I knew that the high-priced classes were attended by Puerto Ricans who wished to learn bomba from one of the best dancers on the island.

The primo *(lead drummer) watched intently, and his gaze remained strong and unbroken as new dancers entered the circle and moved with controlled, upright torsos and skirts that flowed with the small flicks of their wrists.*

The participants at this bombazo seemed to have been Tata's students; many of them knew each other, greeting each other with the Puerto Rican customary kiss on the face. They were all well-dressed before changing into their colorful bomba skirts. There were four *buleadores* and one main drummer. The drumming group was intergenerational and included a female drummer (which is rare, except for in Raúl's classes.) Tata led the *coro* (chorus) through the typical call and response style as she played the customary single maraca. One small girl, who appeared to be a white Puerto Rican, danced in the circle the most often; perhaps her youth did not allow her to recognize the importance of taking turns in the middle of the circle. The first adults to *pasear* (pass through the bombazo) were a couple, a man and a woman. The couple saluted the drum and they began to dance. Her partner then took his turn. He had white hair and moved with grace, confidence, and smoothness, yet he was somewhat stiff. He was the only older man who danced that evening. The couple ended their dance together. A few other little girls began to dance, students from Tata's children's class. After they took their turn, a mother entered the circle and danced with her daughter in her arms. She had dark skin, and so did her daughter. They did not have skirts and looked very different than the sea of lighter faces in the room; she appeared to be the only black woman who danced that night.

The song's rhythm slowed to a stop and then a new one started, like an ocean wave receding and then a new one pushing upon the shoreline. The drummers began to play the *quembé* rhythm. A younger man, perhaps a teen or in his early 20s, began to dance. He was both serious and deft. He took out a cloth and wiped his brow as part of the dance performance. I noticed that he was also one of the singers who responded to Tata's lyrical lead. The *primo* (lead drummer) watched intently, and his gaze remained strong and unbroken as new dancers entered the circle and moved with controlled, upright torsos and skirts that flowed with the small flicks of their wrists. The movements could have been carefully choreographed as each dancer pulled from the same arsenal of steps I had been taught in my dance classes with Caridad and Raúl. At Tata's school, the bomba rhythms poured into the cobblestone streets that run between the structures in Puerto Rico's government center, though the dancers remain inside the walls of the studio. Here, the Cepeda bomba style that has always dominated the San Juan area influences the participants as they tell embodied stories that intersect colonialism, race, and class.

The archival oceanic is present in this bombazo in Old San Juan and in the performance of the Cepeda family on national television, reminding us that Puerto Rico's colonial history under Spanish and then U.S. control is one of protest and power. Because the archival oceanic is a space of living memory, "lo africano" is not relegated to Africanness in the ancestral past; it lives in the everyday fiber of material being, shifting and flowing not only through veins of Puerto Ricans, but through the living culture of bomba. Even amongst the buildings that provided fortress for Spanish settler colonizers, the performance of Africanness, punctuated by Spanish "colonial" posturing and dress, is a tangible representation of ancestral lineage and convergence of cultures without erasing "lo africano." The archival oceanic exists as a site of powerful physical and nonphysical remnants of Africanness, which materialize during the moments in which bomba ebbs and flows through the veins of the island's culture, then emerging as a powerful force which keeps swelling and subsiding through performance of folklore.

Localized Blackness

Loíza, a town about 15 miles down the coast from the touristy, wealthy Isla Verde community, is widely considered a fixed locale of Blackness because its population is of more obvious African descent. It is, in fact, one of the few sites of a localized manifestation of African elements that still remain on the island. Because the area has less infrastructural development than other parts of the island, many critics believe that the town's status as the poorest in Puerto Rico is due to structural racism and a general lack of concern for the area. (Hernández Hiraldo 2006). "Black sites" like Loíza, are kept separate from the popular understanding of what it means to be modern and Puerto Rican.

Conversations with Isar during my field research facilitated my understanding of bomba as a site where Puerto Ricans center black bodies as the most authentic form to practice bomba, yet the characteristics of bomba are crystallized into the Puerto Rican imaginary as unchanging and static. Blackness becomes tangible in places like Loíza, yet *blanquemiento* (whitening) and racism localize Blackness only to these geographic areas, separate from the larger island. During the 2011 conversation mentioned earlier Isar suggested I consider the ways that bomba, as an art form, is associated with Loíza as a site of Blackness and how people imagine Loíza through bomba. She explained, "Loíza gives more authenticity to Blackness; people can authenticate what they are saying."

As I mentioned earlier, during my field research it was not uncommon for people to tell me "black people live in Loíza" and point to the town as a fixed area with clear social and physical boundaries. The complicated dialectic of tangible yet localized Blackness in Loíza has informed the nature of bomba's development in the area. On one hand, Loíza is an undeniable site of long-standing communities with lived black embodiment at their core. Loiceños have their own unique cultural formations, webs of interrelationship, and daily experiences of Puerto Ricanness. Caridad described the close-knit familial atmosphere of Loíza when she said, "The people in Loíza still maintain—different from the city—a village mindset. Everyone knows each other. Everyone knows what goes on everywhere."

I experienced very similar articulations of community formation when I lived with a family in Loíza. Black embodiment is represented in the wider community in ways that it is not in the more racially and class variegated Santurce. Blackness is made tangible in Loíza through embodiment. On the other hand, through places like Loíza, Blackness can be contained and localized to specific spaces. In this process of localization, racist discourses erase, hide, silence, and keep Blackness separate from the image of "true" Puerto Ricanness.

While I understood that Loíza is site of Blackness and separate from "true Puerto Ricanness" in the larger cultural imaginary, I began to learn about the ways that Loíza's bomba legacy reifies this separation even within the bomba community. Similar to Loíza, Blackness is both localized and made tangible in bomba through black bodies in rhythm, flow, interrelationship, and the heightened visibility of black embodiment.

Because bomba in Loíza is considered more authentic, Blackness is made tangible through the dancing bodies engaging the "more African" performance style.

The renowned Ayala family, far more insular than the Cepedas, are from the geographically and ideologically separated Loíza. They have maintained the cultural lineage of the art form in the town and have kept prominent the preservationism and authenticity in the bomba community. Likewise, bomba participants with whom I spoke envisioned *seis corrido,* the traditional bomba style of Loíza, as something different and set apart from other bomba rhythms in the same ways the town is set apart from the larger Puerto Rican imaginary. Because bomba in Loíza is considered more authentic, Blackness is made tangible through the dancing bodies engaging the "more African" performance style.

When I finally had the chance to attend a class with Caridad, I learned more about the differences in Loíza-based bomba performance. The class was held in a dive bar with a stage for local bands to perform for Old San Juan audiences; the space was poorly lit, had concrete floors, and there were large bright paintings on the walls. On that day, we focused mainly on the bomba style. We lined up in rows behind Caridad as she demonstrated the *paso básicos* and her drummer, just the primo, played. She explained that seis corrido was different from the more colonial-inspired bomba form in the rest of the island, noting that seis corrido is more aggressive, originated in Loíza, and doesn't use skirts. Bomba is a part of the culture in Loíza, Caridad tells the class; even in dance, it seems, Loíza is set apart. Caridad taught about how to enter the batey in seis corrido: one must circle the current dancer twice, breaking contact with the drummer in a "move over girl" fashion. Then the drum/dance conversation begins.

The Ayalas of Loíza are living, embodied, tangible representations of the intersection of Blackness and Puerto Ricanness. This family uses the fluid engagement of dance and communalism through social gatherings to perpetuate ancestral legacies of survival. The archival oceanic provides a hermeneutic to understand the ways that bomba community gathering provides a platform for black embodiment to be reimagined and self-designed in a framework that honors, rather than erases, Blackness.

5. Dance Differentials

Raúl ran a weekly bomba drumming and movement class at a dance studio in Santurce. He had a low haircut, was light-skinned, and wore glasses. I often saw him in a t-shirt that hung over his thin frame. Raúl was originally from Orlando, Florida, and had a Puerto Rican parent. He had moved back to the island several years before to learn more about his culture and, after proving himself, had become one of the leaders in bomba. Like Caridad, he had his own bomba group and was a patient teacher for those of us who knew little about the art form.

Raúl informed me of the differences in bomba between the two areas represented by the Cepedas and the Ayalas. This night he had a medium brown-skinned woman teaching the dancing portion of the class. She demonstrated for us the pasos básicos (basic steps) for *sicá* and *yubá*, which are salutes to the drummer as one begins one's solo dance. The brown-skinned woman reviewed all of the basic rhythms before having me perform the basic steps for the student who chose to take the drumming portion of the class. The buladores, the larger groups of background drummers who keep the rhythm, had lower pitched drums. The primo, the main drummer, had a higher pitched, smaller drum. I learned though action that this is the one with whom you keep eye contact.

In an interview, Raúl discussed the Cepeda and the Ayala bomba families. Despite their differences, both groups influenced his training and entry into the bomba community. Raúl explained the differences thusly:

There's different dynamics of how they play, totally. How they work as family units, there's different dynamics. As you can see the Cepedas have a bunch of offshoot groups. The Ayalas kind of have one group and they've kind of stuck together. Singing, dancing is totally different. I'm sure you've noticed that too. [Raúl]

There were indeed noticeable differences between the Cepeda and the Ayala branches of performance styles. The seis corrido rhythm, which originated in Loíza and is maintained by the Ayala family, encourages performative fluidity, improvisation, and African stylistics in ways that other rhythms do not. For many participants, *bomba* in Loíza is "more authentic" than the more "colonialized" styles in places like Santurce and Ponce. Raúl explained:

> **Yeah, the dancing in Loíza is obviously more grounded [or low to the ground].... In my opinion more what it was, or more true to what it probably was when it first got here, [when] it first started getting spread around Puerto Rico. And that's obviously because Loíza was separate. Then the stuff that happens over here (in Santurce) with the skirt and the posture and stuff like that, in my opinion is more like imitating high society dances if you want to say that, like contradanza. [Raúl]**

In the styles of bomba that participants described as "more colonial" or that Raúl calls "high society dances" that developed on various parts of the island, the torso is more upright, and movement is more controlled. Within bomba in Loíza, however, the movements are closer to the ground with looser bodily form and much faster footwork, akin to traditional African styles that feature dancers engaging the music with quick movements of the hips, a lower torso, and bent legs. When this significantly faster rhythm begins to play, the fast-paced, polyphonic cadence insists that one move quickly and energetically, commanding the attention of those who watch.

During my fieldwork, I was a participant observer in many different bombazos. The one in Loíza and the one in Old San Juan hosted by Tata Cepeda's school told different stories of the historical influences on raced, classed, and gendered identities. In San Juan, students attending Tata's Cepeda's school and subsequently the bombazo were more likely to have a higher socioeconomic status than the ones attending the bombazo in the Loíza community. It is significant that many people in the San Juan bombazo were able to pay for the classes where they would learn the movements expected of a trained bomba dancer. In Loíza, a town known for its poverty and lack of resources, the dancers were less likely to have been taught in a studio. These bomba lessons received outside of a formal setting were more likely to inspire unique personalized movements. It was in these spaces where the performances veered from the rigid boundaries of prescribed bomba movements that are taught in a classroom that the tone of the bombazo could shift from performance for spectators to transformative event.

Blackness in the Batey

One Sunday afternoon, a bomba group called Tambores Calientes organized a community bombazo in the Pinoñes area of Loíza behind El Boriqua, the most popular kiosko in Loíza. They had four drummers and microphones behind them. The drummers sang along in the typical call-and-response format songs. Tambores performed demonstrations of each rhythm one by one, calling them out before they played them; however, they mostly played seis corrido. The crowd members took turns entering the circle and dancing. No one had a skirt except for one woman who passed her skirt to a friend to use. The crowd was welcoming and anyone could join. The community was engaged as the gathering was held out in the open.

The moves in the Loíza bombazo were much less calculated than in the Old San Juan event described earlier. An old man drunkenly staggered to the middle of the circle and began to move to a stiff, staccato rhythm. He had his own style of intoxicated moves. Several younger men danced, one with the more delicate movements characteristic of female dancers. The loud drumming cut through the open air and freed itself like the dancers who moved as they pleased. It was not contained by indoor walls like the Tata Cepeda's bombazo. One could hear the drums as they drove on the road usually packed with cruisers on the weekend. This was a community event.

In Loíza, black bodies move in and out of the bomba circle, and movement is less rigid and confined than in San Juan.

A bomba classmate of mine from San Juan was there, and she asked me why I was "not out there dancing." I admitted to her that I was too shy to dance in the circle outside of the classroom environment. She pointed out that the dancers in the batey were not doing movements that we learned in class. I realized at that particular bombazo that there is something different about learning bomba in community and family gatherings instead of in classrooms. In Loíza, black bodies move in and out of the bomba circle, and movement is less rigid and confined than in San Juan. As mentioned, bomba performance in Loíza does not have the same type of upright, rigid posturing and prescribed dance moves defined by many people as "more colonial." Those who entered the circle to dance were more inclined to develop their own style and expression. Dance becomes a creative strategy of resistance for black Puerto Ricans who are subject to the politics of erasure and whose materiality is often bound by the rigid ideologies associated with Blackness in the Puerto Rican imaginary. The fluidity and dynamism of the black dancing body in the batey represents the archival oceanic at work. The materiality of the archive and transforming power of the oceanic emerge in the Loíza bombazo where mostly black Puerto Ricans converge in order to free themselves through movement and communalism. The black bodies in motion become a living archive.

6. Bomba as Religious Experience

What are other implications for the archival oceanic in bomba? Specifically, how might memory and healing inform each other in the context of the batey? While a participant observer, I noticed the mood of the batey beginning to reflect that of ecstatic religious experience in other parts of the African diaspora. Although the bombazo often begins as a social event or as "secular entertainment with aesthetic expression," it moves steadily toward religious experience as intensity builds like a wave that breaks once it crosses a threshold into the realm of the spiritual (Daniel 2011, 144). After the initial rhythms set the mood for the event, it was common for a shift to occur where dancers appeared to be in a trance-like state while moving within the circle of spectators. Raúl describes this "tranciness":

I just think it has that whole root, like you hear the singing and the gospel singing and it's totally [like] bomba and it's how they feel it...tranciness...and I've gone to churches in the [U.S] south and been part of that and just been blown away and feel certain things that I felt over here, of that tranciness and getting into it and just letting go. I think that's what ties in religion and bomba. One of the things that really ties in is the trance. The rhythms are all cycles and they're all trancy, they're all—you know just to separate and also the singing. It's real back and forth, back and forth.... And same with the gospel singing, they're singing so angelic on this level that you get so into that you see people starting to get into it and you're like dude that's Afro. That's not European stuff. That's real, what's going on right there. And I saw that from a young age. [Raúl]

The "tranciness" that Raúl describes, or moments of ecstatic worship found in bomba, connects it with other experiences within the African diaspora. Most notably, the spirit manifestation and embodied worship styles from Brazil to the U.S. south are characterized by fully engaged, rhythmic movement informed by music, song, and transcultural materialities. It is in these moments that religion and bomba do not just overlap, but the experience of bomba itself blurs the line between secular enjoyment and religious experience. Raúl describes his experience further:

I guess it would be more like a personal thing but for me, it would be a connection with God, with the earth, Gaia, all that energy and all the energy of the people who fell before us and who died before us and who are in the earth. It just has to do with all of that for me. Everyone else would have their own take on it and not in a religious [way] at all. I'm not into all that. It's all spiritual. It's all one god. It's all one. I try to leave my religion and stuff far away from this. I don't like having walls because I think that's what religion does a lot, puts walls and barriers on things. And this is like in my opinion nothing to do with religion. [Raúl]

I've always seen different colors and felt things and people are always saying when they dance bomba and I do too, I say it as well, me *curé*, I got cured. That's something here, *me quiero curar*, I want to play. It's a term that's used unconsciously but it's real. It's so real the way that we use it because it's like me cure, like I cured myself. I'm cured, that's what it is. That's what the word means. [Raúl]

Raúl's decision to "leave [his] religion and stuff far away" is informed by his belief that religion has impermeable walls and guidelines, something that he believes should not be a part of bomba. His use of the term "spiritual" demonstrates a differentiation from the term "religion." While I am hesitant to categorize bomba itself as religious, I characterize the participants' experiences as religious. As occurs in religious experiences, Raúl has "seen different colors" and "felt things," and experienced healing in the bombazo. Caridad's transition away from atheism was informed by bomba's ability to give her a new way to understand aspects of spirituality:

...the singing, dancing, and drums create the feeling you want to manifest.... Even I have had to recognize my spirituality through the practice of bomba. Before it, I was an atheist...all my life I was an atheist. Then bomba gave me another perspective of feeling energy and manifestation.... [Caridad]

Her new "perspective of feeling energy and manifestation" signals the presence of energetic power and transformational abilities of the art form. While bomba may not be religious, we see through Caridad's story that it has the capabilities to allow participants to feel an energetic power through its practice. At the moment when bomba becomes something more than entertainment or secular performance, participants are met with the power of healing and feelings of full-body enjoyment. This is the archival oceanic at work. While practitioners may not identify bomba with religion proper, the most transformative moments happen when the lines are blurred between artistic genre and religious experience. It is experiences like these that ebb toward ecstatic worship, mirroring the embodied religious experiences of the African diaspora.

7. Bomba, Ancestral Memory, and Healing

Healing processes in bomba are both related yet also in contrast to other religious rituals of healing in Puerto Rico, where a person seeking the restoration or maintenance of health consults an individual who has experience in these practices (Romberg 2003; Nuñez Molina 2001). I find parallels between bomba and other Puerto Rican traditions in which ancestral spirits play a role in these healing processes, specifically in the way that ancestral memory is key in participants' ability to finding healing through the practice of bomba. The power of bomba's therapeutic aspects is in the participants' ability to recall events, people, or places of significance while in the bomba circle, process the impactful emotions, and then move beyond the pain they once experienced. The archival oceanic reminds us not only that ancestral memory serves as an entry point for healing through bomba, but also that healing is a fluid process with "unclaimed richness for possibility" (Spillers 1987, 72). It was the process of recalling the fondness of those they had lost that helped them to engage their pain and aided in participants' healing.

Raquel Z. Rivera, in personal communication with bomba expert Alex LaSalle, has written about the relationship between memory and medicine in bomba (Rivera 2012). She writes, "LaSalle's exercise in memory is not bound by nationalist concerns.... He proposes bomba as 'medicine' not only for Puerto Rican African descendants but for all African descendants...” (Rivera 2012, 13). Rivera goes on to write that for LaSalle, African-derived religious practices have long been part of bomba and “paying homage to and communicating with deceased ancestors” is an integrated part of these religious practices (Rivera 2012, 14). Through memory, participants are transformed, their psyches are healed, and they experience freedom and a release from the worries that plague them every day. The powerful processes of memory, and honoring those who have died, link bomba to other African diaspora practices and religious traditions: “Remembrance in bomba, therefore, is not just an exercise in nostalgia. For many, it is not even much of a choice: it is a spiritual imperative. Given that the dead walk among the living, charged with guiding us just as we are charged with honoring them” (Rivera 2012, 14). Caridad explains,

> I learned from my children. [They are] six years to ten years old. It became easier to [heal from] violence through dance. [For one student] that was his life and suddenly he went out dancing a quembé or yubá very strongly, but perfectly. I asked, “Do you think of something to take you to this kind of emotion?” And he told me he thought about when his brother was killed. And he went out dancing bomba and danced with rage, suddenly the bomba worked as a therapy...and as a moment of relief that he did not have anywhere else. [Caridad]

The above passages depict specific ways participation in the bomba circle can help ease troubles that participants may encounter. In the first example, Caridad describes the ways she learns from the youth she teaches. They are able to express themselves through the various rhythms in bomba, particularly the stronger rhythms (as opposed to the smoother, slower ones). Each rhythm has a mood or purpose and memory plays a role in the healing process. Upon her asking the children what they think about while dancing, one of them explained that he is thinking about/remembering his brother who was murdered. For them, bomba functions as therapy because they are able to remember a painful past in order to move forward. Raúl described an important moment in the batey when a friends mom visited thusly,

> His mom came and everyone was down and then when we started playing. Everyone just connected, it was like for those two hours nothing else mattered. Everything was love and everyone was good, and it was a moment in time for all of us that just broke us out of that whole depression of what had happened and be like no, everything is okay. He’s here with us. It’s hard to explain but that would be in my opinion one of the times I was real strong that I felt it like that, like the whole week we were down and crying like man what’s this? What’s going on? I can’t believe this and all of a sudden we get together and play bomba and it was like he was there and it was great. [Raúl]

It's important for me because of what I was saying; it's like a healing genre. It gives people who aren't aware of the genre, aren't aware that we have this type of method of healing, the opportunity to be part of it and partake in it. [Raúl]

The experiences in the batey helped Raúl and his group of friends deal with the loss of a loved one. The acute memories of his friend allowed them to feel his ancestral presence in the bombazo after he had passed away. For these reasons, Raúl confirmed, bomba is a "healing genre." The archival oceanic— marked by ancestral memory *as a practice of healing*—becomes a method through which colonized peoples seek wholeness, practicing what Rivera names liberation myths, or the descriptions of the world through which African diasporic subjects seek to "control the present injustices...and... craft dreams of freedom for the future." In the archival oceanic, participants can engage the past and present as constructive tools for designing a future replete with "personal and collective liberation from oppression, injustice, sadness, and/or fear" and recognize that their circumstances as oppressed populations are not static (Rivera 2012, 9).

The Kongo cosmogram provides a helpful visual representation of the experiential shift for bomba participants who are able to access the realm of the sacred, and operationalize the archival oceanic. The cosmogram, accessed in Kongo-derived religious communities throughout the Caribbean, maps the development of the human across the cyclical process of life. One begins in the state of the unborn then cycles through childhood, adulthood, and then back to the state of "ancestorhood." The reincarnation cycle begins again. The cycle also reflects the path of the sun, traveling through the four stages of each full day before it makes its ascent again. Visually, the cosmogram is a "spherical image" divided into four even sections by a vertical and horizontal line (Stewart 2016, 12). Both the human and the sun are believed to travel counterclockwise through the cosmological map, with each point representing a state of existence. The lower half, or two bottom quadrants, is the immaterial realm of the ancestors, or the "kingdom of the dead" (Thompson 1983, 109). The top half is the realm of the living, material world. The middle horizontal line, then, is a transformational boundary. This boundary, or *kalunga*, represents the point where one shifts from living human to ancestor, material to immaterial.

Further, the potential for healing in bomba lies at the experiential point of kalunga, when the performance is no longer secular, but moves into spiritual experience.

In bomba, the point where the mood shifts from secular enjoyment to religious or spiritual experience can be imagined as kalunga in the Kongo cosmogram, and the richness of ancestral memory and healing in the archival oceanic. It is beyond the metaphorical point of kalunga, or the transitional barrier in the mood activity of the batey that true transformation takes place. Further, the potential for healing in bomba lies at the experiential point of kalunga, when the performance is no longer secular, but moves into spiritual experience. It is no coincidence, then, that the healing moments for my interviewees took place though the process of remembering deceased loved ones, or those who have moved beyond the land of the living to the land of ancestors. It is in these moments that one can access the healing and transformative power of bomba.

Beyond the transitional point of kalunga, when one is able to access the alternative realm of nonliving existence, healing through memory becomes the medicine. The healing is in spiritual, immaterial realm. It is important to note that I am not claiming that bomba participants are actively employing the Kongo cosmogram in bomba performance. Instead, I propose that the cosmogram as a visual representation can elucidate the connection between bomba performance, healing, remembering loved ones who have transitioned, and the potential of accessing the immaterial, spiritual realm.

8. Conclusion

Not unlike its historical role among enslaved populations in Puerto Rico, bomba remains a powerful cultural form in which participants can alter societal norms, engage ancestral memory, and gather for a communalistic engagement. Similar to folk religions on the island, bomba developed from the lived, oppressive experiences of the working class and enslaved Afro-Puerto Ricans and functioned as a form of resistance and healing. Bomba continues reflect as powerful element of Puerto Rican culture, but is also constructed as a site of negotiating both Blackness and Africanness. To be sure, in Puerto Rico "lo africano" or the African, is part of the national cultural identity. According to popular discourses on race and ethnicity in Puerto Rico, "lo africano" does not live and thrive in contemporary society, Africanness is seen as a distant part of Puerto Rican identity. Paradoxically, it is still present and undeniable. Blackness is often distanced from the popular culture and localized in specific regions, towns, neighborhoods, and bodies across the country. As a result of this distancing of Blackness from the larger Puerto Rican culture (and simultaneously localizing Blackness only to certain sites), Afro-Puerto Ricans are often marginalized and exoticized.

During my time as a participant observer, I learned that bomba is more than just a site of historicity or a performed interrelationship between a black drummer and dancer. These ways of viewing the activities in the batey limits its reach and influence. The role of the bombazo in participants' lives reaches beyond its immediate songs, dances, or its evidence of black African historical elements. A bomba gathering pragmatically serves as the site and an activity of healing through ancestral memory. The moments where the mood shifts from the secular to the sacred—represented by kalunga in the Kongo cosmogram—can be liberatory for those in the bomba community. A reflection on the ocean, which began this article, also serves to conclude this work. Perhaps Omise'eke Tinsley' words, "The wateriness is metaphor and history, too" (2008, 191), can further inform a new way of imagining the power of the art form. The archival oceanic offers an approach for reading African diasporic religious and cultural practices as well as those rituals that remain in their shadow, those activities—like bomba—that bear the distinguishable features of a transatlantic imprint through movement, music, or participant disposition.

NOTES

[1] Although readers may be able to identify these community leaders by their descriptions, I chose these pseudonyms in adherence to the interview guidelines of the Institutional Review Board.

REFERENCES

Alamo-Pastrana, Carlos. 2009. Con El Eco de Los Barriles: Race, Gender and the Bomba Imaginary in Puerto Rico. *Identities* 16(5), 573–600.

Alexander, M. Jacqui. 2005. *Pedagogies of Crossing: Meditations on Feminism, Sexual Politics, Memory, and the Sacred*. Durham, NC: Duke University Press.

Barton, Halbert. 1995. The Drum-Dance Challenge: An Anthropological Study of Gender, Race and Class Marginalization of Bomba in Puerto Rico. Ph.D. dissertation, Cornell University.

Briggs, Laura. 2002. *Reproducing Empire: Race and Sex, Science and U.S. Imperialism in Puerto Rico*. Berkley: University of California Press.

Crowell, Nathaniel H., Jr. 2002. What Is Congolese in Caribbean Dance. In *Caribbean Dance from Abakuá to Zouk: How Movement Shapes Identity*, ed. Susanna Sloat. 11–22. Gainesville: University Press of Florida.

Cyrille, Dominique. 2002. Sa Ki Ta Nou (This Belongs to Us): Creole Dances of the French Caribbean. In *Caribbean Dance from Abakuá to Zouk : How Movement Shapes Identity*, ed. Susanna Sloat. 221–46. Gainesville: University Press of Florida.

Daniel, Yvonne. 2011. *Caribbean and Atlantic Diaspora Dance: Igniting Citizenship*. Urbana: University of Illinois Press.

Davies, Carole Boyce. 2013. *Caribbean Spaces: Escapes from Twilight Zones*. Urbana: University of Illinois Press.

Dinzey-Flores, Zaire Zenit. 2013. *Locked In, Locked Out: Gated Communities in a Puerto Rican City*. Philadelphia: University of Pennsylvania Press.

Dulitzky, Ariel E. 2005. A Region in Denial: Racial Discrimination and Racism in Latin America. In *Neither Enemies nor Friends: Latinos, Blacks, Afro-Latinos*, eds. Anani Dzidzienyo and Suzanne Oboler. 39–60. New York: Palgrave Macmillan.

Findlay, Eileen. 1999. *Imposing Decency: The Politics of Sexuality and Race in Puerto Rico, 1870-1920*. Durham, NC: Duke University Press.

Freud, Sigmund. 1962. *Civilization and Its Discontents*. Translated by James Strachey. New York: W.W. Norton & Company.

Godreau, Isar. 2015. *Scripts of Blackness: Race, Cultural Nationalism, and U.S. Colonialism in Puerto Rico*. Urbana: University of Illinois Press.

Gomez, Michael Angelo. 2001. *Exchanging Our Country Marks the Transformation of African Identities in the Colonial and Antebellum South*. Chapel Hill: University of North Carolina Press.

Hernández Hiraldo, Samiri. 2006. *Black Puerto Rican Identity and Religious Experience*. Gainesville: University Press of Florida.

King, Rosamond S. 2016. *Island Bodies: Transgressive Sexualities in the Caribbean Imagination*. Gainesville: University Press of Florida.

Moreno Vega, Marta. 1999. Espiritismo in the Puerto Rican Community: A New World Recreation With the Elements of Kongo Ancestor Worship. *Journal of Black Studies* 29(3), 325–53.

Rivera, Raquel Z. 2012. New York Afro-Puerto Rican and Afro-Dominican Roots Music: Liberation Mythologies and Overlapping Diasporas. *Black Music Research Journal* 32(2), 3–24.

Rivera-Rideau, Petra R. 2015. *Remixing Reggaetón: The Cultural Politics of Race in Puerto Rico.* Durham, NC: Duke University Press.

Rivero, Yeidy M. 2005. *Tuning out Blackness: Race and Nation in the History of Puerto Rican Television.* Durham, NC: Duke University Press.

Rodríguez-Silva, Ileana M. 2012. *Silencing Race: Disentangling Blackness, Colonialism, and National Identities in Puerto Rico.* New York: Palgrave Macmillan.

Romberg, Raquel. 2010. *Healing Dramas: Divination and Magic in Modern Puerto Rico.* Austin: University of Texas Press.

Sharpe, Christina Elizabeth. 2016. *In the Wake: On Blackness and Being.* Durham, NC: Duke University Press.

Spillers, Hortense J. 1987. Mama's Baby, Papa's Maybe: An American Grammar Book. *Diacritics* 17(2), 65–81.

Stewart, Dianne M. 2016. Kumina: A Spiritual Vocabulary of Nationhood in Victorian Jamaica. In *Victorian Jamaica,* eds. Tim Barringer and Wayne Modest. 602–21 Durham, NC: Duke University Press.

Thompson, Robert Farris. 1983. *Flash of the Spirit: African and Afro-American Art and Philosophy.* New York: Random House.

Tinsley, Omise'eke Natasha. 2008. Black Atlantic, Queer Atlantic: Queer Imaginings of the Middle Passage. *GLQ: A Journal of Lesbian and Gay Studies* 14(2–3), 191–215.

VOLUME XXXI • NUMBER II • SUMMER 2019

La música como herramienta política de los *condenados*: un acercamiento a la bomba puertorriqueña

JUAN GUDIÑO CABRERA

ABSTRACT

Puerto Rican bomba is part of a constructed and institutionalized historical heritage that requires a decolonial look. This essay rehearses a rapprochement towards a genre that transcends being posited as merely "national culture." I will demonstrate how bomba can be the subject of what Aníbal Quijano calls "the coloniality of power:" simultaneously an instrument of subversion and of resistance, or a tool of decolonial political and identity struggles. I will then address the issue of including this music in the racialized creation of "puertorricanness." I will examine how this discursive apparatus emerges out of a state-sponsored racialized identity. Finally, I will explain how bomba is not simply a music or a dance genre, but a way of seeing the world, of expressing oneself politically, and of crafting historical memory of "the other," an other that has been further "othered" by the state and by Puerto Rican society more broadly. [Keywords: Puerto Rican bomba, decolonial thinking, cultural nationalism, great Puerto Rican family, modernity/coloniality, race/racism]

The author (juan.gudino03@gmail.com) is an independent scholar based in Puerto Rico. He has a bachelor's degree in political science with an emphasis on comparative politics and international relations from the University of Puerto Rico, Río Piedras. Among his research interests are cultural policies, cultural management and administration, decolonial thinking, ethnomusicology, and music therapy. He is a workshop facilitator and a dance and percussion instructor at the Dr. Modesto Cepeda Bomba and Plena Cultural Center, in Villa Palmeras, Santurce.

I. Planteamientos preliminares

En este ensayo exploratorio pretendo realizar un breve análisis de la música africana-boricua bajo la mirada de la subversión y resistencia como herramienta de lucha política e identitaria. Por ello, creo necesario partir desde el análisis del pensamiento decolonial para *re-pensar* la bomba en Puerto Rico. Abordaré el tema de la inclusión de esta música en la creación racializada de la puertorriqueñidad como esta surge de una identidad estatizada. Explicaré cómo la bomba no es sencillamente un género musical o de danza sino una visión de mundo, de expresión política y de memoria histórica tanto *otra* como *otroeada* por el estado y por la sociedad puertorriqueña. También analizaré cómo la bomba sumultáneamente sirve de instrumento de resistencia descolonial más allá de cómo el discurso de cultura nacional la intenta encasillar.

II. El pensamiento decolonial como una contra-respuesta hacia el pensamiento hegemónico-moderno-occidental

"Me quieren hacer pensar que soy parte de una trilogía racial
donde to' el mundo es igual sin trato especial..."
—Tego Calderón, "Loíza"

Para poder enmarcar la problematización de cómo el significado de la bomba en Puerto Rico, dentro del imaginario auspiciado por las instituciones culturales estatales y bajo el discurso del "nacionalismo cultural", es profundamente colonial, tenemos que adentrarnos en la crítica de la modernidad/colonialidad utilizando el pensamiento decolonia*l*.[1] No obstante, debemos conocer los inicios de la primera idea, categoría y práctica social —previamente inexistente— de la modernidad, la raza (Quijano 1991, 1–2). Ese hecho histórico de conquistas, esclavitud y muertes a finales del siglo XV, determinó no solo un posicionamiento de poder del colonizador, sino que determinó la evaluación, el aprendizaje a lo largo de toda la historia del conjunto de especies y la subjetividad de las mismas. No es que la desigualdad humana haya nacido a la par con este hecho histórico. Empero, esta nueva categoría, trascendió y transformó esas desigualdades, causando una diferenciación en términos naturales —un ser humano es superior y el otro es un objeto, una cosa— y propició la creación y producción de nuevas identidades históricas (Quijano 2014, 757).

Estas relaciones de dominación están enmarcadas en lo que Quijano denomina como la colonialidad del poder (Quijano 1991, 2). Según Quijano, este patrón de poder "se funda en la imposición de una clasificación racial/étnica de la población del mundo, y opera en cada uno de los planos, ámbitos y dimensiones, materiales y subjetivas, de la existencia cotidiana y a escala social" (Quijano 2007, 93). A la vez que, "establece la idea de que hay diferencias de naturaleza biológica dentro de la población del planeta, asociadas necesariamente a la capacidad de desarrollo cultural, mental en general" (Quijano 1999, 6). Anteriormente, la división de la especie humana se plasmaba en dominador-dominado. Una vez acuñada la idea de raza, la especie humana se re-clasificaría dentro de esta práctica, aunque sin obviar el elemento dominador-dominado, es decir, se constituye un nuevo patrón histórico de poder al determinar que unas personas son "naturalmente" inferiores a otras en todo lo que constituye la cotidianidad de la vida humana (Castro 2005; Maldonado-Torres 2013; Mignolo 2003; Quijano 2000). La creación de este patrón de dominación estructural supone la noción del racismo. No debemos olvidar que antes de la concepción racista por color de piel, tenemos la concepción racista por religión donde se destacan los primeros debates sobre la especie humana. Aquí sigo las aportaciones de Ramón Grosfoguel cuando menciona:

> El gran debate de los primeros cincuenta años del siglo XVI español era si los "indios" tenían alma o no. La categoría de "indio" constituye una nueva invención identitaria que homogeneiza toda una heterogeneidad de identidades a partir de la idea errada de los españoles de creerse haber llegado a la India. Ese debate fue el primer debate racista en la historia mundial y la identidad de "indio" fue la primera identidad moderna. La pregunta sobre si los "indios" tenían alma o no era ya una pregunta racista que remitía directamente en la época a la pregunta de si eran humanos o animales [...] El resultado del juicio en la Escuela de Salamanca en 1552 es también conocido: el estado imperial español decide que los "indios" tienen alma, pero son bárbaros por cristianizar. Por tanto, es un pecado a los ojos de Dios esclavizarlos [...].

Más adelante en su escrito continúa argumentando que:

> Los "indios" pasaron de trabajo esclavo a una nueva forma de trabajo coercitivo conocido como la "encomienda". Desde entonces el imperio español re-articuló la división internacional del trabajo a partir de la idea de raza de una manera más sistemática. Mientras los "indios" hacían trabajo forzado en la "encomienda", el trabajo esclavo se asignaba a los "africanos" que eran clasificados como "pueblos sin alma" [...] Con la esclavización africana en las Américas el discurso racista religioso se transformó en discurso racista de color. (Grosfoguel 2012, 90–1)

Es en este momento donde se circunscribe todo un andamiaje de esclavitud por concepto de raza y color, entendiendo el racismo como una jerarquía-institucional-estructural de poder donde se denota la superioridad e inferioridad de todas las formas de existencias del ser humano. Esta estructura institucional de poder desprende la naturalidad del ser humano y lo clasifica como humano o no-humano. El mismo condicionado, definiendo y delimitando la medida de lo humano, zona del ser, y lo no-humano, zona del no-ser (Gordon 2009, 217). Esas formas de existencias que priorizan formas de pensar, de sentir, de actuar; formas de vidas o nociones occidentales, son "superiores" al resto (zona del no-ser o formas otras de existencias[2]). Ya el objeto del racismo deja de ser el hombre particular y sí una cierta manera de existir delimitando la subjetividad-personalidad del racializado-colonizado (Fanon 1956, 38–44).

Estas relaciones de dominación y poder crean la base para la justificación de una estructura de dominio colonial y en ciertas especificidades: la epistemológica (colonialidad del saber) y la ontológica (colonialidad del ser). En el escrito "(Re) pensamiento crítico y (de)colonialidad", Catherine Walsh aborda el concepto de la colonialidad del saber[3] entendida como "la represión de otras formas de producción del conocimiento (que no sean blancas, europeas y "científicas"), elevando una perspectiva eurocéntrica del conocimiento y negando el legado intelectual de los pueblos indígenas y negros, reduciéndolos como primitivos" (2005, 19–20). Una de las acciones de esta estructura de poder, es la creación de "*categorías binarias*: oriente-occidente, primitivo-civilizado, irracional-racional, mágico/mítico-científico y tradicional-moderno, que justifican la superioridad e inferioridad —razón y no razón, humanización y deshumanización (colonialidad del ser)— y que suponen el eurocentrismo como perspectiva hegemónica del conocimiento (colonialidad del saber)" (Quijano, 2000, 210–1, citado en Walsh 2010, 90). Estas categorías binarias una vez instauradas como hegemónicas, se des-naturalizan y des-valorizan todo modo otro de sentir, pensar, conocer y disfrutar la vida. No se re-conocen las formas otras de "inteligencia" o "razón" y se sigue proliferando y legitimando la retórica moderna como pensamiento único-universal por las universidades occidentalizadas (Grosfoguel 2013, 51–6).

Boaventura de Sousa Santos, indica que estas acciones tuvieron orígenes en lo que define como "epistemicidio". Se trata de la destrucción y exterminio de formas otras de crear y transmitir conocimientos propios de los pueblos, causadas a raíz del colonialismo (Santos 2010, 7–8). Grosfoguel nos habla sobre cuatro eventos que constituyeron la justificación cartesiana del "yo pienso, luego existo" originaria del "yo conquisto, luego existo"[4] y el "yo exterminio, luego existo"; uno de estos fue contra los africanos, con el comercio de cautivos y su esclavización:

> Se prohibió a los africanos en el continente americano que pensaran, rezaran o practicaran sus cosmologías, conocimientos y visiones de mundo. Se los sometió a un régimen de racismo epistémico que proscribió su conocimiento autónomo. La inferioridad epistémica fue un argumento crucial usado para aducir la inferioridad social biológica por debajo de la línea de lo humano. (Grosfoguel 2013, 38–9).

Por ejemplo, la filosofía cartesiana del "yo pienso, luego existo/soy" selló una complejidad no reconocida en dicha formulación mediante la noción de que "otros no son" o están desprovistos de ser: "Yo pienso (otros no piensan o no piensan adecuadamente), luego existo/soy (otros no son, están desprovistos de ser, no deben existir o son dispensables)" (Maldonado-Torres 2007, 144). Aquí se circunscribe la otra esfera del dominio colonial, la colonialidad del ser. Continuando con las aportaciones de Walsh, si se toma conjuntamente las anteriores colonialidades (del poder y del saber) el concepto de la colonialidad del ser (*v.* Maldonado-Torres 2007) se puede plantear como una fuerza mayor, por el simple hecho de que, "históricamente ha negado ciertos grupos, específicamente los pueblos afrodescendientes, pero en menor medida también los pueblos indígenas, el estatus y consideración como gente" (Walsh 2005, 22–3). Nos menciona Maldonado-Torres que, "a partir de Descartes, la duda con respecto a la humanidad de otros se convierte en una certidumbre, que se basa en la alegada falta de razón o pensamiento en los colonizados/racializados" (Maldonado-Torres 2007, 145). Esa negación se circunscribe en la no-existencia, la existencia dominada, la deshumanización, en una concepción discriminatoria y violenta para con los considerados "inferiores" o como alude Fanon, los de la zona del no-ser, los condenados de la tierra.

El pensamiento decolonial sería sólo una de varias respuestas a ese cambio paradigmático y a ese modelo global hegemónico.

Este modelo colonial-institucional-estructural continúa enraizado en el actual Puerto Rico.[5] Empero, "un paso importante para comenzar a contrarrestar este modelo es comprender que este no es un fenómeno natural ni perpetuo, sino un sistema discriminatorio producto de un deshumanizante capítulo en nuestra historia, que puede transformarse a favor de un mejor presente" (Godreau 2013, 21). El pensamiento decolonial sería sólo una de varias respuestas a ese cambio paradigmático y a ese modelo global hegemónico. Sería una manera contundente de contrastar los esquemas y categorías "universales" creadas por el modelo colonial, dando así paso a formas *otras* de pensar, sentir y ser en la vida.

III. La colonialidad en la creación y marginalización de *la gran familia puertorriqueña*

"Pa' esos niches, que se creen mejores por sus profesiones
o por tener facciones de sus opresores."
—Tego Calderón, "Loíza"

En esta sección abordaré el tema de cómo esa jerarquía-institucional de poder instaura un imaginario colonial en las instituciones culturales estatales, utilizando la bomba como vehículo para legitimar toda una condición colonial. Utilizaré el siguiente esquema para representar visualmente una síntesis de lo expuesto anteriormente, dándole un giro al contexto de cómo este concepto de modernidad/colonialidad se enmarca en el discurso identitario de la bomba en Puerto Rico.[6]

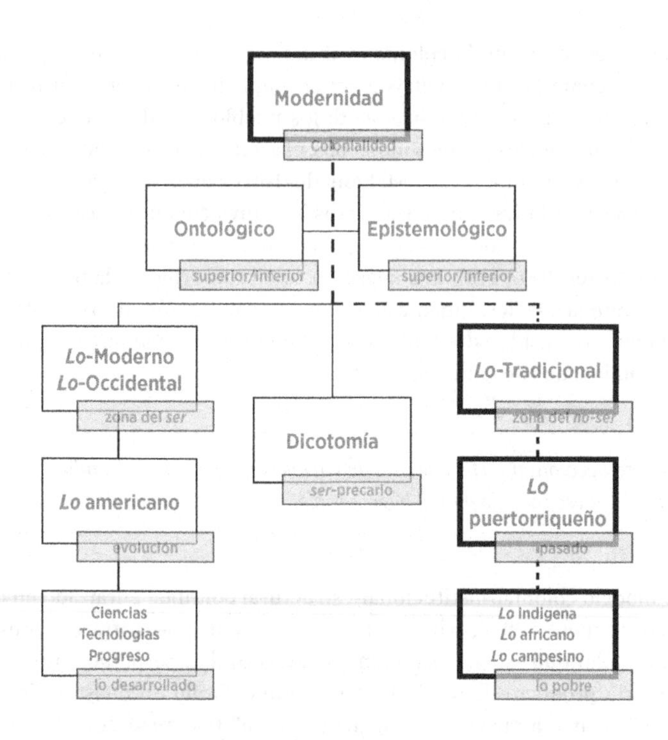

Para sustentar este argumento, es importante contextualizar varios puntos. Aquí sigo las aportaciones de Enrique Toledo cuando menciona que:

> **[...] los primeros 50 años del s. XX, el poder colonial de EEUU se manifestó a través de políticas de americanización que presuponía que el obstáculo para la "libertad" y "prosperidad" del puertorriqueño era su propia condición racial-cultural-histórica".[7] [...] la institucionalización de este poder colonial sobre *lo* puertorriqueño, no toma hasta la aprobación de la constitución del ELA en centralizarse como estructura de poder [...] el ELA no solamente definió una identidad puertorriqueña (como "pobre" o "subdesarrollada" contrario al "rico" y "desarrollado" EEUU) mediante sus circuitos burocráticos como por ejemplo el Instituto de Cultura Puertorriqueña (ICP) [...]. (Toledo 2011, 36–40).[8]**

El ICP fue el instrumento por el cual se creó, se desarrolló y se institucionalizó esa identidad estatizada, diseñada por una élite político partidista, el cual se moldearía y se utilizaría dependiendo del partido en el poder en el momento (Dávila 1997; Martínez Báez 2012). lba Iris Pérez indica que "el proyecto cultural y la concepción imaginada como nación puertorriqueña estuvieron en manos de varios intelectuales de la llamada *generación del treinta* [*v.* Arriví 1972] y fue el sujeto sobre el cual se consolidó el poder político y económico del Partido Popular Democrático"

(2009, 23). La autora destaca que, ya instauradas estas discusiones dominadas por el dirigismo cultural, representan la oportunidad de que las élites se inserten en estos proyectos, asegurándose un espacio desde donde pueden ejercer su autoridad:

> [...] los letrados se apropiaron del aparato estatal, construyeron un "pueblo" y le imprimieron el imaginario que heredaron de la clase social de la cual provenían. En ese proceso lograron convertir a una masa en sujeto histórico, propiciando su identificación con un denominador común que la agrupó en una identidad [...] Esa estrategia de formular una cultura exclusiva, con unos predecesores específicos, [...] se ve en discursos que se amparan en metáforas totalizantes como "la gran familia", "la herencia hispánica", etc., en tanto que cada uno es una manera de aunar al pueblo en una sola identidad, que borra las diferencias étnicas y culturales. Ese discurso procura dar un sentido de unidad a los ciudadanos, en el que nadie se piense excluido, a pesar de que los discursos homogeneizantes se caracterizan, precisamente, por las exclusiones. (Pérez 2009, 22-5)

Teniendo en mente que la bomba en Puerto Rico[9] precede la creación de este "nacionalismo cultural o identidad estatizada"—es decir, la bomba existió cientos de años antes de dicha mezcla de tres razas— es importante analizar dos puntos esenciales, primero, cómo la colonialidad fue insertada en la bomba a través del diseño de este discurso institucionalizado, y segundo, cómo trascendió la bomba decolonial a través de toda su historia y sus manifestaciones.

Siguiendo el patrón de las categorías binarias creadas por la modernidad, en Puerto Rico, la inferiorización y enajenación, es tal —donde lo que conocemos como "lo normal" no se piensa e internaliza críticamente— que todavía se sigue legitimando el racismo en la cotidianidad y en todas las esferas de estructuras, entiéndase: a nivel institucional (gobierno, universidades, ámbito laboral), colectivo (comunidades, organizaciones, familia) e individual (percepciones, prejuicios). Dentro de esta jerarquía-institucional de poder, lo ontológico representa la zona del no-ser y la zona del ser. Lo epistemológico representa la distinción entre sujeto y objeto (o cosa). Lo que se considera *lo tradicional* está en contraposición con *lo moderno* (lo occidental), *lo pasado* está relacionado con *lo atrasado* y *lo desarrollado* está relacionado con *el progreso*. Esta estructura-jerárquica-colonial supone una dicotomía que, en el caso de Puerto Rico, entra en comparación y confrontación *lo puertorriqueño* con *lo americano*. Por ejemplo, lo ontológico representa la zona del ser (americano) y la zona del no-ser (el colonizado puertorriqueño). Entendiéndose que para el colonizado puertorriqueño, el ser necesita vincularse con el ser-americano. Lo mismo ocurre en el esquema epistemológico, se circunscribe el puertorriqueño como el objeto frente al sujeto o ser-americano, que en calidad de ser-sujeto o que lo consideren como tal, necesita del progreso, del desarrollo, de lo moderno. Así las cosas, el discurso de la identidad estatizada (e.g. música folclórica-tradicional; "la gran familia puertorriqueña"; la mezcla de tres razas o mestizaje) queda inscrito en lo tradicional, lo atrasado, lo pobre, el objeto y en la zona del *no-ser*. Como añade

Marisel Moreno, "the cultural myth of *la gran familia puertorriqueña*, thus emerged as a predominant narrative grounded on principles of exclusion" (2010, 76). De hecho, Arlene Torres en su ensayo "La gran familia puertorriqueña: 'ej prieta de beldá – the Great Puerto Rican family is really really black." indica que:

> The process of *blanqueamiento* specifically encourages Puerto Ricans to identify with the *mestizo* [...] By employing these ideologies of *mestizaje* and *blanqueamiento* to gain conditional acceptance by nonblacks, racism is perpetuated [...] such a perspective does not negate the existence of black culture but confines it to the realm of the "popular" [...] In the Puerto Rican context, by defining black cultural contributions within the context of slavery and the expressive realm, naturalized stigmata that set black people apart from the rest of Puerto Rican society are continually reproduced. (1998, 296–7).

Aunque dentro de esa "gran familia puertorriqueña" se tiende a exaltar lo "blanco-occidental" como "baluarte" o como "riqueza cultural" o "alta cultura" (la danza, la música clásica, etc). En comparación con este planteamiento divisorio, Montes-Pizarro (2015a) detalla que:

> The African cultural influence is not denied in the official discourses about Puerto Rican culture [...] Rather than denying it, the hegemonic national discourses, both in Puerto Rico and in Colombia, devalorize African heritage and generally circumscribe it only to specific cultural and musical practices and spaces.

Paradójicamente, dentro de esa *identidad estatizada* se desliga toda conexión, hibridación y/o aportación de la afrodesendencia.[10] Las aportaciones de Montes-Pizarro claramente demuestran que este discurso hegemónico moderno-occidental entra en categorizaciones abstractas, homogéneas, simplistas y divisorias —cimentadas en fanatismos radicales— que perdemos de perspectiva la importancia del cómo nos relacionamos culturalmente y nos enajena de esa riqueza cultural en toda su amplitud. Por ende, el discurso "nacional-cultural" bajo la identidad estatizada de lo puertorriqueño, está definida e inmersa en una retórica moderna-occidental donde, en este caso, la bomba (colonial) es considerada, de forma implícita, como lo pobre, lo antiguo, el folclore, lo atrasado, lo estático, el objeto, el no-ser. Al enmarcar este género social-musical bajo este discurso, enaltecerlo en fiestas de una vez al año, donde por diseño institucional fue enseñado superficialmente en el sistema público educativo, no solo se niega toda una visión de mundo completamente diferente a la impuesta e inferioriza todo conocimiento otro que no sea el del ente dominador, sino que se utiliza este género social-musical como un medio de legitimización de todo este sistema colonial.[11]

En la próxima sección haré una introducción a esa otra visión de mundo negada, detallando la importancia de la música como herramienta de trans-resistencia, el rol que juega el ser y el tiempo en esta dinámica, preparando un horizonte y situando a la bomba (decolonial) como un ente enunciador del condenado.

IV. Los tambores sagrados de la liberación

"Mi pueblo está enclavado en el corazón de la selva ecuatorial [...] Su follaje está
lleno de sabiduría, música, narración [...] Allí, la protección de la naturaleza
y el respeto a los valores humanos no son sólo la ciencia,
sino un modo de vida ancestral, que se deriva de
una filosofía antigua".
—Emmanuell Tina Asseng, cuentista y músico senegalés.[12]

Varios mitos son frecuentemente utilizados como consecuencia de esta historia colonial que pretende homogeneizar y categorizar civilizaciones otras. Por ejemplo, el hecho de que se considere al "continente Africano" como un monolítico y "subdesarrollado" o el hablar de forma abstracta, esencialista y anacrónica sobre las culturas africanas y sus músicas sin conocer de las riquezas de las conexiones entre estas y las afrodescendientes. Montes-Pizarro describe que esa historia de las conexiones afrodiaspóricas y las culturas africanas no es sólo una cuestión de raíces comunes ni de un momento "fundacional" durante el período de la esclavitud.[13] Más adelante menciona:

> [...] conviene que integremos a nuestros estudios las historias de las músicas africanas realmente existentes y de nuestras historias compartidas desde sus comienzos hasta la actualidad. Esto nos permitirá entender mejor lo que llamamos "africanía", trascender estereotipos racistas que circunscribe lo africano a un pasado estático y reconocernos a nosotros mismos como partícipes de culturas que se han forjado en un ir y venir de influencias constantes [...] para que comencemos en Puerto Rico a ampliar nuestras miradas hacia las historias que compartimos todas las comunidades afrodescendientes [...] también podremos entender mejor cómo nuestra propia herencia y actualidad cultural se inserta en esas historias de diálogos y conexiones múltiples. (Montes-Pizarro 2012, 97)

Dentro de la cosmovisión de estas culturas, el cuerpo y el espacio-tiempo juegan un rol importante. Albert Kasanda Lumembu señala que "el concepto negroafricano del cuerpo es tributario de la cosmovisión vigente en África. Por lo general, ésta se despliega dentro de una configuración particular de referencias simbólicas, políticas y religiosas cuya noción básica es la vida" (2002, 103). De cara a una naturaleza hostil, el africano se preocupa por la manera de asegurar su propia existencia (Kasanda 2002, 103).[14] Dentro de esta cosmovisión se desarrolla un pensamiento dualista, no separatista, sino integrador.[15] En el escrito "Siento, luego existo", Vergara expone lo siguiente:

> Esta concepción del mundo, los términos de su doble realidad, la visible y la no visible, no son excluyentes entre sí. No hay antagonismo, sino complicidad [...] Hay en ello una noción intrínseca de continuidad, de multiplicidad de conexiones e identidades que no se refieren a una realidad unívoca sino más bien a una cadena que une los

unos a los otros [...] no hace distinción entre lo biológico y lo espiritual, es decir, en el cuerpo subsiste un dinamismo vital entre ambos espacios [...] Tener un cuerpo significa vivenciarlo [...]. (2014, 45).

Por otro lado, el ritmo, la música, el baile y la espiritualidad, fungen como elementos constitutivos entrelazados y armónicos de esta cosmovisión ancestral y diaspórica. El componente unificador es la libertad individual y colectiva que emana en la integración de estos elementos. Dentro de este razonamiento, Kasanda hace referencia al coreógrafo, bailador e investigador Alphonse Tierou cuando este menciona que:

la tradición africana se caracteriza por el hecho de sacar sus recursos del universo. Bailar a la manera africana es reconocer que el hombre es inseparable del universo, es una chispa divina. Es saber que éste último no puede desligarse de lo fundamental: su participación en el cosmos se concretiza mediante su participación en la vida comunitaria. Es descubrir su cuerpo, vivirlo, obedecerlo y seguir sus experiencias naturales. Es respetar las leyes que no son siempre lógicas ya que el lenguaje del cuerpo es uno de los más irracionales. Es también la facultad de aceptar el placer: en el baile africano, las relaciones se cargan automáticamente de significados nuevos. La alegría y la felicidad constituyen la base, purifican los sentimientos, los hacen más nobles y más espirituales a la vez. (Kasanda 2002, 111–2)

Por otro lado, el cuentista y músico camerunés Emmanuel Tina Asseng, en una entrevista del documental *Rumba y Candela 2013: The Spirit of Rumba* (2013), nos comenta sobre la comunicación dentro de los bailes ancestrales:

All the movements in our traditional dances are meant as communication. We communicate with the body, we communicate with the music. Each dance step has meaning. The slaves were able to keep that. They kept all those movements. Today they are mixed with what they learnt from their masters [...] these dances are danced in a different way now but the roots are the same.[16]

Esta heterogeneidad sigue un patrón en *los Caribes*[17] a consecuencia de los asentamientos coloniales, la libre movilidad y los intercambios culturales en dichas regiones. En la música ligada a esta “africanía” (*v.* Montes-Pizarro 2012) uno de los instrumentos fundamentales es el tambor.[18] El tambor pasa a ser un portavoz de mensajes, una extensión de la corporalidad y por tanto, un texto que espera ser leído e interpretado por un agente externo. El tambor evoca emoción y exuberancia en la música, resalta momentos en el tiempo que puede conducir un mensaje político o una llamada para la liberación física y emocional. Es por esto que en la mayoría de las regiones en los Caribes y en las Américas, se prohibían los toques de tambor (Johnson 2001; Quintero 2009). Don C. Ohadike presenta una compilación entre músicas, religiones y bailes, en África y su diáspora, bajo la mirada de la resistencia:

> Moreover, it was religion and music that first unified the African exiles in the Americas. These Africans had come from hundreds of different nations and language groupings, where they might also have belonged to different religious affiliations [...] without religion and music, the initial problem posed by language and religious differences would have been difficult to surmount [...] European slave owners and colonial authorities that prohibited drumming and certain forms of verbal expressions did not know that Africans could transmit messages with their bodies [...] As a communication device, dance uses different types of gestures, body movements, body decorations, and even masks. Dance could serve as a form of record keeping. (2007, 5-11)

Eran estos los momentos de encuentros e intercambios que suscitaban la sublevación para encontrar la libertad despojada. En "Esclavos rebeldes y cimarrones" Javier Laviña detalla que:

> La fiesta y el tambor sirvieron como medios de comunicación entre los esclavos de las haciendas para preparar las sublevaciones, para recordar un continente del que habían sido brutalmente arrancados, para convertirse de nuevo en seres humanos. Una parte importante de las sublevaciones se dieron después de una fiesta donde el tambor dejaba de ser un instrumento para convertirse en el protagonista de la llamada a la sublevación. Los toques, códigos de comunicación, anunciaban la llegada de la hora. (2011, 26)

Estos medios de la cotidianeidad de estas culturas se vieron vinculados a una nueva práctica o método de resistencia debido a los procesos causantes por la esclavitud (e.g., enajenación, asimilación, negación, etc.) que jamás habían experimentado en su tierra. Ohadike reconoce que no todas las músicas o bailes en África estaban ligadas a la resistencia ya a que para muchos africanos, la música es un elemento de puro entretenimiento y una herramienta para transmitir mensajes culturales, es un medio de expresión individual y colectiva (Ohadike 2007, 8-11). La música y el baile son por ende un texto, una forma de inscripción cultural que uno puede aprender a imprimir con su propio cuerpo.

V. "Candela, candela le damos"[19]

La gente que tenía dinero estaban en contra de que nuestra música, que hoy en día se pasea por todos sitios, estuviera [...] Ellos vivían en ciertos sitios donde más abajo vivían pobres [...] y ellos le decían a la policía: "vayan que allá hay un baile que están bailando esa gente negra de allá y no dejan dormir aquí a la gente". Esas personas que estaban dispuestas a solamente oír música de violín, sentir ese "tún-tún-tún" les molestaban el oído. Entonces ellos como eran gente pudiente mandaban a la policía, la policía llegaba sin preguntar y caían a palos, rompían las panderetas y les caían a palos a la gente y muchos que terminaron en el hospital con las cabezas rajadas y tenían que quedarse callados porque si decían algo, enseguida, los encerraban por alteración a la paz. (Rafael Cepeda Atiles en *Plena is Work, Plena is Song* 1989)

Como ya explicamos, el baile y la música como expresión individual y colectiva, constituyen ciertas funciones políticas y se utilizan como vehículos que van más allá de la resistencia entendida como tal. Son vehículos de trans-resistencia: trasmiten mensajes, preservan o construyen identidades, alivian el peso de la opresión particular y colectiva, combate la opresión colonial y sobreviven ante la violencia sistemática-moderna. Esta trans-resistencia es parte de una construcción colectiva en respuesta a lo establecido como lo universal-hegemónico-dominante sobre otros modos de pensar-sentir-vivir. La bomba decolonial —pensándola, sintiéndola y viviéndola de esta manera— es una forma de trans-resistencia individual y principalmente colectiva. La proliferación, desarrollo y evolución de este género social-musical en Puerto Rico han estado atados, en algunos casos, por diferentes factores: primero, pudiéramos llamarle "moda", segundo, por problematizar ese discurso nacional, y tercero, por dar un giro a la reafirmación de una historia negada y subyugada. Sea cualquiera el medio por el cual la bomba se ha inmiscuido en todas las esferas —con la proliferación de escuelas[20] y centros culturales, agrupaciones musicales, cursos académicos, y la promoción de la bomba como herramienta política—, lo cierto es que representan modos de combatir el discurso colonial. Éstos reafirman la valorización y respeto a este otro modo de sentir, pensar y ser; son así, formas de trans-resistencia. Estas dinámicas no solo se dan en Puerto Rico; la diáspora es un componente importante de proliferación y preservación de la bomba decolonial.

En una entrevista a Roberto Pérez, co-director del grupo Bomba con Buya de Chicago, comentaba sobre el video de la canción "Candela" que grabaron en la ciudad de Chicago y en el pueblo de Ponce, Puerto Rico. El video apela a los cimientos de una música que en su momento, estaba la necesidad de comunicarse para sublevarse, luchar, escaparse de la opresión y rescatar esa libertad arrebatada. Transmite una comparación de espacio-tiempo que invoca la realidad e interconectividad del pasado, presente y futuro.

Our project is deeply informed by both the symbolism and historical context of the song because of its capacity to engender dialogue about institutionalized oppression, resistance, collective mobilization, and self-determination. The socio-historical and political content mobilized and embodied by Buya urgently directs our attention to various contemporary injustices that still permeate across the country. Through video we aim to connect coordinates found between Puerto Rican and African diasporas while mapping entrenched racial and political violence and protest. This explains our site specific work in Chicago and Ponce, Puerto Rico. For example, Ponce is well known for the Massacre of 1937, where over two hundred people were wounded and nineteen unarmed Nationalists were executed by the state police. We would like to suggest that the Ponce Massacre of 1937 and the current climate of police brutality and state sanctioned violence across the United States share political and racial dimensions (e.g. Ferguson, Baltimore, and New York City). Therefore, each location will provide an opportunity to engage these issues through performative and discursive means, using

Candela as a platform to theorize how African-rooted performance practices such as bomba might simultaneously operate as technology of diasporic citizenship and vehicle for social activism. (Gudiño Cabrera 2017)

Con el propósito de conocer otras iniciativas que actualmente Bomba con Buya está gestando en Chicago, le preguntaba a Pérez cómo Buya utilizaba la bomba como herramienta de cohesión social y movilizadora en Chicago:

Chicago is also very segregated [...] in a beautiful way we've been able to leave our community, leave our comfort zone, and we've been very successful in collaborating with other musical jammers. ***Por ejemplo, hemos tocado con un grupo Haitiano, un grupo Jamaiquino, uno de Belice Garífuna, conexiones con grupos de la costa de México, Veracruz —todo esto ocurriendo en Chicago.*** **We really try to collaborate with these groups and show commonalties than necessary differences, and we're being able to play outside of our little area, so we're very much welcome in the Mexican community and the African American community,** ***nos buscan bastante*****, almost I think more than even in our own community, and I think it's because of what we speak, we speak about commonalities we don't speak about differences, we speak about the same causes, the same struggles we're facing. (Gudiño Cabrera 2017)**

Este solo es un ejemplo, de cómo la bomba decolonial en tiempos presentes se está gestando en la diáspora boricua de las diferentes ciudades de los Estados Unidos. Teniendo en mente las diferentes vicisitudes sociales que se generan en territorios separados,[21] esta música trasciende estas barreras del espacio-tiempo, transformando esas "diferencias" en harmonías, cohesiones y unidades, perpetuando el toque de bomba como conexión intrínseca donde se encuentran el pasado, el presente y el futuro. Es ese el *pensamiento fractal* (Glissant 1977),[22] donde los encuentros son generados por y en la relación afectiva de las diferencias. Esto trasciende la trinchera del nacionalismo-individualista-insularista, coartador de visiones transversales entrelazadas en la afectividad colectiva, entendiendo que, dentro de estas visiones de mundo(s), hay infinidades de espacios y de infinitas oportunidades.[23]

VI. "Con el eco de mis barriles, calmo la pena que me persigue"[24]

La intención de este ensayo exploratorio fue abordar el tema de la bomba bajo una perspectiva decolonial, donde la crítica subyace en que, mientras se constituya y circunscriba la Bomba como parte de esa identidad estatizada —producto del pensamiento moderno/occidental— la misma sigue siendo colonial, legitimando toda esa construcción socio-histórica-cultural la cual niega maneras otras de ver-pensar-sentir el mundo. Siendo la bomba antecesora de dicha identidad estatizada, en Puerto Rico, el tabú del racismo institucional en todas las esferas (e.g. lo educativo, lo cultural) ha perpetuado ese discurso enajenante y excluyente. Afortunadamente, y a consecuencia de una extensa historia de luchas, existe en Puerto Rico y en la diáspora, exponentes de esta visión y defensores de esta historia negada y marginada, en otras palabras, hacedores de la trans-resistencia. La mayor importancia de esta propagación hacia un interés por adentrarse en la bomba no radica en la proliferación en sí por una simple "moda" sino en el genuino interés por transmitir y conocer su significado histórico y social más allá de las trincheras banales de la exclusividad, coartadoras de la necesidad de vernos como parte integral de estas músicas hermanadas. El objetivo tiene que estar centrado en la problematización de estos conceptos que damos como "lo normal", con el propósito de elevar la conversación hacia una enseñanza y prácticas antirracista, entablando diálogos *otros* que integren visiones *otras* al hablar de estas músicas hermanadas e identidades culturales. Reconociendo las distinciones de los acontecimientos históricos y contextos sociales entre épocas, la bomba ha ido evolucionando y gestándose de formas *otras* con el pasar del tiempo. La bomba, seguirá siendo una música de tambor, de este conglomerado de músicas hermanadas, que perpetúa una expresión libertaria de esta cosmovisión negada que, al llegar a los Caribes, se entrelaza y, a su vez, constituye ese crisol de experiencias vivenciales. Más que el género social-musical de mayor historia en Puerto Rico, la bomba es parte del acervo de vidas y pensamientos ancestrales que se desarrollaron y evolucionaron en estas regiones. Dentro sus diferentes matices, existe en ella ese *manana*[25] que es el elemento unificador y característico, resultante de esos conocimientos *otros* que han ido gestándose y evolucionando, pero manteniendo y preservando, esa memoria histórica de nuestros ancestros y creando nuevos presentes.

NOTAS

[1] Aquí sigo las aportaciones de Walter Mignolo (2007) cuando menciona que "el pensamiento decolonial emergió en la fundación misma de la modernidad/colonialidad como su contrapartida [...] la genealogía del pensamiento decolonial se estructura en el espacio planetario de la expansión colonial/imperial [...] es *pluriversal* (no *universal*). Así, cada nudo de la red de esta genealogía es un punto de despegue y apertura que reintroduce lenguas, memorias, economías, organizaciones sociales, subjetividades, esplendores y miserias de los legados imperiales. La actualidad pide, reclama, un pensamiento decolonial que articule genealogías desperdigadas por el planeta y ofrezca modalidades económicas, políticas, sociales y subjetivas *otras*".

[2] "La zona del ser y no-ser no es un lugar geográfico específico, sino una posición en las relaciones raciales de poder que ocurren a escala global entre centros y periferias, pero que también ocurren a escala nacional y local contra diversos grupos racialmente inferiorizados" (Grosfoguel 2012).

[3] Para más información sobre este concepto, véase Lander y Castro-Gómez (2000)

[4] "Enrique Dussel (2005) responde a estas preguntas con el siguiente argumento: El "yo pienso, luego existo" de Descartes está precedido por 150 años de "yo conquisto, luego existo". El *ego conquiro* es la condición de posibilidad del *ego cogito* de Descartes. Según Dussel, la arrogante e idólatra pretensión de divinidad de la filosofía cartesiana viene de la perspectiva de alguien que piensa en sí mismo como centro del mundo porque ya ha conquistado el mundo. ¿Quién es este ser? Según Dussel (2005), es el *Ser Imperial*. El "yo conquisto", que comenzó con la expansión colonial europea en 1492, es el cimiento y la condición de posibilidad del "yo pienso" idolátrico que seculariza todos los atributos del Dios cristiano y reemplaza a Dios como nuevo fundamento del conocimiento. Una vez los europeos conquistaron el mundo, el Dios de la cristiandad se hizo desechable como fundamento del conocimiento. Después de conquistar el mundo, los hombres europeos alcanzaron cualidades «divinas» que les daban un privilegio epistemológico sobre los demás" (Citado en Grosfoguel 2013).

[5] Durante este ensayo exploratorio no estaré abordando detalladamente la historia del racismo y la esclavitud en Puerto Rico. Para más información sobre este tema, véase: Baralt (1985); Díaz Soler (1995); Figueroa (2005); Sued Badillo (1986).

[6] Esquema creado con la ayuda de Enrique Toledo-Hernández a quien agradezco toda su guía y consejos durante esta significativa travesía.

[7] "Uno de los primeros gobernadores militares estadounidense de la isla decía a principio del siglo XX que: "*the inhabitants, all of foreign races and tongue, largely illiterate and without experience in conducting a government in accordance with Anglo-Saxon practices,* [...] *were not deemed to be* [...] *qualified* [...] *to fully appreciate the responsibilities* [...] *of complete self-government*" (Citado en Toledo 2011, 36).

[8] "Un grupo de prominentes líderes y educadores del PPD, preocupados por la creciente americanización y por lo que denominaban la erosión del patrimonio cultural [que generaba el proceso de industrialización], se dedicó a organizar entre círculos oficialistas un movimiento de afirmación de los valores y la creación cultural puertorriqueña. Este proyecto de promoción de una "cultura nacional" como parte de la estructura política del Estado Libre Asociado [...] se cristalizó mediante la creación, por ley de 1955, del Instituto Cultura Puertorriqueña [...]" (Citado en Toledo 2011, 40).

[9] Durante este ensayo exploratorio, no estaré abordando los orígenes de la Bomba en Puerto Rico ni su definición como género musical. Para referencias sobre este tema, véase: Barton (1995); Dufrasne-González (1985); McCoy (1968); Rivera Rivera (2013); Vega Drouet (1979); Ferreras (2005); Abadía-Rexach (2015).

[10] No podemos circunscribir el continente africano como un continente monolítico u homogéneo. El mismo es un pluriverso de culturas e historias entrelazadas. El pensamiento moderno-occidental perpetuó en su discurso mitos y categorías binarias deshumanizantes que permean en la actualidad. Por ejemplo, en el escrito del sociólogo Juan A. Giusti Cordero, "Dos mitos sobre África y algunas sorpresas" (1994), menciona que: "Ninguna parte del mundo ha estado tan sujeta a tantos mitos y falsedades como África, como resultado de la ignorancia y racismo. De los muchos mitos sobre África que circulan en nuestra cultura, hay dos que sobresalen: primero, que África es una gran selva, y segundo, que África no tiene historia".

[11] En este ensayo exploratorio pretendo incitar la conversación para tener una base en donde se pueda ir solidificando el tema de lo colonial y decolonial dentro de la cultura musical puertorriqueña. Partiendo de un análisis inicial, esto sería un excelente tema para gestar una serie de investigaciones extensas y abarcadoras al cual invito a examinar en detalle dos planteamientos. Primero las diferentes políticas culturales desde la creación del ICP enmarcadas en lo colonial, y segundo, profundizar en la agencia y el rol de bombeadorxs en ese contexto histórico, enmarcado en varias preguntas como, por ejemplo: ¿estaban conscientes del poder y sus consecuencias de la creación de esta identidad estatizada?; ¿fueron manipulados implícitamente por parte del estado para continuar con el diseño de esta creación?; ¿de qué otras maneras pudieron darle un giro a este discurso para continuar con la gestión cultural educativa?; ¿cómo desarrollaron esa agencia y capacidad para resistir y luchar dentro de este andamiaje estatal?

[12] Traduccíon del autor del siguiente texto original: "Mon village est niché au coeur de la forêt equatoriale [...] Son feuillage regorge de sagesses, musiques, contes et légendes [...] Là-bas, la protección de la nature, et le respect des valeurs humaines ne sont pas que des sciences mais un mode de vie ancestral, qui découle d'une philosophie millénaire".

[13] No podemos olvidar el tránsito por todo el mundo (en especial en los Caribes y las Américas) de los negros libres.

[14] A esto, el autor añade: "La preocupación por la vida no es específica del pueblo africano, se trata de algo compartido por todos los pueblos. Sin embargo, la diferencia entre éstos consiste en la forma (técnica, metafísica) como se aborda la problemática." (Kasanda 2002, 103*n*4).

[15] Kasanda menciona que "a diferencia del pensamiento occidental, no se desarrolla relaciones de exclusión entre ambas realidades; de lo contrario, se piensa en términos de una inclusión recíproca." Más adelante en el escrito añade que: "Contrariamente al "Yo" de Descartes que se construye en base a su dimensión racional, "Yo pienso, luego existo", el ser negroafricano pone énfasis en su inserción en la red existencial, en el tejido de correspondencias con la naturaleza, lo divino y los demás seres mediante la energía vital. En este sentido, anticipadamente, podemos decir que el concepto de cuerpo remite aquí a la totalidad de los cosmos. El cuerpo se percibe como un universo en pequeño" (Kasanda 2002, 105).

[16] Para información sobre Asseng, véase: <http://tinaemmanuel.wix.com/tina-wix1#!contes-a-ecouter/> o <http://www.dapper.fr/fiche-spectacle.php?id=157/>.

[17] Me refiero a la región del Caribe como *los Caribes* por su heterogeneidad cultural y pensamientos *otros*. Como menciona Antonio García de León Griego: "En el sentido de más larga duración, el Caribe fue y sigue siendo un crisol de culturas, razas y costumbres, un espacio intrincado que prefiguró en los primeros siglos coloniales mucho del cosmopolitismo actual, así como los primeros avances universales de los que hoy conocemos como modernidad" (Citado en Montes-Pizarro 2015a).

[18] Normalmente se tiende a simbolizar las músicas africanas con el instrumento del tambor,

pero los instrumentos de cuerdas y viento son parte integral en estas músicas (*v.* Montes-Pizarro 2015b).

[19] Extracto de la canción "Candela" interpretada por el grupo musical de bomba Buya. "Se cree que la canción, originalmente en español y criollo francés, se jugó como parte de la tradición Bambula que se trajo a Samaná, República Dominicana de Nueva Orleans como parte de los múltiples intercambios entre los exiliados de Luisiana y otras comunidades Afro-diáspora en todo el Caribe. Estos intercambios formaron la conceptualización de la identidad pan-africana, y los esfuerzos posteriores dirigidos por Marcus Garvey durante el siglo XX" (Torres-Figueroa y Smith 2015).

[20] Para información sobre el surgimiento y proliferación de escuelas independientes de Bomba, véase Rivera-Rivera (2015). El surgimiento de escuelas de bomba independientes ante la ausencia de enseñanza en el currículo oficial del sistema de educación en Puerto Rico.

[21] Me refiero a que la proliferación de métodos de resistencias —aunque no se proyecten explícitamente como tal o porque sus ejecutantes no lo aprecien como tal— pueden ocurrir en contextos y espacios completamente diferentes. El hecho de que la bomba sea transversal —se practique, enseñe o se integre en otros espacios— ya es un ejemplo de que la misma trasciende la resistencia, propiciando la oportunidad de crear un espacio de encuentro, traduciéndose en un proyecto político.

[22] Édouard Glissant (2008) define que: "la propia medida de lo que se llama civilización cede más bien ante el entrelazamiento de las culturas de las humanidades, cada vez más cercanas e imbricadas unas con otras. Los detalles engendran totalidad por todas partes. Al conjunto de estos elementos inextricables e inesperados lo he denominado: Todo-mundo".

[23] Estas infinidades de espacios están ligadas en la armonía de la colectividad. Por ejemplo, en la mayoría de las culturas africanas, el término *omundu/muntu* o *ubuntu*, abraca cuestiones de respeto y dignidad humana bajo el entendimiento de que la humanidad de un individuo, está interconectada con la dignidad humana de los otros. Schoeman (2012) señala que: "Within Africa, humanity is not just an anthropological concept, it is a moral term and reflects the association between all people with shared aims and interests. This relationship goes beyond ethical and racial divides and recognizes humanness as the single criteria that constitutes all human beings into one universal family of humankind which adheres to the morality of a shared family".

[24] Los Rebuleadores de San Juan, *El Eco*. Recuperado de: <https://www.youtube.com/watch?v=B3nLC2fseBs/>.

[25] La palabra *manana* se utiliza con mucha frecuencia en la rumba cubana. La connotación e historia que se le otorga a la palabra *manana* es diversa, en una entrevista realizada por *Manana Cuba* (2016), Alain García Artola comenta sobre los orígenes de esta palabra: "Manana era la esposa de un general de la guerra de la independencia, un general dominicano pero que vino a Cuba y se unió a la causa cubana, su nombre (Máximo Gómez) es bien recordado por la historia de Cuba. Su mujer se llamaba Manana y estuvieron separados por mucho tiempo por cuestión de la guerra y de los problemas de la guerra, entonces, cada vez que ella le escribía una carta, al final le escribía, con sentimiento, Manana. Y entonces los rumberos, a principios cuando la rumba se estaba creando, era una expresión que usaban mucho para reflejar lo que sentían, y para siempre decir que todo lo que hacían, lo hacían *con sentimiento manana*, de ahí viene el origen de esta palabra". Por otro lado, uno de los grandes exponentes de este género y percusionista, Maximino Duquesne expresaba: "¡Tengo la virtud de que estas manos me han salido buenas! Y toco, toco con un sentimiento. Se llama *manana*, sentir lo que tú estás haciendo y que te llegue

[...] esa armonía y melodía te tiene que llegar y que te guste, o si no, tú no eres rumbero" (*Rumberos de Cuba* 2016). Utilizo ese significado extrapolándolo a la Bomba por dos razones, primero, como parte de esta integración de músicas hermanadas y, segundo, por mi experiencia de vida con la Bomba cuando la bailo, toco, y transmito a futuras generaciones para que la valoren y preserven tal y como me enseñaron en mi barrio de Villa Palmeras.

OBRAS CITADAS

Abadía-Rexach, Bárbara I. 2015. Saluting the Drum! The New Puerto Rican Bomba Movement. Tesis doctoral, University of Texas.

Arriví, Francisco. 1972. *La Generación del treinta*. Ciclo de Conferencias sobre la Literatura de Puerto Rico. San Juan: Instituto de Cultura Puertorriqueña

Baquero, Sergio A; Ortiz, Julián A, y Noguera, Juan R. 2015. Colonialidad del saber y ciencias sociales: una metodología para aprehender los imaginarios colonizados. *Político* 85: 76-92.

Baralt, Guillermo A. 1985. *Esclavos rebeldes: conspiraciones y sublevaciones de esclavos en Puerto Rico 1795-1873*. San Juan: Ediciones Huracán.

Barton, Halbert E. 1995. The Drum-Dance Challenge: An Antrhopological Study of Gender, Race, and Class Marginalization of Bomba in Puerto Rico. Tesis doctoral, Cornell University.

Castro-Gómez, Santiago. 2005. *La Hybris del Punto Cero: Ciencia, Raza e Ilustración en la Nueva Granada (1750-1816)*. Bogotá: Editorial Pontificia Universidad Javeriana.

Castro-Gómez, Santiago; Grosfoguel, Ramón. 2007. *El giro decolonial: reflexiones para una diversidad epistémica más allá del capitalismo golbal*. Bogotá: Siglo del Hombre Editores;

Dávila, Arlene. 1997. *Sponsored Identities: Cultural Politics in Puerto Rico*. Philadelphia: Temple University Press.

Díaz Soler, Luis M. 1995. *Historia de la esclavitud negra en Puerto Rico*. San Juan: Editorial de la Universidad de Puerto Rico

Dufrasne-González, J. Emanuel. 1985. La homogeneidad de la música caribeña: sobre la música comercial y popular de Puerto Rico. Tesis doctoral, University of California, Los Ángeles.

Fanon, Frantz. 1956. Racismo y cultura. *1er. Congreso de Escritores y Artistas negros en París*. Publicado en número especial de *Présence africaine*, 8: 22-131.

________. 2009. *Piel Negra, Máscaras Blancas*. Madrid: Akal.

Ferreras, Salvador E. 2005. Solo Drumming in the Puerto Rican Bomba: An Analysis of Musical Processes and Improvisational Strategies. Tesis doctoral, University of British Columbia.

Figueroa, Luis. 2005. *Sugar, Slavery, and Freedom in the Nineteenth Century in Puerto Rico*. San Juan: Editorial de la Universidad de Puerto Rico.

Giusti Cordero, Juan. 1994. Dos mitos sobre África y algunas sorpresas. MS

Glissant, Édouard. 1997. *Poetics of relation*. Traducido por Wing B. Michigan: The University of Michigan Press.

________. 2008. Conferencia magistral de la Universidad de Cartagena con motivo de la recepción del doctorado honoris-causa y del Coloquio Internacional Caribe, Archipiélago de Influencias. 17 de junio. Cartagena, Colombia. <http://www.festivaldepoesiademedellin.org/es/Diario/05_18_05_09.html/>.

Godreau, Isar. et al. 2013. *Arrancando mitos de raíz: Guía para una enseñanza antirracista de la herencia africana en Puerto Rico*. Cayey: Instituto de Investigaciones Interdisciplinarias UPR-Cayey.

Gordon, Lewis. 2009. A través de la zona del no ser. Una lectura de *Piel negra, máscaras blancas* en la celebración del octogésimo aniversario del nacimiento de Fanon. En Frantz, Fanon. *Piel Negra, Máscaras Blancas.* Madrid: Akal.

Grosfoguel, Ramón. 2012. El concepto de racismo en Foucault y Fanon: teorizar desde la zona del ser y la zona del no ser. *Tabula Rasa,* 16: 79-102.

________. 2013. Racismo/sexismo epistémico, universidades occidentalizadas y los cuatro genocidios/epistemicidios del largo siglo XVI. *Tabula Rasa,* 19: 31-58.

Gudiño Cabrera, Juan. 2017. Entrevista a Roberto Pérez. 16 de febrero.

Iris-Pérez, Elva. 2009. Un discurso dramático para la nación puertorriqueña 1934-1955. *El Amauta; Universidad de Puerto Rico recinto de Arecibo,* 4.

Johnson, Chris. 2001. *Drums Rising: The Drum as Myth and Symbol in African American Culture.* New York: Manuscript.

Kasanda-Lumembu, Albert. 2002. Elocuencia y magia en el cuerpo. Un enfoque negroafricano. *Memoria y Sociedad* 6(12), 101–20.

Lander, E. y S. Castro-Gómez. 2000. *La colonialidad del saber: eurocentrismo y ciencias sociales: perspectivas latinoamericanas.* Buenos Aires: CLASCO

Laviña, Javier. 2011. Esclavos rebeldes y cimarrones. En Gallego-Andrés, J. *Tres grandes cuestiones de la hisotria de Iberoamérica: ensayos y monografías.* Madrid: Fundación Ignacio Larramendi.

Maldonado-Torres, Nelson. 2007. Sobre la colonialidad del ser: contribuciones al desarrollo de un concepto. En S. Castro-Gómez, & R. Grosfoguel (eds.). *El giro decolonial. Reflexiones para una diversidad epistémico más allá del capitalismo global.* (págs. 127-167). Bogotá: Siglo del Hombre Editores.

Manana Cuba. 2016. Entrevista a Alain García Artola: Where does the word 'Manana' come from? 18 de febrero. <https://www.youtube.com/watch?v=lUDsxTrElAQ/>.

Martínez Báez, Rubiam. 2012. La relación entre la cultura y la política en Brasil, Argentina y Puerto Rico. *El Amauta* 8/9(enero).

McCoy, James. 1968. The Bomba and Aguinaldo of Puerto Rico as They Have Evolved from Indigenous African and European Cultures. Tesis doctoral, Florida State University.

Mignolo, Walter. 2003. *The Darker Side of the Renaissance: Literacy Territoriality & Colonization.* Ann Arbor: Michigan University Press.

________. 2007. El pensamiento decolonial: desprendimiento y apertura. En *El giro decolonial. Reflexiones para una diversidad epistémico más allá del capitalismo global,* eds. Santiago Castro-Gómez y Ramón Grafosfoguel. 25–46. Bogotá: Siglo del Hombre Editores.

Montes-Pizarro-Pizarro, Errol. 2012. Viajes de la música afrodescendiente: Más allá de la metáfora de raíz. En Duprey, M (Ed.), *Memorias de Bomba que Rumba: Memorias del Primer Simposio sobre la Bomba y la Rumba,* (97-119). San Juan: Publicaciones puertorriqueñas.

________. 2015a. The Paradox of Puerto Rican 'Trova Jíbara' in Colombia: Builing Bridges over 'Blanqueamiento'across the Americas. *VI Congreso Internacional Música, Identidad y Cultura en el Caribe.* Santiago de los Caballeros: Instituto de Estudios Caribeños y Centro León.

________. 2015b. Conservatorio en el Saramanda Club. YouTube <https://youtu.be/E_J_jTS4R1Y/>.

Moreno, Marisel. 2010. Family Matters: revisiting 'la gran familia puertorriqueña' in the works of Rosario Ferré and Judith Ortíz Cofer. *CENTRO: Journal of the Center for Puerto Rican Studies* 22: 75-105.

Ohadike, Don. C. 2007. *Sacred Drums of Liberation: Religions and Music of Resistance in Africa and the Diaspora.* Trenton: Africa World Press .

Plena is Work, Plena is Song. 1989. Pedro A. Rivera y Susan Zeig, directores. Recuperado de <https://www.youtube.com/watch?v=iAsX3qi0Kg8&t=508s/>.

Quijano, Anibal. 1991. Colonialidad y modernidad/racionalidad. *Perú indígena,* 29: 11-21.

________. 1999. ¡Qué tal raza! *Ecuador Debate. Etinicdades e identificaciones* 48: 141-152.

________. 2000. Colonaliadad del poder, eurocentrismo y América Latina. En: Lander, E. (comp.). La colonialidad del saber: eurocentrismo y ciencias sociales. Perspectivas latinoamericanas. Buenos Aires: CLASCO.

________. 2007. Colonialidad del poder y clasificación social. En Castro-Gómez, Santiago y Grafosfoguel, Ramón (eds.). *El giro decolonial. Reflexiones para una diversidad epistémico más allá del capitalismo global.* (págs. 93-126). Bogotá: Siglo del Hombre Editores.

________. 2014. Raza, Etnia y Nación en Mariátegui: cuestiones abiertas. En *Cuestiones y horizontes: de la dependencia histórico-estructural a la colonialidad/descolonialidad del poder*. Buenos Aires: CLACSO.

Quintero Rivera, Ángel. 2009. *Cuerpo y cultura: las músicas "mulatas" y la subversión del baile.* Madrid: Iberoamericana.

Rivera Rivera, Pablo L. 2013. Orígenes culturales y el desarrollo de la bomba en Puerto Rico. Tesis doctoral, Centro de Estudios Avanzados de Puerto Rico y el Caribe.

Rumba y Candela 2013: The Spirit of Rumba. 2013. Recuperado de: <https://www.youtube.com/watch?v=m3nzABX30_I&t=1310s&list=WL&index=9/>.

Rumberos de Cuba. 2016. Havana Club International S.A. [HavanaCultura]. 16 de febrero. <https://www.youtube.com/watch?v=HF3C2Df2JZ0/>.

Santos, Boaventura de Souza. 2010. *Descolonizar el saber, reinventar el poder.* Montevideo: Ediciones Trilce.

Sued Badillo, Jalil. 1986. *Puerto Rico negro*. San Juan: Editorial Cultural.

Vega Drouet, Héctor. 1979. Historical and Ethnological Survey on the Probable African Origins of the Puerto Rican Bomba. Tesis doctoral, Wesleyan University.

Toledo-Hernández, Enrique. 2011. *La burocratización del poder colonial: de la americanización a la tecno-buroqueñización del territorio no incorporado de Puerto Rico & el informe del "Task Force" de la Casa Blanca sobre el estatus político de Puerto Rico.* Río Piedras: Archivo Sociedad Sinergia .

Torres, Arlene. 1998. La gran familia puertorriqueña: 'ej prieta de beldá' - the Great Puerto Rican family is really really black. En A. Torres, & N. E. Whitten, *Blackness in Latin America and the Caribbean* (págs. 287-306). Bloomington: Indiana University Press.

Torres-Figueroa, Brenda y Arif Smith. 2015. Candela. *Chicagoartistsmonth.com*. Consultado el 19 de enero 2017. <http://www.chicagoartistsmonth.org/candela/>.

Vergara, P. B. 2014. "Siento, luego existo". Cuerpo y meociones en dos personajes afrodescendientes en la literatura chilena. En Pizarro, Ana y Benavente, Carolina. *África/América: Literatura y Colonialidad* (págs. 45-54). Santiago: Fondo de Cultura Económica.

Walsh, Catherine. 2005. (Re)pensamiento crítico y (de)colonialidad. En: Catherine Walsh (ed.), *Pensamiento crítico y matriz (de)colonial. Reflexiones latinoamericanas.* (págs. 13-35). Quito: Universidad Andina Simón Bolívar-Abya-Yala.

________. 2010. Interculturalidad crítica y pedagogía de-colonial: In-surgir, re-existir y re-vivir. *Entrepalabras,* 3. Revista de Educación en el Lenguaje, la Literatura y la Oralidad. La Paz: Universidad Mayor San Andrés.

VOLUME XXXI • NUMBER II • SUMMER 2019

INTERVIEW / ENTREVISTA

The Bombazo-Fandango: An Interview with Hector Luis Rivera (aka HecOne, aka HecVortex)

JADE POWER-SOTOMAYOR

I sat down with bombero Hector Luis Rivera, a Bronx Boricua living on the West Coast, to talk with him about his work in co-organizing the Bombazo-Fandango. Together with his wife and partner Melody González-Chávez, a Chicana cultural worker and educator, they envisioned and produced four Bombazo-Fandango events between 2009 and 2014 in Melody's home town of Santa Ana, California. The Bombazo-Fandango was—and as discussed below, may someday be again—a week-long event bringing together master teachers and practitioners from both bomba and son jarocho communities. Consisting of workshops, performances, exhibits, dialogues, and many all-night "after-parties," the event aimed to strengthen and deepen community connections by creating complex musical exchanges and cultural dialogues about what these African diasporic practices share and the distinct function that they serve in their respective communities.

The Bombazo-Fandango initially emerged from the interpersonal intimacy experienced across Boricua and Chicanx communities and the particular experience of practicing bomba on the West Coast, specifically in Santa Ana, what Rivera calls "a Puerto Rican desert," but also a city with a strong Mexican presence. Santa Ana, the

The author (powersoto@gmail.com) is an Assistant Professor in the Department of Theatre and Dance at the University of California, San Diego. She is a Cali-Rican performance scholar and a bomba cultural worker and dancer. Research interests include: Latinx theatre and performance, dance studies, epistemologies of the body, feminist of color critique, bilingualism, and intercultural performance in the Caribbean diaspora. Her current book project, *¡Habla!: Speaking Bodies in Latinx Dance and Performance*, theorizes Latinidad and Latinx communities of belonging as constituted through doing versus being.

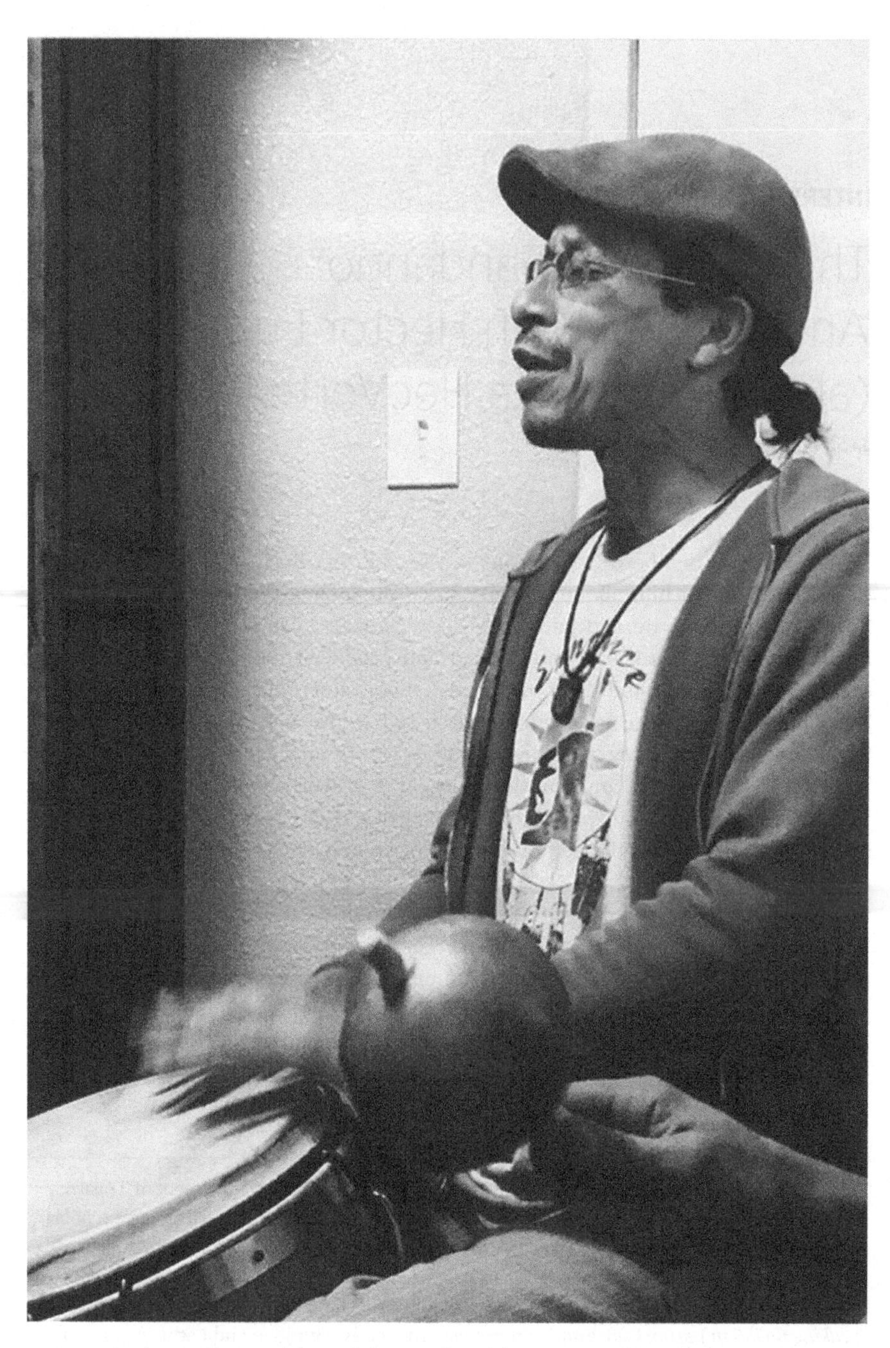

Hector Luis Rivera. Photograph by Melody González Chávez. Reprinted by permission.

Puerto Rican desert," but also a city with a strong Mexican presence. Santa Ana, the county seat of the notoriously conservative and very wealthy Orange County, stands in sharp contrast as a city where 78 percent of the population is Latinx, many are immigrants, poverty levels are high, and Spanish is widely spoken in public. Having myself participated in and benefitted from the Bombazo-Fandangos as a *bombera* from down the road in San Diego, I witnessed the profound ways this event both drew upon and consolidated bomba communities on the West Coast. At the same time, it also deepened and forged lasting ties with *jaraneros*, providing a context to understand and appreciate *son jarocho* as a practice.

These Santa Ana events were not the first examples of bomba and son jarocho collaborations in the US, but certainly they were the most thoughtfully articulated and purposefully curated. In other words, while bomba and son jarocho had come together through the happenstance of shared space and shared community in other places and at other moments, the Bombazo-Fandango came into being through a conscious choice to celebrate and examine these genres alongside each other. Hector shares that the original impulse for creating the event emerged from a desire for togetherness, a relational building that is both personal (romantic) and communal. "Looking for an excuse to be together" refers to the practical realities of manifesting shared time and space for what was at first a long-distance relationship between him and Melody. However, it also recognizes that the success of interpersonal relationships comes from the support of community networks of belonging. Thus, the success of the events—because indeed they were successful in creating a web of connections and in sharing diverse knowledges—comes from the fact that in enacting this trans-diasporic, intra-Latinx *convivencia* they highlighted the following:

- Music, dance and signing activate a shared sense of belonging that can both help name and heal the traumas of living in a racist, xenophobic society in the US, as well as articulate and enact a political stance of resistance in relationship to the dominant culture. Both bomba and son jarocho communities have done this.
- The enslavement of Africans that took place widely throughout the Americas and the forced movement of Black bodies in and following the transatlantic slave trade led to a complex circulation of African diasporic cultural practices that continue to mark the histories and experiences of Black people and their descendants throughout the Americas. Bomba and son jarocho are two such examples. More specifically, they share Congo origins.
- The appropriation of practices marked "Black" and "Indigenous" by nation-building projects has in many cases led to the folklorization of said practices, rendering them "objects" frozen in time and estranged from the contemporary experiences of the descendants of their originators. Parallel movements to de-folklorize bomba and son jarocho have prioritized community participation and practice outside the context of the staged performance.
- Given the parallel movements to center the *batey* and the *fandango/huapango*

over staged enactments, diasporic practitioners of both bomba and son jarocho similarly navigate mandates to maintain the fundamental aspects of the form and adequately "represent tradition" while at the same time attending to the political, cultural, and geographic realities in which they are living.

- Despite living alongside each other and crossing paths in a variety of community circles, Boricuas and Chicanxs do not often have the opportunity to learn the particularities of each other's histories and experiences. Through the embodied knowledges offered by bomba and son jarocho, members of these groups have been able to learn ways of being together that are determined outside the logics typically offered through political coalition building.
- Because developing the skills necessary to create and maintain bomba and son jarocho communities requires access to space, practitioners have relied on fostering important relationships with cultural centers and communal hubs that may often be private residences. As such, bomba and son jarocho communities enact long-term embodied relationships to space and place that extends beyond simply "using a rehearsal space."

The crossings imagined by the Bombazo-Fandango, and the relationships and alliances it produced, inspired other musical/dance solidarities that have since taken place in distinct locations. For instance, Seattle hosted a "Bombango" and continues to develop bomba practice in large part via networks established through the local son jarocho project. At the annual Fandango Fronterizo, a bi-national son jarocho event held on both sides of the US-Mexico border, bomberxs have been present to play both bomba and plena on different occasions. Even when these exchanges are not purposefully orchestrated, familiarities with the protocols and languages unique to bomba and son jarocho have created ways to connect in improvisation whenever and wherever these communities and practitioners may find themselves together.

Hector Luis Rivera is an important figure in contemporary diasporic bomba practice, especially through his many song compositions

---

Despite the many utopic possibilities offered by the Bombazo-Fandango and its offshoots, it should be clear that these exchanges have been far from idyllic: a collection of love-filled moments of song and dance, harmonies and discordant syncopations, of mistranslations and misunderstandings, hand-holdings and embraces, protective respectful distance-taking, of behind-closed-doors whispers of doubts, and public declarations of solidarity. They have required physical, artistic, social and intellectual labor, deep listening, and bravery. Most of all they are born of a shared inspiration and commitment to bomba and son jarocho and the histories they breathe life into, the ancestors and communities to whom they are responsible. Hector Luis

Rivera is an important figure in contemporary diasporic bomba practice, especially through his many song compositions. Together with Melody, he has been instrumental in envisioning and carrying out these possible crossings. In the interview that follows, he traces his journey from hip hop and poetry to bomba, reflects on bomba's healing properties, relates his own experiences as a bombero now living on the West Coast, and shares how he planted the seeds for and now envisions growing the Bombazo-Fandango.

February 24, 2017

Jade Power-Sotomayor: This is a question that Pablo Luis Rivera asks his guests in his show for Radio Bonita *Repicando*. What does bomba mean to you? *¿Como tú defines la bomba?*

Hector Luis Rivera: Yea. That question always strikes me as the perfect question. You know who the first person that made me think of it was Reynaldo [Rodríguez], the artist, when he did his exhibition in Florida. And I got to meet up with him. And he had done a piece of me playing the *cua*.

To me bomba is medicine. Its around. You know anything that's around for hundreds of years, there's a good reason for it. Bomba is around for hundreds of years because it's medicine for our people.

Culture is medicine too. To be rooted like a tree. And so bomba is that, to be rooted in who we are. I met the poet Mayra Santos Febres when I was at Cornell, and I remember she wrote about Puerto Rican culture being in the air. In the airwaves. She's talked a lot about that give and take of diaspora and the so-called mainland. The main island, our motherland. And what culture is in between that, and also the play between those. I also see it spiritually that way too. It's just energy. And that expression of who we are, in order to become more human. And that's part of it, the Puerto Rican trying to express themselves, more humanly. And that's bomba.

So bomba is medicine. When the so-called DNA, or whatever molecules of bomba in me got reignited, when I saw bomba in...I think it was in 1995 at Bronx Museum of the Arts. There was an exhibition of *casitas*. I forget who curated it, but it was an exhibition of casitas, replicas of little casitas that neighborhood gardens would have, like La Casita de Chema, Rincón Criollo. They were all over the barrio and the Bronx and all the other boroughs too. Maybe even in Philly and other places. I know Chicago has one. There was this exhibition, and the Pleneros de la 21 were playing. They performed with a big replica of a casita. It was real dope. The dance is what struck me. It was like what I would have considered back then in my frame of reference: *¡oh se montó*! It was really spiritual. And I started to cry right there. I think the song was even about someone that had passed away. And I was moved at the energy and the delivery. And it resonated. For me, that was part of reconnecting the seams. Now I realize that my father is from a place that is known for bomba, and knew all great dancers that people are talking about now, went to school with them, played baseball with them, down the block: *O sí, este tal don Miguel... que si esto que si lo otro*. And my aunt on my mother's side has played bomba along with other folkloric music in a group called Guateque from Corozal, for over 35 years. And so it was just reignited, you know.

But it came through poetry first actually. Through a love of poetry, Nuyorican poetry. Again, just that same desire that people have in general to express themselves and find a voice.

And so through Poetry eventually, and the love of percussion and drum, came bomba. So bomba to me is my medicine.

JP-S: Did you imagine that you would be playing bomba every day when you first saw it? Heard it?

HLR: Probably my subconscious did. Was like, Yes this is what I like, I love this! But no really, I would have never imagined, I am so happy, it's such a blessing. To find community everywhere. That's part of the medicine, is that bomba brings the people together. That's what the batey is, a circle, and it's not broken. There's that reminder. There is that Native American teaching about the circle being broken and needing to fix it. And these practices, these so-called "restorative practices" that we've been practicing forever, that uplift our resilience. And bomba is one of them. It's all over the diaspora, that's the most beautiful thing. Thanks really to a lot of families and people, my generation and younger who did a lot of work in terms of researching and bringing together a lot of information, interviews. A lot of different people. People from Emmannuellis, to Vélezes, to Ferraos, to Pablo Riveras, to LaSalles and to the families who kept it, and began schools when it wasn't something that was cool, you know, and it was still a struggle. Not that it's on the radio now, but it wasn't something super popular that was going to make you rich or nothin'; it was for the love. And that says a lot about bomba itself. It brings all of that energy with it. It brings all of the hundreds of years of the songs that started on the plantations. It brings that same energy of trying to write new songs about what's happening now. That same dichotomy of slave/not slave. Free/not free. Love/hate, hurt/community. It's the same energy.

JP-S: How did you first start studying bomba then?

HLR: I was a poet with The Welfare Poets. We ran into this dude, I forget his name. He was on the Banco Popular video playing next to Giovanni, light-skinned dude, playing in that scene [Ramón Gómez]. He was at Cornell. I remember one day, cuz we loved percussion, we would play rhythms without having no teachings, just playing drums, kinda copying what Last Poets had done and all the music that was living through us. Someone would teach us a *tumbao* here or there. And so one day this dude brought a *barril* and taught us some rhythms. So that was the first time. But really in New York with The Welfare Poets, there were a lot of the members of the wonderful bomba groups and the Antillean groups, and we got to perform with them. With members of these groups and people that would become the groups. I started writing bomba songs and plena for Welfare Poets by around 2003-4. And I was surrounded by all these groups developing at that time, Yerbabuena, for instance, and my brother [Flaco Navaja] started singing with them and then there was Alma Moyó eventually. These are all the same generation of people who were learning and also researching. And in 2006 big there was a big *bombplenazo*. And the *Raíces* video [Banco Popular Special] had already come out. It was all just a big turning point, bomba was spreading in all these ways, there was a lot of growing. And that was when I moved to Chicago. And that's when I really started. I talked to Rubén [Gerena] from Nuestro Tambó, and I said I think I could write songs. I said "I write poetry, I like bomba, I'd like to be part of the group, I'd like to learn." *Y ahí me pusieron. Y ahí seguí.* And ever since then, anywhere, everywhere. Just playing and I love it. It's a fix. You know how we do it: bomba zombie all day! And that's why I teach. It's not because I'm finished as a student by far. There are so many times that as a teacher when I say something I'm like, "Oh, I gotta rememeber that!" *Firmeza,* oh my gosh, I keep forgetting. Things like that.[1]

And when you do that together as a community, it transforms energy.

As a teacher, I share because it brings people together. There is a magic that comes when you just bring people together. But there *are* tendencias...like the name of the group in Puerto Rico...I love the name....the different aspects, like in dance firmeza, *postura*, different rhythms, different approaches to the rhythms. That's a key to expressing something. And when you do that together as a community, it transforms energy. That's why I keep saying its medicine. Teaching it is to create that possibility. That's why I like to teach it and do it here in Santa Ana, in what might be considered a Puerto Rican desert. Ha!

JP-S: Was there a point you felt like you actually became a *bombero*?

HLR: There was music in my house growing up but nothing formal. I never had an instrument, just breakdancing and dancin' and things like that (*laughs*). So, I probably became a bombero when I moved to Chicago, 'cause it was everywhere and every week I was playing bomba. I already love percussion, played on every window sill, chair, table, like "Stop playing!" But once I start playing every day, it becomes part of everyday life, part of eating, how I walk, how I walk to the bathroom. I could practice singing a song, writing a song because I was around it all the time. It's like this. The people I am around love it. I am going to a bombazo; I don't feel well. I am going to go, and the power of bomba is that I am going to sing this *coro* without announcing, and we're going to get it *y de ahí sale—"Me curé, me curé, con la bomba me curé."*[2] It just becomes part of life; let's do it together. Community was a pillar for me in that moment, to help me get through things that were happening.

JP-S: So why did you start Buya?[3]

HLR: Well I was playing with Nuestro Tambó for a while. And you know it's like a lot of musical families in New York and other places, where it's just one general family of musicians who love this type music and want to keep learning and playing it. It was the same thing in Chicago. One big family of people who play it. Some of us were in Nuestro Tambó; a lot of us, all together. There a family of bomberos in Chicago, from the people of AfriCaribe, to the people who were playing bomba with Grupo Yubá with Eli Samuel [Rodríguez] and Centro Cultural Ruíz Belvis to even some other groups before that. There is whole trajectory in Chicago. I was lucky enough to be invited to play with Nuestro Tambó, Grupo Yubá.[4] So there was a point where a couple of us bomberos who weren't necessarily in a group but were living together, and of course still living bomba. So we said let's start a group! It's interesting. I'm glad you asked me about Buya. I think it's an important group, not because I claim anything with them; they are amazing on their own. But how it started, the foundation is important. Berto, one of the co-founders, said something very important: "There was the *época* of bomba *de* plantations/ then, the epoca of bomba *de familias* and we are in the epoca now of bomba *de grupos*." But Buya is also a familia. I agree with that, that's the way it started. I was living with Piro [Teo López], one of the members. Of course, Ivie [Iveliesse Díaz] is his sister, Berto [Roberto Pérez] is a *compay*. So we started Buya. (*Laughs*). Buya means *espíritu bueno*. We really just want to bring this spirit to bomba. I was with them not even a year before I moved to Cali. And then it was right after that they got the blessing of meeting Rafa and Pablo and Gío [Jiménez].[5] And they ate it up and grew exponentially and just continued. That says a lot about the teachers and ambassadors of bomba that Rafa [Maya] and Pablo [Rivera] and Gío are. Gío, Rest in peace. Their mastery of the genre, their mastery of history and talking about it visa-vis other musics, but also their inviting ways of teaching and building community. It's so important. It's all important, but I think their visits have really helped in this Puerto Rican desert to keep it fertile. And other visits, so many visits. Of course, the founding visits that planted seeds were from the Cepedas who came to the Bay.

JP-S: So what happened when you moved to Santa Ana, and how did it feel to be a Boricua in Aztlán, specifically a Bronx Boricua?

HLR: It's great; I feel blessed because I have good roots. I've been in different places throughout my life. I went to boarding school and was among the rich. I had to figure out who I was when I went to Cornell. That's always the wonderful struggle for a Boricua in the colonial condition, especially in the diaspora. In Santa Ana I felt blessed because I had Melody who was already beloved here. And so that was easy! We did an event before I even moved out here. Bombazo Fandango, the first one, was here, 2009. *La misma idea, una excusa pa' vernos*. Bring people together, and bring the rest of our communities together. We brought Buya with us, and then we also brought the *fandangueros*, the people who play son jarocho, the huapango, all the ways they call it. Son del Centro and all the extended family that came through that community. It was a big event...that's how we met you for the first time! So yea, being in Santa Ana, there was a dope community of music. At the same time, like always, the joy of finding Boricuas everywhere and anywhere. I once saw a book that talked about Puerto Rican migration and Latino migration throughout California and Southern California, 1990 something, and there were like 90,000 Puerto Ricans. So, *estamos por ahí y por allá*.

And we have important history, events important to this country from this region like Boricuas, Afro-boricuas Felícita Méndez and her daughter Sylvia Méndez.[6] So Santa Ana has been awesome. But, of course, I am always thirsty for our people. So that's been great to have the family. San Diego, LA, and the Bay. And again, the excuse always to bring us all together, all of it, that we love, what my partner Melody loves, what I love, what we both love, is the *bombazo fandangos*. That's how it formally became.

JP-S: What would you say have been your goals in playing bomba especially in terms of performance and the dynamics between the so-called professionalization of genre and the community-based practice? What do you make of that dynamic of bomba as performance, like when people find out you play bomba, they invite you to perform, they want bomba at their event and you want to present a certain quality. You want to respect the genre by presenting a certain quality, but also you want to continue to value and promote its place in the community and keep it open. How do you navigate that?

HLR: That's a good question. *Pues, la intención*. First intention is to play and have fun. To bring people together. I love it. As far as my experience in California and in Chicago, in any group, if we perform and are exchanging energy and money for it.... It's almost like it's a given; it's so we keep doing it. Because there is a passion to share it, to share it with others. As a teacher, it's also to keep learning and teaching to build a community. And to be real, there's times where you just have three or four people, that's the nature of it out here. And we still want to continue it, and not let the fire die out. That's real; it's exactly just like that. The fire is going to die out if we don't keep it lit. And so we play, we play with what we've got. And then there's times where we can push ourselves and say hey, let's bring it. And we have it. Let's bring the best representation of bomba to this school. That's where groups materialize. It's a real tension though. It's good. I remember receiving an email from a great teacher who had seen a video posted and wrote kinda calling us out, saying: Hey, there is a great responsibility with what you are doing.... And I was like: it's true. But there's more to it too; let's build a relationship because we are in a desert. This is what we've got. There's more to it too. But it's not hurting nobody. I get it. But at the same time I've seen crazier stuff in Puerto Rico in videos that I see circulating all the time. Just saying....

JP-S: What do you most love about bomba? As a practitioner, do you have frustrations?

HLR: That we don't get to play longer, that there's not enough spaces, that we're not close together. That's the longing, the yearning for it. All day every day. I love the challenge of the dance. For me, it's big. To be able to reclaim my body in dance. To work it and control it, while still being graceful. To be able to use it to express whatever different emotion. Grace or power. *El reto del baile*. I love the connection of *primo* with the dancer, that energy. I love being in brotherhood and sisterhood with the drummers, with the *buleo*. Together. How it affects the whole room to be in resonance together. Same thing with the great piece of the *coro*; that's church. And singing—well, it's so fun. Its *sacando* emotions with tones. I don't have the best

Spanish vocabulary, but that's what I am aiming for, and I think of songs all day long about what emotion I want to express. I think because I don't have that big Spanish vocabulary, then anyone can interface with my songs differently. Hopefully. It's a blessing when other people like my songs and, well, sing them. That's the intention. To have them sing.

JP-S: What was your first interface with son jarocho?

HLR: Well, subconsciously, Ritchie Valens...but then really for real like in fandango in Chicago. In fact, I met a lot of the folks from Santa Ana in Chicago with the CIW [Coalition of Immokalee Workers] and with Melody.[7] Chicago has a big community of Boricuas *and* Mexicans. And they live close together.

Not a mash up but to show "This is how we celebrate when we get together, when we have a party it's called a bombazo, when you all have a party it's called a fandango."

JP-S: Did you attend events where bomba and son jarocho had been played together?

HLR: Before I got to Chicago there was an event with AfriCaribe and Gina Pacheco (Maya's mom), but when I was there...we had events on the same bill...in Little Village...nothing big. Well, one of the biggest was when the CIW won the campaign against McDonald's, and we were supposed to play bomba. It was huge because it was also the reunion of Zach [De La Rocha] and this dude from Rage Against the Machine [Tom Morello]. It was like an overnight victory. It was supposed to be a protest and a victory party celebration the next day at the House of Blues. *Y fue un revolú,* all packed, overbooked, tight. They said you can't perform. And we were like: "drop the *barriles* and take the *panderos*!" And we just got on stage and started playing. That was an event with a lot of son jarocho. It was mostly Son del Centro from Santa Ana.

JP-S: What gave you the idea for organizing the bombazo-fandango, or even calling it that?

HLR: Well the idea was because I was going to visit Melody! [In Santa Ana].

JP-S: So, it was like, let's have an event and bring my people together with your people?

HLR: Well we already knew that the bombazo was our jam, and the fandango was their jam, and it was going to be a jam, a get together. Not jam in the sense of putting all these instruments together but get together and bring our musics and our community together. Not a mash up but to show "This is how we celebrate when we get together, when we have a party it's called a bombazo, when you all have a party it's called a fandango." So, it was a bombazo-fandango. It was intentional. We brought a lot of people together! It was a lot. Ten members of Buya came, San Diego came (at that time, the group was called Areito Borincano), from LA Atabey came, from the Bay Bomberas de la Bahía came. And just like us in California and in Chicago, there was this family of bomba developing "pan states." The same thing in son jarocho. When they were going to make a call, it was going to be to fandangueros from Santa

Ana, and it was going to be a call to all fandangueros. So, by nature it became a way of bringing many different people together when really the original, bottom-line intention was: "Hey, Melody, I want to see you, I love you." *Y de esa semilla sigue creciendo.*

JP-S: And how did it continue to develop over the years, how did it change?

HLR: Well, we got more intentional with what we could offer. In the first one we offered workshops in both bomba dance and *zapateado*. The next year we had raised funds to bring *maestros* from the respective locations: Puerto Rico and Veracruz. That's when we brought Pablo and Rafa for the first time. At the same time, we had other maestros from Veracruz. We always worked together and just figured it out. We brought Patricio Hidalgo. It developed into workshops and a photography exhibit, a great dialogue with over seventy people. More than twelve workshops in a day. Performances by different groups that came through. And then a bunch of after parties throughout. Sometimes as many as two hundred musicians. The last one we had the Quenepas, the kids group from the Bay.[8] It was the best thing ever. Here it is, the seeds, keeping this music three thousand miles away.

JP-S: So, in bringing people from Mexico and Puerto Rico *and* from other parts of the diaspora, do you think it's important for this to take place in the US as opposed to in México or Puerto Rico?

HLR: Truthfully, anywhere and everywhere. It didn't start here. This type of *encuentro* happened when Paracumbé performed in Veracruz. And I know Tito Matos was over there too. There's a video of a *fandanguera* doing zapateado and Nellie [Lebrón] from Paracumbé singing, "*Chupa chupa chupa, la condenada*" [son jarocho song]. So it's happening, and it's happened before, and it's happening more and more. It happened in 2006 at the Smithsonian Folkways Festival with AfriCaribe from Chicago and Son de Madera from Veracruz, playing together for a song.[9] It's happened in Chicago, before there was ever a bombazo-fandango here. My dream for the next one, the fifth one, is to activate people in those communities where it's already happening. Be part of the same *jornada de* bombazo-fandango. Do it around the same month or months. Create a nexus. Possibilities are: workshops, dialogues, performances. There was already something in New York, Chicago. In Florida let it happen, in the Bay, in Seattle. And the last week we party down the West Coast and end up in Mexico! After parties all the way.

JP-S: It's like the Fandango Fronterizo that has people doing parallel events at the same time across the world.[10]

HLR: Which is also very connected to the Bombazo-Fandango, it's part of the same movement really. It's the same communities!

JP-S: But, again, do you think there is some particular value in doing it in the diaspora?

HLR: *Es una manera de nutrir las comunidades.* For instance, Rafa, my compay and great teacher and musician and friend, he expresses a lot of gratitude about the diaspora. The truth is though that it's always been part of our identity, the development of the flag, to great writers like Jesús Colón writing in New York, to Ismael Rivera going back and forth. It's part of our identity as a colony. In expressing ourselves fully, we have to include the diaspora. That's the push-pull. The music has always developed that way. Los Pleneros de la 21, a hugely important group: they're from New York! Like Mayra says, "Identity is in the air." That's our reality. My son is a Bori-Mex, and he's not the only one, even way back when like Sylvia Méndez. These communities have been meeting and building together forever. The same way that it happens in the Antilles. Betances: his mother and father were Dominican. You know who said it best: Patricio Hidalgo, the great singer and composer from Veracruz. In a bombazo-fandago he said, "*Un fandango sin proposito puede fracasar.*" So I take that to mean that you have good intentions, you bring people together, good things happen. We find dancers in the dialogue, we see ourselves in the exhibit, we learn from each other, learn new songs and moves and get inspired. In general, that's the beautiful thing about bomba spreading everywhere. And there's always the fear, which I understand, about bomba getting away from us. That's the beast of consumer culture, of capitalism, but with a good seed we shouldn't worry. Like that teacher who wrote to me: "Don't worry; you've planted a great seed already. And your father, and your father's father and mother." Keep walking that walk and learning and doing it will be ok.

JP-S: So how do you think that values of tradition and innovation play out in the bombazo fandango? Since it *is* in the diaspora, you have all these communities that practice away from the source. They are away from having a lot access to seeing practitioners and communities that have been doing it a long time. So, they develop their own ways of doing it, that are around a *fundamento* but sometimes, just different.

HLR: I feel like I am one of those people that participates a lot in bomba yet didn't have a really close teacher. I had to just be in it to learn it. Every now and then the reflections of other people served as my teacher; and then, from that, I tried to be better. I think that's what most people have experienced. Not everyone has a close teacher or comes from a family of bomberos. So yea, in terms of the tension between tradition and innovation, that's a dialogue in both communities. The huapango/fandango and in the bomba communities. It boils down to the same thing: strong *fundamentos*. The truth is, though, is that it is constantly changing. The barril we have today is not the one we had back then. People dress differently. And yes, we are three thousand miles away! But we influence each other.

JP-S: *En navidades* in Puerto Rico I saw three people dance with skirts and every other woman I saw danced without a skirt. Norms change. Which is also, in part, influenced by the diaspora.

HLR: But there is also something about the material conditions. There is no bomba store to go buy a *falda*. There is a consumerist culture that just wants to buy in order to access. They just want to dance and maybe sometimes want immediate access that also reflects a fast-paced society. So it is important in a culture that is fast and doesn't take its time to respect and honor the elders and the sacrifices, the conditions endured, to keep this music alive. It didn't come from a jukebox, from the studio. This is in my DNA, and instinctively that gives me a way to survive the attempted genocide. *Punto*. In the *cañaverales*, the plantations, I am going to take the space, create the space, the batey. And that's why its magic, that ceremonial space.

JP-S: So is the batey—what you would say—is the most productive aspect of the bombaza-fandango overall? Or what is?
HLR: That people feel good. That's all. That people feel like community, that it highlights the reality that we live together and feel each other (*laughs*). There's someone from the son jarocho community who whispers and tells me, "I think I love bomba more." And I'm like "Ahhh I'm going to tell everyone!!" (*laughs*). No, but it's beautiful. *Sirve*. It's something that makes everyone feel good. There's even been moments of bringing the music together.
JP-S: Does it work?
HLR: Of course it works. Some of it I like more than other times, but it's just about finding it and continuing to dialogue and figuring it out.
JP-S: What have been some of the challenges in organizing and executing the event?
HLR: Most of the challenges are my own. It's come out great, but finding resources is always a challenge. But being resourceful makes it all come together. There are more skills that I need to learn and to involve other people and share the loads. I would like to bring more people in and make it more self-sufficient. One real challenge is that things happen within the communities themselves that then get in the way, that stop communication and dialogue between groups that make this community even exist in the first place.
JP-S: So the best part is also the most challenging part: community.
HLR: Yup. That's why we have to do the next bombazo-fandango. For more healing.
JP-S: What do you think the musical genres have in common? Because you just can't put anything together. Clearly bomba and son jarocho have lots of things in common. You hear this is in the dialogues, the musical practice, the music making. But also, how are they different? Because they are also very different. The musics but also the communities. They have a lot in common but also differences. This is something that I have observed at the bombazo-fandangos; there is a sense of coming together, but also a clear sense of difference. Not all households are Bori-Mex *pa' decirlo así*.
HLR: Not all households are Bori-Mex. This is true. But part of the beauty is that there is a healthy curiosity. And that healthy curiosity can help this world more generally. Like: "Oh wow, look at the Boricuas and how they are"; and "Oh wow, look at the fandangueros, and all the people that love it."
JP-S: Look at the fandangueros that don't get tired playing!
HLR: Playing til the sun comes up! Amazing. ¡*Y siguen cantando*! So yea there's a healthy curiosity that is dope. But it's also complex because there is still difference in that. Not all fandangueros are alike. There's folks from Veracruz whose families have been playing forever and talk about "*los tiempos de antes*" and are like "you all are playing too fast." Which is very similar to things we hear in our community. So this healthy curiosity lends to the dialogue of what our similarities are. Musically there are so many. In both, the dancer makes music, zapateando or with *piquetes*. But there's also differences there. Also through the words. Patricio Hidalgo looks at the word "fandango" and the root "ango" as having Congo, Bantu origins. Which of

course is one of the strongest roots of bomba. From my perspective, as someone not really in the son jarocho community, the tension around innovation seems different. Like they play mostly old songs. It's part of a project of *rescatando* and bringing them to light. So there is less emphasis, from my relatively uninformed perspective, on new compositions. While in bomba, there are a lot of new compositions more and more every day.

One of the things that is often cited is that both of these genres are afrodescendientes, and that is also part of why it makes sense to hold them in the same space, that shared history.

JP-S: You already kind of answered this, but do you enjoy playing the two genres together, or do you prefer them to be in the same space but played separately?
HLR: Same space but separately. And if we continue to dialogue, we will find something. I have had different levels of enjoyment of attempts to do that. For instance, I liked when you all in Bomba Liberté did a song together. We did some moments with Atabey and Quetzal in Pomona. But more dialogue is necessary. There hasn't been enough. The last bombazo-fandango was when we actually felt like "*vamos a atrevernos.*" There's been a real respectful intention to meet but not try to "mash it up." There was an article that came out around the time of the bombazo-fandango where they interviewed us, and when it came out, it was framed as a "mash up," and I was like: No! That's not what this is.
JP-S: A mash up of two communities maybe.
HLR: Maybe. It's still more complex than that.
JP-S: *¿Y tú nunca has tratado de aprender son jarocho*?
HLR: I'm intimidated. I would love to. It seems like I'm a repetitive record: but also, more than anything, just to be part of that community.
JP-S: I feel you.
HLR: And I love music of course, I love *décimas*, and that poetry that I wish I could unlock within me. I think about it all the time but I am intimidated.
JP-S: But I think you see more Chicanos trying to do bomba, *atreviéndose* but then...
HLR: *Bueno* one of Buya's members started off playing son jarocho....Jonathan Pacheco. He was one of the Jarochicanos in Chicago. One of first times I seen son jarocho through CIW. And he was part of them, and they were like, yea, *es* Boricua, and we were like *vente pa' acá*. But he was in the South side, or another neighborhood and eventually they connected. But he was a little kid, and he's still young, but he was a little kid then, really talented as a musician, rocking playing primo.
JP-S: But I think we could agree though that there are more jaraneros interested in playing bomba than there are bomberos interested in playing son jarocho. What's your theory?
HLR: Out here it makes sense because we are thirsty for our own stuff, and then we're a curiosity to them. And so we're still just thirsty for our own stuff (*laughs*). That's cool,

but I gotta play bomba! In Chicago those communities are closer together, and there's a lot more of them. For example, at times there have been four or five bomba groups, same with son jarocho. It's not like that out here, though, bomba is the novelty.

JP-S: Ok. So here's another question: How do you think ideas about race, blackness specifically, circulate in conversations at and around the Bombazo-Fandango? Do you think there is a way that bomba is seen as more Black? One of the things that is often cited is that both of these genres are afrodescendientes, and that is also part of why it makes sense to hold them in the same space, that shared history. But then is there one that is seen as "more Black?" And does that matter? I would say that people tend to see bomba as "*más negro*" to some extent, from both communities perhaps. Do you think that matters? How do you see that playing out?

HLR: Yea.... Anywhere that there is a manifestation of blackness in the African diaspora, it's alive despite harsh conditions.... I don't know about discussions of things being more Black or less Black...it's tough. Now there is more public discussion of Africans in Mexico. There were more Africans that went to Mexico than the United States! Of course, the Caribbean was the first stop and got the most.

JP-S: There is also a longer trajectory of naming blackness in the Caribbean, so there is a way to name it.

HLR: Like in Cuba, Brazil. So, it's beautiful that in Mexico they're talking about it more.... When it becomes problematic is when we bring the psychosis of how we look at race in the United States.

JP-S: I think it's important to recognize that just because you are Mexican, or Puerto Rican, Afro-Puerto Rican or Afro-Mexican, we bring these ideas with us to the practice.

HLR: When I studied Africana studies, it was important for me to realize the difference between race and culture. The intersections but also the differences. My great-grandmother was blacker than most people saying Black Power, but I can't say that a cop is going to see me as a black person. At all. But Black culture, that's different.

JP-S: That's an interesting dynamic that surfaces in both bomba and son jarocho: *¿Y tú abuela donde está*? But at the same time varying levels of privilege in relationship to anti-black violence exist.

HLR: I always remember this one time, a Black Dominican woman in LA wrote to me about an event we were doing. Then, a few days later, she wrote to me again, and a conversation ensued about authenticity. There was a dialogue about "Oh, there's white people playing bomba," because they saw Kelly or who knows, and it was around the time that Pablo was here. And I wound up having problems with myself, explaining "But, no, Pablo's here." And eventually I was like: "You know, what we're going to have a good time, *quédate en casa si quieres*, we're playing bomba. I've been playing bomba this long, my grandmother's Black, here is a Black teacher that is going to come teach class, Kelly's [Archbold] Puerto Rican." I was answering all these petty questions. But I had a lot of empathy for her because I understand it. It's part of the psychosis of our identity here where for safety we have to have these lenses because of the violence of being Black, because of white supremacy. Hopefully one day she will come back, and we'll still be playing bomba. I did see her once, she was way in the back at an event we did.

JP-S: Do you think that playing bomba does something specific for Puerto Ricans, and do you think that it does something different for non-Puerto Ricans? And the same for son jarocho even if *tú no vas a opinar*.

HLR: Well it's interesting. There's this Mexican woman who might consider herself Chicana, loves modern dance and ballet and jazz, but there is something about bomba that touches her in a profound way, she loves it. And there are different entrances for different people. I think we are blessed, especially out West, with individuals that are practicing bomba with very good intentions. It's been about sharing it and having it grow in a responsible way and of course bringing people together. So what does it do for us? Well, there's a pride to it of course, connecting us back. Three thousand miles away. And the rest, it depends on the individual. It might be body freedom, it might be that feeling of Church singing coro. Of course, all the benefits of playing the drum. It might be the community of course. Like spending the night at each other's house, banquet the next morning, our kids growing up together, writing songs. And that's contagious to anybody. So like tonight, when we do this bomba class, more than likely there will be mostly non-Puerto Ricans there *pero a gozar. Lo aprecian, es la verdad*. People talk about Diasporicans and how we are extra-nationalist. So on that note we gotta study extra hard.

JP-S: So, will you organize another bombazo-fandango?

HLR: Hell yea, definitely. But it's going to take a lot of planning. Two years out in advance.

JP-S: Also, why not just organize the big West Coast bombazo? Is it because you tap into more community resources if you make it a bombazo-fandango? Because there are so few of us out here, don't we need the rest of the community to help us out?

HLR: That's a good question that I have often asked myself. *Pero no se...*I always dream big. *Invita a todo el mundo*. I'd like to do an album of son jarocho and bomba. Maybe we can continue it yearly officially, and everything else is magic because everyone is already connected, and so do your thing in your city, playing, learning from each other. So yea, let's do it. Events throughout the country. West Coast jornada, North to South, all the way to TJ (Tijuana) Workshops, dialogues, kids, exhibits. All of it. We'll bring Berto to cook and have a showdown with another jarocho cook. Luis Guzmán hosting! We'll do it all.

NOTES

[1] The Welfare Poets was a popular Afro-Caribbean hip-hop group co-founded in the 1990s at Cornell University by Hector Luis Rivera together with Ray Ramírez and others. Yerbabuena was an "urban *jíbaro*" group founded in New York by Tato Torres. Nuestro Tambó was founded by Rubén Gerena and Ángel Fuentes in Chicago. Alma Moyo is a bomba group founded in 2002 by Alex LaSalle.

[2] A song that Hector composed in the rhythm of yubá and is widely sung across the diaspora and the island.

[3] Bomba con Buya is one of the most active, visible and respected groups in the diaspora at this time.

[4] AfriCaribe is a cultural project founded by Evaristo "Tito" Rodríguez in 2000, and Grupo Yubá was founded in 1991 with Eli Samuel Rodríguez.

[5] Giovanni Jímenez was the talented singer for the group Desde Cero from Puerto Rico who was brutally murdered in 2010.

[6] The *Mendez v. Westminster* case set the precedent at the federal level for overturning *Plessy v. Ferguson* and desegregating schools with *Brown v. Board of Education.*

[7] The internationally recognized worker-based human rights organization.

[8] Quenepas is part of the Bay Area Bomba & Plena Youth Project directed by Shefali Shah and Hector Lugo.

[9] See <https://youtu.be/UhEmrfJsL80/>.

[10] The Fandango Fronterizo is a bi-national son jarocho fandango event that has been held on both sides of the San Ysidro/Tijuana border fence since 2008. Fandanguerxs come from all over the country to participate in this communal protest that denounces the violence of the border, showing how music and dance permeates and deactivates borders. A midday fandango is held at Friendship Park with musicians and dancers exchanging verses and danced solos through the metal fence under the scrutiny of the Border Patrol and a second evening fandango takes place in Tijuana where the son jarocho community gathers until dawn. Southern California bomberxs have participated and demonstrated solidarity in various ways by attending and sometimes by playing bomba afterwards as an extension of the event.

VOLUME XXXI • NUMBER II • SUMMER 2019

Bomba goes to College—How is that Working Out?

SHANNON DUDLEY

ABSTRACT

Although academic disciplines such as ethnomusicology, folklore, and cultural studies have helped legitimize scholarship on vernacular culture, the concept and practice of "art" in the university is still fundamentally different compared to most community settings. This article explores the nature of that difference and its implications for the inclusion of Afro-Puerto Rican bomba in the university. Based on literature review, interviews, ethnography, and the author's experience organizing community artist residencies, the article focuses primarily on the challenges and rewards of teaching bomba in university music programs, using a residency by Pablo Luis Rivera at the University of Washington as a case study. The more interdisciplinary and integrated practices of community arts activists, both inside and outside of the academy, in the U.S. and Puerto Rico, are also considered. [Keywords: Bomba, public scholarship, participatory music, community engagement, arts activism]

The author (dudley@uw.edu) is Professor of Ethnomusicology at the University of Washington, Seattle. His publications include *Music From Behind the Bridge: Steelband Spirit and Politics in Trinidad and Tobago* (Oxford, 2008), *American Sabor: Latinos and Latinas in U.S. Popular Music* (University of Washington Press, 2017), and other writings on Caribbean music. In Seattle he plays son jarocho and bomba, and is active in promoting dialogues between arts artivists in the U.S., Puerto Rico, Mexico, and elsewhere.

Although academic disciplines such as ethnomusicology, folklore, and cultural studies have helped legitimize scholarship on vernacular culture, the concept and practice of "art" in the university is still fundamentally different compared to most community settings. In this article I explore the nature of this difference and its implications for the inclusion of Afro-Puerto Rican bomba in the university. Because bomba integrates music, dance, poetry, community-building and social activism, it needs to be engaged from diverse disciplinary perspectives. As an ethnomusicologist teaching in a university school of music, however, I face the immediate practical challenge of how to teach bomba in my own discipline. I therefore focus here especially on the relationship of bomba to university music programs, but I also consider the possibilities of modelling university curriculum on the more integrated practices of community arts activists ("*artivistas*" or "artivists"), both inside and outside of the academy.

This inquiry is situated both in music studies and in a wider discourse about removing barriers between universities and their surrounding communities, and valuing diverse forms of knowledge. National initiatives to promote public scholarship and public engagement through the arts include Imagining America, a coalition of "publicly engaged artists, designers, scholars, and community activists working toward the democratic transformation of higher education and civic life" (<http://imaginingamerica.org/about/>). Another such initiative is the Hemispheric Institute, the brainchild of NYU Performance Studies scholar Diane Taylor, whose conferences and on-line archive explore the possibilities for activism through art and scholarship across the Americas (<http://hemisphericinstitute.org/hemi/>). In the specific realm of music, a discipline called "Community Music" is emerging, especially at universities in the UK (Higgins 2012).

While a desire for change is thus in the air, the academy is also conservative, and defends its values and procedures. Somewhat paradoxically (given the boundary-crossing nature of music in our modern world), music continues to be an especially conservative discipline, causing members of a recent College Music Society task force to ask, "Why, after 50 years of appeals for reform, have we not witnessed more substantive curricular change in music?" (Sarath et al. 2017, 65). To help think about this question, and about new models for academic music studies, I draw on two ethnographic studies of university music schools/departments (Kingsbury 1988; Nettl 1995) and on a recently published report by a task force of the College Music Society (Sarath et al. 2017). I also draw on my own involvement with bomba and fandango activists[1] during the last decade, on conversations with university colleagues in various disciplines, and especially on my collaboration with Pablo Luis Rivera, who served as a Community Artist in Residence at the University of Washington, where I teach.[2]

The Institutional Culture of Classical Music

By characterizing as I do the culture of music schools, departments, and conservatories, I realize I am oversimplifying and stereotyping. Certainly some things have changed in the last few decades. More university music departments have hired ethnomusicologists, for example. The inclusion of jazz in college and university music departments has also had significant impact on the way performance is taught. At my own university, for example, there is an emerging focus on "improvised music" that encourages contemporary (avante garde) musicians to collaborate with jazz musicians. Nonetheless, the culture of music in the academy remains so strongly rooted in Western art music (WAM), commonly referred to as "classical music," that it is important to recognize some general features of this model.

I grew up in the classical music tradition, playing cello and participating in orchestras and choirs, and I benefited from it in countless ways. Ultimately, though, I needed to escape it, which I first did by playing in a steelband at Oberlin College. I say "escape" because classical music is taught and transmitted through a system that protects its practitioners from other kinds of music. This resistance to teaching about other repertoires, even those that are popular in the wider society, is cited by Robin Moore as evidence that U.S. musical institutions remain "ideologically colonized" (2017, Introduction). I would add that it also reflects a specifically American agenda of racial exclusion, an argument that I will try to make briefly here.

Lawrence Levine, in his seminal book, *High Brow Low Brow* (1988), traces the urgency to protect classical music to the latter 19th century in the United States, when WAM was actively distanced from popular music. One of the ways this happened was through subsidizing municipal symphonies, beginning with Chicago's in 1889. Financial backing from wealthy patrons and businesses enabled symphonies to sign musicians to exclusive contracts and freed them from the constraints of popular taste. The European repertoire of the symphony was privileged through an ideology that Levine calls "sacralization," a term that also appears in ethnographic studies of late 20th-century conservatories in the U.S. Henry Kingsbury, for example, speaks of "the intensely sacralized distance between the audience and the performer" (1988, 87–8) and notes:

> **The notion of 'serious music,' a phrase that is widely used to designate Western art music, provides an insight to the 'sacred' character of this musical idiom. It should be self evident that the word serious in the phrase serious music is not to be taken as contrasted with say, funny, frivolous, or silly. If anything, it is understood as a contrast to 'popular' music, or perhaps to folk music, rock, or jazz. (1988, 142)**

Bruno Nettl relates the sacred character of classical music to the exalted position of the composer, noting that "the quintessential importance of the relationship between a work of art and its creator is a major characteristic of Western classical music, literature, and art" (1995, 14). Nettl explains how the great European composers are imagined as a "pantheon" in which Mozart and Beethoven are the "chief deities," and in which the composers' distinctive personalities and stories constitute a mythology: Mozart is a composer of effortless genius, Beethoven is one who struggled to achieve greatness, Wagner is brilliant but terrible, Haydn is a fatherly mentor, etc. (Figure 1).

Figure 1: A concert hall on the campus of Pomona College enshrines the pantheon of European composers, including Wagner, Chopin, Beethoven, Bach, and Schubert.

Related to this reverence for the great composers is a reverence for musical notation—the score. Christopher Small, who famously urged scholars to pay more attention to "Musicking" (1998), argues that when we conceive music as a written score we devalue the activity and relationships that produce what we hear. This implies, among other things, that the physicality of musicking is undervalued. When we define a piece in terms of its written score, we define it in terms of the intellectual work of the composer, rather than the physical work of the performer. This may help explain why music is largely separated from dance in the academy and in the concert hall, and why audiences are expected to sit silent and motionless.

As Levine demonstrates, such constraints on audience behavior were not a part of United States concert culture in the early 19th century, when symphony conductors had to cater to diverse and interactive audiences. The effort to change this in late 19th century was based partly on an antipathy towards popular music, which, in the words of the Chicago Symphony's first director, Theodore Thomas, is "the sensual side of the art and has more or less the devil in it" (Levine 1988, 136). Thomas' alarmed depiction of popular music would certainly have been influenced by the songs of the blackface minstrel show and ragtime that were popular in the second half of the 19th century. This suggests that racial fears played a part in his impulse to separate the high brow from the low brow.[3] The moral consequences of "syncopation," for example (a widely acknowledged feature of African American music), were debated by musical authorities such as Paul Carr, who in 1901 wrote in the journal, *Musician*: "There is no element of intellectuality in the enjoyment of ragtime. It savors too much of the primeval conception of music, whose basis was a rhythm that appealed to the physical rather than to the mental senses" (Carr quoted in Berlin 1980, 43).

This elevation of intellectuality over physicality is a persistent trend in critiques of African American music. It has been renewed by guardians of European tradition in reaction to the advent of jazz, rock and roll, and hip hop. Tricia Rose recounts a 1989 conversation with a university music department chair who told her, "Well, you must be writing on rap's social impact and political lyrics, because there is nothing to the music" (1994, 62). Conspicuously absent in this professor's evaluation of hip hop is any consideration for one of its most important functions: dancing. His omission is representative of a general skepticism in music scholarship about the artistic value of physicality and dance. The following statement by Polish esthetician Roman Ingarden makes this skepticism explicit: "We may doubt whether so-called dance music, when employed only as a means of keeping the dancers in step and arousing in them a specific passion for expression through movement, is music in the strict sense of the word" (quoted in McClary and Walser 1994, 75).

All of this is to say that, in insulating itself from popular music, WAM culture is characterized by skepticism toward performances that foreground rhythm, movement, and sensuality. This attitude has European precedents but is reinforced by a specifically American context of racial anxiety. Bomba, as an African diasporal practice in which sound and movement are inextricably linked, thus presents a challenge to some systemic ideological biases in the way music is taught and performed in the academy. To help think about how to address and overcome such bias, I will begin by reviewing the work of a musician who arrived in academia by a very different route than I did.

A Bomba Activist

In winter quarter of 2014 I had the privilege of working with Dr. Pablo Luis Rivera during his term as a Community Artist in Residence at the University of Washington School of Music. Part of what brought Pablo to my attention in the first place, and what made him successful as a university faculty member, was the extraordinary variety of his experience and collaborations. Pablo had studied and performed with important figures in the bomba tradition; he had gathered information from many more bomba practitioners, as well as scholars, in the course of his research for a Ph.D. dissertation on the history of bomba; he had promoted bomba and Afro-Puerto Rican culture in schools and other educational contexts, as well as media; and he had collaborated with artists and cultural activists of diverse backgrounds in projects to promote bomba in the public sector. Pablo's trajectory, which I will review briefly before describing his residency at UW, exemplifies the synthesis of education, activism and art that has made bomba into a dynamic cultural force over the last two or three decades.

Pablo Luis Rivera was born in 1975 in the barrio of San Antón, Carolina, on the eastern outskirts of the San Juan metropolitan area. Carolina is part of a larger region

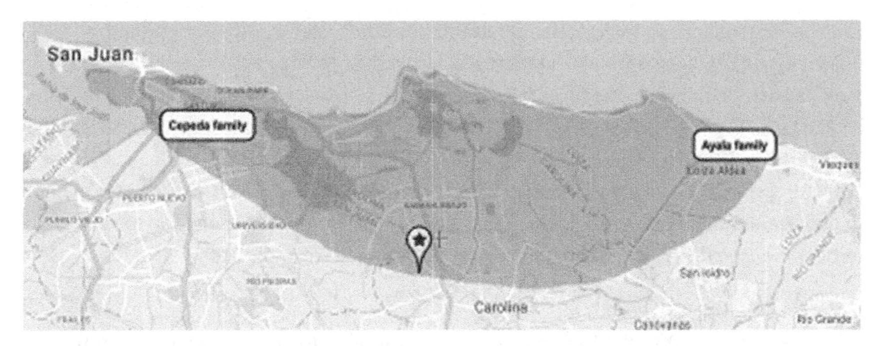

Figure 2: The shaded area corresponds to the general region of Cangrejos, settled by free black people beginning in the 17th century. Despite the proximity of Pablo Luis Rivera's neighborhood of San Antón (marked with star) to important bomba families, the Cepedas and the Ayalas, he did not learn about this Afro-Puerto Rican music and dance tradition until he was in high school.

called Cangrejos that was settled by free black people beginning in the 17th century and is an important region for Afro-Puerto Rican culture (Berríos-Miranda and Dudley 2008). Although Pablo grew up relatively close to bomba tradition bearers (including the Cepeda family in Santurce and the Ayalas in Loiza) he never saw it in school or at public events (Figure 2). His entrance into performing arts came through *declamación* (poetry recitation), which he began practicing in elementary school. It was not until high school that his friend Luis René García suggested he add music to his declamación. When Pablo asked what kind of music would work, Luis said he should use bomba.

Luis took Pablo Luis to the Cepeda family school in Santurce, where he was mesmerized by the improvisation between drummer and dancer, astonished that a dancer's movements could be sounded simultaneously on the *primo* drum. Pablo Luis had already learned that culture was a tool he could use to motivate people, and in bomba he found a powerful expression of the Afro-Puerto Rican culture and history that he sensed had been missing from his education and from representations of Puerto Rico generally. Although music did not come to him easily, he worked hard to learn how to dance, drum, and sing.

In 1993, four years after he began learning bomba with the Cepedas, Pablo Luis was invited by Norma Salazar to join the group Plenibom. Salazar was a prolific culture worker who created folk art, published articles about Afro-Puerto Rican culture, and helped organize many community arts projects and events, including the island-wide Encuentro de Tambores. Pablo Luis also received valuable advice from her husband, the revered salsa composer Tite Curet Alonso, about stage performance and the entertainment business. During this time Pablo Luis also played with Jesús Cepeda's group, Bombalele, and in Tierra Viva, who performed regularly on television on Channel 6. The mid-90s were thus a time when Pablo's vision expanded immensely, as he interacted with diverse people in diverse performance contexts.

Tener la experiencia de tarima, de televisión, de actividades particulares privadas y públicas, pues te hace entender el mercado, y también te hace pensar en cosas que puedes hacer y en cosas que hace falta hacer... y eso te lleva a crear tu propio concepto. (Pablo Luis Rivera 2017)

[To have experience on stage, in television, and in private and public events helps you to understand the market, and also makes you think of things you could do or that need to be done ... and that is what leads you to develop your own concept.]

In the late 1990s Pablo began to focus this vision through several innovative projects. One of them was a project of "participatory action research" organized by anthropologist Hal Barton, a post-doctoral fellow at the University of Puerto Rico, Río Piedras. With funding from the Rockefeller "Caribbean 2000" project, Barton teamed with brothers Jorge, José, and Víctor Emmanuelli and their bomba group, Raízes Eternas, to form the Centro de Investigación Cultural Raízes Eternas (CICRE). CICRE's principal mission was the "Bombazo project," aimed at getting young people involved in *doing* bomba, expanding the performance tradition beyond the presentations of traditional bomba families such as the Cepedas and the Ayalas. To that end they launched a "pub tour"—a series of performances in different pubs around the island with a group they called Bombazo de Puerto Rico, beginning in May of 1998 (Barton 2004).

Having participated and learned in these pub sessions, Pablo and some other musicians took an important new step in late 1998 by establishing a regular Sunday evening *bombazo* at the Rumba Café, in the Calle San Sebastián in old San Juan. The clientele were mainly young people who came for live music on weekends, including both salsa and rumba. With the group Son de Batey Pablo performed three sets every Sunday night at Rumba. In between their sets, dancers took to the floor with a DJ. When Son de Batey played, though, the youths cleared a space in front of the drummers to create the *batey,* the circle. They began to learn the protocols and dancing skills of bomba: a single dancer makes his or her *paseo* into the middle of the *batey*, accompanied by the drums and the call and response singing; the dancer salutes the *primo* player and begins to create phrases of rhythmic movements, *piquetes,* that the primo sounds; all the while the *buleadores, cua,* and *maraca* keep a steady rhythm.

The Sunday night bombazo at Rumba Café was a regular event from 1999 to 2003. It became a destination for tourists, and even for celebrities such as singer Marc Anthony, actor Edward James Olmos, and TV news anchor Carmen Jovet. For Pablo Luis, though, the importance of these Sunday bombazos at Rumba was that they opened up bomba as a recreational opportunity for a whole new generation of young people and brought them into the bomba tradition.

Al principio, el núcleo de la bomba no iba a vernos. Porque era como una mirada a algo, como un tipo de sacrilegio tú llevar la bomba, que era algo que se miraba como algo que no podía transgredirse y llevarla a un pub, que es un lugar donde van jóvenes, donde hay bebidas alcohólicas, donde se dan unas circunstancias que no se entendía que eran favorables para la bomba.... Son del Batey estuvo años tocando ahí los domingos. Y el público al principio eran jóvenes, jóvenes, jóvenes, jóvenes. De hecho, al pasar del tiempo muchos de los integrantes de los grupos en la diáspora que ahora están organizados, venían a ver ese espectáculo de Son del Batey en Rumba. Y fue como un impacto fuerte y ya, con el pasar del tiempo, la gente de la bomba que al principio tenían una resistencia, empezaron a ir frecuentemente y a participar y a compartir. (Pablo Luis Rivera 2016)

[At first the core of the bomba community didn't come to see us. Because they looked at it askance, like a kind of sacrilege that we would take bomba, which was seen as something that couldn't be defiled and brought into a pub, where young people go and drink alcohol, a place whose atmosphere was not seen as appropriate for bomba.... Son de Batey played for years there on Sundays. And the audience at first was just youths, youths, youths, youths. In fact, many of the members of groups that are now organized in the diaspora, used to come to see Son del Batey at the Rumba club. It had a powerful impact, and after a time the bomba people who at first had resisted began to come often and participate and share.]

The other initiative that Pablo Luis helped launch in 1998 was Restauración Cultural. Inspired by the way Hal Barton and the Emmanuelli brothers had created CICRES to procure grants and institutional support, and confident now in his own abilities as a performer and educator in diverse contexts, Pablo—along with Felipe "Junito" Febres and Lourdes Colchado—formed Restauracion Cultural to pursue educational projects involving bomba. Among other things, they procured a grant from Fundación Puerto Rico to help school teachers integrate bomba into their curriculum. In 2006 they began teaching a class for adults in the plaza of Carolina, which they called Gigantes de la Bomba, which attracted active and retired university professors who in turn helped to organize public dialogues, and contributed in other ways to the dissemination of bomba practice and knowledge.

In 2009 Restauracion Cultural member Rafael Maya proposed a new initiative to connect both with Puerto Ricans in the diaspora and with practitioners of Afro-diasporic traditions in other countries. Over the next few years this new initiative, Proyecto Union, took Pablo and his associates to Chicago, New York, Cleveland, Los Angeles, San Diego, and San Francisco. The groups they worked with in these places included some of the diasporal Puerto Ricans that Pablo had first met at the Rumba Café ten years earlier, including Alex Lasalle in New York, Roberto Perez in Chicago, and José Fusté in San Diego. Proyecto Union also made trips to the Dominican Republic, St. Croix, Peru, Mexico, Martinique and Guadeloupe to teach and to engage in cultural exchanges.

As he expanded this cultural work, Pablo turned to academia for training that could help him with grant-writing and administrative work. In 1993 he began a bachelor's degree in business administration at the University of Puerto Rico (UPR) in Carolina, followed by a correspondence MBA with the University of Phoenix. Keenly aware of the lack of historical information about bomba, he ultimately embarked on a Ph.D. in history at the Centro de Estudios Avanzados de Puerto Rico y el Caribe. In 2013 Pablo successfully defended his doctoral dissertation on the history of bomba. During this time he also worked in a series of staff positions at the university, beginning in the office of Human Resources at UPR Carolina in 1996 and later working with the registrar and the financial aid office.

In addition to performances, workshops, and presentations with the groups described above, Pablo initiated a series of "conversatorios" oriented especially to the community of artivistas and to the youth he sought to reach.

Although the university provided him with training and degrees, it did not immediately provide him a teaching position, so Pablo has continued to perform much of his cultural and educational work outside the academy. In addition to performances, workshops, and presentations with the groups described above, Pablo initiated a series of "conversatorios" oriented especially to the community of artivistas and to the youth he sought to reach. They began with a pair of events organized at a Piñones community center, COPI (Corporación Piñones se Integra), titled "Jovenes en la Bomba," which invited young Afro-Puerto Ricans to exchange ideas about their culture and their ambitions. Building on the success these events, Restauración Cultural organized two more conversatorios in San Juan and Mayaguez before finally settling on a permanent home for the series at the Centro de Recreación in Carolina. To date they have held over fifty conversatorios—public conversations with university professors, lawyers, politicians, musicians, and other professionals and cultural workers on themes such as bomba history, regional styles of bomba, drum-making, Afro-Caribbean culture, and racism.

Bomba Residency at the University of Washington

I first met Pablo Luis in 2007 when we were introduced in Puerto Rico by Pedro "Capitol" Clemente, a long-time artivista and co-founder (in 1973) of the Festival de Bomba y Plena. I subsequently interviewed Pablo about his work in promoting bomba, and attended a bombazo in Piñones where I saw him in action with his colleagues and students. Several years later, when he was on the verge of finishing his doctoral dissertation, Pablo received a call from me out of the blue inviting him to be a visiting artist at the University of Washington (UW). He later admitted that he couldn't place the name when he talked to me on the phone, but true to his inquisitive and adventurous nature he accepted our invitation and came to Seattle for winter quarter 2014.

Figure 3: Playing bomba on the University of Washington campus, from left to right: Chicago bombera Ivelisse Díaz, Pablo Luis Rivera, the author, graduate student Iris Viveros, and Pablo's wife Yadilka Rodriguez. Photo by Scott Macklin. Reprinted by permission.

The planning for Pablo's residency included arrangements with the UW Dance program for Pablo to teach Dance 231, Folk-Social Dance Forms. This gave Pablo access to the Dance program's spacious and beautiful studios. We were fortunate to obtain the services of Ricardo Güity, a Honduran Garifuna drummer, to play primo for Pablo's dance class, but it took some convincing because the dance department paid only $50 per class. They were accustomed to hiring "accompanists" for their dance classes, but they didn't have the budget to invest in a highly expert musician. Their normal procedure was not well suited to a genre such as bomba, in which the music has to be taught just as expertly as the movement.

In the School of Music, Pablo taught Musap 389/589, World Music, in which students have private or small group instruction with a visiting artist one hour a week and also meet once a week for an ensemble class. Interestingly, Pablo's ensemble class for the music students ended up being mostly dancing, despite the cramped space in our music classroom. This helped them learn the relation between movement and sound much better than they could have learned by just playing drums. Music students had the additional option to play drums and sing in the Dance classes, which several of them did.

Another goal of Pablo's residency was to contribute to the arts scene off campus. During three months in Seattle, Pablo's duties included helping to direct a community *"bombango"* (combined bombazo and fandango, Figure 4) and leading two community bomba workshops, as well as a presentation at UW's Tacoma campus.

Figure 4: Community members along with UW faculty and students gathered for a "bombango" (bombazo and fandango) at Casa Latina in Seattle. Photo by Scott Macklin. Reprinted by permission.

He spent time with other community arts groups, including the Seattle Fandango Project, Grupo Bayano, FICA capoeira, and Movimiento Afrolation de Seattle (MAS). Pablo's UW dance classes also drew some community participation, as did his final concert in the School of Music.

Exchanges between UW students and community members were a key accomplishment of Pablo's residency. In both UW classes (which together comprised almost 50 people) students were required to make at least one visit to a community bomba event. Some attended one of the weekly bomba workshops conducted by Grupo Bayano, and others went to one of Pablo's community workshops at sites off campus. At the end of the quarter we partnered with the Seattle Fandango Project to organize a "bombango" (combined bombazo and fandango) at Casa Latina, a support center for seasonal workers in Seattle. For this event we invited Ivelisse Díaz, a bombera from Chicago, to conduct a workshop and help animate the dancing at the bombango. UW student reports about these community engagement experiences included the reflections below.[4]

"One of the biggest differences between this [community] event and our class was that there were also various people from the local bomba community there. They each had their own style that was unique to them, and it was very interesting to see how different people interpret the same culture, and dance.... Overall, I learned that going to a community event in addition to our regular classes is very important in really understanding the culture, and the dance. Seeing the way everyone interacted with each other and had fun with the music made me appreciate bomba a lot more."

"While the group weekly classes and private lessons allowed me to build up my drumming and dancing skills I quickly learned at [community workshops] that these are not the only things that make up bomba; a lot of it comes from the community and the people and the energy that comes alive during these events."

"I was absolutely floored by the concept of the primo creating music in real time to match the dancer and his or her moves and intensity. I find this idea astoundingly beautiful especially because I feel that with the exception of jazz there is so little opportunity for improvisation in the music that I study and there are especially few opportunities for this improvisation spanning across different art forms like dance and drumming together."

"What I was able to experience was truly fantastic. This is not to say that our classroom experience was not equally powerful and necessary, [but] classroom environments encourage you to overthink everything: what you hear, where you are, what you are doing, etc. These environments in the community place the emphasis on sensory experience and feeling and as a result engage you as a participant differently."

"I know the skill I gained from this course was more than just rhythm. It was also the ability to use music to connect with people."

As these reflections suggest, students' engagement with bomba challenged and enriched them on both a musical and a social level. The protocols of bomba required them not only to improvise but to connect sound with movement. They also had to work on all the different performing roles that comprise bomba, including percussion, dancing, and singing. Finally, by participating in community events, they were presented with a diversity of approaches and styles that they could not have learned from a single instructor. And they had fun.

Broadening the Concept of Art in the University

The student experiences recounted above run counter to how arts are typically taught in a university, and they suggest how participatory arts can bring new depth and vitality to academic music studies. To elaborate on this I will use bomba, and Pablo's residency in particular, to illustrate some of the ways that university music culture can productively integrate aspects of "community music" culture. The paradigm of community music I use here is shaped especially by my experience during the past ten years with people who practice fandango and bomba.

Contrasting paradigms

UNIVERSITY MUSIC		***COMMUNITY MUSIC***
Composition-centered	....	**Activity-centered**
Creation of "works"	....	**Creation of relationships**
Presentation	....	**Participation**
Separation	....	**Integration**

Composition vs. Activity

Although composition happens in all music, the role of the composer in Western art music is unique. A single composer, often reaching from his grave, controls the minute details of what will happen in a given performance. We can predict the exact sequence of notes that every musician in the orchestra will play when they perform Beethoven's 5th symphony, for example. At a bombazo, on the other hand, one can make no such prediction. What is important in a bombazo is the creation of a space where people engage one another creatively; sound and choreography are the unpredictable results of that engagement. While the university concert promises the performance of a specific composition, that is, the bombazo promises a creative social activity.

Promotion criteria must reward work that is activity-centered and collaborative, and to acknowledge as "peers" (for the purpose of review and evaluation) experts who may not have traditional academic degrees or certifications.

The metaphor of composition can also be extended to think about the broader university culture. While the role of the composer has its own logic and history in western art music, it also fits into a university culture where individual faculty are expected to plan and achieve predictable results. Faculty achievements are measured by evaluating the products of their research, including books and scientific discoveries, as well as musical compositions. The academy is less good, however, at measuring outcomes such as happiness, healthy personal relationships, and networks of community support that faculty might achieve through community arts projects. Furthermore, even if the university could measure such things we would be left with the problem of deciding which of the many people involved in a bombazo get credit for its success. It is easier for the university to reward the single author of a book, or the featured soloist in a concert. The criteria for reward and promotion in academia, that is, do not favor collective work. They privilege product over activity, composer over facilitator.

Some rethinking of the concepts of "research" and "publication" is therefore required to create incentive and support for community arts work in the university. Promotion criteria must reward work that is activity-centered and collaborative, and to acknowledge as "peers" (for the purpose of review and evaluation) experts who may not have traditional academic degrees or certifications. This is the goal, for example, of a report by the Imagining America coalition titled, "Scholarship in Public: Knowledge Creation and Tenure Policy in the Engaged University." The authors of this report argue that "Enlarging the conception of who counts as 'peer' and what counts as 'publication' is part of something bigger: the democratization of knowledge on and off campus" (Ellison and Eatman 2008, iv). They stress that it is not a question of relaxing academic standards but rather defining "excellence" in a way that can apply to engaged public scholarship as well as traditional peer-reviewed publication.

Works vs. Relationships

Much of the effort of university music faculty and students centers on the creation (by composers) and interpretation (by performers) of "works." Although works are experienced through their performances, they are also imagined to have an identity that is independent of any specific performance. Bomba musicians and dancers, on the other hand, use the protocols of the batey to initiate and explore relationships between the performers. What endures is not a reproducible work of art, but rather a series of relationships created through playing, singing, and dancing together. For example, Son de Batey's weekly performances at the Rumba café over four years generated relationships that continued to bear fruit in the form of other projects and exchanges between *bomberos* in Puerto Rico and bomberos in the U.S.

My work with Pablo Luis and other Community Artists in Residence has connected me in productive and lasting ways to international networks of artivistas, especially in the fandango and bomba movements. Similarly, this work has connected me to local artists and communities, and to colleagues and students in other departments of my university. What I have learned through these relationships has profoundly impacted the way I think, teach, and make music—more so than any traditional "research" project I have undertaken. Community arts networks also provided a wealth of contacts, stories, and photographs for my most recent book project (Berríos et al. 2018). My own experience is nicely captured in the words of architecture professor Gail Dubrow:

> What I've built are sustained relationships and out of those relationships come a plethora of interesting projects of many forms: student theses, classes, weekend events, and books. What I'm trying to sustain are the partnerships and relationships over time transcending any particular project. And those are the skills I try to teach, because they're critical to the work and are needed in the curriculum. (Ellison and Eatman 2008, 7)

Our "knowledge" basically consists of what we learn through particular relationships—to people, to projects, to institutions, to works of art, etc.—and indeed it can be said that knowledge is relationship (Wilson 2008, 22). As technologies of relationship-building, therefore, participatory music genres such as bomba represent an

Figure 5: Students playing bomba in Brechemin Auditorium at the University of Washington School of Music.

enormous and under-exploited potential for university music programs to contribute to the creation of knowledge.

Presentation vs. Participation

Ethnomusicologist Thomas Turino has emphasized the importance of distinguishing presentational performance from participatory performance, and understanding how their esthetics and goals differ (e.g., Turino 2008). University music performances are generally presentational, characterized by a clear division between performers on a stage and audience members listening from their seats. Bomba is sometimes staged in a presentational way (Power Sotomayor 2015), but it is fundamentally a participatory tradition whose protocols give everyone present the opportunity to take an active part, whether it be through playing an instrument, dancing, or singing.

Presentational and participatory modes of performance can combine and overlap in myriad ways. At Pablo Luis Rivera's Visiting Artist concert at the University of Washington, for example, his students danced in a group, performing previously rehearsed choreographies that would satisfy the expectations of an audience who had come to see a "show." At the end of the show, however, he invited students as well as audience members to dance individually, transforming the stage into a sort of batey. We had to adapt the batey's traditional circle to leave an opening through which the seated audience could watch, but even so this arrangement encouraged the audience to get involved in a different way, shouting and applauding in reaction to special moments in the dancing.

Applause is generally discouraged in the presentational culture of the classical music concert, except at designated moments, so that the audience can become completely immersed in what is happening on stage. It is also true, however, that a responsive audience helps a musician to grow as a performer. A jazz musician, for example, learns from shouts and applause when she has connected with listeners. In bomba, the response of the drummer to the dancer teaches intense lessons about connecting through sound and movement (Power Sotomayor 2015, 718). These kinds of experiences are also beneficial to classical musicians. In fact I would suggest that the concept of "talent" that is considered ineffable and unteachable in Western art music culture (Kingsbury 1988, 60–3) is often conferred on musicians who have an instinct for how to connect with their listeners. Participatory traditions such as bomba, in which feedback and exchange are more spontaneous, offer a way for musicians and dancers to develop their talent for communicating and connecting through their performances.

Unlike band or orchestra ... many community music traditions have protocols that accommodate people of different skill levels.

Separation vs. Integration

As an institution dedicated to specialization and expertise, the university tends to separate the arts into different components. The departmental structure of a university typically expects music, dance, drama, visual art, and poetry to be taught by separate faculties, with separate budgets, and even separate buildings. Such a separation of the arts complicates the teaching of a performance tradition such as bomba in which music, dance, and verse are interrelated and simultaneous. Indeed the very concept of "music" as a distinct art is unintelligible to some people whose languages do not have separate words for dance and music. For example, the East African word *ngoma* is cited by the CMS Manifesto as a conceptual category that unites dancing, singing, and drumming, and as a principle that could repair the "fragmentation" of the arts in American universities (Sarath et al. 2017, 66). The case of Pablo Luis Rivera's residency at the UW shows how bomba can challenge departmental structures and promote integration of music and dance. We worked actively to achieve this by arranging for Pablo to teach in two departments, integrating music and dance in both the classes, and requiring students to get outside their departmental environment: music students could attend the dance class to help with the drumming and singing, and all students were expected to spend some time learning in a community context where musicians, dancers and singers work together.

The university also separates people according to musical skill. By the time students reach the university, music performance studies are largely limited to an elite few who have had years of private instruction and school ensemble experience. This selection process starts with school band programs where students are auditioned and divided into beginning and advanced ensembles, ideally allowing the advanced students to play at a more expert level. In community music scenes, also, there are musicians who seek the opportunity to play at a more expert level. Unlike band or orchestra, however, many community music traditions have protocols that accommodate people of different skill levels. In bomba, for example, a high degree of skill is required to interpret the dancer's movements on the primo, while competent percussionists can play the steady rhythms of the buleador or cua. The song leader has to be good at improvising, but everyone present can sing the chorus. Dancers may differ in their grace and creativity, but they can make the best of whatever skills they possess. This diversity of roles and styles makes the batey an inspiring learning environment, as the comments of Pablo's students testify.

As it does in all disciplines, of course, the university also separates people by age. Young children are scarce on campus, and while not all community music scenes encourage children to participate they are generally more kid-friendly than the concert hall. Many community arts events on our campus in recent years have included young children, a refreshing change from the university's adult culture, and something that makes it easier and more comfortable for mothers to attend events. Community arts traditions also tend to stress respect for the knowledge and presence of elders, which is somewhat different from the university's stress on respect for "expertise".

The Future(s) of Bomba in the University

Pablo Luis' bomba residency at the University of Washington produced positive outcomes and a lasting impact, but the question of how bomba might be taught in the university going forward is a larger one. To begin answering this question I will start with the College Music Society's recently published study, *Redefining Music Studies in an Age of Change: Creativity, Diversity, and Integration* (Sarath et al. 2017). While this so-called "Manifesto" does not reflect consensus among university music faculty, it is the product of a national task force of music performers, scholars, composers and educators. Its authors address what they see as three "core deficiencies" of university music programs: 1) the prevalence of "interpretive performance," in which students focus most of their energy on acquiring the technical skills needed to interpret the works of composers; 2) the ethnocentricism of a Western art music-dominated curriculum, which the CMS task force characterizes as "nothing short of a social justice crisis" (see also Ellison and Eatman 2017, 61); and 3) the fragmentation of the arts. For each of these deficiencies, the authors propose a principle of reform, and each of those principles would seem to apply well to bomba, as indicated in the chart.

Recommendations of the College Music Society task forceon the Undergraduate Music Major (Sarath et al. 2017)

DEFICIENCY	SOLUTION
Interpretive Performance	**Improvisation**[5]
[improvisation is at the center of bomba dancing and drumming]	
Ethnocentrism	**Diversity**
[bomba diversifies the university culture]	
Fragmentation	**Integration**
[bomba integrates music, dance, verse, and activism]	

In this perspective participatory music/dance genres have much to offer, but integrating bomba into the curriculum requires thinking outside the conventional norms of university music study. One model for how it can be done is the Community Artist in Residence program at the University of Washington (Campbell and Dudley 2018), where Pablo Luis Rivera taught in 2014 and Amarilys Ríos taught in 2019. Other university programs, such as dance or Latin American and Caribbean Studies, participate and support the residency. Local arts groups with whom we collaborate benefit from the energy and expertise of having a visiting artist in town for three months. Students benefit from this expanded community of learning. Students in ethnomusicology and music education, particularly, get degree credit for studying with Community Artists in Residence and are therefore more strongly represented in these classes compared to students in other divisions (classical music performance, jazz, musicology, etc.).

In addition to their function in the School of Music, Community Artists in Residence have an impact in the wider university and also off campus. Each Community Artist Residence is organized in collaboration with another university program or department that helps with funding, course offerings, symposia, etc. Collaboration with a community arts group creates a larger and more diverse learning community in which university students may form lasting relationships. Community participants in past Community Artist Residencies include the Seattle Fandango Project, the Women Who Rock collective, Movimiento Afrolatino de Seattle (MAS), Garinagu Houngu, Grupo Bayano, the International Capoeira Angola Foundation. University programs we have collaborated with include Music, Dance, Communications, Performance Studies, Ethnic Studies, Latin American and Caribbean Studies, Gender, Women and Sexuality Studies, and more.

This raises the question of how bomba can be taught in other departments, or through interdisciplinary coalitions. Some answers to that question can be sought in the experiences of community-based groups who perform and do workshops on college campuses. In a university environment that may be difficult or even hostile for students of color, bomba and other community arts such as fandango provide them a familiar and supportive cultural space. For example, the Welfare Poets, who later went on to record several albums and performed/workshopped extensively on the college circuit, were founded by Hector Luis Rivera and Ray Ramirez at Cornell University in the early 1990s. They integrated hip hop and bomba to create a forum where students of color could share their feelings about racism, African heritage and current political issues such as the anti-apartheid campaign (Hector Luis Rivera 2019). The group Buya has developed lasting relationships with several universities in the Chicago area, and Buya member Ivelisse Díaz explained to me that faculty and staff at these institutions have come to recognize Buya as a valuable "pipeline" for students of color to connect with the local Puerto Rican, Mexican and African American communities (Díaz 2019). Like the Welfare Poets and Buya, other bomba groups began responding to student interest in bomba before it had any place in the regular curriculum.

More recently a number of community arts activists have attained university faculty positions and have begun to make a place for bomba and fandango in the course curriculum. These include Hal Barton (Anthropology, Long Island University), Micaela Díaz-Sanchez (Chicano Studies, University of California, Santa Barbara), José Fusté (Ethnic Studies, University of California San Diego), Alexandro Hernandez (Music, UC Santa Barbara), Jade Power Sotomayor (Theater and Dance, University of California San Diego) and Raquel Rivera (Sociology, Tufts University, and elsewhere).

University programs that recognize playing, singing, and dancing together as a form of discourse and knowledge production may be more receptive to the inclusion of bomba or fandango in the curriculum.

Fandango practitioner Martha Gonzalez is a tenured professor in the Intercollegiate Department of Chicano Latino Studies at Scripps College in Claremont, CA. When I asked her what it was like teaching fandango in a "non-arts" department she replied, "I don't think Chicano studies is a 'non-arts' discipline. It is interdisciplinary so art is always referenced" (Gonzalez 2017). She also pointed out that a course like hers, in which she teaches the fandango arts in combination with reading and discussion, is more likely to be supported in a university department that gives recognition and importance to the "embodied knowledge" transmitted through participatory music and dance. Paradoxically (because music performance programs are deeply invested in transmitting embodied knowledge) music scholars have generally been slow to grant embodied knowledge the same academic authority as texts and scores.[6] "Teaching through [embodied] practices even rearranges the thought process and urges non-linear thinking strategies, which can lead to more interesting arguments," says Gonzalez (2017). Similarly Jade Power Sotomayor recognizes that playing bomba in her Interdisciplinary Arts classes at the University of Washington, Bothell,[7] "enacts certain relationships" that facilitate a different kind of learning than reading and discussion (2017). University programs that recognize playing, singing, and dancing together as a form of discourse and knowledge production may be more receptive to the inclusion of bomba or fandango in the curriculum.

In addition to being a model for this kind of integrated learning, Gonzalez' own course, Fandango as a Decolonial Tool, centers social justice concerns that are important in contemporary bomba and fandango movements. Like interdisciplinarity and embodied knowledge, social justice is often given more importance in area studies or ethnic studies programs than in music programs. When I tried to explain my interest in community engagement to one of my music colleagues, for example, I was told, "This is the School of Music, not the School of Social Work." At the risk of painting with too broad a brush, I would say that response spoke for a significant portion of university music professors who are invested in the idea of art for art's sake, and who may be tired of hearing that they are privileging dead white men's music. In short, disciplines like Latino Studies or Women Studies generally tend to place more emphasis on social justice than do music programs. This tends to make them receptive to what community arts activists have to offer.

The experience of bomba activists who offer workshops and performances on college campuses can also tell us something about which disciplines are most likely to want bomba. Through conversations with Raquel Z. Rivera (formerly a member of Alma Moyó), Ivelisse Díaz (of the Chicago-based groups Buya and Las Bompleneras), Hector Luis Rivera (of the Welfare Poets), and Julia Loíza Gutierrez-Rivera (of Los Pleneros de la 21, and Redobles de Cultura), I learned that most of the funding for their college visits has come from departments other than music, or from student organizations. Gutierrez-Rivera noted, however, that working with music students was as rewarding and fruitful, in its own way, as working with students in other disciplines and with community members: "You can work on engaging folks who ... already have an [affinity for] the culture, whereas dance/music-focused groups can have the benefit of learning more about their own crafts using different languages and frameworks. Both contribute to expanding knowledge and appreciation of the cultures in different manners" (2017).

Gutierrez-Rivera's recognition that dance and music students are interested in "their own craft" is, I believe, another important consideration for the integration of bomba into the university. Music and dance are not what draw students to most Chicano Studies or Womens Studies classes, nor is performing expertise usually a significant factor in hiring faculty in such departments. Chicano Studies professor and bomba/fandango practitioner Micaela Díaz-Sánchez values dance and music as an "embodied pedagogical method," but also recognizes that "as teachers and practitioners who are operating outside of [music] departments, there are other critical epistemic and pedagogical approaches" (2017). Despite the innovative use of embodied practices by scholars such as Díaz-Sánchez and Gonzalez, many of their colleagues still place more importance on those other pedagogical and epistemic approaches. In the experience of Ethnic Studies professor and bomba musician José Fusté, for example, he has not felt encouraged to integrate bomba into his teaching, and in general he sees his discipline as being more concerned with critical thinking than doing (Power Sotomayor and Fusté 2017).

Music departments and schools, by contrast, place a lot of emphasis on doing. Music students who encounter bomba in a class or workshop may not always see it as part of their heritage, but they embody what they learn, and perhaps incorporate it into "different languages and frameworks." While humanities and social science scholars are likely to affirm the academic value of embodied knowledge, that is, musicians are likely to put it into practice. Despite the advantages of teaching bomba or fandango in other departments, therefore, there are also reasons to seek a disciplinary home for bomba in university music (or dance) programs.

Ultimately, strategies for integrating bomba or fandango into a university curriculum should be tailored to the particular institutional structures and the particular people involved. This would ideally include community-based experts whose pedagogies are rooted not in academic disciplines but in the culture and practice of bomba. Anthropologist Hal Barton, who integrates bomba extensively into his teaching at Long Island University, notes:

> **If [students] are serious, they need to become aware that there is an entire "community-based" bomba curriculum (regionally variable and Diasporic, but with many common threads) in which codes (honor, respectability, etc.) and communal ethos of a word-of-mouth 'oral tradition' are still paramount—where it's never 'just' about bomba in the narrow sense, but often much more! (2017)**

Nowhere are the community resources for bomba more abundant than in Puerto Rico, and I would like to conclude with a brief consideration of the way bomba is being taught at universities on the island. In 2016 I met and talked with students at the Conservatorio de Música de Puerto Rico, and also had some conversations with music students at the University of Puerto Rico in Río Piedras, and others at the Universidad Interamericana de Puerto Rico. My impression was that these students generally had more diverse musical interests and experiences than music majors at the University of Washington. In a class where I was invited to give a presentation about Trinidadian music, the Conservatorio students were quick to sing along with a calypso song, and played Afro-Caribbean rhythms with ease. I understood that most of these students were studying classical music, but they also had the opportunity to play Caribbean music styles in the Taller de Música Afro-Caribeña and the Taller de música Puertorriqueña. Students at the Universidad Interamericana de Puerto Rico, Recinto Metropolitano, also receive instruction in popular music, including a bomba and plena ensemble taught by saxophonist Ricardo Pons that performs dance band arrangements in the tradition of bands like Cortijo and Viento de Agua.

Although students in these ensembles learn some bomba rhythms to apply to stage performing, those with a deeper interest in bomba must learn in community settings. Amarilys Rios, who served as Community Artist in Residence at the University of Washington in winter of 2019, is an example. She learned to play the drum in the early 2000s with Jerry Ferrao, who taught students informally on the University of Puerto Rico campus. Later she found a mentor in Victor Emmanuelli, and in 2007 Ríos became the primo player for Nandí, the first all-women bomba group in Puerto Rico. In 2009 she enrolled at the Conservatorio where she earned a degree in percussion, and this helped her become more musically versatile and professional (Ríos is currently director of the all-female fusion group, Émina, musical director for Tego Calderon, and arranger for Héctor "Coco" Barez, among other projects that go beyond traditional bomba). Students at the Conservatorio can learn some basics of bomba drumming from a faculty percussionist, but those like Amarilys who have really learned to play bomba have done so outside the Conservatorio. Neither the Conservatorio nor the Universidad Interamericana offers instruction in the participatory and improvisatory way of playing of bomba.

Like Martha Gonzalez' fandango class at Scripps, Pablo's class is a first of its kind for bomba, and it is not taught in a music program.

The only university class in Puerto Rico I know of where students can learn bomba in an integrated way is taught by Pablo Luis Rivera at the University of Puerto Rico, Carolina. Although his position there is primarily administrative, Rivera has developed a class for university credit in which students learn to dance, play, and sing bomba and also study about its history and its place in Puerto Rican culture. Like Martha Gonzalez' fandango class at Scripps, Pablo's class is a first of its kind for bomba, and it is not taught in a music program. He has had conversations with administrators at the Conservatorio, though, about teaching there in the future. He has also expanded his teaching to offer history classes at the Universidad Interamericana in Fajardo, where the university sponsored him to teach a community bomba class in February 2018.

Opportunities for university students in Puerto Rico to learn bomba in community settings are growing, and bomba is also having some impact on the university curriculum. Nonetheless bomba faces some of the same constraints at universities in Puerto Rico that it faces at universities in the mainland U.S. University music programs in Puerto Rico are still strongly influenced by WAM culture, and their tendency to treat bomba as a musical performance instead of centering it in the drum-dance relationship reinforces fragmentation of the arts. Inevitably there will be differences in the way people learn music in an institution, compared to community settings, and perhaps that is as it should be. But the work of Pablo Luis Rivera and other bomba activists challenges universities to examine these differences, and to think in new ways about how we create relationships and knowledge through art.

Conclusion

The culture of the university presents certain obstacles to the inclusion of participatory music and dance traditions such as bomba. Those of us who want to see this inclusion happen therefore need to think strategically. While our strategies must respond to the specific conditions and people with whom we work, this list may be a helpful start:

- build participatory music experience into degree requirements
- hire visiting artists to bring depth to the teaching of diverse traditions
- broaden the learning community by partnering with community artists and groups
- collaborate between disciplines to support a more integrated perspective on community arts
- document the impact on student learning and community engagement
- revise promotion criteria to support faculty who want to do activity-centered and collaborative work
- be present.

The last strategy in this list is the simplest, and yet the most important for building relationships. Being present regularly at community events can be challenging for professors who are busy with university teaching and research (as it is for most people with jobs and families), but nothing can replace the trust and understanding that develops between people who music and dance together repeatedly, who stay engaged despite disappointments and disagreements, and who simply share the same space on a regular basis.

Having noted some things we should do to make a place for bomba in the university, it is also important to note that bomba is already doing fine. Bomba has always presented a challenge and an alternative to dominant institutions, and it remains rooted in communities of practice outside the university. Bomba doesn't need the university to protect it. As Ernesto Rodrigues of the group Alma Moyó says, "This saved us. We didn't save it. This is indestructible" (Raquel Rivera 2012, 19). It is rather the case, as I have argued here, that bomba has much to offer the university. The university in turn can become an ally in community arts activism, help create broader awareness about Afro-Puerto Rican culture and history, and share institutional resources with bomba artists and communities.

The culture of bomba and the culture of the academy have some common ground upon which to build. An important mission of the university is to connect diverse people, disciplines, and ways of knowing, and through these challenging encounters to advance our understanding. This impulse to connect and unify is also reflected in bomba's extraordinarily diverse cultural history. Over hundreds of years, bomba has adapted to and incorporated countless inter-cultural encounters (Berríos-Miranda and Dudley 2008). That process of innovation continues in the work of contemporary bomba artivistas, such as Pablo Luis Rivera, who use art to forge relationships between musicians, dancers, intellectuals, educators, media workers, social workers, politicians, impresarios, and people making art in different regions and countries. Bomba in this way helps people to make sense of a changing world. Ideally, then, bomba and college have at least this in common: They are disciplines that challenge us to learn, so that when we step into the *batey* of life and salute the drummer we will know who we are, and what we are doing.

ACKNOWLEDGEMENTS

I am grateful to colleagues who contributed to this article by responding to my questions about teaching bomba and fandango in university and community settings. Thanks especially to Noel Allende-Goitía, Hal Barton, Marisol Berríos-Miranda, Jaime Bofil, Ivelisse Díaz, Micaela Díaz Sanchez, Quetzal Flores, José Fusté, Martha Gonzalez, Julia Loíza Gutiérrez-Rivera, Jade Power Sotomayor, Amarilys Rios, Hector Luis Rivera, Pablo Luis Rivera, and Raquel Z. Rivera.

NOTES

[1] For an overview of bomba and fandango (or son jarocho) as activist movements, see Berríos-Miranda, Dudley and Habell-Pallán (2018, Chapter Five).

[2] In winter quarter 2019 the UW hosted another bomba artist, Amarilys Ríos, as a Community Artist in Residence. This article was already submitted and reviewed at that point so I have not added reflections on her residency.

[3] Indeed these terms originated with the pseudo-science of phrenology, in which they refer to the skull shape of Europeans (high brow) and Africans (low brow).

[4] I have also included several comments from students who studied with Amarilys Ríos during her Winter 2019 Community Artist Residency at UW, which included weekly community workshops as well as a participatory community bombazo.

[5] The scheme used in the book actually says "creativity" rather than "improvisation," but I want to avoid the implication that interpretive performance is not creative.

[6] I have several ideas about why this is so (including the WAM tradition's tendency to elevate the intellectual over the physical, explained above) but that is the topic of another discussion.

[7] Power Sotomayor has since taken a new position in the department of Theater and Dance at the University of California, San Diego.

REFERENCES

Barton, Halbert. 2004. A Challenge for Puerto Rican Music: How to Build a *Soberao* for Bomba. *CENTRO: Journal of the Center for Puerto Rican Studies* 16(1), 69–89

__________. 2017. Personal communication, November.

Berlin, Edward. 1980. *Ragtime: A Musical and Cultural History*. Berkeley: University of California Press

Berríos-Miranda, Marisol and Shannon Dudley. 2008. El Gran Combo, Cortijo, and the Musical Geography of Cangrejos/Santurce, Puerto Rico. *Caribbean Studies* 36(2), 121–51

Berríos-Miranda, Marisol, Shannon Dudley and Michelle Habel-Pallán. 2018. *American Sabor: Latinas and Latinos in U.S. Popular Music*. Seattle: University of Washington Press

Campbell, Patricia and Shannon Dudley. 2018. A University Commitment to Collaborations with Local Musical Communities. In *Oxford Handbook of Community Music*. New York: Oxford University Press.

Díaz, Ivelisse. 2019. Phone interview, May.
Díaz Sánchez, Micaela. 2017. Personal communication, November.
Ellison, Julie and Timothy Eatman. 2008. *Scholarship in Public: Knowledge Creation and Tenure Policy in the Engaged University.* <http://imaginingamerica.org/wp-content/uploads/2015/07/ScholarshipinPublicKnowledge.pdf/>.
Gonzalez, Martha. 2017. Personal communication, November.
Gutiérrez-Rivera, Julia Loíza. 2017. Personal communication, November.
Higgins, Lee. 2012. *Community Music: In Theory and in Practice.* New York: Oxford University Press
Kingsbury, Henry. 1988. *Music, Talent and Performance: A Conservatory Cultural System.* Philadelphia: Temple University Press
Levine, Lawrence. 1988. *High Brow Low Brow.* Cambridge, MA: Harvard University Press
McClary, Susan and Rob Walser. 1994. Theorizing the Body in African American Music. *Black Music Research Journal* 14(1), 75–84.
Moore, Robin, ed. 2017. *College Music Curricula for a New Century.* New York: Oxford University Press
Nettl, Bruno. 1995. *Heartland Excursions: Ethnomusicological Reflections on Schools of Music.* Urbana: University of Illinois Press.
Power Sotomayor, Jade. 2015. From Soberao to Stage: Afro-Puerto Rican Bomba and the Speaking Body. In *The Oxford Handbook of Dance and Theater*, ed. Nadine George-Graves. 706–28. New York: Oxford University Press.
Power Sotomayor, Jade and José Fusté. 2017. Personal conversation, November.
Rios, Amarilys. 2017. Personal communication, November.
Rivera, Hector Luis. 2019. Phone interview March.
Rivera, Pablo Luis. 2016. Personal interview, Santurce, Puerto Rico, 13 July.
__________. 2017. Telephone interview, 9 March.
Rivera, Raquel Z. 2012. New York Afro-Puerto Rican and Afro-Dominican Roots Music: Liberation Mythologies and Overlapping Diasporas. *Black Music Research Journal* 32(2), 3–24.
__________. 2017. Personal communication, November.
Rose, Tricia. 1994. *Black Noise: Rap Music and Black Culture in Contemporary America*, Hanover, NH : University Press of New England
Sarath, Ed, David Myers and Patricia Campbell. 2017. *Redefining Music Studies in an Age of Change: Creativity, Diversity, and Integration,* New York and London: Routledge
Small, Christopher. 1998. *Musicking: The Meanings of Performing and Listening,* Hanover : University Press of New England
Turino, Thomas. 2008. *Music as Social Life,* Chicago: University of Chicago Press
Wilson, Shawn. 2008. *Research Is Ceremony: Indigenous Research Methods,* Halifax and Winnipeg: Fernwood Publishing

VOLUME XXXI • NUMBER II • SUMMER 2019

MEMOIRS / MEMORIAS

Inventario de la serie "Conversatorios sobre la Bomba y la Cultura Puertorriqueña" instituidos por la organización Restauración Cultural

PABLO LUIS RIVERA

Desde el 2007, se han llevado a cabo en Puerto Rico una extensa serie de conversatorios sobre la bomba puertorriqueña convocados por Restauración Cultural, una organización que ayudé a fundar en 1998 y que está dedicada a resaltar los valores culturales de Puerto Rico a través de clases, conferencias, publicaciones, actividades, presentaciones y todo tipo de acción educativa, musical o artística de impacto social. Instituimos todo esto ante la escasez de enseñanza de nuestra cultura en el sistema educativo puertorriqueño, especialmente los temas relacionados con la afrodescendencia. Al armar estos espacios de diálogo originalmente, pretendíamos establecer un motor para revelar y difundir información sobre la bomba mayormente ignorada u olvidada, provocando la discusión, la plática y la investigación, en beneficio de la comunidad y los amantes de la cultura. Nuestra intención siempre ha sido recopilar datos sobre algunas de nuestras prácticas culturales desatendidas por la academia oficial de una manera organizada y profunda pero también accesible para todo tipo de público. Es importante destacar que los invitados que propiciaron los distintos temas a discutir lo hicieron voluntariamente por la amistad que los vincula con Restauración Cultural.

The author (xiorro@gmail.com) holds a Ph.D. in history from the Centro de Estudios Avanzados de Puerto Rico y el Caribe. He is a teaching researcher in the educational system of Puerto Rico, director of the Restauración Cultural organization, and co-director of the AFROlegado Educational Program and the Proyecto Unión. He is a well known bomba performer, composer, presenter and social activist, and has offered university credit-bearing courses on bomba at the University of Washington and the University of Puerto Rico.

La bomba puertorriqueña es un género caracterizado no solo por una diversidad de ritmos, sones y seises, además de estilos, pero también por su bagaje cultural complejo. La cultura como concepto representa las expresiones que nos caracterizan como pueblo y definen nuestra identidad. Desde muy temprano en el proceso de colonización y conquista, arribaron a Puerto Rico africanos y luego afrodescendientes oriundos de sociedades de plantación y otros territorios en otras partes del Caribe y América continental. Muchos llegaron esclavizados pero otros eran personas libres que migraban por múltiples razones. Por siglos, estos flujos poblacionales nutrieron el entorno cultural puertorriqueño con diversas experiencias y tradiciones. Sin embargo, el hecho de que los opresores o aventajados tienden a ser los que escriben la historia (silenciando así saberes y vivencias de poblaciones oprimidas) ha provocado un vacío en el estudio de nuestros orígenes africanos y las prácticas que de ese gran continente heredamos. África también es madre patria, pero se discute vagamente su legado.

Aparte de subrayar su afrodescendencia, cabe recordar que la bomba es uno de nuestros géneros de música y baile más antiguos en Puerto Rico. No olvidemos tampoco que nos conecta con otros lugares que poseen tradiciones centradas alrededor del tambor. La esclavización de personas, el cimarronaje, la libertad, la resistencia, la identidad, el resurgir, se sumergen en el relato constante, en la presencia indiscutible de este género que se niega a morir y, al contrario, está más vivo que nunca varios siglos después de su génesis. Por esto continúa despertando curiosidades entre practicantes y apasionados de la bomba que buscan entender mejor sus interioridades y así fortalecer aún más sus fundamentos.

Hablemos de bomba

A pesar de reconocer que este género ha formado una parte fundamental de la historia de Puerto Rico y que se encuentra en una fase de resurgimiento notable, la bomba necesita ser entendida mejor por el público general. Por lo ordinario, dentro de los espacios donde se practica públicamente, existen muchos que disfrutan de sus canciones, de su baile, de sus idiosincrasias y sutilezas como práctica artística accesible pero también emocionantemente compleja e intensa. Sin embargo, son menos los que reconocen su valor histórico y comprenden su desarrollo, sus usanzas, sus intimidades y fundamentos. Para ayudar a remediar esto, Restauración Cultural lleva más de dos décadas organizando múltiples proyectos educativos sobre la bomba tanto en la isla como en la diáspora.

Entre estos está Bomba de Oro, proyecto en el cual se le ofrecen clases a personas de edad avanzada en todo Puerto Rico. También continúa el programa educativo municipal en Carilina Los Gigantes de la Bomba en el cual se le ofrecen clases de bomba a todas las personas que acudan a la plaza de recreo de dicho municipio. Este ha sido fundamental y puntual en el proceso de aprendizaje de miles de personas que han participado. El municipio auspicia el pago de los integrantes de Restauración Cultural que actúan como maestros para que los participantes puedan toman los cursos gratuitamente. También ofrecemos talleres en escuelas e instituciones que solicitan nuestros servicios educativos dentro de la jurisdicción de Carolina. Organizamos también el Proyecto Unión, con el cual se les ofrecen talleres, apoyo, conferencias y actividades de integración con personas radicadas en la diáspora, tanto, personas puertorriqueñas y de otras nacionalidades. Así mismo comenzamos AFROlegado que se ha convertido en el brazo educativo de la organización Restauración Cultural y con el cual se ofrecen clases, se difunde material didáctico, se realizan intercambios, se efectúan alianzas educativas e institucionales y se crean currículos y clases mayormente a nivel universitario.

Finalmente, a partir del 2007, iniciamos nuestros Conversatorios sobre la Bomba Puertorriqueña aquí desglosados. Los mismos fueron inspirados por los Festivales de Bomba y Plena que a partir del 1972 fueron organizados anualmente por el productor Pedro "Capitol" Clemente en compañía de un grupo de estudiantes universitarios (la mayoría de la Universidad de Puerto Rico) quienes iniciaron un proceso sumamente importante: la realización de actividades que buscaban dar a conocer estos dos géneros (la plena y la bomba) dentro y fuera de Puerto Rico. Estos incluían presentaciones, exhibiciones, conferencias, actividades gastronómicas y eventos de tarima llevados a cabo por diferentes artistas experimentados y aprendices. El festival utilizaba estos recursos para educar al público en distintos lugares y contó con prestigiosos investigadores y artistas como Isabelo Zenón Cruz, Silvia del Villard, Marcelino Canino, Marie Ramos entre otros quienes indagaban sobre el trasfondo histórico de la bomba, los elementos característicos de la plena, la importancia de la afrodescendencia y datos útiles que buscaban fortalecer el conocimiento de los receptores. También ponían a disposición del festival sus escritos para ayudar a la difusión de su mensaje. Conocía de estos festivales y asistí a muchos de ellos, y luego hemos participado de los mismos como artista y conferenciante y, formando parte de la junta directiva, pero algo que también me inspiró a co-organizar los conversatorios de bomba fueron otros los congresos dedicados a la bomba que se llevaron a cabo en el Centro de Estudios Avanzados de Puerto Rico y el Caribe mientras realizaba mis estudios doctorales allí. Estos fueron organizados por personas como el maestro Jesús Cepeda Brenes y la educadora Hilda Hernández. También participaban agrupaciones y personas de todo Puerto Rico.

De este modo, le hemos dado voz y visibilidad a figuras que en muchas ocasiones pasaban desapercibidas en la historia pero que poseían una información sumamente valiosa.

Todo esto sumado a nuestras experiencias en conferencias, clases, presentaciones y talleres, donde palpábamos el interés, pero a la vez, el gran desconocimiento que existía sobre la la bomba nos inspiró a crear nuestros propios conversatorios para continuar dialogando sobre las interioridades de este gran género. De este modo, le hemos dado voz y visibilidad a figuras que en muchas ocasiones pasaban desapercibidas en la historia pero que poseían una información sumamente valiosa. Durante los últimos doce años, hemos expandido este tipo de actividades para valorizar aún más las experiencias, vivencias y saberes de personas y grupos que han dedicado gran parte de su vida a la ejecución, practica e investigación del género de la bomba y la cultura afrodescendiente. Aquí expondremos la información de algunos de los más importantes.

Primer conversatorio

El primer conversatorio convocado por Restauración Cultural fue un evento que nos generó grandes expectativas. Se llevó a cabo el 12 de octubre del 2007 en las facilidades de la Corporación Piñones se Integra (COPI). La primera vez que se realiza una actividad así es compleja pues uno no se imagina que puede suceder, quien puede participar, cuantas personas vendrán, quienes aceptarán el reto. Manteníamos una excelente relación con COPI dado que en ese momento ofrecíamos clases allí, realizábamos toques de bomba en su espacio y dirigíamos su grupo de bomba local llamado Majestad Negra. Por esto, decidimos realizar este primero conversatorio en este lugar emblemático, a las orillas de la Boca de Cangrejos, al lado del puente que divide la costa de Isla Verde de Piñones, un área perteneciente al municipio de Loíza que es considerada la capital de las tradiciones afrodescendientes y del legado Taíno de la isla. Por generaciones, esta área se ha asociado con el cimarronaje de los afrodescendientes puertorriqueños Es un palenque de diversidad y resistencia. No teníamos duda de que sería una actividad exitosa, pero jamás nos imaginamos que se instauraría como un evento y espacio regular indispensable para la discusión y el flujo de actividades sobre bomba orientadas hacia el enriquecimiento académico. Maricruz Rivera Clemente y el equipo de trabajo en COPI siempre estuvieron muy dispuestos a colaborar para el éxito de la actividad.

Este primer conversatorio fue titulado "Los jóvenes en la bomba." En él participaron: Felipe "Junito" Febres Rivera, ex miembro del grupo de la Familia Cepeda y de Son del Batey y codirector y cofundador de Restauración Cultural; Víctor Emmanuelli Náter, en ese momento integrante del Centro de Investigación y Cultura "Raíces Eternas" (CICRE) y del Bombazo de Puerto Rico; Oxil Febles, directora de Nandí, el primer grupo de bomba femenino en Puerto Rico; Pedro Colón Amaro, integrante de la Escuela de Bomba y Plena Rafael Cepeda Atiles dirigida por el Dr. Modesto Cepeda Brenes y finalmente Héctor Calderón, director del Taller Folclórico Yuba Iré.

La primera actividad sirvió de modelo para las demás. Se trabajó a manera de panel donde estaban los invitados arriba mencionados y este servidor como moderador. Se colocó un micrófono para preguntas y comentarios. Grabamos con una cámara de video para documentar los hechos (todos los conversatorios están grabados y en posesión del que suscribe). La sorpresa fue muy grande al ver la gran cantidad de personas que asistieron, un grupo muy nutrido de amantes de la cultura tanto de Puerto Rico como de Estados Unidos.

La discusión giró en torno a los procesos de cambio que sufrió la bomba, especialmente, desde los inicios de los ponentes en este ambiente cultural y su participación en la escena bombera. También los cambios al vivir en carne propia el resurgir de este género. Ellos relataron sus comienzos, su participación amplia, los aciertos, las frustraciones, la importancia de conocer el fundamento, de valorar a los precursores, la resistencia que ponían muchas personas a los cambios que se iban dando, y como se podían abrir camino en un mundo tan competitivo. El público realizó muchas preguntas, comentarios constructivos y nos demostraron el interés para que se continuaran realizando actividades de este tipo.

Segundo conversatorio

En enero del 2008 decidimos realizar una actividad que denominamos Fiesta Nacional de la Bomba. Aprovechando la conmemoración del día feriado de Martin Luther King Jr., decidimos realizar otra actividad educativa en COPI. Nuevamente Piñones fue el escenario de tan importante actividad. Tuvimos conferencias a cargo del Lic. Ebenezer López Ruyól. Este nos habló sobre la importancia de conmemorar las hazañas de Martin Luther King pero lo discutió en el contexto de un prócer olvidado en Puerto Rico, el cangrejero Arturo Alfonso Schomburg, aprovechando el hecho de las coincidencias en fechas de nacimiento de ambos insignes luchadores, aunque Schomburg nació en 1874. También conseguimos que la emisora WKAQ Radio trasmitiera hablando de las actividades y los temas relacionados a la bomba en los programas que trasmitían todo ese día. Algunas de las personas de la emisora nos ayudaron con esto fueron el Prof. Juan Manuel García Passalacqua, el periodista Julio Rivera Saniel, el Lic. Luis Pabón Roca y el Lic. Carlos Díaz Olivo. A pesar de haber sido un día lluvioso, estuvo muy concurrido. Las agrupaciones musicales que se presentaron fueron: Bomba Tour de Restauración Cultural, Desde Cero, Son del Batey, Yagüembé, RumbaCuembe, Nandí y Majestad Negra. Fue una actividad llena de mucha acción bombera, artesanías, gastronomía y grandes emociones. La unión estuvo presente y el interés y compromiso de los participantes se sintió. El conversatorio en esta ocasión estuvo a cargo de Pedro "Capitol" Clemente el cual estuvo discutiendo los detalles de cómo comenzó el Festival de Bomba y Plena en la década de los 70, los grupos que surgieron, las entrevistas a grandes ejecutantes identificados en las diversas regiones, la aportación de la prensa y el gobierno para lograr su realización, el proceso educativo y como este festival se convirtió en modelo de otros festivales y actividades en todo y el país y fuera de este. Los intercambios culturales, la promoción del arte a través de sus carteles y otros eventos, y la constante discusión de los temas vinculantes a nuestra herencia africana. Fue todo un éxito y nuevamente consiguió despertar el interés por los temas históricos. Reiteradamente se consiguió reconocer la importancia de valorar y reconocer a los precursores de tan importante evento.

Tercer conversatorio

El primer traslado de un conversatorio organizado por Restauración Cultural fuera del área metropolitana se dio en área oeste, específicamente en el pueblo de Mayagüez. Para realizar un mejor trabajo y poder involucrar a los protagonistas en la escena de bomba de esta región dialogamos con el amigo Alberto Galarza, historiador, fotógrafo y ejecutante para que colaborara en esta gestión. Galarza no dudó en proponernos varias ideas para hacer realidad este sueño. Se encargó de crear un afiche y lo dialogó con los amigos y amigas del grupo de bomba en el que el participaba como integrante activo en ese momento: Yagüembé. Dialogamos con Ramón "Papo" Alers, director del mismo y ejecutante experimentado y sin dudarlo nos ayudó también. Aprovechamos la disyuntiva de la conmemoración del día de la abolición de la esclavitud del año 2008 para realizar dicho evento. Queríamos que fuera una actividad de conciencia estableciendo las bases históricas de lo que era la historia de la bomba mayagüezana. Se invitaron a figuras emblemáticas: Edwin Albino, historiador y enlace con el Instituto de Cultura Puertorriqueña en el área oeste; Ramón Alers del Grupo Yagüembé y eventual director de la escuela de bomba en ese municipio; Rubén Cepeda, uno de los organizadores del Festival de Bomba y Plena de Mayagüez y ejecutante de varios grupos de esta región; Isabel García, bailadora y reconocida ejecutante de bomba; Lucas Buyé, afamado ejecutante de la bomba mayagüezana y Agapito Soler, otro ejecutante emblemático del oeste isleño.

La discusión se llevó a cabo en el Centro Cultural Baudillo Vega Berrios en Mayagüez y fue intensa. Se recordaron lugares donde se practicaba la bomba antigua, se relataron experiencias y eventos de antaño y como había variado la ejecución con el pasar de tiempo. Estuvimos trabajando en la moderación en compañía de la maestra de baile Jamie Pérez. El público participó muy activamente y cuestionaban constantemente el que no se discutieran estos temas en el sistema educativo. Luego de homenajear a los participantes, se efectuó un gran toque de bomba donde participaron integrantes de los diversos grupos de Mayagüez, e incluso, integrantes de Majestad Negra, Restauración Cultural, y de la Escuela Caridad Brenes. Fue una actividad muy estimulante que definitivamente nos motivó a organizar conversatorios subsecuentes. Había que saciar la sed de aprender y conocer más profundamente.

Cuarto, quinto y sexto conversatorio

Luego de realizar la Fiesta Nacional de la Bomba nos sucedieron muchas cosas buenas. Una de ellas fue que mientras estábamos tocando bomba una tarde de domingo en Loíza, unos empleados del Municipio de San Juan, específicamente de la Oficina de Turismo y Arte, se nos acercaron porque asistieron a la actividad realizada en COPI (Fiesta Nacional de la Bomba) y querían que se replicara en San Juan. Así que les sometimos una propuesta que fue eventualmente aprobada y en 2008 realizamos la actividad Sonido de Tambores en la Capital. Esta actividad congregaba a varios grupos de bomba y artistas plásticos en la Plaza de Armas en el viejo San Juan convocados por Restauración Cultural. El primer año se realizó un conversatorio ofrecido por Marién Torres y Frederick Ríos. Fue tan buena la reacción del público que en el 2009 al repetirse la actividad se volvió a efectuar otro conversatorio, esta vez contando con la presencia de Isabel Albizu y su Grupo Bambalué de Ponce. Doña Isabel habló de sus experiencias en el sur de Puerto Rico y cómo la bomba de esta región ha evolucionado hasta nuestros días. También discutió las influencias de personas de la bomba con las que tuvo contacto desde infancia no solamente en Ponce, sino en otros lugares de la región sur como Arroyo, Guayama y Salinas. También habló de ejecutantes de otras regiones que los visitaban. Fue muy importante que los asistentes conocieran la bomba desde la perspectiva de una de las más importantes y queridas bomberas de nuestros tiempos.

En el 2010 se realizó con mucho éxito el tercer evento Sonido de Tambores en la Capital. Aquí el conversatorio fue sobre los fundamentos de la bomba y las múltiples distorsiones que existen relacionadas a los conocimientos sobre este género. Este servidor dialogó con el público sobre los detalles relacionados al fundamento de la bomba, lo relevante de conocer claramente las sutilezas del género y su importancia histórica y como bandera de identidad nacional.

Conversatorios en Carolina

Luego de observar las actividades que se realizaron en Piñones, San Juan y Mayagüez decidimos que era importante establecer conversatorios regulares para satisfacer a un público con mucha hambre de intercambiar más conocimiento sobre la bomba. Dado que estábamos dirigiendo el proyecto municipal Los Gigantes de la Bomba nos pareció excelente atar las actividades a este programa educativo. Los conversatorios fueron acompañados de poesía, toques de bomba, proyecciones de películas y documentales, talleres y conferencias, entre otras actividades. En estas prestezas se proyectaron documentales tales como: *Raíces*, *Con sabor a Mayagüez*, *Nenén de la ruta mora* y otros relacionados a la bomba. También tuvimos la participación de la declamadora Elsa Costoso Mercado, La Rondalla Carolina, Pedro Rodríguez y Los Gigantes de la Salsa. También en estos conversatorios regulares, contamos con la presencia de un sinnúmero de bomberas y bomberos aquí mencionados.

Conversando en el 2011

En el 2011 se realizó el primero de los más de treinta conversatorios que tuvimos en el edificio de Recreación en Carolina. Ya a que estábamos trabajando con la Oficina de Recreación y Deportes, convencimos a la administración a que nos ayudara con estos eventos. Tuvimos la colaboración de Felipe Febres y Rafael Maya, además de la asistencia y apoyo constante de los estudiantes de los Gigantes de la Bomba. Se preparaba el lugar acomodando todo para pasar una tarde inolvidable.

Continuando con los Conversatorios en el 2011 se realizó un conversatorio dedicado a la gran aportación de las mujeres en la bomba y el grupo Paracumbé.

El primer conversatorio de esta serie fue efectuado por la historiadora Lidia Milagros González. En este se discutieron asuntos muy importantes relacionados a la bomba de Loíza. Para Lidia fue muy importante discutir esta información con un público muy interesado en conocer las interioridades de sus investigaciones, su punto de vista y detalles importantes publicados en su libro *Elogio a la bomba* (2004) donde discute aspectos relacionados a la bomba de la zona noreste de la isla. Desde aquí y en adelante, se creó un sistema donde los integrantes del proyecto Gigantes de la Bomba no solo disfrutaban de estas visitas, también se encargaban de agasajar a los invitados, incluso al público que asistía de otros lugares. El Departamento de Recreación del Municipio Autónomo de Carolina también prestaba las facilidades y materiales para la puntual realización de esta actividad.

Otros conversatorios efectuados en el 2011 fueron en los que estuvieron como invitados Tadeo “Tato” Conrad y Raúl Berrios. Ellos estuvieron dialogando sobre un libro escrito por Raúl titulado *Bambula* (2011) y trajeron a colación aspectos importantes de su visión de lo que es la bomba y su conexión con el Caribe. Continuando con los Conversatorios en el 2011 se realizó un conversatorio dedicado a la gran aportación de las mujeres en la bomba y el grupo Paracumbé. Este estuvo a cargo de la profesora Nelie Lebrón Robles acompañada de atinadas intervenciones del profesor Emmanuel Dufrasne. Fue un momento donde se dialogó sobre las experiencias de este grupo, sus investigaciones y elementos innovadores que este conjunto ha aportado a la historia de la bomba.

Conversando en el 2012

Ya en el 2012 se reanudan los conversatorios dominicales con grandes aportaciones al quehacer cultural. Una de estas aportaciones se dio por personas como el melómano Ing. Raúl Román Normandía. Este, contribuyó presentando sus experiencias y conocimientos vinculados a las grabaciones que incluyen el género de la bomba, músicos olvidados o poco conocidos como Kito Vélez y aportaciones que muchas personas desconocían. Román trajo muy buenos ejemplos sobre la música orquestada, participación de la bomba en conjuntos, incluso ejemplos de bomba cruda o con instrumentos tradicionales. Fue el primero en traer su presentación proyectada.

Este año hicimos una excepción y realizamos un conversatorio sobre Rafael Hernández Marín en ocasión de la develación de una obra de arte dedicada a este. El conversatorio fue ejecutado por el Dr. Ismael Rodríguez Tapia quien realizó su tesis doctoral sobre este tema. El mismo se efectuó en las antiguas facilidades de la Escuela y Centro Especializado de Restauración Cultural en la Urbanización Dos Pinos en Río Piedras, lugar que albergaba a la organización (CEDICE) dirigida por Carmen Villanueva Castro.

Los lazos que nos unen con la diáspora cada vez son más fuertes. De hecho, la bomba ha tomado un auge increíble fuera del territorio puertorriqueño. Es por esto que no podíamos omitir la experiencia de los grupos que allí transcurren.

Aprovechando la gira promovida por el Proyecto Unión, recibimos al Grupo Buya de Chicago. Sus integrantes dialogaron sobre sus aciertos, desaciertos y situaciones fuera de la Isla. Definitivamente plasmó un puente desarrollado por el sonido de los tambores. El compartir fue memorable.

Interesante por demás estuvo el conversatorio relacionado con las conexiones con el Caribe. Lester Nurse, profesor universitario retirado, trajo buenos ejemplos de música de tambor en diversos lugares del Caribe. Lester problematizó trayendo a colación discusiones interesantes sobre el origen de la bomba puertorriqueña y el concepto autóctono en la misma. Afirmando que la bomba tiene una conexión muy amplia con el Caribe. Este invitado enfatizó la importancia de conocer las etnias africanas que impactaron nuestra región, la conexión e intercambio constante de Puerto Rico con el Caribe, el papel que juega San Mateo de Cangrejos (actualmente Santurce) en este proceso y la discusión importante sobre la bomba actual como cultura viva y no un género de museo ni folclórico.

La fundadora de la actividad denominada Encuentro de Tambores y directora del grupo Plenibom, la Profa. Norma Salazar nos acompañó en otra ocasión para dialogar sobre la bomba en las letras de su compañero de vida el compositor guayamés Catalino "Tite" Curet Alonso. El público se deleitó con una información sumamente valiosa. Tite era conocido más bien por sus composiciones de salsa, así que enfatizar la diversidad musical que su trabajo fue sumamente importante.

La bomba en el oeste de Puerto Rico tuvo un notable resurgir por varias razones que incidieron en ese proceso, creando una estructura que contemplaba la tradición, pero que también le inyecta nuevos recursos. Bomberos jóvenes de esa área han recuperado canciones antiguas a través de la investigación pero también crean nuevos temas cantados. Además, el interés por aprender promovió una nueva ola de escuelas, presentaciones y proyectos en esa región. Para entender más claramente este proceso invitamos a Alexandra y Javier Muñiz, Christian Galarza Boyrie y Randy Zorrilla. En este conversatorio se discutieron las nuevas corrientes en el oeste y los distintos puntos de vista de los invitados.

La vasta experiencia de Idalina Rodríguez, maestra de profesión, fue fundamental para entender las transiciones entre los grupos y los ejecutantes, en espacios comunitarios versus la experiencia en tarima, lo folclórico y lo tradicional. Estos elementos eran importantes a la hora de evaluar las prácticas relacionadas a la ejecución de la bomba. Su conversatorio ayudó a entender los factores a considerar a la hora de practicar la bomba por gusto o por participar de una agrupación.

Conversando en el 2013

El 2013 nos permitió realizar otros conversatorios importantes. Uno de ellos estuvo a cargo de uno de los bailadores más emblemáticos de Puerto Rico, José Antonio "Nuno" Calderón. Este nos relató sobre sus experiencias desde que comenzó en el famoso grupo Familia Cepeda de San Mateo de Cangrejos. Su diálogo fue muy impactante. Nos habló sobre las transiciones que él ha experimentado y vivido desde que se inició en el género cuando joven hasta lo que ha llegado a ser el baile de bomba hoy. También discutió la importancia de conocer el fundamento para poder crear cosas nuevas.

Este año también nos permitió continuar conociendo las profundidades históricas en la región loiceña. En esta ocasión y para discutir este tema estuvo el ejecutante, historiador y compositor Marcos Peñaloza Pica. Marcos estuvo adentrándose en los asuntos relacionados a la historia, lo que lo inspira a componer, sus experiencias en múltiples grupos y la discusión de sus producciones musicales.

La experiencia y vivencias en la familia Cepeda y luego en diversos grupos han hecho de Vilma Sastre una de las bailadoras más emblemáticas de la bomba puertorriqueña. Su relación directa con la familia y los años que estuvo vinculada a esta agrupación le permitieron realizar un conversatorio lleno de información y detalles importantes.

Cada vez se intensificaba más la discusión. Mayagüez volvió a tener un turno para la discusión cuando invitamos a David González (catedrático asociado, UPR Mayagüez), quien nos presentó su documental titulado *Con sabor a Mayagüez*. Esto creó un ambiente de discusión muy importante luego de que este explicara como surgió este trabajo, y dialogara sobre los artistas y lugares que se mencionan. Este día fue especial porque fue la primera vez que se presentó plena en un conversatorio con una participación importante de Norberto Sánchez, Víctor Vélez, Santos Benítez, Raúl Román y Juan Emilio Martínez entre otros.

Es la bailadora o el bailador quién realiza una de las partes musicales más importantes de cada canción dado a que el tambor afinado más agudo llamado "primo" o "subidor" marca los pasos de la persona que baila.

El último domingo de cada mes presentaba una nueva sorpresa para los amantes de la cultura. Con el favor del público que visitaba Carolina de diversas partes, fue muy emocionante recibir a Dennis Lebrón, Rhenna Lee Santiago y Lara Serrano estudiosos y practicantes de la bomba del sur. Ellos discutieron aspectos importantes relacionados a las sutilezas vinculadas a su participación en el afamado grupo Paracumbé y sus investigaciones.

Uno de los elementos importantes a la hora de practicar la bomba es el baile. Es la bailadora o el bailador quién realiza una de las partes musicales más importantes de cada canción dado a que el tambor afinado más agudo llamado "primo" o "subidor" marca los pasos de la persona que baila. Dado a esta dinámica complicada, para llegar a ser diestro en el primo o subidor hay que conocer cabalmente su práctica. Incluso, hay personas que pueden interpretar como una falta de respeto el que se toque este tambor sin dominar plenamente su ejecución. Para concebir mejor este tema se invitó a Víctor Emmanuelli Náter y Héctor Calderón, tocadores experimentados, para un conversatorio denominado Dialogando con el Tambor. Los presentes aclararon muchas dudas sobre esta relación tan importante.

Este año fue uno lleno de mucha información y la maestra y bailadora Jeanitza Avilés contribuyó a enriquecer nuestro conocimiento. Además de hablar y mostrar elementos relacionados a las técnicas útiles sobre el baile, habló sobre su tesina la cual detalla estos conceptos bailables. Otro conversatorio resaltó el canto de bomba y cómo sus cantos y letras tienen mucho que revelar. Aprovechando la visita del proyecto Taller de la Isla desde Aguadilla. invitamos a Víctor Vélez para que dialogara sobre diversas canciones en la bomba y las historias que cuentan.

También invitamos al artesano y artista Kenneth Meléndez a que nos ofreciera una explicación muy completa relacionada a la confección de máscaras en las distintas regiones de Puerto Rico y comparándolas con las confeccionadas en diversos lugares de América. Además dedicamos un conversatorio a el Grupo Calabó que jugó un papel importante en el desarrollo de otras agrupaciones durante la segunda mitad del siglo XX. Para esta sesión, invitamos a su directora, la Dra. Marie Ramos Rosado (UPR, Río Piedras), quien nos habló del proceso de desarrollo del grupo, los espacios educativos que tuvo este colectivo y como su grupo se inserta en los temas políticos, de protesta y la realización de denuncias importantes especialmente encaminadas a erradicar el racismo.

Conversando en el 2014

Este año también estuvo lleno de visitas interesantes. Una de estas fue la del Grupo desde Cero dirigido por Rafael Maya Álvarez. Explicaron cómo surgió la agrupación, literalmente desde cero hasta llegar a ser uno de los grupos más representativos que interpreta la bomba contemporánea en Puerto Rico. Conocer su génesis en el 2007, y ver cómo fueron engranado hasta ser competitivos profesionalmente fue sumamente importante. También nos relataron sobre la realización de su producción discográfica. El 2014 también tuvo la visita de la bailadora y maestra Yinaidarys Rivera Beltrán. Rivera discutió aspectos relacionados a las técnicas de baile y sus experiencias con diversos grupos culturales. También habló de sus vivencias internacionales.

Uno de los conversatorios más esperados fue el de Felipe "Junito" Febres por ser uno de los maestros en el Programa Gigantes de la Bomba. Esto porque los estudiantes no suelen escuchar al denominado "caballero de la bomba" conversando sobre sus experiencias y vivencias. Entre experiencias y su acostumbrado sentido del humor relató lo que le parece es importante conocer para tener una mejor ejecución y ser más competitivos a la hora de aventurarnos en un proyecto relacionado a la bomba; paciencia, practica y disciplina.

De los artesanos de tambores uno de los más conocidos y de mayor experiencia en Puerto Rico es Iván Dávila. Él se convirtió en un investigador apasionado y no se limitó a fabricar instrumentos sino que también se dedicó a componer canciones y ejecutar la música de Puerto Rico. Fue muy interesante escuchar sus relatos sobre sus variadas experiencias visitando las distintas regiones donde se práctica la bomba.

Uno de los grupos emblemáticos en el proceso de resurgir de la bomba lo fue Son del Batey. Este conjunto que surgió a finales de los años noventa rompió muchas barreras en la bomba. Por ejemplo, fue de los primeros que se empezó a presentar regularmente en negocios nocturnos frecuentados por gente joven. Omar "Pipo" Sánchez director de Son del Batey se sinceró y nos habló del surgimiento del grupo, su desarrollo, evolución y transformaciones. Nos trasmitió los eventos que llevaron a buscar la mejor ejecución de la agrupación.

Las mujeres han ocupado un papel imprescindible en el desarrollo de la bomba. Ese rol ha variado con el pasar del tiempo, así que era importante invitar a dos de las bomberas más reconocidas hoy día en la isla: Marién Torres López y Amarilys Ríos. Ellas discutieron aspectos vinculados a como la mujer pasa de meramente bailar o cantar a destacarse en la percusión. Hablaron francamente sobre las barreras con las que se toparon y como pudieron superarlas para así ampliar el protagonismo femenino en el género. Ambas fueron integrantes de Nandí el primer grupo de bomba en Puerto Rico exclusivamente integrado por mujeres y ahora participan con otra agrupación femenina llamada Ausuba.

Conversando en el 2015

El 2015 trajo consigo una serie de iniciativas muy interesantes. Una de ellas fue el programa *Repicando* en Bonita Radio. Se nos ofreció producir este espacio radial que se trasmite por espacios cibernéticos. Este programa fue creado por los bomberos Otoquí Reyes y Naomi Vázquez. Estos realizaron su primera serie. Para su segunda año, aceptamos la misión de continuarlo y expandirlo por ser una idea original que permitía tener a los exponentes de los conversatorios expandiendo y difundiendo sus discusiones. También, nos permitía entrevistar a personas que no pudieron dialogar en los conversatorios y así descubrir nuevos talentos. En nuestro caso moderábamos el espacio, pero sumamos a Felipe Febres Rivera para conducir el mismo. Esto nos ha permitido entrevistar además de las personas que han participado de los conversatorios a figuras como: Raúl Ayala, Modesto Cepeda Brenes, Shannon Dudley, Juan José Vélez, Milagros Barez, Jorge Martínez, Maritere Martínez, Lero Martínez Roldan, Héctor Rivera de Jesús, Manuel Pérez Kenderich, Jade Power-Sotomayor, José I. Fusté, Elia Cortes, Virgen "Choco" Orta, Manuel Carmona, Héctor Lugo, Hiram Abrante, Pedro Colón, Ángel Alomar y Mirta Salazar, entre otros invitados.

Mientras desarrollábamos este programa, continuamos los conversatorios en el Centro de Recreación y Deportes en Carolina. Recibimos al Dr. Luis Manuel Álvarez quien realizó dinámicas musicales que involucraron el conocimiento de las raíces africanas, españolas, árabes y como estas influyeron en la bomba. De Mayagüez recibimos a Liz Saira Díaz Nadal directamente desde la Escuela de Bomba mayagüezana y con ella asistieron los integrantes del grupo Botucos de la Bomba. Estos jóvenes demostraron su aprendizaje, validando así la calidad de la enseñanza y el amor por las tradiciones. La experiencia en Mayagüez, en la escuela y el resurgir ascendente en estos últimos años en esta región fueron temas que discutió la invitada con suma claridad.

Luego de este ofrecimos otro conversatorio sobre la Escuela Rafael Cepeda y el Centro Modesto Cepeda Brenes, instituciones emblemáticas en la enseñanza de la bomba, con una estructura fija donde las personas podían asistir y aprender las intimidades no solo de la bomba, también de la plena. Esta escuela en San Mateo de Cangrejos (Santurce) sirvió de modelo para los sistemas de enseñanza de la bomba en Puerto Rico. Todavía es dirigida por el maestro Dr. Modesto Cepeda quién no pudo estar con nosotros. Su familia asistió a conversar sobre el desarrollo de este proyecto educativo. Nos visitaron Gladys Cámara, Brenda Cepeda, Sandra Hernández, el Dr. Daniel Martínez, Mónica Cruz y Pedro Colón. Esta experiencia logró explicar cómo fue el proceso de crear una estructura nueva, y como de ser la escuela Rafael Cepeda, pasó a ser el Centro Dr. Modesto Cepeda. Las anécdotas nos llevaron a dialogar sobre el gran sacrificio y esfuerzo de cuatro décadas y la satisfacción de haber fomentado el amor por la cultura en tantas personas.

Cuando se habla de bomba hay que mencionar al continente África, así que fue muy interesante conocer sobre la raíz bantú en conversatorio que tuvo practica musical.

También en el 2015 recibimos a Javier Muñiz y Alberto Galarza directamente desde Mayagüez. Su presentación estaba dirigida a conocer la historia de la bomba mayagüezana con imágenes, documentación y fotos que nos transportaron a la sultana del oeste. Este conversatorio reforzó los conocimientos relacionados al trasfondo y la tradición en esta región. Cuando se habla de bomba hay que mencionar al continente África, así que fue muy interesante conocer sobre la raíz bantú en conversatorio que tuvo practica musical. Por esto, durante otro conversatorio el músico y artista gráfico Beto Torrens nos transportó hacia la región bantú en el continente africano y discutió la relación con países como Brasil. Finalmente, ese año hablamos sobre el programa *Alborada* en Radio Universidad, uno de los espacios que por más de dos décadas ha fomentado el apoyo a los trabajos culturales de los artistas del patio. Andrés Pérez Camacho, su moderador, estuvo con nosotros discutiendo las experiencias de un programa solidario con la cultura y comprometido con el desarrollo de los exponentes de la bomba, la plena y otros géneros puertorriqueños.

Conversando en el 2016

En el 2016 recibimos al Dr. Emmanuel Dufrasne González quien hablo de Paracumbé, grupo que se honra en dirigir. También nos relató sobre sus investigaciones y en particular, sobre la dinámica en pueblos como Loíza y San Mateo de Cangrejos (Santurce). Nos mostró los ritmos que documentó en esta región, canciones y elementos importantes de la bomba. También este año nos visitó el Dr. Hugo Viera, antropólogo y catedrático asociado en la Universidad Ana G. Méndez, Recinto de Cupey, quien explicó sus hallazgos vinculados a la visita de John Alden Mason a Puerto Rico entre el 1914-15. Otro recurso importante que participó de los conversatorios fue el Dr. Noel Allende Goitia, catedrático de música en la Universidad Interamericana.

Este realizó una exposición histórica sobre los temas musicales, figuras importantes a través de los siglos que documentan la bomba y el vínculo con África.

La familia de Ponce volvió a ser representada por los amigos de Bambalué ya a que en otra ocasión habíamos recibido a Alberto "Beto" Santiago, esta vez su padre Wilfredo "Ito" Santiago, Cesar Hernández y José Archeval nos visitaron. Nos relataron sus experiencias en este grupo, además de discutir las grandes trasformaciones que han vivido al crear proyectos como la Escuela de Bomba Isabel Albizu y el grupo Bomba Iyá. También discutieron aspectos relacionados a las producciones musicales y como el área sur está en pleno desarrollo.

Este año se realizó también un conversatorio sobre el son jarocho mexicano. En esta ocasión Jazmín Cansio fue nuestra invitada y explicó los elementos importantes relacionados a este género tradicional de Veracruz. De esta manera se ampliaba la discusión cultural considerando otras latitudes y explicando el trabajo realizado en los bombazos fandangos/bombangos entre comunidades latinas en la costa oeste de los Estados Unidos.

Conversando en el 2017

En el 2017 se realizaron varios conversatorios. Uno de ellos fue se efectuó a manera de panel en ocasión del decenio de la afrodescendencia promovido por la UNESCO. Tuvimos exposiciones a cargo de la Dra. Doris Quiñones, la Dra. Ada Verdejo, el Dr. Manuel Febres y el Lic. Ebenezer López Ruyól. El contexto de la afrodescendencia fue discutido para entender las realidades que van más allá de solamente los aspectos musicales de nuestra herencia cultual. Se discutieron asuntos relacionados a los temas de educación, racismo, derechos civiles entre otros. Esta serie la cerramos con un conversatorio sobre técnicas de investigación aplicadas a la bomba ofrecido por este servidor.

Además del programa *Repicando* en Bonita Radio vinculamos los conversatorios con actividades universitarias. Una de las actividades es el Foro de Educación, Historia y Afrodesendencia. Al día de hoy, este evento se ha realizado en tres ocasiones con una participación muy concurrida. En el primero se discutieron varios temas a manera de panel: "Los rumbones de esquina en Santurce," realizado por la Dra. Marisol Berrios Miranda, "Educación y cultura" ofrecido por la Dra. Ada Verdejo Carrión y "El resurgir de la bomba" realizado por el que suscribe. Este evento se efectuó en ocasión del cierre de la clase de bomba con créditos realizada en la Universidad de Puerto Rico. El segundo Foro de Educación, Historia y Afrodescendencia también se efectuó en la UPR y los invitados fueron la Dra. Bárbara Abadía Rexach (UPR, Río Piedras) quien habló sobre los cuatro pisos o etapas históricas de la bomba y Marcos Peñaloza Pica que hizo una exposición sobre la historia de la bomba de Loíza. El tercer Foro se trasladó a la Universidad Interamericana en Fajardo y fue un homenaje a la vida del Dr. Modesto Cepeda. Otros eventos vinculados fueron las conferencias dedicadas a las cuatro décadas del festival de bomba y plena original auspiciadas por la Fundación de las Humanidades y el National Endowment for the Arts.

Tuvimos el honor de dirigir este proyecto que contó con la participación de la Dra. Barbara Abadía Rexach, el artista Nelson Sambolín, el Dr. Ismael Rodríguez Tapia, la Dra. Doris Quiñones, la Dra. Ada Verdejo, el fotoperiodista José Rodríguez y el productor del Festival Pedro "Capitol" Clemente. Las actividades se realizaron en el Centro de Estudios Avanzados, la Universidad de Puerto Rico y en la Universidad Interamericana en Fajardo. También foros como el ofrecido en la Universidad Ana G. Méndez en Carolina sobre el Caño Martín Peña, Rafael Hernández Marín y la Bámbula ofrecido por Nelson Fred, Ismael Rodríguez Tapia y este servidor.

La internacionalidad de los conversatorios

Llevar la discusión de los temas de la cultura puertorriqueña no es tarea fácil. Sin embargo, hemos tenido la oportunidad de llevar la discusión a otros lugares. Además de las conferencias ofrecidas en actividades vinculadas con asociaciones y universidades a nivel mundial, en California en el año 2012 se realiza el 3er Bombazo-Fandango, una actividad que involucra a distintas figuras vinculadas al son jarocho mexicano y la bomba puertorriqueña. En colaboración con el comité organizador pudimos participar de un conversatorio en el que estuvimos varios gestores de la cultura incluyendo a: Patricio Hidalgo, Luis Alberto Sarmiento, Roberto Pérez Mayda Alexandra del Valle, Rafael Maya y el que suscribe. Esta actividad moderada por Melody González y Héctor Luis Rivera se discutieron aspectos importantes de la historia y desarrollo de la bomba y el son jarocho, pero también se discutieron aspectos vinculados a las prácticas en lugares lejos del lugar de origen de estas prácticas culturales. también se dialogó sobre el enfoque de los músicos y ejecutantes diseminados fuera de Puerto Rico y Veracruz.

En Martinica también realizamos un conversatorio donde varios integrantes de Restauración Cultural, la Mansión del Belé y los maestros y ejecutantes más longevos practicando el Belé en la vecina isla. Participaron: Benoit Rastocle, Constant Velasques, Félix Caserus, Pier Dru, Stella Zetwal Isabelle Florenty, Apollon Vallade, Marien Torres, Lero Martínez, y el que suscribe.

Fuimos invitados a participar en un panel organizado en la Universidad de Bielefeld, Alemania junto a los docentes Dr. Ángel "Chuco" Quintero Rivera (UPR, Río Piedras), el Dr. Juan José Vélez (académico puertorriqueño que enseña en esta última universidad) y la profesora Yadilka Rodríguez gracias a la Universidad y el Black Americas Network. Aprovechando esta invitación acudíamos también a la Universidad de Bremen, donde realizamos un conversatorio en compañía de Yadilka Rodríguez Ortiz y los estudiantes del Dr. Vélez. En esta ocasión hablamos de la cultura afrodescendiente en Puerto Rico y el impacto social del proyecto AFROlegado. Luego pudimos reproducir un panel similar en la Universidad de Puerto Rico añadiendo al Prof. Patrik Scanlon y a la Dra. Doris Quiñones como moderadora. El panel presentado en febrero de 2019 se llamó Música y Resistencia: Sonidos y Diálogos en el Caribe Afroantillano. Finalizamos este ciclo colaborando con el grupo Al Son de Bomba dirigido por Javier Muñiz ellos organizaron una actividad titulada Conversando entre Café y Bomba en febrero de 2019 en K-fe Luna en Rincón para los estudiantes de dicho Proyecto. Fuimos invitados y en este conversatorio discutimos la faceta histórica de la bomba basándonos en nuestra tesis titulada: "Orígenes culturales y desarrollo de la bomba puertorriqueña".

En este relato tratamos de mencionar la mayor parte de los datos y sucesos mas relevantes de lo que sucedió en este proceso educativo.

Conclusión

Los conversatorios se convirtieron en un espacio de discusión importante para conocer más profundamente nuestra herencia cultural, la bomba y nuestras tradiciones. Se dieron gracias al trabajo colectivo y el compromiso de múltiples personas. Es sumamente importante conocer más sobre nuestra historia, los protagonistas de las distintas estancias y los eventos que han marcado nuestra identidad como país. La discusión, la interpretación, el pensamiento crítico, los eventos, las sutilezas, las regiones, la evolución son solo aspectos importantes que requieren un estudio y difusión colectivo. Ante la ausencia de enseñanza general sobre nuestros géneros culturales, estos espacios juegan un papel indispensable. Escuchar diversas visiones y experiencias nos nutre y enriquece. Pronto estaremos realizando un nuevo ciclo en las facilidades de AFROlegado respondiendo a las nuevas realidades históricas y necesidades de los receptores. Este evento demuestra el compromiso con la educación y la identidad de nuestro país. Los espacios de intercambios de ideas son fundamentales para el desarrollo de nuestras tradiciones. ¡¡¡Que viva la cultura puertorriqueña!!!!

Conversatorios Restauración Cultural

	Nombre	Tema	Lugar	Año
1°	Oxil Febles, Felipe Febres, Héctor Calderón, Víctor Emmanuelli, Pedro Colón	Los jóvenes en la bomba	Corporación Piñones se Integra (COPI)	2007
2°	Pedro "Capitol" Clemente	El festival de bomba y plena original	Corporación Piñones se Integra (COPI)	2008
3°	Ramón "Papo" Alers, Edwin Alvino, Rubén Cepeda, Isabel García, Lucas Buyé y Agapito Soler	La bomba mayagüezana	Centro Cultural Baudillo Vega Berrios, Mayagüez	2008
4°	Marién Torres y Frederick Ríos	El baile en la bomba	Plaza de Armas, San Juan	2008
5°	Isabel Albizu y Bambalué	La bomba del sur	"	2009
6°	Pablo Luis Rivera	Fundamentos de la bomba y las múltiples distorsiones	"	2010
7°	Lydia Milagros González	Elogio a la bomba de Loíza	Edificio de Recreación y Deportes, Municipio Autónomo de Carolina	2011
8°	Raúl Berrios y Tadeo "Tato" Conrad	Bámbula	"	2011
9°	Nellie Lebrón Robles	Las mujeres en la bomba y el grupo Paracumbé"	"	2011
10°	Raúl Román Normandía	La bomba en las producciones musicales	"	2012
11°	Ismael Rodríguez Tapia	Rafael Hernández Marín: canta-autor de la patria	"	2012
12°	Grupo Buya	La bomba en la diáspora	"	2012
13°	Lester Nurse Allende	La bomba y su conexión con el Caribe	"	2012
14°	Norma Salazar	La bomba en las letras de Tite Curet Alonso"	"	2012
15°	Idalina Rodríguez	Del batey a la tarima	"	2012

Conversatorios Restauración Cultural

Nombre		Tema	Lugar	Año
16°	Javier Muñiz, Christian Galarza Boyrie, Alexandra Muñiz y Randy Zorrilla	Nuevas corrientes de la bomba del oeste	"	2012
17°	José Antonio "Nuno" Calderón	Vivencias y experiencias	"	2013
18°	Marcos Peñaloza Pica	Historia de la bomba loiceña	"	2013
19°	Vilma Sastre	Baile y experiencias	"	2013
20°	David González, Norberto Sánchez y Juan Emilio Martínez Román	Con sabor a Mayagüez	"	2013
21°	Dennis Lebrón, Rena Lee Santiago y Lara Serrano	Expresiones de la bomba del sur	"	2013
22°	Víctor Emmanuelli y Héctor Calderón	Dialogando con el tambor	"	2013
23°	Víctor "Sorpresa" Vélez	Las canciones en la bomba	"	2013
24°	Kenneth Meléndez	Confección de máscaras tradicionales	"	2013
25°	Marie Ramos	Calabó	"	2013
26°	Jeanitza Avilés	Técnicas de baile integradas en la bomba I"	"	2013
27°	Grupo Desde Cero	Dialogando con el grupo Desde Cero	"	2014
28°	Yinaidarys Rivera Beltrán	Técnicas de baile integradas en la bomba II	"	2014
29°	Felipe "Junito" Febres	Vivencias en la bomba	"	2014
30°	Iván Dávila	Confesiones de un barril	"	2014
31°	Omar "Pipo" Sánchez	Son del Batey	"	2014
32°	Marién Torres y Amarilis Ríos	Las mujeres en la bomba	"	2015
33°	Luis Manuel Álvarez	Influencias musicales en Puerto Rico	"	2015

Conversatorios Restauración Cultural

Nombre		Tema	Lugar	Año
34°	Liz Saira Díaz Nadal	Escuela de bomba de Mayagüez	"	2015
35°	Gladys Cámara, Brenda Cepeda y Daniel Martínez	Escuela Rafael Cepeda y Centro Dr. Modesto Cepeda	"	2015
36°	Javier Muñiz y Alberto Galarza	Historia de la bomba mayagüezana	"	2015
37°	Beto Torrens	La raíz bantú	"	2015
38°	Andrés Pérez Camacho	Alborada	"	2015
39°	Emmanuel Dufrasne González	Dos tradiciones de bomba: Loíza y Santurce	"	2016
40°	Hugo Viera Vargas	La Colección de John Andel Mason a Puerto Rico"	"	2016
41°	Alberto "Beto' Santiago, José Archeval, Wilfredo "Ito" Santiago, Cesar Hernández	Bambalué y la expresión sureña	"	2016
42°	Jasmín Cancio	Conociendo sobre el son jaracho de Vera Cruz	"	2016
43°	Doris Quiñones, Ada Verdejo, Manuel Febres y Ebenezer López Ruyol	Afrodescendencia	"	2017
44°	Pablo Luis Rivera	Técnicas de investigación aplicadas a la bomba	"	2017

Nota: Estos conversatorios están grabados digitalmente y en poder del que suscribe.

Writing Puerto Rico. Our Decolonial Moment

By Guillermo Rebollo Gil
Palgrave Pivot, 2018
ISBN: 978-3-319-92975-0
116 pages; $69.99 [paper, hardcover]

Reviewer: Manuel S. Almeida, Universidad del Este

Known Puerto Rican poet and sociologist Guillermo Rebollo Gil's most recent book, *Writing Puerto Rico. Our Decolonial Moment*, might constitute the future of fully ethico-politically engaged and militant cultural and social critique: a sort of gunslinger cultural critique. Or better, a quick draw cultural critique. That is, a critique that regardless of its situated and immediate urgency (thus, the necessary quickness), has the ability to hit on target. I say this fully conscious of how *awkward* that may sound, since proper critique requires patient rational reflection. But hey, this is book is –by its author's own admission– an endeavor in being "awkward". Awkward, though, in the sense of certain feminist activists' sense of awkwardness "as a political disturbance" (cited in p. 7).

In fact, this book might disturb customary and hegemonic academic sensibilities given its complex form. It swings freely from disciplinary discourse to disciplinary discourse, drinking from whichever critical well that might help better illuminate a particular social, cultural, economic, or political problem in the present conjuncture of contemporary Puerto Rico. Thus, he states at the beginning:

> **"Thinking" in this book mines sociological, autobiographical, literary, pop cultural, and activist registers. In doing so, it takes the form of chronicle, memory, metaphor, and speculation" (p. 9).**

And I might also add using autoethnography, among other forms. In this sense, *Writing Puerto Rico* continues with the type of social and cultural critique first rehearsed in his previous two books, *Última llamada* (Carolina: Ediciones UNE, 2016) and *Los actos gratuitos* (Carolina: Ediciones UNE, 2018).

This book's urgency is no joke, though. Puerto Rico, a 120-year old territorial colony of the United States, is currently under duress besieged by the U.S. federal law PROMESA, the Puerto Rico Oversight, Management, and Economic Stability Act, which re-inscribes the colonial nature of Puerto Rico's territorial relation to the US. PROMESA places an oversight board over the Puerto Rican government, which in fact, more than mere oversight, is a governing board over Puerto Ricans, since they can, in reality, effect changes on the local Puerto Rican budget (or impose its own recommended budget), public policy, among other stuff. This oversight board is commonly called by Puerto Ricans as "la Junta."

Though PROMESA, the *Junta*, our local government's incompetence and reactionary policies, as well as global capitalism's objective and structural violence, permeate the whole backdrop of the book, the focus is on the little things. Not little as in meaningless or less meaningful, but more as those little things which, when put under a magnifying glass, help elucidate wider and more comprehensive power dynamics. Thus, for example, Rebollo Gil's uses from his own personal life experiences as a student in a privileged Jesuit high school to elaborate and illuminate on the complexities and subtleties of the enacting and construction of white privilege.

There is a similar approach when he elaborates on the construction of the notion and subjectivity of the "middle class" in contemporary Puerto Rico. The notion of a middle class is seen in one of the chapters of the book as one that is posited through the construction of a frontier between a middle class which is meant to feel in their present precariousness as being held unfairly responsible for the supposedly laziness and unproductiveness of the popular classes seen as living the good life out of public (local or federal) handouts. Rebollo Gil discusses these popular sectors through the articulation of the pejorative, classist, racist, and misogynist stereotype of *la yal*, "a lower class, dark or darkened young mother whose sexual proclivities, lack of fashion sense, and/or questionable ethics are supposed to symbolize the gravity of our present predicament in socio-cultural terms" (p. 41). The Puerto Rican contemporary *yal* is a sort of local version of Reaganism's 'welfare queens' of the 1980s. Around these issues, he injects intensity and politicizes an otherwise forgetful local play. In a similar vein he does when using Rafael Acevedo's excellent short novel, *Guaya guaya* (pp. 53–62), where he politically charges the novel's plot and characters as a way to speculate on whether the revolutionary subject is not necessarily who and what we expect him (yes, typically *him*) to be, but more a random somebody, a *qualunque* (a nobody, an anybody) who somehow finds himself acting out a revolutionary or politically relevant act.

And thus we reach *the decolonial moment*, as can be articulated throughout the book's propositions. The decolonial moment is a fleeting one, but one that can be enacted or reenacted potentially at any moment, particularly in these times of—to use Gramscian terms—'organic crisis," where the old is dying and the new has yet to be born. Decolonial moments seem to be those where, at any unsuspected point in time, quotidian acts are politically or ethically potentiated or charged in such a way that they successfully, though briefly and always tendentially ending in failure, disrupt normality (normality being the hegemonic social order in which there are always oppressors and subalterns). I say at any unsuspected point in time, since, as Rebollo Gil states "It [the decolonial moment] could easily be missed. But, though fleeting, it is both worthy and withstands repetition (on stage, in a text, and/or on the street). And it demands of us equal bursts of critical, creative thought" (p.74).

Even though these decolonial moments tend to end up in failure, they could regardless provide for important political pedagogy, as for example when the author argues for a re-reading of a failed university student strike as important, regardless of ist outcome, even if it is to show the limits of helplessness (pp. 91–2). It is in part these continual acts of resignification, of re-cognition, that do not necessarily comply with the usual standards of Western modern parameters of reading or interpreting that associates what the author means by decolonial to that by now pretty abundant literature on decolonial thinking.

Toward the end of the book the author questions, almost as an afterthought, the supposed authority of those that, though are not located specifically in the author's space and time: say, in post-hurricane María Puerto Rico, where his location is not only his, since as Rebollo Gil reminds us at times he writes from a complicit stance but maintaining a perspective of "we and I." He questions, for example, those academics or *experts* who after their brief research stays of a week, two weeks (funded by their respective institutions or federal grants), conscious or unconsciously intend to tell us how to feel, how to organize ourselves, how to resist, how to solve our problems, how to understand our current conjuncture, so that we can impose the epistemological and even emotional discourses and codes with which to understand our place in Puerto Rico's current predicament. Of course, the author's intentions in this questioning is not out of a silly exclusivist perspective, in which it is said, "If you're not living it, you can't speak about it," It is more about how in the present hegemonic formation, there is always a privileging of those who can speak for them; them (us) being in this case, Puerto Ricans under the hardship of the debt, PROMESA, the Junta, the effects of María, so on and so forth.

This is an important book, both in its content and in its form. It illuminates what otherwise (and usually is) missed in current social and cultural analysis on Puerto Rico. The author's unapologetic partisanship and engagement in the matters of which he speaks of is also refreshing. It is something that one awkwardly misses, because they lack it, in the usual reports or opinion pieces on Puerto Rico's present juncture by the so-called experts: the sense of urgency that the situation mandates, and the sense of necessary partisan engagement needed to fully grasp it.

Concrete and Countryside: The Urban and the Rural in the 1950s Puerto Rican Culture

By Carmelo Esterrich
University of Pittsburgh Press, 2018
ISBN: 978-0-822-96539-8
207 pages; $27.95 [paper]

Reviewer: Ivis García, University of Utah

After Hurricane Maria devastated Puerto Rico on September 20, 2017, developers are seeking to build new housing. A large percentage of the Community Development Block Grant Disaster Recovery funds that the island has received and will be receiving will be dedicated to these purposes. But even when more than 20 percent of all housing in Puerto Rico remains vacant, the construction industry is not looking into rehabilitating abandoned homes in urban centers. Homes in commercial business districts (CBD) of the metro area—that is, Río Piedras, Santurce, etc.—are still considered not ideal places to live by most Puerto Ricans. There is the impression that these spaces are criminal and unsafe while areas outside of the CDB are the places where one should grow up, raise a family, and age. The construction industry as a whole respond to the cultural inclinations of Puerto Ricans, which seem to be very different from that of the U.S. new urbanist and smart growth tendencies, where density is more desirable than suburban and rural environments. In his book *Concrete and Country Side: The Urban and the Rural in the 1950s Puerto Rican Culture*, Carmelo Esterrich examines how citizens, academics, writers, musicians, theater, and film producers viewed the urban and rural in the island more than half century ago.

In particular, Esterrich examines the period from 1947 when Operation Bootstrap started to the 1960s when Puerto Rico was still believed to be the showcase of the American modernization project. All of this era was characterized by a central figure, Luis Muñoz Marín, who was Governor from 1948 to 1964. As the population grew in the 1930s and the sugar industry collapsed during the Great Depression, the island suffered from high unemployment. To overcome despair in the poverty-stricken island, in the late-1940s, Luis Muñoz Marín, envisioned, named, and implemented Operation Bootstrap, his economic development plan based on industrialization—a period already taking place around the world in the mid-twentieth century. This model was not a matter of choice. It was a new social structure and part of what became an evolutionary process of all modern societies. Puerto Rico, a U.S. territory, was not to escape these changes under Muñoz leadership.

During this time, Puerto Rico's GDP per capita grew dramatically, making it one of the wealthiest countries after the U.S. and Canada, and thus, a showcase of not only the Caribbean but all of North America. The new economic model based on tourism, industrial agriculture, and manufacturing, lifted the standards of living for many in the form of access to schooling, healthcare, personal income, and so on. Although it created jobs for people in Puerto Rico, it was mostly in urban settings. A large number of households move close to industry, choosing a new way of life in the city—now, a privileged space regarding employment location. Individuals and families settled either in state-sponsored public housing or self-help homes. San Juan, the capital of Puerto Rico, became a growing and buzzing metropolis characterized by hotels near the coast, modern buildings, and "slums"—that is, self-help construction which was viewed as substandard, not up to zoning codes, and informal. The modern era conceives of formal housing as the standard to follow and informal housing as something to eradicate. In a way, both of these forms were merely part of the urbanization process. Still, in the eyes of most, migration to urban areas was equated to slum living and arduous living, a rough life. Thus, many rejected the adoption of urban culture by romanticizing rural life, a *parcela* (piece of land) and a *casita* (house) in the mountains. Similarly, subjects like *el jí*baro (the peasant) was to be idealized. Ironically, the symbol of *el jí*baro, la pava (straw hat) became the icon of the Popular Democratic Party and Luis Muñoz Marín's Operation Commonwealth.

Even though Operation Commonwealth was creating modernization, at the same time, Luis Muñoz Marín's Operation Serenity through radio and commercial music were popularizing the bomba and the plena, music forms that were "conservative" in nature, perhaps, anti-modern. Dr. Esterrich dedicates his book to understand Operation Serenity, which is often ignored by academics. Governor Muñoz Marín envisioned Operation Serenity as a way to bring peace and tranquility after the economic and political changes brought up by Operation Bootstrap and Operation Commonwealth, respectively. Operation Serenity was to be operationalized by the Institute of Puerto Rican Culture, the Division of Community Education, and the Puerto Rico Communications Authority.

The primary goal of the Division of Community Education was to educate adults through the modern film; then, mostly used by American soldiers in the island to document peculiarities of the territory. Puerto Ricans started to film brought by the Americans to tell Puerto Rican stories about baseball, romance, comedy, and horror. The Division also produced movies to educate the public about hygiene, voting, among other topics that were important for development. Similarly, the Puerto Rico Communications Authority spread government messages of modernization through public radio and television channels.

In *Concrete and Countryside,* Carmelo Esterrich notes that through programming and popular music the Institute of Puerto Rican Culture was trying to create a single national identity. This identity needed to be along the lines of "we are all Puerto Ricans, we are not divided by race." In this vein, the Institute emphasized that Puerto Ricans had three identities—Spanish, African, and Indigenous. Before the only identity promoted was to be very proud of being Spanish descent. Academics and writers embraced this idea of Puerto Ricans composed equally of three races as a way to reject modernity and what was perceived as an American project. In this view, being of Spanish descent was to be "modern" while to be African, and Indigenous was the opposite, to be "communal" or "traditional." Embracing the African and Indigenous roots became then a way of rejecting Americanization. It also became a way to reject Operation Commonwealth.

At the time many academics and writers criticized the development narratives of a modern Puerto Rico, they disapproved Operation Commonwealth and Operation Bootstrap. At the same time, they got on board with projects of Operation Serenity and idealized, instead, rurality and "community" as opposed to "society," to use Ferdinand Tönnies conceptualization. There were a lot of contradictions in Operation Serenity and in the thought processes of the people who were leading it. For example, Esterrich analyzes the music of "Cortijo y su Combo," who popularized bomba and plena by playing it live on television shows. Although Cortijo grew up in San Juan, his lyrics would romanticize *el jí*baro by singing, "yo no soy de la ciudad, soy del campo" (I am not from the city, I am from the countryside).

One of the most interesting analytical frameworks of Carmelo Esterrich is that he puts the literary text of René Marqués alongside those of José Luis González. On the one hand, René Marqués is a central figure against Operation Commonwealth, but paradoxically, he worked at the Division of Community Education which led the modern cultural project of the Free-Associated State, which he so vehemently rejected. On the other hand, José Luis González saw the materialistic prospects of the industrial revolution. René Marqués rejected the urban while José Luis González was more inclined to acknowledge the possibilities of urban life. Marqués seminal play *La carreta* (the Oxcart) (1953) was about a countryside family that moved to La Perla, an infamous slum in Old San Juan (Act I). When they realized that they did not find the better life that were hoping for—the male main character ends up incarcerated and the female figure, pregnant after a sexual assault (Act II). In Act III both characters move to El Bronx in New York to solve their incremental difficulties. Ironically, once in the big city, the male character dies at the hands of a machine in the factory, and the female character becomes a prostitute. Overall, the play shows that Marqués loved the countryside and was critical of industrialization and urbanization. Like many others in Puerto Rico, he treated the old way of life and its traditions nostalgically. According to him, modernity was changing us and stripping us from our traditions.

González was a Marxist, and like most Marxist, he seems to believe that capitalism "rescued a considerable part of the population from the ***idiocy*** of rural life" (emphasis mine, Marx and Engels, 1848). Like other Marxist thinkers, José Luis González was critical of class inequalities. In one of his best known, short stories "En el fondo del caño hay un negrito" (At the bottom of the creek there is a black boy) (1950) González exposes the precarious conditions where informal settlers lived in. In this story, a black toddler ends up jumping into a creek, where his parents had built an informal and substandard house on top of a septic water canal between mangroves and garbage. Like one of the main characters of *La carreta*, the toddler González story also loses his life. The lesson here is that regardless if rurality was better or worse, urbanization and modernization had terrible consequences. Marqués and González were on agreement on this regard.

Humanities and Cultural Studies Professor Esterrich analyzes these and many others cultural productions created during midcentury Puerto Rico to see how people understood the changes that they were facing—like Marqués most perceived it negatively, while some like González recognized its positive implications. A general belief characterized the modern era that as a society we would be able to solve all problems through science and industry. When this conviction was not materialized, people started to get a sense of general malaise. This is what philosopher Jean-François Lyotard labeled as post-modernism—a realization that science and industry do not represent the end of history. Carmelo Esterrich exposes the post-modern thought during a modern era. In a way, Esterrich analysis is a post-modern one. That being said, this book will be of interest to those who enjoy reading about modernism, post-modernism, capitalism, industrialization, urbanization, migration, and cultural production as well as how it manifested itself in midcentury modern Puerto Rico.

The Constitutional Evolution of Puerto Rico and Other US Territories, 1898-Present

By Gustavo Gelpí

Inter American University of Puerto Rico, 2017
ISBN: 978-0-986-44875-1
241 pages; n.p.

Reviewer: Luis Galanes Valldejuli, Universidad de Puerto Rico, Cayey

With the publication of *The Constitutional Evolution of Puerto Rico and Other US Territories, 1898-Present*, Gustavo Gelpí contributes yet another text to the already numerous list of texts written about the Insular Cases and the governance of the US territories. These include, to cite just a few among the most renowned and the most recent: Carman F. Randolph's *The Insular Cases* (1901); George F. Edmunds's *The Insular Cases* (1901); José A Cabranes's *Citizenship and Empire: Legislative History of American Citizenship for Puerto Ricans* (1979); Juan R. Torruella's *The Supreme Court and Puerto Rico: The Doctrine of Separate and Unequal* (1985); José Trías Monge's *Puerto Rico: The Trials of the Oldest Colony in the World* (1997); the collection of essays included in *Foreign in a Domestic Sense: Puerto Rico, American Expansion, and the Constitution* (2001), edited by Christina Duffy Burnett and Burke Marshall; Thomas Alexander Aleinikoff's *Semblances of Sovereignty: The Constitution, the State and American Citizenship* (2002); Bartholomew H. Sparrow's *The Insular Cases and the Emergence of American Empire* (2006); Lanny Thompson's *Imperial Archipelago: Representation and Rule in the Insular Territories under U.S. Dominion after 1898* (2010); Krishanti Vignarajah's "The Political Roots of Judicial Legitimacy: Explaining the Enduring Validity of the Insular Cases" (2010); the collection of essays delivered at Harvard's 2014 Conference on The Insular Cases, and collected in *Reconsidering the Insular Cases: The Past and Future of the American Empire* (2015), edited by Gerald L. Neuman and Tomiko Brown-Nagin; or the more recent collection of essays published by *Centro Journal* in their Special Issue (2017, Vol. 29, No. 1), entitled *Citizenship in Puerto Rico: One Hundred Years after the Jones Act.*

But, for those thinking that, with this massive amount of writing and publishing, everything that needed to be said on the issue has already been said, Gelpí's book holds a big surprise. With a keen eye that can only come from a US District Judge of the United States District Court of Puerto Rico with thorough knowledge of constitutional law, and who has been reflecting and writing on issues of the territorial status since his college years, Gelpí provides a particular interpretation of the history and evolution of the island's relation with the US which is fresh and novel, and which makes him unique among his peers. It is also an interpretation that places him at odds with other more commonly held narratives of exactly the same events, and particularly with the condemnatory view shared by "statehooters" and *independentistas* alike. Thus, while these latter see in the events of history a pattern of unconstitutional treatment of a colonial type, and of general exclusion, Gelpí will see in the development of those same events a movement in the opposite direction, that is, indicating a desire of eventual full incorporation. The process, Gelpí will sentence, has reached a level where Puerto Rico has already become a "de facto state."

The book is arranged as a collection of different essays and court opinions written by Gelpí over the past years, all in English, and all concerning the issue of the constitutionality (or lack of it) of the territorial status. Adopting a comparative approach, the essays discuss the territorial treatment of Puerto Rico in relation to other territories held by the US over the past century, including the Philippines, American Samoa, the Panama Canal Zone, and the US Virgin Islands. The book also compares the judicial treatment given to territories against that given to American Indian reservations. Included in the text are also substantive commentaries by key political figures of the island, including texts from former governors Rafael Hernández Colón and Pedro Roselló. It is also a very readable book, intelligible to the general public, but without abandoning the technicalities of the legal language nor the standards of formal academic writing.

The argument in favor of the de facto state develops more or less as follows: In the Foraker Act of 1900 and the Jones Act of 1917, Congress not only granted US citizenship to Puerto Rican residents, but also established a local government "paralleling that of a state, with three branches of government... [and] a federal district court" (119). With the establishment of the Commonwealth of Puerto Rico in 1952, Congress once again "took the position that the Island's measure of self-government under a republican form of government and own constitution conferred upon the US territory separate, state-like sovereignty from that of the federal government, just as that of the States" (213). More significantly yet, in 1966 Congress moved (through Public Law 89-571 80 Stat. 746) to transform the Article IV federal district court in Puerto Rico to an Article III court; a move which, as Gelpí points out, "was implemented not as a request of the Commonwealth government, but rather at the repeated request of the Judicial Conference of the United States" (124-125). The appointed Puerto Rican federal judges are on a par with the several other Puerto Ricans that, commencing in 1961, have been appointed by the President, following the advice and consent of Congress, to act as ambassadors of the US in foreign countries. "Such trust," Gelpí argues, "as is the case with Article III judges, can only be placed in the hands of persons whom the President and Congress clearly understand are an integral part of the American Nation" (127). Moreover, when Congress established an Article III federal court in Puerto Rico, it did not extend such benefit to the then other US territories, the Virgin Islands, Guam, and the Panama Canal Zone.

For a person coming from outside the legal profession, this latter action of Congress may seem inconsequential. But, as Gelpí warns us, one should not underestimate its relevance, nor the power that the written word carries with it in this big "Lettered City" that is the US federal government, to use Angel Rama's characterization allegorically. But, in establishing an Article III court in Puerto Rico, Gelpí adds, Congress's "actions speak louder than words," and what they convey is an implicit intention of full incorporation projected into the future.

> The several aforementioned Congressional acts evidence that Congress for over a century has not intended to govern, and in fact has not governed, Puerto Rico "temporarily." To the contrary, the ties between the United States and Puerto Rico have significantly strengthened to the effect that Puerto Rico's system of government and laws resembles that of a federated State of the Union... From a juridical perspective, the Puerto Rico of present is, thus, one which Congress... has chiseled in the very image and likeness of the United States system of government and laws... into a de facto state. (125–26, 131, 139)

This does not mean, however, that Gelpí is blind to those other instances where Congress has also moved, in contradictory manner, to give discriminatory treatment to the territory vis-à-vis the States. In *Lastra v. New York & Porto Rico S.S. Co.* (1924), for example, the Court of Appeals for the First Circuit concluded "that the admiralty jurisdiction of the United States did not extend to Puerto Rico *ex proprio vigore*" (60-61). Moreover, in *Califano v. Torres* (1978) and in *Harris v. Rosario* (1980), the US Supreme Court sided with Congress in its decision to restrict the health benefits that are granted to Puerto Rico through the Medicaid program. More evidently yet, in *Puerto Rico v. Sánchez-Valle* (2016), the Supreme Court argued, regarding the application of the double jeopardy clause to Puerto Rico, that the United States and Puerto Rico do not enjoy separate sovereignty (as is the case with states), but rather that the sovereignty of the latter derived from the sovereignty of the former. "This position," Gelpí will argue, "—its effects being that Puerto Rico remains a colony, subject to the plenary powers of Congress—was wholly contrary to that historically argued by the United States in federal courts, as well as in the United Nations" (215). Moreover, the fact that this opinion was issued in the context of a possible restructuring of a $74 billion debt, and after Puerto Rico had already defaulted on payments to its bondholders, as Gelpí insightfully adds, served to set the stage for the even more intrusive measures implemented under PROMESA law, taken only six days after *Puerto Rico v. Sánchez-Valle*. In approving PROMESA, Congress went as far an establishing an oversight board for Puerto Rico, made up of members appointed by the President, and with "super veto" powers over the use of local governmental funds. Thus, Gelpí asserts: "PROMESA is just but another example of a congressional experiment in territorial governance" (219).

While Gelpí does not turn a blind eye on these cases, he will see them mainly as "anomalies in a sea of federal uniformity," as well as opposite "to that historically argued by the United States in federal courts, as well as in the United Nations" (215).

An alternative interpretation

When all these different Congressional mandates and court opinions are taken collectively, an alternative interpretation of them is also possible: one that moves Puerto Rico neither closer to a de facto state nor farther away from it, but rather in a direction which is perhaps best described as ambivalent and erratic, with no clear destiny in view. One only needs to stop and dwell momentarily on the very linguistic formulas employed by Supreme Court judges and congressmen in their bewildering attempts at reaching a definition of this so-called "territorial" status during the early stages of the relationship, in order to grasp the dimensions, as well as the original source, of this ambivalent and confusing way of proceeding. The confusion, for example, was well established by Representative Amos Cummings of New York who, during the debate leading to the signature of the Foraker Act in 1900, declared:

> Now, Mr. Chairman, Puerto Rico is either in the United States or out of it. If the island is out of the United States, we have no business legislating for her here in any way whatsoever, and if she is in the United States, she is in the same condition as Arizona, New Mexico, Oklahoma and the other Territories [incorporated through the Northwest Ordinance Act of 1787]. (Archives of the US House of Representatives)

The confusion would remerge once again in the 1901 landmark Insular Case *Downes v. Bidwell* (182 U.S. 244). On this occasion, the Supreme Court judges found it difficult to agree on a definition of the island status, as can be evidenced by a five to four split vote, and five separate written opinions, three in favor and two dissenting. The court's majority decision established that "the island of Puerto Rico is a territory appurtenant and belonging to the United States, but not a part of the United States" and that, as Justice Edward D. White (in his concurring opinion) put it, Puerto Rico was "foreign to the United States in a domestic sense." Thus, in an attempt to erase the ambiguity surrounding the definition of Puerto Rican status, the Supreme Court judges in *Downes v. Bidwell* ended up creating what Gervasio Luis García has called a "fabricated jurisdictial fiction" (2000: 44), that is, a definition of the territorial status that is surrounded by ambivalence and confussion, defying all attempts at interpretation. The ambivalence and vagueness of such definition was condemned by dissenting Justice John Marshall Harlan in the following terms:

> This idea of "incorporation" [of Puerto Rico] has some occult meaning which my mind does not apprehend. It is enveloped in some mystery which I am unable to unravel (Archives of the US House of Representatives).

The Jones Act of 1917 did little in terms of helping Puerto Ricans exit the political limbo in which they were inmersed. In fact, it could be argued that the Jones Act only helped increase the level of confusion, as the form of citizenship that it granted to Puerto Ricans was as ambivalent and confusing as was the status granted through the Foraker Act, and ratified by the Supreme Court in *Downes v. Bidwell* (182 U.S. 244). In 1924, seven years after the Jones Act, a *Washington Post* reporter was still able to complain that "what the ultimate status of Porto Rico will be is a matter still lying in the capacious laps of the gods" (Territories 1924: 6).

A similar confusion, Boyer points out, will characterize the status granted to Virgin Islanders through the Organic Act of 1927. Even when the Treaty of the Danish West Indies of 1916 explicitly stated that "citizenship in the United States" would be granted to the inhabitants of the newly purchased islands, the State Department would not take long in making a distinction between citizenship "in" and citizenship "of" the United States, the first one implying American "nationality" but not full "citizenship." Thus, as Boyer puts it, it was "for the want of a two-letter word" ("of" instead of "in") that the State Department denied Virgin Islanders full constitutional protection (2010: 140-41). Indeed, a *New York Times* editorial of June 14, 1925 (eight years later) underlined that "the best experts consulted [were] not prepared to say whether the islands are a possession of or a part of the United States" (Archives of the US House of Representatives). The confusion continues on to this date.

If there are moments in the life of language when it serves a function different from that for which it was intended, that is, for the transmission of meaningful contents, when language is employed to say what cannot be said, when it assumes the form of what Mikhail Bakhtin has called "heteroglossia," this is certainly an exemplary one. As Boyer has put it, it must have required a "strained semantics and a tortuous exegesis of the English language" (2010: 141) in order to arrive at these linguistic formulas. And it is in these linguistic formulas that we can find the foundational ambivalence of the whole confusion, from where all the posterior ambivalences feed on and attempt to emulate.[1]

But the argument that Gelpí is attempting to put forward is more complex than simply favoring one interpretation over another. For what he really intends to argue is that, regardless of which of the alternative interpretations one wishes to adopt, if we concentrate momentarily and exclusively on those actions of Congress that have moved us closer to a de facto state, one must conclude that Congress has already crossed a point-of-no-return on the road toward statehood. In establishing an Article III federal court in Puerto Rico, Congress crossed that point-of-no-return. From then on, for Gelpí, the problem is one of time, and of time alone. It's a matter of "when, not if." And it is precisely this claim that makes Gelpí's arguments both novel and polemical.

In claiming this, we must add, Gelpí's line of argumentation is not unrelated to the increasingly generalized view of the present moment as a "critical point" in the political history of the island. In fact, it was a view held by many of the participants in the 2014 Harvard Conference on The Insular Cases. Gorrín Peralta, for example, will define the present situation as "a crisis situation or point in time when a critical decision must be made" (2015). Several contemporary events serve to give credit to this opinion. First, two recent status referendums (2012 and 2017) revealed, if not a clear desire of Puerto Ricans for statehood (given the low voting participation), at least a dissatisfaction with the current status. Second, the possible restructuration of Puerto Rico's debt, which, while fueling the perception that Puerto Ricans are unable to govern themselves, also serves to push the status debate to the forefront. But above all, the passing of the 100 years milestone. All these events, it is argued, conflate to provoke that "point in time when a critical decision must be made."

And yet, what makes Gelpí's arguments novel is not so much his adherence to this "critical point" theory, but rather his conviction that, from a judiciary perspective, a point-of-no-return has already been crossed by Congress. At this stage, any measure taken to find a final resolution to the conflict that does not contemplate granting Puerto Ricans the option of full incorporation is no longer an option for the US.

The "temporality" debate

Perhaps the only way one could justifiably legitimate the limited matter in which fundamental constitutional rights are granted to the inhabitants of the territories, and to the inhabitants of Puerto Rico in particular, is by arguing that it is a "temporary" arrangement. In fact, many of the states who joined the Union through the Northwest Ordinance Act of 1887 were also subjected to similar temporal arrangements before becoming states. Yet, while there does not exist an explicit time limit for this "temporary" arrangement, the 1901 Supreme Court did warn Congress about the limits of its powers over time, while also placing (perhaps inadvertently) the time span of "a century" as a figurative time limit. In *De Lima v. Bidwell* (1901), the Supreme Court sustained that the idea that a territory is simultaneously a foreign country, and ought to be treated as such by law,...

> **...[and] presupposes that territory [a foreign country] may be held indefinitely by the United States... That this state of things may continue for years, for a century even, but that until Congress enacts otherwise, it still remains a foreign country. To hold that this can be done as matter of law we deem to be pure judicial legislation. We find no warrant for it in the Constitution or in the powers conferred upon this court (205—emphasis added).**

Moreover, after the Insular Cases, two other cases (also discussed by Gelpí) have drastically changed the legal landscape in which the dispute over the territories should be redeemed. The first one is *Brown v. Board of Education* (1954), which put an end to the "separate but equal" doctrine first applied to Afro-Americans, and then emulated for the territories in the Insular Cases. More significant yet is *Boumediene v. Bush* (2008), regarding the extension of constitutional rights to detained enemy combatants aliens held in Guantanamo Bay, Cuba. In this case, the US Supreme Court not only recognized that fundamental Constitutional rights do apply to these enemy combatants detained in the territory, but (once again) warned both the President and Congress about the limits of their powers over time:

The Constitution grants Congress and the President the power to acquire, dispose of and govern territory, not the power to decide when and where its terms apply... Abstaining from questions involving forward sovereignty and territorial governance is one thing. To hold the political branches have the power to switch the Constitution on and off is quite another. (118)

The question, thus, is not whether Congress is actually "switching on and of the Constitution" at will, as it evidently is in the case of Puerto Rico. The question is for how long can this "fallacy" be sustained. "How long may Congress 'temporarily' hold a territory when the territory has evolved into a model of a federal state without having been formally admitted into the union?" (97). Congress has imposed a territorial status on Puerto Rico for approximately 120 years now. While there is no formally established timeline for Congress, Gelpí reasons, and even when technically they could continue holding the territorial status indefinitely, the fact is that it will to be very hard for them to continue doing so for an unreasonable amount of time. And perhaps a century is a good estimate of what constitutes an inordinately lengthy amount of time. A century was, in fact, and as stated earlier, the time span inadvertently suggested by the 1901 Supreme Court in *Lima v. Bidwell*—"for a century even." Apart from the unique case of the Panama Canal Zone, also discussed by Gelpí extensively, never in its history has the US relinquished sovereignty over a territory it has held for a whole century. After a century of territorial status for Puerto Rico has well passed, the time is more than past due for the US to amend its position. And the final resolution of the conflict, Gelpí anticipates, will need to come from the judiciary branch. Thus, from a judiciary perspective, the question translates to this: How long will the judiciary branch "continue permitting Congress *per secula seculorum* to switch on and off the Constitution"? (135). At some point, sooner or later (perhaps sooner than later, considering that 120 years have already elapsed), the United States will have to come to reason and abide by its own Constitution.

Ingenious arrangements alternative to statehood

Another issue that is relevant to the debate has to do with the idea of a "discriminatory" treatment. From a judiciary perspective, it is evident that Congress discriminates against Puerto Rico, in the sense that it grants differential treatment to the territory vis-à-vis the other states. But not all of these discriminatory acts are prejudicial to Puerto Ricans, and some are highly cherished by them. Thus, it is precisely because Puerto Rico is a territory, and not a state, that it could grant federal tax exemption to manufacturing corporations establishing operations on the island for the period 1976-2006, through the 936 Internal Revenue Code. It is precisely because Puerto Rico is a territory that its inhabitants are generally exempt from payment of federal taxes. It is precisely because Puerto Rico is a territory that it is able to sell municipal bond with "triple exempt status" (which is part of the reason why it was able to amass a $74 billion debt it cannot now pay). For many, it seems evident that, even under statehood, some form of discriminatory or differentiated treatment would still need to be kept in place, even if only for logistical or economic reasons. In fact, most Puerto Rican economists share the idea that the economic well-being of the island is dependent on such form of discriminatory treatment. Perhaps this is also one of the reasons why US Congressmen and Supreme Court Judges have proven adamant to take the necessary step towards full incorporation of Puerto Rico, having fallen for the idea that the continued need of some form of differentiated (preferential) treatment serves as an indication of Puerto Ricans unpreparedness for self-government, and consequently for statehood—as if an ideal moment for that could ever be established.

Because Gelpí's book approaches the issue of Puerto Rican status exclusively from a judiciary perspective, these other pragmatic considerations of full incorporation are mostly left aside. And there is nothing wrong with that, considering the author's background and area of expertise, as well as the explicit objectives of the book. Nonetheless, it is not without relevance that, when discussing the judiciary relevance of the presidential vote, Gelpí will mention, perhaps unwittingly, that it is paramount that Puerto Ricans "participate in the national lawmaking process, by way of formal statehood *or any other ingenious arrangement*" (190; emphasis added).

To be sure, an "ingenious arrangement" of some sort is what Puerto Rico might need. The idea is not new to the Puerto Rican pro-statehood sector. It was first put forward by former pro-statehood governor Luis A. Ferré back in 1968, in the form of what he called a "*Jíbaro* Statehood" (*Estadidad Jíbara*). But there is a question—and a question that also begs for a judicial interpretation—regarding whether US federalism has space, or ought to have space, for such types of arrangements. The general agreement is that it does not, and ought not. As one US Congressman eloquently put it: "Puerto Ricans have to understand that there is only one flavor of statehood, plain vanilla." But the debate continues on, and in fact forms the backbone of the critique put forward by "communitarians" and multiculturalists against the liberal idea of "individual rights," as opposed to "group rights." While a discussion of their work is beyond the scope of this review, it will suffice to say here that the right to be different, and to be treated as different, could also come to be considered a fundamental right. As Ana Lydia Vega has reminded us, on this issue "equality [*igualdad*] and equalization [*igualamiento*] are not synonymous. Equality demands reciprocal respect. Equalization implies mimetic conformism" (2018).[2] Thus, if Gelpí's work helps to remind us of the possible imminence of statehood status, then the next question of a judicial nature that Puerto Ricans will need to answer will be related to the possibility of incorporating ingenious arrangements under the particularities of US federalism—that is, the possibility of a state different from the "plain vanilla" type.

This question, in fact, has already been posed by Thomas Alexander Aleinikoff, who has highlighted the need for a new constitutional law suitable "for the twenty-first century"--that is, one that holds "understandings of sovereignty and membership that are supple and flexible, open to new arrangements that complement the evolving nature of the modern state." while at the same time reminding us that "our [current] constitutional law, at least as declared by the Supreme Court, is moving in the opposite direction, adopting wooden conceptions of sovereignty and membership as citizenship and statehood are brought into close —almost congruent—association" (2002: 5).

Concluding Remarks

In Gelpí's book there subsides the idea of a teleology at work in the history of the relation between Puerto Rico and the US which gradually but progressively, little by little, has helped Puerto Rico move closer to the image of a state, and whose final end-point would be statehood status or, more specifically, the option of statehood status. Moreover, such teleology also reveals that, *from a constitutional standpoint*, a point-of-no-return has already been crossed by Congress.

Despite the novelty of these propositions, Gelpí's text suffers one major shortcoming, and one that potentially threatens to destroy his whole argumentative edifice: namely, its critical lack of engagement with the vast literature that exists on the issue. In this sense, Gelpí's text is not, properly speaking, an academic book, and it is perhaps best conceived as an individual's reflections on US constitutional law, thinking mostly in solitary. Unfortunately, suck lack of engagement leaves a door open to criticism that serious scholarship would undermine his ideological arguments; even more so when one considers that such vast literature almost unanimously follow argumentative lines moving in the opposite direction (therein resides part of the novelty of Gelpí's book, in the sense that it is saying something different to what the majority of scholars are saying). Thus, where a majority of scholars see a consistent pattern of discriminatory constitutional treatment throughout history, and adopt a condemnatory tone accordingly, Gelpí sees a sequence of events, some discriminatory and some not, but that, when taken together, also reveals a pattern of gradual concessions in self-government and integration leading to a de facto state.

But, beyond whatever disagreements one may have regarding the proper interpretation of past history—i.e., a history of colonial discrimination, or of gradual concessions, or rather of ambivalent and erratic treatment, as we have suggested—there is also in Gelpí's book a line of questioning that points not toward the past but toward the future, and that, in our view, also contributes to its novelty. At this point in the argument, the question is no longer whether there is a past history of unequal treatment (which evidently there is), but rather whether it is possible, *from a constitutional perspective*, to derpive Puerto Ricans the option of statehood status in the future, once the presumption of a red line has been established and crossed. At this point in time, having traveled the road already traveled—Gelpí seems to be saying—it would be constitutionally inconceivable that a final resolution of the status conflict of Puerto Rico could be possible without the US granting the option of full incorporation.

We remain skeptical of Gelpí's propositions, and do not underestimate the capacity of the US Congress and the US Supreme Court to continue adopting an ambivalent posture toward Puerto Rico, nor to continue devising linguistic formulas to say what cannot be said, *per omnia saecula saeculorum*. Be as it may, the general ideas put forward by Gelpí in his *The Constitutional Evolution of Puerto Rico and Other US Territories, 1898-Present* are certainly novel, and at points also daring, and therefore merit consideration—even if one is eventually doomed to reject them. And, because of the novel and polemical nature of its propositions, one can only anticipate the oncoming debate that the book will surely generate.

NOTES

[1] Elsewhere we have documented, through an analysis of voting patterns in status plebiscites, and of the discourses produced around these events, how the use of ambivalent and heteroglossic language is not an exclusive property of the metropolitan power brokers, as it is also reproduced by the same colonized subjects who are condemned to live inside the Puerto Rican limbo. In these events, we have argued, Puerto Ricans assume the role of what we Richard Rosa and Doris Sommer have called "undecided heroes" (Galanes Valldejuli and Capetillo 2016; on the language issue, see also Galanes Valldejuli 2017). But what we wish to highlight here, in connection with Gelpí's book, is that whatever ambivalences Puerto Ricans exhibit can always be traced back to the foundational ambivalence established by the Supreme Court in the early 1900s.

[2] Original text in Spanish reads as follows: "...igualdad e igualamiento no son sinónimos. La igualdad exige respeto recíproco. El igualamiento implica conformismo mimético" (Vega 2018).

REFERENCES

Aleinikoff, Thomas Alexander. 2002. *Semblances of Sovereignty: The Constitution, the State and American Citizenship*. Cambridge, MA: Harvard University Press.

Archives of the US House of Representatives. <http://history.house.gov/Exhibitions-and-Publications/HAIC/Historical-Essays/Foreign-Domestic/Puerto-Rico/>.

Boyer, William W. 2010 [1983]. *America's Virgin Islands: A History of Rights and Wrongs*. Durham: Carolina Academic Press.

Galanes Valldejuli, Luis. 2017. *Tourism and Language in Vieques: An Ethnography of the Post-Navy Period*. Lanham, MD: Lexington Books.

Galanes Valldejuli, Luis and Jorge Capetillo. 2016. Le « héros indécis » : Porto Rico et les îles Vierges américaines. [The Undecided Hero : Puerto Rico and the American Virgin Islands]. *Cahiers des Amériques latines* 81, 179–98.

Garcia, Gervasio Luis. 2000. I Am The Other: Puerto Rico in the Eyes of North Americans, 1898. *Journal of American History* 87(1), 39–64.

Territories and Statehood. 1924. *Washington Post* 23 June.

Vega, Ana Lydia. 2018. Se busca un mito. *El Nuevo Día* 4 February.

CARIBBEAN STUDIES

Revista bianual del Instituto de Estudios del Caribe
Universidad de Puerto Rico

ÍNDICE • CONTENTS • SOMAIRE

Vol. 45, Nos. 1-2 (January-December 2017)

Special Issue: Language Contact, Creoles, and Multilingualism: Stigma, Creativity, and Resilience

Introducción • Introduction • Introduction

Artículos • Articles • Articles

Ensayo bibliográfico • Review essay • Compte rendu

Reseñas de libros • Book reviews • Comptes rendus

Centro Publications

2019 CATALOGUE

NEW

Liberalism and Identity Politics: Puerto Rican Community Organizations and Collective Action in New York City

José E. Cruz
ISBN 9781945662089 | LCCN 2017006438
$24.99; $9.99 Kindle

This book is a recollection and analysis of the role of ethnic identity in Puerto Rican community institutional development and collective action in New York City between 1960-1990. The book demonstrates that through institutional development and collective action, Puerto Ricans articulated and promoted a liberal form of identity politics in which ethnic identity and the idea of group rights provided a platform for the production of both individual and collective goods.

NEW

Not the Time to Stay: The Unpublished Plays of Víctor Fragoso

Víctor Fragoso; Edited, Translated and with an Introduction by Consuelo Martínez-Reyes
ISBN 9781945662249 | LCCN 2018034538
Pbk. 2018; 244 pages
$24.99; $9.99 Kindle

Not the Time to Stay brings to light for the first time the marvellous work of Puerto Rican playwright Víctor Fragoso. Eight plays, edited and translated by Consuelo Martínez-Reyes, portray the socio-cultural issues Fragoso sought to expose: the choice and difficulties of migration, the clash between American and Puerto Rican societies, the oppression suffered by Latinos in the USA, homelessness, and domestic violence, among others. Fragoso played a key role in the New York City theatre scene in the 1970s, and in the overall interrogation of Puerto Rican and Latino identities in the USA.

FORTHCOMING FALL 2019

Patria: Puerto Rican Revolutionary Exiles in Late Nineteenth Century New York

Edgardo Meléndez
$24.99

Patria examines the activities and ideals of Puerto Rican revolutionaries exiles in New York City at the end of the nineteenth century. The study is centered in the writings, news reports, and announcements by and about Puerto Ricans in the newspaper *Patria*, of the Cuban Revolutionary Party. The book looks at the political, organizational and ideological ties between Cuban and Puerto Rican revolutionaries in exile, as well as the events surrounding the war of 1898. The analysis also offers a glimpse into the daily life and community of Puerto Rican exiles in late nineteenth century New York City.

Centro Publications

2019 CATALOGUE

FORTHCOMING FALL 2019
Fighting on Two Fronts: Puerto Rican Soldiers in the Korean War

Harry Franqui-Rivera
$24.99

Tens of thousands of Puerto Rican soldiers took part in the Korean War as combat troops. Many of these soldiers fought as part of the 65th U.S. Army Infantry Regiment, "el sesenta y cinco." Its men were known as the Borinqueneers. During the war, the 65th became a national icon on the island and among the growing Puerto Rican communities in the mainland. The island-based press and political figures made reference to the 65th as a catalyst for forging a modern person and a modern Puerto Rico, while the community in New York highlighted the Puerto Rican soldiers' heroic efforts and sacrifices to counter racial discrimination. The Borinqueneers helped established a bridge between New York and the island. These Puerto Rican soldiers' service required them to fight on two fronts. They fought relentlessly North Korean and Chinese soldiers in fierce combat. They also fought brutal racial discrimination within the U.S. Armed Forces. Their story is a neglected chapter in the history of the Puerto Ricans.

Race, Front and Center: Perspectives on Race Among Puerto Ricans

Edited by Carlos Vargas-Ramos
ISBN 9781945662003
LCCN 2016030601. Pbk. 2017; 403 pages **$24.99**

Race, Front and Center is a collection of essays that captures in a single volume the breadth of research on the subject of race among Puerto Ricans, both in Puerto Rico, in the United States and in the migration between the two countries. Its twenty-two chapters divided into seven sections address the intellectual, aesthetic and historical trajectories that have served to inform the creation of a national identity among Puerto Ricans and how race as a social identity fits into the process of national identity-building.

Before the Wave: Puerto Ricans in Philadelphia, 1910–1945

Víctor Vázquez-Hernández
ISBN 9781945662027
LCCN 2016047262. Pbk. 2017; 129 pages **$19.99**

This book recounts the genesis of the Puerto Rican community in Philadelphia during the interwar years (1917–1945). It connects the origins of this community to the mass migration of the post-WW II years when Puerto Ricans consolidated their presence in Philadelphia (1945–1985). This study compares the experiences of Puerto Ricans with that of the Italians, the Polish, and African Americans in Philadelphia during the early twentieth century.

Centro Publications

2019 CATALOGUE

Rhythm & Power: Performing Salsa in Puerto Rican and Latino Communities

Edited by Derrick León Washington, Priscilla Renta and Sydney Hutchinson
ISBN 9781945662164
LCCN 2017038687. Pbk. 2017; 88 pages **$12.00**

The story of New York salsa is one of cultural fusion, artistry, and skilled marketing. A multi-disciplinary collective of scholars illuminate how immigrant and migrant communities in New York City—most notably from Puerto Rico—nurtured and developed salsa, growing it from a local movement playing out in the city's streets and clubs into a global phenomenon.

State of Puerto Ricans 2017

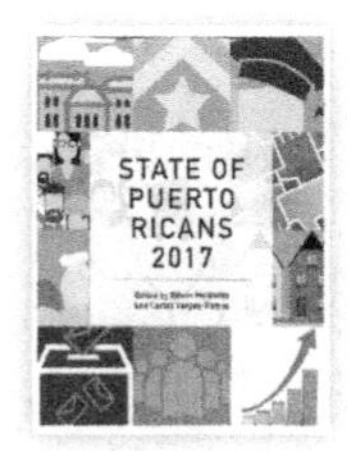

Edited by Edwin Meléndez
and Carlos Vargas-Ramos
ISBN 9781945662126
LCCN 2017021705. Pbk. 2017; 138 pages **$20.00**

This book provides an updated overview of some of the most salient subjects and themes about the Puerto Rican population in the United States at present. It highlights the continued mobility and expansion of the Puerto Rican population throughout the country, including state-to-state migration, migration from Puerto Rico in light of the economic crisis in the island, as well as the role of service in the armed forces in anchoring new areas of settlement.

Almanac of Puerto Ricans in the United States

Editors Jennifer Hinojosa and
Carlos Vargas-Ramos
ISBN 978-1945662072
LCCN 2017002040. Pbk. 2016; 167 pages. **$20**

Learn more about the recent changes in the Puerto Rican community on the mainland United States through national and state-specific demographic data. The almanac compiles information on social, economic, and civic conditions of the Puerto Rican population in nine key states, and includes maps, tables, and descriptions of the population nationwide.

The Bodega: A conerstone of Puerto Rican Barrios (The Justo Martí Collection)

Carlos Sanabria
ISBN 978-1945662065. Pbk. 2016; 43 pages. **$15**

This photo book is a compilation of photographs of bodegas in 1960s New York City shot by Cuban photographer Justo Martí. The photos are part of Centro's Justo Martí collection, which documents the life and activities of the individuals, families and organizations that made up the Puerto Rican experience in New York.

Centro Publications

2019 CATALOGUE

Gilberto Gerena Valentín: My Life as a Community Activist, Labor Organizer, and Progressive Politician in NYC

Edited by Carlos Rodríguez Fraticelli; Translated by Andrew Hurley; With an Introduction by José E. Cruz
ISBN 9781878483744; 2013; 315 pages. **$20**

Gilberto Gerena Valentín is a key figure in the development of the Puerto Rican community in the United States, especially from the forties through the seventies. He was a union organizer, community leader, political activist and general in the war for the civil-rights recognition of his community. In his memoirs, Gilberto Gerena Valentín takes us into the center of the fierce labor, political, civil-rights, social and cultural struggles waged by Puerto Ricans in New York from the 1940s through the 1970s.

Puerto Ricans at the Dawn of the New Millennium

Edited by Edwin Meléndez
and Carlos Vargas-Ramos
ISBN 978187848379-9. Pbk. 2014; 319 pages. **$24.99**

This edited volume features chapters by Centro researchers and outside scholars presenting new research on social, economic, political and health conditions of the Puerto Rican population in the United States and highlighting the improvements and the challenges in this rapidly changing and growing community.

Soy Gilberto Gerena Valentín: memorias de un puertorriqueño en Nueva York

Gilberto Gerena Valentín; Edición de Carlos Rodríguez Fraticelli
ISBN: 9781878483645—ISBN: 9781878483454 (ebook); 2013; 302 pages.
$20 (print); $6 (ebook)

Gilberto Gerena Valentín es uno de los personajes claves en el desarrollo de la comunidad puertorriqueña en Nueva York. En sus memorias, Gilberto Gerena Valentín nos lleva al centro de las continuas luchas sindicales, políticas, sociales y culturales que los puertorriqueños fraguaron en Nueva York durante el periodo de la Gran Migración hasta los años setenta.

http://www.centropr-store.com

Centro Publications

2019 CATALOGUE

The AmeRícan Poet: Essays on the Work of Tato Laviera

Edited by Stephanie Alvarez and William Luis
ISBN: 9781878483669; 2014. Pbk. 2014; 418 pages. **$24.99**

A collection of thirteen essays, an introduction and a foreword by fifteen established and emerging scholars. The essays discuss diverse aspects of Laviera's life and substantial body of work that includes five published collections of poetry, twelve written and staged plays, and many years of political, social, literary and healthcare activism. The book also includes four unpublished poems and the play King of Cans.

The Stories I Read to the Children: The Life and Writing of Pura Belpré, the Legendary Storyteller, Children's Book Author, and New York Public Librarian

Pura Belpré; Edited and Biographical Introduction by Lisa Sánchez González
ISBN: 9781878483805—ISBN: 9781878483454 (Kindle). 2013; 286 pages.
$20 (print); $7.99 (Kindle)

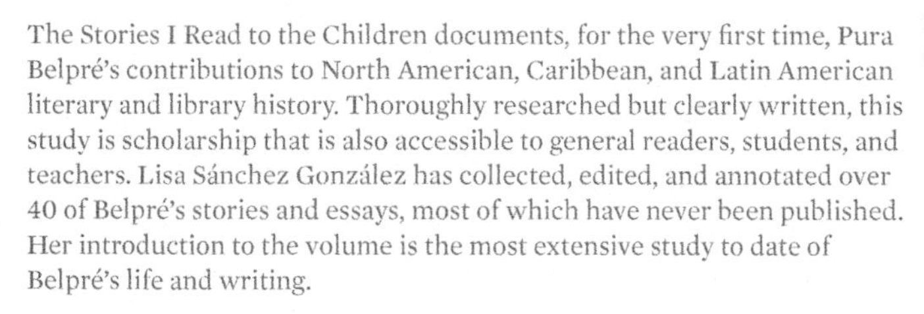

The Stories I Read to the Children documents, for the very first time, Pura Belpré's contributions to North American, Caribbean, and Latin American literary and library history. Thoroughly researched but clearly written, this study is scholarship that is also accessible to general readers, students, and teachers. Lisa Sánchez González has collected, edited, and annotated over 40 of Belpré's stories and essays, most of which have never been published. Her introduction to the volume is the most extensive study to date of Belpré's life and writing.

The State of Puerto Ricans 2013

Edited by Edwin Meléndez
and Carlos Vargas-Ramos
ISBN: 9781878483720; 2013; 91 pages. **$15**

The State of Puerto Ricans 2013 collects in a single report the most current data on social, economic and civic conditions of the Puerto Rican population in the United States available from governmental sources, mostly the U.S. census Bureau.

http://www.centropr-store.com

Made in the USA
Monee, IL
07 October 2023